The Commedia dell'Arte

For

Franco and Ada

The Commedia dell'Arte

A Documentary History

KENNETH RICHARDS AND LAURA RICHARDS

Published by Basil Blackwell for
The Shakespeare Head Press

First published 1990

Basil Blackwell Ltd
108 Cowley Road, Oxford, OX4 1JF, UK

Basil Blackwell Inc.
3 Cambridge Center
Cambridge, Massachusetts 02142, USA

British Library Cataloguing in Publication Data

A CIP catalogue record for this book is available from the British Library.

Library of Congress Cataloging in Publication Data

Richards, Kenneth, 1934–
The commedia dell'arte.

Bibliography: p.
1. Commedia dell'arte – History and criticism.
I. Richards, Laura, 1937–. II. Title.
PQ4155,R48 1989 852'.0523'09 88-25761
ISBN 0-631-19590-4

Typeset in 10 on 12pt Linotron Bembo
by Wyvern Typesetting Ltd, Bristol, England.
Printed in Great Britain by Butler and Tanner Ltd., Frome, Somerset

Contents

List of Plates

Preface

THIS STUDY of the *commedia dell'arte* is neither a history nor a comprehensive survey of all aspects of the Italian professional theatre between the mid-sixteenth and mid-eighteenth centuries. As its subtitle indicates, it is a more modest documentary account, bringing together for English readers a selection of the most important documents illustrative of the activities of the *commedia dell'arte* players and companies: some of these have been translated before, but are scattered through a number of books and articles; many have not been translated into English hitherto. It is hoped that by making them available in a single volume, readers without Italian will be better able to appreciate important aspects of what in the twentieth century has been one of the most influential dramas of the older European theatre. To that end the documents are gathered under a number of chapter headings which focus on specific aspects of the *commedia dell'arte*, and each chapter is prefaced by a brief introduction intended to place the documents in context. At the same time, however, chapters are not discrete units, and many individual documents in each chapter necessarily contain information relevant to areas treated of in other chapters: as far as possible we have cross-referenced.

Documentary material bearing on the *commedia dell'arte* is considerable: Vito Pandolfi's collection, for example, runs to six substantial volumes, yet is far from exhaustive. We have therefore had to be highly selective in our choice of what to include. That choice has perforce been conditioned by our own views of the subject, and what we think to be relevant, and has been determined too by our wish to make the account of interest and value to both the reader wanting a general introduction to the subject, and to the needs of those consulting it for more specialist purposes. We have tried to keep the translations as literal as possible, but on occasions have had to diverge somewhat from the originals in order to convey the sense: in addition to difficulties presented by the plurality of Italian dialects at this time, an inescapable problem in some documents is that their authors were actors, not men of letters, and their writings are not wanting in grammatical and stylistic idiosyncracies. Ideally we should have liked the translations to have been accompanied by the Italian originals, but that would have made the book unmanageably long and expensive. We have, however, provided source references for those wishing to consult the originals, and refer to much Italian commentary in the Notes.

This work had its beginnings some years ago when preparing material for the Open University Drama course, we read Enzo Petraccone's collection of basic documents; that suggested to us the utility of a somewhat comparable, although wider-ranging gathering for English readers; we are grateful to the Open University for permission to include here a small part of what we wrote then. In preparing a documentary account of this kind we have inevitably incurred many obligations to other theatre historians: those we have tried to acknowledge both in the text and the notes throughout; if there are omissions they are inadvertent, and we apologise in advance. We wish particularly to remark here our dependence on the work of recent Italian theatre historians like Siro Ferrone, Sara Mamone, Ferruccio Marotti, Cesare Molinari, Elena Povoledo, Mirella Schino, Ferdinando Taviani, Roberto Tessari and Lodovico Zorzi, whose work over the past two decades or more has substantially illuminated understanding of the subject. Our thanks are also due to those doyens of English scholars of the improvised drama, Kathleen Lea and Allardyce Nicoll, and to the staff of many libraries, more particularly those of the British Library, the John Rylands University Library, Manchester, the Biblioteca Nazionale, the Biblioteca Casanatense and the Biblioteca Teatrale Burcardo, Rome, the Biblioteca Nazionale and Biblioteca Marucelliana, Florence, the Biblioteca Nazionale Braidense and the Biblioteca Ambrosiana, Milan, the Biblioteca Comunale, Perugia, the Biblioteca Palatina, Parma, the Biblioteca Correr, Venice, and the Bibliothèque Nationale, Paris. We are pleased to acknowledge the help of a grant from the British Academy for work in Italy, and the support of the Universities of Manchester and Salford. Last, but far from least, we are particularly grateful to Claudette Williams and Thelma Wright for their skill in typing with such good humour from our indecipherable hands, and to David Martin, Philip Carpenter, Andrew McNeillie Anne Bone and Sophie Hartley of Basil Blackwell for their great patience.

Chronology 1545–1763

1545 First record of the formation of an Italian professional acting troupe, at Padua.

1548 Francesco Andreini born.

1552 A. F. Grazzini (Il Lasca) refers to improvised playing at Florence.

1558 *(Accession of Queen Elizabeth.)*

1562 Isabella Andreini born.

1563 Birth of Pier Maria Cecchini.

1564 *(Shakespeare and Marlowe born.)*

1565–6 First references to *commedia dell'arte* figures like *Zanni* and *Pantalone* in connection with acting companies.

1567 References to acting companies led by *Graziano, Flaminia* and Vincenza Armani at Mantua.

1568 First mention of the Gelosi Company, playing in Milan. Massimo Troiano's description of an amateur improvised performance in Bavaria.

*c.*1570–80 Paintings, probably of the Dutch School, depicting *commedia dell'arte* figures, notably *Pantalone* and *Zanni*.
The fifty-four *Recueil Fossard* engravings, probably depicting scenes from improvised plays, date from the 1570s.

1571 The Gelosi Company makes its first visit to Paris, where it acts at the house of the Duke of Nevers before Charles IV, then before the King and Queen at Nogent-le-Roi.
The Company of Zan Ganassa (Alberto Naseli) also performs in Paris this year, possibly playing quite regularly through to early 1574.
These visits mark the beginning of the foreign touring

that was to become a singular feature of the work of many of the leading players and companies for some two hundred years.

The first illustration we have of an *Arlecchino* figure (possibly Zan Ganassa). Now in the Bayeux Museum.

1572 Further fleeting records of Italian (possibly Florentine and Venetian led) companies in France.

The frescoes at Castle Trausnitz in Bavaria possibly date from this year: they depict figures from the *commedia dell'arte* and may have been based on an actual performance.

1573 The Gelosi perform in the first production of Tasso's *Aminta* at Ferrara.

(Ben Jonson born.)

1574 The Zan Ganassa Company is in Madrid, and probably travelling through other towns in Spain giving performances.

The Gelosi Company is invited to play in Venice before the French King Henry III at his request; also in Vienna in this year.

First record of the Confidenti Company, acting in Cremona, Pavia and Milan.

Italian performers in England at Windsor and Reading.

1576 First mention of the Company of Pedrolino, in Florence, Pisa and Lucca. Henry III calls an Italian company, and more particularly 'the Magnifico' he had seen in Venice, to perform in Paris.

(James Burbage opens the Theatre in London.)

1577 The Gelosi Company is again in France; its performances are opposed by the French Parliament, but it is protected by the King, before whom it played at Blois and in Paris.

(The Curtain theatre opened in London.)

1577–8 The Company of Drusiano Martinelli performs in London. Italian comedians may in earlier years have occasionally accompanied Queen Elizabeth on her summer progresses.

1578 First mention of the Uniti Company, at Ferrara.

The Andreini (Francesco and Isabella) probably members of the Gelosi by this date. When Francesco became leader of the troupe is uncertain, but by the 1590s he, and particularly his wife, Isabella, were among the leading players of Italy.

1581 First mention of the Desiosi Company, by Montaigne in his *Voyage en Italie*.

1584 Last mention of the Zan Ganassa troupe in Spain.

(Edward Alleyn begins acting career.)

1585 Tommaso Garzoni describes street entertainers in *La piazza universale*.
Palladio's Teatro Olimpico completed.

1587–8 The Confidenti Company is in Spain.

1588–9 (*Marlowe*'s Tamburlaine, Parts I and II *performed.*)

1589 *Zingana* (with Vittoria Piissimi in the lead) and *La pazzia d'Isabella* (with Isabella Andreini in the lead) acted at Florence as part of the great theatrical spectacle mounted to celebrate the marriage of Ferdinand I and Christine of Lorraine.
(*Kyd*'s Spanish Tragedy *performed.*)

1590 First mention of the Accesi Company, although it was probably active before this date.
(*Shakespeare*'s Titus Andronicus, Richard III, Love's Labours Lost, Romeo and Juliet, *and* A Midsummer Night's Dream *performed c.1589–95; English actors in Leiden; London theatres closed by plague 1592–3; Shakespeare a member of the Lord Chamberlain's Men.)*

1594 Vecchi's *Amfiparnasso* published with illustrations of Italian performers.
(Lope de Vega's El Maestro de danzar *performed.)*

1597 *(Peri's* Dafne *performed.)*

1599 Last mention of the Desiosi Company in Verona. For a time this Company may have been led by the celebrated actress, Diana da Ponti.
(The Globe Theatre opens in London.)

1600 The Accesi Company is in France for the marriage celebrations of Henry IV and Maria de'Medici; it remained in Paris throughout 1601.

1601 Tristano Martinelli, a celebrated early, and possibly the first, *Arlecchino*, probably responsible for publishing *Compositions de rhetorique* at Lyons; it includes important early illustrations of *Arlecchino*.
The paintings of *commedia dell'arte* figures now in the Theatre Museum at Drottningholm probably date from this time.
The Fedeli Company is formed by G. B. Andreini (Lelio), the son of Francesco and Isabella; it was perhaps the most distinguished Italian troupe of the early 17th century.
(Shakespeare's Hamlet *performed.)*

1603 *(Death of Queen Elizabeth and accession of James I.)*

1604 Returning to Italy from France Isabella Andreini falls ill at Lyons and dies. Her husband, Francesco, leader of the Gelosi Company, gives up the profession and the troupe is disbanded.
(Inigo Jones introduces Italianate stage scenes and machines to English court theatricals.)

1604–7	*(Shakespeare's* Othello, King Lear, Macbeth *and* Antony and Cleopatra *performed.)*
1607	Francesco Andreini publishes *Le bravure del Capitano Spavento*. *(Monteverdi's* Orfeo *performed.)*
1607–8	The Accesi spend most of these two years in France playing before the King at the Hotel de Bourbon, and publicly there and at the Hôtel de Bourgogne. *(Shakespeare's Company, the King's Men, leases the indoor Blackfriars Theatre.)*
1611	Flaminio Scala publishes *Il teatro delle Favole rappresentative*, the first, only published, and therefore the most important, collection of *commedia dell'arte* scenarios. *(Shakespeare's* The Tempest *performed.)*
1613	The Fedeli visit Paris in this year. *(Lope de Vega,* Fuente Ovejuna.*)*
1614	*(Webster's* The Duchess of Malfi *performed.)*
*c.*1614–5	About this time the actor Pier Maria Cecchini writes two essays on the improvised comedy, *Brevi discorsi intorno alla commedia ai commedianti* and *Discorso sopra l'arte comica e il modo di ben recitare.*
1615–20	Basilio Locatelli gathers the scenarios now in the manuscript collection of the Biblioteca Casanatense in Rome. The Corsini collection of scenarios, with their highly illuminating 'primitive' water-colour illustrations, were gathered about this time; written by an unknown author or authors probably well before this date.
1616	*(Death of Shakespeare.)*
1618	Made about this date were the feather-book illustrations of *commedia dell'arte* figures now in the McGill University Library. *(Giacobbi's* Andromeda, *performed at Salzburg, the first opera done outside Italy. The Thirty Years War breaks out.)*
1619	Flaminio Scala's, *Il finto marito* published in Venice. The two prologues are important for their discussion of actors, acting and improvisation in relation to the techniques of the literary drama. *(Death of Richard Burbage.)*
1620–26	*(English actors performing on the Continent.)*
1620–22	Jacques Callot's *Balli di Sfessania*, highly stylised engravings of the *commedia dell'arte*; probably prepared from sketches made during his residence in Italy some years before.
1624	Death of Francesco Andreini.
1625	*(Death of James I and accession of Charles I; from 1626 Inigo Jones designs changeable scenery for plays at court, and after 1631 uses* commedia dell'arte *figures in court masques.)*

1626 *(Death of Alleyn.)*

1627–8 The Fedeli troupe on foreign tour, acting in Prague and Vienna.

1628 Last mention of the Accesi, at Parma. Pier Maria Cecchini's *Frutti delle moderne commedie* published.
Niccolò Barbieri prepares his *Discorso familiare*, the first version of *La Supplica*, a vigorous defence of the improvising players.

*c.*1630 Compilation of MS of 51 scenarios by an anonymous author-editor, now in the Museo Correr, Venice.

1630 Death of Tristano Martinelli.

1632 Sir Aston Cockain sees the Affezionati perform in Venice.

1633 *(Ford's* 'Tis Pity She's a Whore *performed.)*

1634 Italian players perform in Warsaw.
Niccolò Barbieri's *La Supplica, discorso famigliare di Niccolo Barbieri detto Beltrame* published.

1635 *(Calderon's* La vida es sueno *performed.)*

1636 *(Corneille's* Le Cid.*)*

1637/40 Some time between these dates the Fedeli Company broke from its long time patron, the Duke of Mantua.

1637 First public theatre for opera, the San Cassiano, opens in Venice.
Domenico Biancolelli born.

1639 Tiberio Fiorilli, known as *Scaramouche* in France, is possibly in Paris in this year with the Giuseppe Bianchi company.
(Racine born.)

1639–40 Last mention of the Confidenti troupe in Milan and later in Paris.

1642 *(Civil War breaks out in England; the English theatres are closed by Act of Parliament.)*

1643–7 G. B. Andreini spends a considerable time abroad, although possibly not with the Fedeli.

1645 Death of Cecchini.

1645 *(Sacrati's 'machine play'* La finta pazza *is performed at the French court, designed by Torelli and with Italian professional players.)*

1646 Giovan Domenico Ottonelli *Della Christiana Moderatione*, Bk I, published in Florence. Four more volumes published through to 1652.

1649 *(Charles I executed.)*

1652 Last mention of the Accesi troupe, in Milan.)

1653 The Company of Basilio Locatelli is in Paris, Fiorilli playing with them.

1656 *(Davenant's* The Siege of Rhodes *performed.)*

1658 The Comédie Italienne shares the Petit Bourbon with Molière's company, the Compagnie de Monsieur.

1660 *(Charles II is restored to the English throne; the English theatres reopen and actresses are introduced.)*
1661 The *Arlecchino* Domenico Biancolelli is called to Paris.
1664 Formation of Francesco Calderoni's Company, co-directed by his wife Agata (*Flaminia*). It is last mentioned in Vienna in 1703, when it had apparently spent the previous 5 or 6 years abroad.
1664–7 *(Molière's* Le Misanthrope *and* Tartuffe, *and Racine's* Andromaque.*)*
1670s Fiorilli performs several times in London.
1670 *(Dryden's* The Conquest of Granada *performed.)*
1675 *(Wycherley's* The Country Wife *performed.)*
1680 The Hôtel de Bourgogne is given to the Théâtre Italien.
1685 *(Death of Charles II, and accession of James II.)*
1688 Death of Biancolelli.
1689 *(Purcell's* Dido and Aeneas *performed.)*
1694 Evaristo Gherardi publishes *Le théâtre Italien*, a collection of pieces performed by the Italian players in Paris.
1695 Angelo Costantini *La vie de Scaramouche* published in Paris (published in English 1698).
1697 The Italian players are expelled from Paris after a supposed slight to Mme de Maintenon, the mistress of Louis XIV, in the play *La Fausse Prude*.
*c.*1710 Gregorio Lambranzi produces engravings of *commedia dell'arte* figures in dance.
1715 Death of Louis XIV. The Duke of Orleans asks for an Italian company to be sent to Paris.
1716 The Italian players return to Paris. The troupe is led by Luigi Riccoboni, and enjoys considerable but short-lived success with improvised drama.
1716–20 Marivaux writes pieces for the new Théâtre Italien, among them pieces for his mistress, the soubrette Silvia.
1720–28 *(Ludwig Holberg writes plays under Commedia dell'arte influence.)*
1723–24 *(Marivaux's* La double inconstance, *and Metastasio's* Didone abbandonata *performed.)*
1728 Luigi Riccoboni, *Histoire du Théâtre Italien* published in Paris.
1733 Luigi Riccoboni publishes *Le Nouveau Théâtre Italien,* a collection of pieces acted by the Théâtre Italien.
1734 Placido Adriani gathers a collection of *commedia dell'arte* materials.
1737 *(The Stage Licensing Act passed in England.)*
1739 Girolamo Medebach forms a company to perform in Venice; Carlo Goldoni becomes a dramatist for the troupe, and begins his 'reform' of the traditional, improvised comedy.

1742	The great *Arlecchino*, Antonio Sacchi, forms his own company.
1743	*(Voltaire's* Merope *performed.)*
1745	Goldoni writes the first, scenario version of *Arlecchino, servitore di due padroni* for Sacchi.
1753	The Freres Parfaict, *Histoire de l'ancien théâtre italien* published in Paris.
1756	*(Mozart born.)*
1760–5	Carlo Gozzi attempts to revive improvised playing with his *fiabe*.
1762	The Comédie Italienne joins with the Opéra Comique.
	(Gluck's Orpheus and Euridice *performed.)*
	Goldoni leaves Venice to work with the Comédie Italienne in Paris.

Introduction

The *Commedia dell'Arte*

ITALIAN Renaissance drama has often for convenience sake been classified under two broad heads: the *commedia erudita* and the *commedia dell'arte*. The *commedia erudita*, or learned drama, was the literary drama of scripted plays (comedies, tragedies and pastorals), inspired by classical modes and written and performed mainly by *dilettanti*, or amateurs, in socially exclusive courts and academies.[1] The *commedia dell'arte* on the other hand was the drama of professional players: it was improvised, not scripted, mingled masked and unmasked figures, was conspicuously physical and pantomimic, and was given in a wide range of performance places, from the streets and squares of towns, through hired rooms and halls to the gardens, courtyards, great halls and formal theatres of the nobility. While the *commedia erudita* was the preserve of the educated elite, the *commedia dell'arte* apparently appealed to all social levels and has been considered a form of 'popular' theatre. Its seeming tap roots in the culture of the people, and its independence of the dramatist, have given it a reputation for being spontaneous and preeminently of the stage: an example of a once achieved actors' theatre.[2]

However, such divisions into *commedia erudita* and *commedia dell' arte*, elite and popular, can be misleading as well as helpful. The *commedia dell'arte* flourished for well over two hundred years, from the emergence of organized professional acting companies in the mid-sixteenth century through to the mid-eighteenth century, when its decadence was deplored by many, particularly the *letterati*, and the Venetian dramatist Carlo Goldoni furthered its disintegration with his radical reform of the Italian comic drama. In the course of those two centuries or more then *commedia dell'arte* changed in many ways, and was subject to numerous cultural influences, native and foreign. Indeed, so various were its manifestations, and so historically elusive is it, that notwithstanding the considerable attention it has received from theatre historians it remains something of an enigma.

As the mingling in performance of masked and unmasked figures suggests, the improvised drama of the *commedia dell'arte* was stylized and non-naturalistic, and the companies which performed it were composed of actors and actresses who sustained in most of the pieces they performed certain stock figures: two *vecchi*, or old men; two or more comic servants, the *zanni*; a free-ranging figure, often a military man, who could be boasting, obsequious, cowardly and amorous by turns; and two or more pairs of lovers or *innamorati*. Additional figures could include a *servetta*, and sometimes a widow or a courtesan, and there is often call for supernumeraries like tradesmen and constables. The main comic figures, the *vecchi* and the *zanni*, often wore close-fitting leather half-masks covering the upper part of the face; the others were usually unmasked. The plots of the improvised comic plays in which these stage figures appeared turned on mistaken identity, disguise, conflicts between young and old and amatory entanglements. Both the plot lines and the stage figures derived in some measure from classical and Italian learned drama, drew too on medieval and Renaissance *novelle*, on the popular and romance traditions, and on immediate local life. But they were above all rooted in the personalities and stage skills of the performers. The figures created by the players in improvised pieces were further distinctive in their accoutrements and local attributes, as well as for their use of regional dialects. The use of dialects enabled the players to circumvent in some measure the absence in Italy at the time of a unified national language and to develop, where appropriate, familiar colloquial address to complement the more formal, ornate, and even artificial discourse they assimilated from the learned culture.

From the beginning the acting companies were itinerant, the political and linguistic fragmentation of the peninsula and the lack in Italy of any commercially and culturally dominant city comparable to Paris or London obliging the companies to travel in search of markets. The most popular circuits included the main cities of central and northern Italy, particularly Florence, Bologna, Padua, Venice, Milan, Mantua and Genoa, although companies are early found much further south, from Naples and beyond into Sicily. Even when companies were under the direct patronage of the nobility, like the Medici in Florence or the Gonzaga in Mantua, nonetheless some players managed to maintain considerable independence. This independence they achieved by professional skills the quality of which was recognized at all social levels. Indeed the ability of the companies to develop a market for their wares was crucial to their survival. Many troupes were doubtless of very modest means and eked out a living as best they could, disbanding or amalgamating when convenience or necessity required. On the other hand, certain companies and players, inevitably those about whom we know most, achieved great reputation and some social status and were admired and rewarded by royalty and *letterati* alike. Many of the leading companies were welcomed by court and public audiences not only in Italy but abroad, for they undertook not just local but foreign touring. By the end of the sixteenth century *commedia dell'arte* players or companies had visited France, Spain, the German states, the Low Countries and England, and in the next two centuries they travelled even further abroad, as far as Scandinavia, Poland and Russia.

A strong magnet for their talents by the mid-seventeenth century was Paris. The first troupes were there as early as the 1570s, visits became increasingly frequent in the early decades of the seventeenth century and from 1661 a permanent company was based there, the Comédie Italienne. For several decades the Italian players flourished in Paris, enjoying popular and royal approval, but disaster overtook them when in 1697 they were banished from Paris following a supposed slight to the King's mistress, and were permitted to return only in 1716, after the death of Louis XIV. In the eighteenth century new modes of comic theatre evolved, like *opera buffa*, the harlequinade and pantomime, which owed obvious debts in comic types and strategies to the *commedia dell'arte*, for all that in other respects they were largely independent of it. These forms had a tendency to exploit what the visual arts emphasized, the sentimental and decorative elements latent in the figures, costuming and situations of the *commedia all'improvviso*.

During the heyday of the improvised *commedia dell'arte* its influence on the comedy of many nations was substantial, although by virtue of the ephemerality of performance not always readily calculable. What, if anything, it contributed to the Elizabethan and Jacobean comedy is difficult to gauge;[3] its influence on French comedy, particularly that of Molière and Marivaux, is more readily apparent.[4] One thing it certainly did was help to disseminate throughout Europe some of the plot materials and many of the stock situations of the classical and Italian Renaissance learned comedy in a popular and easily receivable form, thus helping to shape much of the content and structure of later European comic drama. It appears too to have stimulated the development of native drama and theatre in countries like Spain and Poland.[5] Its influence on modern theatre – on the work of directors, composers and theatre theorists like Craig, Meyerhold, Reinhardt, Copeau, Prokofiev and Stravinsky, as well as many more recent practitioners – is well documented.[6]

The Records

By any measure the *commedia dell'arte* is abundantly documented, and nowhere more so than in the pictorial records. For no other theatre of the period from 1550 to 1750 is there quite such a wealth of visual material. There are numerous engravings, drawings and paintings of individual players, groups of performers, and open-air and indoor performances. To appreciate how rich this stock of illustration is we need compare it only with the very few extant visual records which depict aspects of the English Elizabethan and Jacobean theatre; we have few portraits of early English players, a mere scattering of theatre drawings and designs, and those mostly by Inigo Jones for court theatricals, scarcely anything reflective of practice on the English public stages.[7] But although abundant, the *commedia dell'arte* illustrative material is not always easy to interpret. None of it can be assumed to have even quasi-photographic authority, and the extent and accuracy of its depiction of actual stage activity or practice is highly problematic.

The interpretative difficulties are many: identification of individual players or troupes is invariably hazardous unless the accompanying text is unambiguous; the provenance of much material is not always clear; both artistic and publishing licence can substantially distort the evidence provided by the material. Jacques Callot's magnificent but very individual *Balli di Sfessania* engravings may be taken as an instance of the ways in which the artistic imagination can so firmly stamp itself upon illustrations that the extent to which they depict the actual remains a constant interpretative difficulty.[8] Etched in about 1618–20 on the basis of drawings made earlier in Italy, the bird-like figures they show are witty, ebullient and grotesque. They doubtless express the spirit of the Italian performers, but at some remove from the real world of street and stage. The vivid frontispiece to the *Balli* (see plate 1) may indeed reflect the appearance of a carnival or fairground fit-up, and certainly confirms the evidence of other, literary sources, that song and dance were characteristic features of performance. But the distinctive Callot style overlays the whole. Another *Balli* engraving (plate 19) shows in the background a trestle stage performance in progress, but foregrounds figures at street level: the worlds of stage, street and carnival are intermingled, and artistic freedom governs what is depicted.

A far remove from Callot's fluent and sophisticated drawings are the water-colour illustrations of stage scenes in the Corsini collec-

PLATE 1 *Frontispiece to Jacques Callot,* Balli di Sfessania *(c. 1620). Permission of The British Library, 1295 h29*

tion of *scenarii* (see plates 20, 24, 30, 32 and 33). These delightful naive paintings are in many respects highly suggestive in their depictions of figures, scenic decoration and stage activity, but we would need to know much more than we do about the occasion of their composition in order to regard them as specifically, rather than generally, informative of regular stage practice. Ascription is similarly uncertain for many of the other early extant paintings and engravings of group and individual figures, for the occasion and purpose of the particular painting or engraving, necessarily conditioning what was depicted, are for the most part now lost to us. Again, it seems certain that the iconographic tradition increasingly became independent of the stage tradition, and exercised a strong influence in its own right on the illustration of *commedia dell'arte* figures and scenes, while that illustrative tradition in its turn came to influence staging in the theatres. This seems to have been the case with early eighteenth century French paintings of *commedia dell'arte* scenes, and may have been the case too with earlier visual depictions. From at least the early seventeenth century there exists at least the possibility of such a reciprocal relationship between the iconographic and theatrical traditions. The extent of that relationship is, by its nature, highly problematic, and thus it is all the more difficult to draw firm conclusions about staging practices from the visual materials.[9]

In addition to the visual materials we have too a large number of *scenarii*, collections of *lazzi* (comic set-pieces), examples of stock literary materials, information about company itineraries, administrative documents and contracts, players' and patrons' letters, and a substantial amount of critical and occasional writing by both sympathetic and hostile commentators (see bibliography, section B). Some of this material is invaluable for the information it provides about relations between the players themselves, between players and their patrons, between the companies and theatre impresarios, about relationships with church and municipal authorities, and about the difficulties encountered by patrons and troupe leaders in attempting to assemble companies. Unfortunately we do not possess any detailed and unambiguous accounts by professional players of performance preparation, nor do we have any really full and analytical descriptions of late sixteenth- and seventeenth-century professional improvised performances.

We find with the *commedia dell'arte*, then, as for other theatre of the same period such as the Elizabethan and Jacobean, that details and technicalities which contemporaries took for granted, or assumed to be known, or uninteresting or irrelevant, are precisely what we would most like to know more about. Specific detail on the economy of the companies and their day-to-day operations is less than abundant. Wanting too is incontrovertably authoritative information about the nature of improvisation itself. As with the visual materials, interpretation of the scripted records can raise many problems. Exactly how much information, for example, can we confidently glean from the extant *scenarii* about actual staging practices? To what extent were those stage materials which actually found their way into print in the early seventeenth century refined and adapted according to literary rather than stage criteria in order to make them fit for publication? To these and many similar questions there can be no definitive answers.

Some Interpretative Problems

For all that we possess a wealth of documentation, literary and pictorial, from its beginnings through to its apparent decline, the *commedia dell'arte* remains elusive. What were its origins? Can it appositely be called a species of 'popular' theatre? Was it characterized primarily by improvised performance, and if so, how was the improvisation executed and how substantial and significant in improvised performance was the literary dimension? Was it above all, as some early commentary and much of the extant iconography suggest, a theatre dominated by the masked actors, the *zanni* and *vecchi*? Since at least the mid-eighteenth century the *commedia dell'arte* has been seen as a very distinctive, autonomous form altogether unique in the history of the European theatre: an actor-based theatrical theatre of masks and improvisation, the polar opposite to the theatre of those professional players elsewhere, in England and Spain for example, who performed the plays of dramatists. It is that image and idea of the *commedia dell'arte* that has underpinned modern interests and imposed itself on modern theatre practice. Much in that view, however, may have been filtered through materials themselves somewhat misleading or open to misinterpretation.

We have remarked above the convenient distinction often made between the *commedia erudita*, and the *commedia dell'arte*. This distinction was made by some of the seventeenth-century commentators, like Pier Maria Cecchini and Andrea Perrucci, and was endorsed by Luigi Riccoboni, who in addition to being a distinguished actor and troupe leader must be considered the first historian of the Italian theatre. In his *Histoire du Théâtre Italien* (1728) Riccoboni wrote of the Italian Renaissance stage:

> During the whole of the sixteenth century until the beginning of the seventeenth century, we see two different theatres: one consisting of mercenary players, who performed *all'improvviso* with Arlequin and other masked actors, and the other of academicians, who acted scripted and regular pieces, which sometimes passed into the theatre of the professionals.[10]

But the situation was more complicated than this apparently neat separation allows, and Riccoboni's final qualification can easily be passed over. Professional actors and actresses performed *all'improvviso*, but so too did the *dilettanti*, and the first description we possess of a performance *all'improvviso*, is of an amateur not a professional event: Massimo Troiano's entertainment at the Bavarian court in 1568 (see below p. 48). Professional players acted in many kinds of scripted drama – in comedies, tragedies, tragicomedies, pastorals, *intermezzi* and *melodramma*. For example, professional players are known to have performed in versions of classical comedy and tragedy; professionals acted in the most celebrated pastoral tragi-comedy of the age, Giovan Battista Guarini's *Il Pastor Fido*; the professional actress Virginia Ramponi in 1608 took the lead role in the Monteverdi–Rinuccini opera *Arianna*. Nor was playwriting confined to the *dilettanti*. A number of professional players who regularly acted *all'improvviso* also wrote fully-scripted plays, often in verse, and had them published as well as performed. One of the most important and prolific was the actor and troupe manager of the Fedeli company, Giovan Battista Andreini, who wrote at least fifteen full-length plays. Other actors who turned their hands to playwriting included Flaminio Scala, Silvio Fiorillo, Fabrizio de Fornario, Bartolomeo Rossi and Pier Maria Cecchini. It is clear then that the divisions between amateur and professional, scripted and improvised theatre, were decidedly less than clear cut.

Riccoboni's history of the Italian theatre, and his later *Reflexions historiques et critiques sur les différens théâtres de l'Europe* (1738), were but two of several *settecento* commentaries which have much influenced modern understanding of the *commedia dell'arte*. Important information is found for example in the letters, play prefaces and memoirs of Carlo Goldoni, and in the *Memorie inutili* and other writings of Carlo Gozzi. French collections and commentaries of the late seventeenth and eighteenth centuries, like those of Gherardi and Gueullette, provide a rich source, too, as do the paintings of Watteau, Lancret, Gillot and others already remarked. All these materials have been influential in colouring modern views of the Italian comedy. There are good reasons however for using some of these records with caution, for in certain respects they may reflect more of what the *commedia dell'arte* had become, or nostalgically was thought to have been, than what it actually was in its heyday between circa 1570 and 1640.

In fact the very term *la commedia dell'arte* was never used of the activities of actors or professional acting companies until the eighteenth century, when we find Carlo Goldoni employing it to distinguish the masked and improvised drama from the scripted comedy of character that as a dramatist he himself favoured.

PLATE 2 *An engraving from Watteau depicting the banishment of the French players from Paris in 1697. Permission of the Bibliothèque Nationale, Paris*

Whether or not the phrase was a Goldoni coinage is uncertain, but it was soon in general currency as a phrase by which to define the work of the professionals. Among modern theatre historians it has been variously interpreted: some take it to mean 'the drama of the profession', indicating that the players were banded together, even if informally, into something equivalent to a trade guild; others have understood it to signify 'the drama of skill' or 'technique',[11] a reading not without difficulty however in a period when 'art' and 'craft' were only beginning to acquire distinct status; yet others have seen it as carrying a combination of the two meanings, the profession of trade being characterized by its mastery of presentational skills. Earlier terms used of the professional players and companies tend to be rather more specific: *la commedia degli Zanni, la commedia a soggetto, la commedia all'Italiana,* or *la commedia mercenaria.* All are fairly precisely descriptive: *degli Zanni* refers not just to the *servo* or *servi* of the comedy, but embraces all the players and characterizes a kind of performance; *a soggetto* similarly points the style or technique of the presentation, the particular mode of production; *all'Italiana* indicates that it was a peculiarly Italian speciality; *mercenaria* defines it as an activity undertaken for payment, and done by those who made their living by performing plays. All these terms save the last could equally well have been used of performance by *dilettanti*; the last, however, clearly indicates the professional nature of the players' work.

Again, it is not until the *settecento*, in the writings of Riccoboni, Goldoni and Gozzi, that we find the *commedia dell'arte* expressly defined as the theatre of the 'masks', and more particularly of the four 'masks' – the two *vecchi* and the two *zanni.* A number of early writers associate the 'masks' and improvisation, and the physical comic 'business' of the Italian players, with 'popular' classical theatre forms, but the evidence they adduce is negligible. Perhaps much more suggestive, however, is the fact that several of the eighteenth century commentators write scathingly of the decline in quality of improvised playing, thereby implying that the performance of their own day was significantly different from what it had once been. Of course we need to allow for exaggeration and nostalgic self-deception in some of these criticisms, which were based on report of what the drama had once been, not on first-hand experience of it. But by the early eighteenth century the long history of the improvised theatre was drawing to a close. It had changed much since its beginnings. Many generations of players had contributed to its evolution, their individual personalities and performer skills and emphases all enriching and shaping its history. It had been affected, too, by social, cultural and political change and the modifications brought about by accommodation to, and incorporation of, diverse foreign preference, most obviously the French. In short, we need to be alert to the possibility that what some later writers identified as characteristic may have been true more for their own age, and, their own ways of seeing, than for the *commedia dell'arte* of the late sixteenth and seventeenth centuries, and that our own understandings may have been conditioned by misconceptions and modern needs and ways of seeing.

The history of the *commedia dell'arte* is peculiarly complicated by the varied nature and extent of the players' activities, both in Italy and abroad, by their ability to respond to the opportunities of many theatrical markets, by their assimilation of materials and staging techniques and strategies from many sources, and by their accommodation of their own native working methods and materials to the requirements of successful foreign touring. Since the seventeenth century many myths have accumulated in many countries about the *commedia dell'arte*: that it was a single entity, that it was artistically self-contained and well defined, that it was spontaneously improvised, drew much on 'popular' materials and was essentially of the 'popular' meridian, that it trafficked mainly in 'low' comedy, and was rooted in the physical and acrobatic antics of the masked players. The historical reality, however, was rather different. The *commedia dell'arte* was the outcome of complex social change, economic necessity and performer opportunism. It was the product of accident, trial and error, and calculated innovation. The practice of specialists, it was at its best a vocally and physically disciplined theatre of distinctly verbal and rhetorical emphasis. It was organized and somewhat hierarchically stratified by companies, and while it drew on, and had certain roots in, the 'popular' and regional, it aspired to, leaned more to, and at its upper reaches gained entry to, the 'high' culture of the courts and the learned academies. It was, too, multi-faceted and diffuse, and cannot be reduced to any particular formula. Its history is not just that of the 'masks' and the improvised drama, which the iconographic tradition and many modern accounts have tended to foreground; it is the history of the actors and the companies, their patrons and audiences, the stages they played on, and the many different kinds of play they performed, both scripted and improvised. It is the history, too, of the players' fortunes abroad and the manner in which their theatre became the victim and myth of its own Europe-wide success.

I

Antecedents

Classical and Medieval Precedents

A NUMBER OF very early comments on the *commedia dell'arte*, dating from the sixteenth century, assume a derivation at least from Roman times, but although they have the apparent advantage of being contemporaneous with the development of the drama itself, they nonetheless carry little real authority, since Renaissance writers were ever ready to find sanction for the interests and activities of their own age in supposed classical precedents. The precedents concerning the *commedia dell'arte* were rather tenous: certain general similarities perceived between the stage figures and comic business of the Italian Renaissance improvised drama and those of early Italian and Roman popular mime and comic entertainment.[1]

Not least of the problems involved in seeking to establish such classical derivation is the sheer elusiveness of this early popular theatre. Next to nothing has survived in the way of play text fragments or written records of the activities of these entertainers, and most of our knowledge is drawn from scenes depicted in extant fourth-century Italian vase paintings (see plate 3); these last, while fascinating and suggestive, are fraught with interpretative difficulties. Farcical parody of Greek tragic drama evidently flourished in Magna Graecia, performed by comic actors called *phlyakes*. These parodies appear to have included the antics of slaves and old men, and were concerned with the adventures of braggart hero-figures like Herakles.[2] Devisers of Atellan farce took over elements of Doric theatre and parody of the myths of Attic drama in fashion-

PLATE 3 *Vase illustration c.350 BC of a* phlyax *farce. Permission of the Antiken museum Berlin, Staatliche Museen Preussischer Kulturbesitz*

ing their own distinctive and local popular comedy which was widespread in Campania about the third century BC, and was the stock in trade of travelling mimes who set up their trestle stages in streets and market places.[3] From Campania they appear to have migrated to Rome, their multiplicity of masks gradually coalescing into four characteristic masked types: Maccus, a gluttonous fool; Dossenus, a crafty hunchback; Bucco, a comic braggart; and Pappos, a ridiculous old man.

The temptation to link these four principal figures with what eighteenth-century and later commentators identified as the four principal masks of the *commedia dell'arte* – the two *vecchi* and the two *zanni* – has remained attractive to some modern scholars, and indeed a link with antique entertainment was made by late sixteenth-century observers, as the following indicates:

> I would never number among plays those things peddled around by such miserable and mercenary creatures as call themselves Gianni of Bergamo, Francatrippa, Pantalone and similar buffoons, were we not able to liken them to Mimes, the Atellanae and the Planipedes of the ancients.[4]

This comment, however, merely perceives a general likeness, and significantly looks to classical precedent in order to give rather reluctant endorsement to the modern comedy. Luigi Riccoboni, in his *Histoire du Théâtre Italien* (1728), likewise remarked connections with early southern Italian farce and classical *histriones*, connections which seemed all the more plausible at the time he wrote as they appeared to be supported by recent archaeological discoveries at Herculaneum.[5] Riccoboni was of course writing at the height of the neo-classical period, and was seeking too, in a sense, to give the weight of classical prestige to a theatre he himself still practised. His arguments were by no means *jejune*, and in discussing derivation he was alert to possible Renaissance as well as classical influences. Derivation from Roman comedy was assumed, too, by the highly influential nineteenth-century historian and recuperator of the *commedia dell'arte*, Maurice Sand, who probably followed Riccoboni in his *Masques et Bouffons* (1862), and the case has been given qualified support by several more recent commentators, including Allardyce Nicoll.[6]

Certainly some of the resemblances and correspondences identified between Atellan farce, later mime entertainment and the Italian improvised comedy are striking, and there are clearly similarities between them in costuming and masking. For those scholars disposed to make sharp distinctions between the literary and improvised drama, it has been tempting, too, to see the *commedia erudita* and the *commedia dell'arte* as the Renaissance equivalents of, respectively, the Roman literary *togata* and *palliata*, and the more plebeian entertainment provided by the *atellanae* and *farsae*.[7] Unfortunately, however, the evidence for such similarities tends to be more general than particular, and the plausibility of the case is the more difficult to accept when so much concerning the characteristics of the Atellan popular theatre remains itself highly conjectural. Not least important in that regard is the problem of the possible connections between the work of such early entertainers and the later Latin scripted comedy. Readily available to at least some of the sixteenth-century professional players were of course the extant comedies of Plautus and Terence, which they could have encountered in printed texts or stage productions. The plays of Plautus in particular are decidedly performer-oriented, and provide numerous pointers to possibilities for actor improvisation on which the Renaissance professionals could, and quite certainly did, capitalize.

Difficulties are further compounded by certain similarities

scholars have perceived between the figures of the improvised *commedia dell'arte* and those of the Turkish puppet theatre, the *Karagöz*, for which direct descent from classical times has similarly been claimed.[8] Unfortunately the transmission of popular theatrical forms in the Near East is equally elusive. It may well be true that modes of both popular and more sophisticated performer entertainment migrated to Italy, and more particularly to Venice and its territories on the lower Adriatic, after the fall of Constantinople in 1543, and that the confluence of these and native Italian kinds helped to generate the improvised drama of the professionals. But the nature, extent and importance of the random and panic-induced cultural displacements from the old Roman empire in the East are virtually unchartable, and important sources of possible record in the Levant remain unexplored or inaccessible. So elusive are the tracks of classical popular theatre influence through the so-called Dark Ages, that modern scholarship on the *commedia dell'arte* has largely turned away from such enquiry. It cannot, though, simply be dismissed out of hand, and could well be re-opened in the future, although as yet no really persuasive, let alone unchallengeable, evidence has been adduced to establish a definite transmission of stage figures, costumes or comic strategies from the early Italian period, through the Middle Ages, to the Renaissance, and on the whole current scholarly opinion considers the case not proven.

Somewhat more plausible, although no less problematic, are those arguments which have sought to link features of the *commedia dell'arte* to certain figures and practices of the late medieval theatre. Quite certainly much from the medieval period fed into, and helped to shape, the later organized professional drama, but, just as with the antique materials, most of it was by its nature ephemeral, unrecorded and often unrecordable. Again, the sheer richness and variety of medieval theatre defeats such speculation. Many elements of streets and *piazza* entertainment were taken into the religious drama, particularly the Florentine *Sacra rappresentazione*, of which there is a substantial body of extant scripted record, and professional entertainers played an increasingly active part in the preparation and performance of these spectacles. That the example of the religious drama was felt in the emergence and early development of the *teatro d'arte* need not be doubted: the agile and scheming comic devils, opinionated elderly counsellors and pompous military men found in the religious plays have something in common with the figures of the improvised *commedia dell'arte* (see plate 4). Indeed it would be very surprising if such a widespread and pre-eminently theatrical form, which levied heavily on the popular and folkloric, had not exercised influence on the later professional theatre, just as it did, however indirectly, on the work of the early *cinquecento* playwrights. Some of the staging techniques too of the *Sacre rappresentazioni* may well have been exploited by the improvising comedians, as they were by the scenic designers and machinists who mounted literary drama in the Renaissance court theatres.[9] That there was some influence, then, can be accepted. But again, as with the supposed classical indebtednesses, correspondences between the character lineaments, plot functions and costuming of certain of the stage figures in the religious and the improvised drama tend to be general, rather than so particular that they show a very clear line of direct derivation.

Carnival and Popular Entertainers

As will be clear from the above, much investigation into the possible origins of certain features of the improvised *commedia dell'arte* has looked more particularly to the example of popular entertain-

PLATE 4 *Miniature from a MS of Renaud de Montauban showing players preparing for a show, and the Devil in a Hell scene, Bibliothèque de l'Arsenal, Paris, MS,5072.f.28r. (photograph: Giraudon)*

ment, and has sought, too, folkloric roots. Many suggestive general correspondences are traceable between the figures, and the stage and staging techniques of the improvised drama, and those of the itinerant entertainers of Carnival, fairs and market-places. Their entertainment, like that of the later organized professional companies, appears to have spanned all social levels, and their performance places, too, ranged from the streets and *piazze* to the halls of the well-to-do. They likewise performed at weddings, birthday celebrations and formal banquets. These peripatetic entertainers included masked mimes, clowns, instrumentalists, singers, dancers, rope-dancers, jugglers and acrobats. At street level their activities constituted the theatrical entertainment dimension of popular culture, a field comparatively little examined by theatre historians, first because it has apparently left only few and scattered traces, and second because theatre history has traditionally been concerned much more with the theatrical concerns of what the anthropologist Robert Redfield has usefully called the 'great' tradition: the culture of the educated elite as opposed to the 'little' tradition, which was that of the mass of the people.[10] The 'little' tradition of pre- or early modern Europe is elusive: much of it was taken for granted, it has left comparatively few written records, and such reports as have come down invariably see it from the point of view of the educated. Popular theatrical entertainment is even more elusive than other popular cultural forms, for theatre is by its nature ephemeral. Further, its practitioners were very diverse, some were amateur, some quasi-professional, some wholly committed to earning what living they could by exercising their entertainer skills. The presence of popular theatrical entertainers in medieval and early modern society was ubiquitous, yet it is signally difficult to get any secure purchase on the nature and extent of their activities and the influence they undoubtedly exercised on the work of the later organized professional players.

However, in the opinion of some scholars the contribution of these itinerant entertainers to the emergence of organized professional companies and to the gradual evolution of the improvised *commedia dell'arte* was crucial. We know that some performed short sketches and mimed playlets which were, in effect, quasi-dramatic shows involving one or more characters, sometimes supported by a musician or a singer who provided a comic or ironic commentary to the action.[11] Other popular entertainers were themselves, or worked in close association with, travelling mountebanks, who from fit-up trestle stages sold a variety of wares, including patent medicines and perfumes, in village squares, at fairs and markets, or in the larger towns during Carnival-time.[12] Colourful and garrulous, many of these charlatans were brilliant entertainers in their own right, some using not only performer skills, but stage decoration, ingenious devices and fire effects in their embryonic theatrical shows. The purpose of these shows was of course to draw audiences, the sale of the mountebank's goods punctuating or following the entertainment, indeed being inseparable from it in that even the sale's pitch was itself a show. Nor was mountebank entertainment confined to the streets; as more than one contemporary observer indicates, skilled performers could rise above trade in cheap wares to provide banquet entertainment of a high order in socially exclusive circles. A number of early commentators, particularly clerics, made little or no distinction between such mountebank performers and the lower denizens of the entertainment world, including itinerant actors: both exploited the attractions of female entertainers and trafficked in the arts of deception; both were classified by their critics as rogues and vagabonds whose activities were socially and morally reprehensible (see chapter 9).

But notwithstanding the views of such moralists, mountebank entertainers seem to have been one thing, professional players banded into organized companies something else. Whether the latter evolved from the former, and if so how, when, and under what conditions, are matters much disputed. There may possibly be a link between these mountebank shows and what was perhaps, as Mario Apollonio has argued, the nucleus of the later, more fully-developed improvised performances of the *commedia dell'arte*, the exchanges between Pantalone and Zanni.[13] This is difficult to establish with confidence although some credence is lent to the possibility by late sixteenth-century engravings depicting comic and grotesque master—servant relationships, where the figures would appear to be the Magnifico, Pantalone, and the Capitano, both involved in antics with Zanni (see plate 5). But as so often with the extant visual materials, it is impossible to be sure that these engravings illustrate or reflect stage activity, their provenance is uncertain, and their dating only approximate.

Nowhere are the interpretative difficulties more evident than when we consider the connections between elements of the folk tradition and the masked figures of Carnival on the one hand, and on the other what have come to be seen as the characteristic masks of the improvised *commedia dell'arte*.[14] Most historians of the improvised drama have assumed that the actors took their masks either from vestigial classical inspiration or from the folk tradition and the world of Carnival. But classical derivation, as we have remarked, is highly problematic, and no less so in this particular area, while none of the literary or visual evidence is conclusive. Carnival engravings certainly show that the actors' masks were popular festival guise, but none of the engravings seems indisputably to predate the formation of the *commedia dell'arte* troupes.[15] Again, some popular literary materials, macaronic verse and the like, which certainly pre-date the companies, refer to figures analogous to the actors' masks, notably the Magnifico and the Zanni.[16]

PLATE 5 Zanni *with a* vecchio*. Late sixteenth century. Permission of the National Museum, Stockholm (photograph: Statens Konstmuseer)*

But such literary traces are much less concrete than the visual evidence provided by engravings and paintings, and most of the correspondences they offer are general rather than particular. If primacy must thus be given to the inconographic evidence, this would seem to suggest that Carnival revellers took over the masks from the stage, for their visually engaging qualities and because the actors had already made them popular and familiar. It would be unreasonable of course to claim that the players conjured their masks out of the air: in devising them it is more than likely that they drew, consciously or unconsciously, on elements of the folk imagination. In their essential lineaments, however, in all that made them such a distinctive feature of the improvised *commedia dell'arte*, the masks seem to have been developed by the actors themselves. If this was indeed the case, then it underscores how complex were the inter-connections between popular materials and the improvised drama, and undermines even more the already less than persuasive arguments of those who, seeing the *commedia dell' arte* as a single artistic entity, would seek the origins of the improvised comedy and its stage figures in Atellan farce, Roman mime and medieval precedents.

Documents

The documents included in the first section below are intended to give an indication of the kinds of argument advanced by commentators who have sought to establish firm links between the commedia dell'arte *and popular classical forms and those who early on questioned the plausibility of such a derivation. The later sections provide a selection of early Italian and English materials descriptive of street, Carnival, banquet and mountebank entertainment.*

ORIGINS

Riccoboni on Arlecchino

The first historian of the Italian theatre, Luigi Riccoboni, made much of the similarities in appearance between Arlecchino and early mimes. The correspondences adduced, however, although he bolsters them by Latin quotation, are rather tenuous.

I believe there is no need to doubt that Arlecchino's costume is that of this species of mimes who had shaved heads and were called *Planipedes*, and I am supported in my conjecture by this passage in Apuleius:

> Quid enim si choragium thimelicum possiderem? num ex eo argumentarere etiam uti me consuesse Tragaedi Syrmate, Histrionis crocota, Mimi centunculo.

In a single phrase, *Mimi centunculo*, the costume of Arlecchino is identified.

There are other factors in Arlecchino's appearance which prove its origin is to be found in the costume of the mimes. For example, his mask depicts the ancient mimes, *fuligine faciem obducti*.

The habit of having the head shaved comes from the fact that *Sanniones mimum agebant rasis capitibus*.

To ensure that we miss nothing let us examine once again this point. *Planipes graece dicitur Mimus, ideo autem latine Planipes quod Actores planis pedibus, id est, nudi Proscenium introirent.* The hair style of Arlecchino is surely described here, his feet are simply wrapped in leather without heels; from head to foot the habit and appearance of Arlecchino are nothing other than that of the Latin mimes.

(From Riccoboni, *Histoire du Théâtre Italien*, 1728, p. 5)

Maurice Sand on the origins of the masks

Equally confident of classical derivation was Maurice Sand, who published his influential Masques et bouffons *in 1862. The son of the novelist George Sand, as a child he took part in family theatricals which drew on the example of the improvising Italian comedians, and he developed a keen, nostalgic interest in their history. The many illustrations to the account he eventually published were not its least influential part, notwithstanding that many were imaginative impressions of the stage figures rather than reproductions of sixteenth- and seventeenth-century illustrative materials. Sand not only drew a sharp distinction between the improvised and the literary drama, but endorsed and developed, too, Riccoboni's speculation that the masked figures of the improvised* commedia dell'arte *were the direct descendants of types formed in ancient farce and mime, even to the detail of their garments, masks and accoutrements.*

Throughout the sixteenth century, down to the seventeenth, two distinct theatres were therefore in existence: one occupied by comedians who played impromptu (*commedia dell'arte*) with Harlequin and other masked actors; the other occupied by the academicians, or academic actors, who performed written and regular pieces (the *commedia sostenuta*) which sometimes passed into the theatre of the buffo-comedians.

[. . .] Pulcinella had never ceased to exist from the days of the Atellanae, in which he went by the name of Maccus, the *mimus albus*.

Casnar, Pappus, the flouted and ridiculous old man, became Pantaloon, and later Cassandro.

The two *Zanni*, Harlequin and Brighella, are the *saniones* of the ancient theatre: the first is a lackey or loutish peasant, stupid and gluttonous; the second is an astute and wily slave, avenging himself upon his masters by robbing them.

The ancient tradition has been preserved down to our own days in the garments of the characters of the Italian comedy. First the mask, which has been but little modified; for the principal types, such as Pulcinella, Harlequin, Brighella, Pantaloon, Coviello, Tartaglia, still wear the mask which, in itself, lends them an ancient character and, except in the case of old men, a nightcap which conceals the hair and so perpetuates the tradition of the shaven heads of the ancient mimes.

The tradition of that other part of the costume worn by the Greek phallophores was preserved by comedy mimes and buffoons down to the time of Louis XIII. It suffices to cast a glance at such illustrations as Callot's *Les Petits Danseurs*, as Cerimonia, Smaraolo, Scaramuccia, Captain Spezza-Monti and others, to realise this.

Most of the characters also wore the mantle (*il tabaro*) and all the lackeys, like the slaves of the Atellanae, appeared in short garments. The toga and the long robes were permitted only to the nobles and the old men.

The club of Pulcinella and the bat of Harlequin are probably no more than modifications of the curved staff of the peasants of the Greek theatre, the attribute of the Muse of Comedy.

Other essential analogies are to be considered. First, La Cantatrice included in all the Italian troupes, who, in the manner of the ancient chorus, came to sing and to explain the scenes. Then the modern *planipes*, the Bolognese Narcisino, who still comes, by way of interlude, to chat with the public and scoff at the manners of the day; finally and chiefly the method of performing impromptu, the actors having memorised no roles and playing after merely having read an outline of the subject nailed up in the wings. These resemblances and many others would prove that the *Commedia dell' Arte* is no more than the continuation of the theatre of Atella with its improvisations and its free and often licentious scenes, mingled with songs and pantomime.

(Sand, *Masques et bouffons*, 1862; from the translation, *The History of the Harlequinade*, London, 1915, vol. I, pp. 26–8)

PLATE 6 *One of five engravings to Alessandro Caravia,* Naspo Bizaro, *Venice, 1565. Permission of the Bodleian Library, Oxford, Douce C322*

J. A. Symonds on classical derivation

Much more circumspect in his discussion of the relationship between the popular classical performers and the figures of the commedia dell'arte *was John Addington Symonds. In the lengthy introduction he provided to his translation of Carlo Gozzi's* Memorie inutili, *Symonds largely maintained the convenient distinction between the* commedia erudita *and the* commedia dell'arte *but cogently questioned the assumption that any direct transmission could easily be assumed from the Latin masks to those of the sixteenth-century Italian comedians.*

Further familiarity with the modern *Commedia dell'Arte* will make it clear how tempting it is to conjecture a direct transmission of these Roman masks from ancient to modern times. Maccus and Bucco bear a strong resemblance to the two Zanni. The very word Zanni seems to suggest Sanniones; although it is probably derived from the Bergamasque name for a varlet – Jack; Zanni being a contraction of Giovanni. Pappus looks uncommonly like Pantalone, and Dossenus like the Dottore. The *Stupidus* has an air of our clown or Mezzettino or Il Villano. Manducus might be any glutton with a huge pair of champing jaws. Yet nothing could be more uncritical than to assume that the Italian masks of the sixteenth century AD boasted an uninterrupted descent from the Roman masks of the fifth century BC. That assumption closes our eyes to a far more interesting aspect of the phenomenon. The fact seems to be that ancient and modern Italy possessed the same mimetic faculty and used it in the same fashion. The peasants of modern Tuscany indulged in their Fescennine jibes, stained themselves with wine-lees, and jumped through bonfires, like their most remote ancestors. The grape-gatherers of modern Nola and Capua ridiculed their neighbours with obscene jests, and pranked themselves in travesty, like the earliest Oscans or the first colonists from Hellas. Out of the same persistent habits emerged the same kind of native drama; and just as the Atellanae of ancient Rome eventually brought the comedy of the proletariate upon the public stage in cities, so at the close of the sixteenth century the *Commedia dell'Arte* worked up the rudiments of popular farce and satire into a new form which delighted Europe for two hundred years.

Many details derived from the *Commedia Erudita* rendered the resemblance between the modern improvised drama and the vernacular comedy of ancient Rome superficially striking. The conventional characters of Plautus and Terence, the *senex*, the *servus*, the *meretrix*, the *mango*, the *ancilla*, the *miles gloriosus*, and the *parasitus* reappeared. In truth, this peculiar and highly complex hybrid combined strains of manifold varieties. Upon the wild and native briar, which in former times produced the *Osci ludi, Fescennini versus,* and *Satura*, and which went on living its own natural life beneath the drums and tramplings of so many conquests, was now grafted the cultivated rose of the *Commedia Erudita*. This, in its turn, contained elements of the *Fabula palliata* and *togata*. The result was a species eminently characteristic of sixteenth-century Italy, and similar to the Atellan farces of the Romans.

(J. A. Symonds, *The Useless Memoirs of Count Carlo Gozzi*, 1890, vol. I, pp. 38–40)

CARNIVAL

Fynes Moryson on Carnival

As remarked above, whether or not organized professional theatre in Italy developed directly out of Carnival entertainment is very much a matter of debate, but it most certainly contributed, at the very least, in helping to cultivate a public taste for theatre and in bringing amateur and professional performers together in common celebrations. Surprisingly few detailed early accounts of Carnival in Italian cities have come down to us, primarily perhaps because what was familiar was not felt to warrant detailed description. The reports of foreigners tend to be particularly vivid, even if often brief. Among them is that of the English traveller Fynes Moryson, who wrote at the end of the sixteenth century. His likening of mountebank entertainment to comedies is particularly interesting, as is his reference to the esteem some stage players enjoyed.

In the tyme of Carnavall all Cittyes use to have publike Comedies acted by Citizzens, and in Florence they had a house where all the yeare long a Comedy was played by professed players once in the weeke and no more, and the partes of wemen were played by wemen, and the cheefe Actours had not their parts fully penned, but spake much extempory or upon agreement betweene themselves, espetially the wemen, whose speeches were full of wantonness, though not grosse baudry (which the Italians like, but neede no such provocation) and their playes were of Amorous Matters, Never of hystoryes, much lesse of tragedies, which the Italyans nature too much affects to imitate and surpasse. And one Lucinia a woman player, was so liked of the Florentines, as when shee dyed they made her a monument with an Epitaphe. Also not only in Carnavall but all the yeare long, all the Markett places of Great Cittyes are full of Mountebankes, or Ciarlatanes, who stand upon tables like stages, and to sell their oyles, waters, and salves, drawe the people about them by musicke and pleasant discourse like Comedies, having a woman and a masked foole to acte these partes with them.

(Fynes Moryson, *Shakespeare's Europe*, 1903, vol. 2, p. 465)

John Evelyn on Carnival in Rome

The English diarist John Evelyn visited Italy in 1643, travelling through France to Marseilles, then on to Genoa and Rome, before returning via Venice and Padua – a journey that lasted nearly four years. In his Diary *he records his impressions of Carnival customs in various Italian cities; the following is his account of Carnival in Rome in February 1645.*

We were taken up next morning in seeing the impertinences of the Carnival when all the world are as mad at Rome as at other places; but the most remarkable were the three races of the Barbary horses, that run in the Strada del Corso without riders, only having spurs so placed on their backs, and hanging down by their sides, as by their motion to stimulate them; then of mares; then of asses of buffalos, naked men, old and young and boys: an abundance of idle and ridiculous pastimes. One thing is remarkable, their acting comedies on a stage placed on a cart, or *plaustrum* where the scene or tiring-place is made of boughs, in a rural manner, which they drive from street to street with a yoke or two of oxen, after the ancient guise. The streets swarming with prostitutes, buffoons and all manner of rabble.

(Evelyn, 1857, vol. I, p. 174)

BANQUET AND CARNIVAL CLOWNS

Balls and banquets, as we have said, were a feature of Carnival and dynastic festivities in the Renaissance, and clown performances were as popular with the social elite as with the lower orders. A celebrated early sixteenth century Carnival and banquet entertainer, who performed too in short intermezzi, *was the buffoon Zan Polo. Very little is known about him or his fellow clowns, but his performances were often* intermezzi *between the acts of classical play productions. There is a tantalizingly brief description of a piece he gave in February 1515 as* entr'acte *entertainment to a performance in Venice of Plautus'* Miles Gloriosus, *acted by the Immortali Academici*:

In the midst of the acts Zan Polo came up with another new comedy in which he pretended to be a sorcerer and in Hell, and he conjured up a Hell with flames and devils: he also pretended to become the God of Love, and was transported into Hell, where he found Domenego Taiacalze [another buffoon who had died two years before] enclosed with the *castroni*; and then he came out with the *castroni* and they all did a dance; then there was music by Nymphs riding on a triumphal carriage, who sang a song to the beat of hammers, each beating time on an anvil, imitating the beating of a heart etc.

(Marino Sanuto, *Diarii*, 1879–1903, XIX, p. 443)

Another remarkable solo performer of the early cinquecento *was the buffoon Cimador. The poet and dramatist Pietro Aretino describes one of Cimador's performances, and his account suggests that this apparently improvised comic sketch contains within itself many of the essential elements of the improvised comedy developed later by the acting companies. This clown mimics in turn figures comparable to a* zanni, *a* servetta *and a* Magnifico, *and by vocal skill and timing conjures up a small comic world at once exaggerated in its emphases, yet rooted in the instantly recognizable. The situation and exchanges are comparable to many of the short scenes the players were later to develop into a visible stage action.*

Nanna: Ha! ha! ha! I'm still laughing about one they called the son of Giampolo, a Venetian I think, who imitated an assortment of voices while concealed behind a door. He did a porter well enough for anyone from Bergamo to have given him the palm. When the porter enquired of an old woman about a lady, in imitating the old woman he would say, 'And what do you want from my lady?' And in reply said to her, 'I should like to speak with her,' and in just the way such a rascal would do he added, 'Madonna, oh! Madonna, I'm dying, and I can feel my lung bubbling like washed tripe.' He could complain like a porter in the most perfect way in the world, and when he began to fondle her he joked away with the sort of remarks sure to spoil her Lent and make her break her fast. Then in the midst of this game who should appear but her senile old husband, who at the sight of the porter made an uproar that sounded like a peasant who finds his cherry tree being robbed – and the porter replied 'Oh sir!, sir! Ah ha!', and laughed and gestured like an idiot. 'Oh, go your way!' said the old man, 'You're a drunken ass!' Then having got the servant woman to remove his boots, he would tell his wife a garbled tale about *Sofi* and the Turk, and made everyone collapse with laughter as, farting all the while, he would swear never again to eat food that gave him the wind. When he had been put to bed, and was snoring away in his sleep, this same buffoon became the porter again, and after much laughing and crying with the lady began to shake her fur [. . .] you'd have howled listening to the noise they made too-ing and fro-ing together, the vulgar remarks of the porter nicely counterpointing the lady's cries of 'Do it to me!'

(Aretino, *I ragionamenti*, 1584, pp. 67–8)

PLATE 7 *Mountebanks in Piazza San Marco, Venice, Late sixteenth century watercolour. Permission of The British Library, MS Egerton 1191*

MOUNTEBANKS AND STREET ENTERTAINERS

Garzoni on mountebanks

During Carnival in particular, but throughout the year, the great squares of the major cities were naturally a magnet for the talents of travelling mountebank troupes with their embryonic professional theatre performances. In his La piazza universale *(1585), Tommaso Garzoni, an indefatigable observer and analyst of the social scene, has left an illuminating account of the whole genus of mountebanks, buffoons and similar itinerant entertainers who swarmed in the Italian cities. Here we cite from J. A. Symond's vigorous, if slightly contracted, translation of Garzoni, (pp. 745–7, 1595 ed):*

[. . .] the curtains of the booth open, and the Tuscan comes forth with his tumbling girl. He begins some silly story in the Florentine tongue, during which the girl draws her circle and puts herself in position, straddling with arms and legs abroad, flinging her body backwards to pick up a piece of money with her mouth from two crossed swords, and tickling the greasy varlets of the market-place by the exhibition of her lascivious graces. Not far away, you may see the Milanese quack, dressed like a noble gentleman, velvet cap on head and white Guelf feathers waving to the wind. He is telling his man Gradello some story of his hapless love. The groom cuts indecent jokes and gibes in the background; then swaggers forward, twirls his moustachioes, vows to uphold his mater's cause against all rivals, and bristles like an enraged bloodhound; but, on a sudden, feigning to see foe-men near, he drops his arms, knocks his knees together, befouls his breeches on the stage and lets himself be soundly drubbed. When that interlude is over, Gradello acts another part. He is a blind man squalling out a ditty, and thrumming on a puppy in his lap instead of a theorbo. The climax of all this buffoonery is a panegyric of some famous pills, which lasts an hour or two, and leaves the charlatan wrangling over cents and farthings with his swiftly dwindling audience. Towards evening the crowd of quacks and blind musicians and acrobats thicken. Here is Zan della Vigna with his performing monkey; there Catullo and his guitar; in another corner the Mantuan merry-andrew, dressed up like a zany, Zottino singing an ode to the pox, and the pretty Sicilian rope dancer. Tamburino spins eggs on a stick; the Neapolitan capers about with brimming bowls of water on his pate; and Maestro Paolo da Arezzo makes his solemn entry with a waving banner, on which you see St Paul, holding a huge falchion in one hand, while the rest of the field is painted over with twining hissing serpents. The mountebank clears his throat and relates his fabulous pedigree. St Paul was his great ancestor, and ever since that accident upon the island of Malta, all the family have possessed miraculous powers over the snaky tribe. Hereupon boxes are opened, and horrid vipers, water-snakes, and adders are drawn forth to the terror of bystanders.

(Garzoni, *La piazza universale,* cited by J. A. Symonds, *The Useless Memoirs of Count Carlo Gozzi,* 1890, vol. I, pp. 77–8)

Coryate on mountebanks in Venice

The English traveller Thomas Coryate was in Italy in 1608 and published an account of his journey in 1611, Coryates Crudities. *In it he gives a vivid description of mountebanks at work in the Piazza San Marco in Venice, the details of which nicely complement those of Garzoni and are remarkably close to the particulars in a contemporary engraving showing such entertainers in the great square (see plate 16).*

The principall place where they act, is the first part of Saint *Marks* street that reacheth betwixt the West front of St *Marks* Church and the opposite front of Saint *Geminians* Church. In which, twice a day, that is, in the morning and in the afternoone, you may see five or sixe severall stages erected for them: those that act upon the ground, even the foresaid Ciarlatans being of the poorer sort of them, stand most commonly in the second part of S. *Marks*, not far from the gate of the Dukes Palace. These Mountebanks at one end of their stage place their trunke, which is replenished with a world of new-fangled trumperies. After the whole rabble of them is gotten up to the stage, whereof some-weare visards being disguised like fooles in a play, some that are women (for there are divers women also amongst them) are attyred with habits according to that person that they sustaine; after (I say) they are all upon the stage, the musicke begins. Sometimes vocall, sometimes instrumentall, and sometimes both together. This musicke is a preamble and introduction to the ensuing matter: in the meane time while the musicke playes, the principall Mountbanke which is the Captaine and ring-leader of all the rest, opens his truncke, and sets abroad his wares; after the musicke hath ceased, he maketh an oration to the audience of halfe an hour long, or almost an houre. Wherein he doth most hyperbolically extoll the vertue of his drugs and confections:

Laudat venales qui vult extrudere merces.

Though many of them are very counterfeit and false. Truely I often wondred at many of these naturall Orators. For they would tell their tales with such admirable volubility and plausible grace, even *extempore*, and seasoned with that singular variety of elegant jests and witty conceits, that they did often strike great admiration into strangers that never heard them before: and by how much the more eloquent these Naturalists are, by so much the greater audience they draw unto them, and the more ware they sell. After the chiefest Mountebankes first speech is ended, he delivereth out his commodities by little and little, the jester still playing his part, and the musitians singing and playing upon their instruments. The principall things that they sell are oyles, soveraigne waters, amorous songs printed, Apothecary drugs, and a Common-weale of other trifles. The head Mountebanke at every time that he delivereth out any thing, maketh an extemporall speech, which he doth eftsoones intermingle with such savorie jests (but spiced now and then with singular scurrility) that they minister passing mirth and laughter to the whole company, which perhaps may consist of a thousand people that flocke together about one of their stages. For so many according to my estimation I have seene giving attention to some notable eloquent Mountebanke. I have observed marveilous strange matters done by some of these Mountebankes. For I saw one of them holde a viper in his hand and play with his sting a quarter of an houre together, and yet receive no hurt; though another man should have beene presently stung to death with it. He made us all beleeve that the same viper was linealy descended from the generation of that viper that leapt out of the fire upon S. *Pauls* hand, in the Island of Melita now called Malta, and did him no hurt; and told us moreover that it would sting some, and not others. [. . .] I have seene some of them doe such strange jugling trickes as would be almost incredible to be reported. Also I have observed this in them, that after they have extolled their wares to the skies, having set the price of tenne crownes upon some one of their commodities, they have at last descended so low, that they have taken for it foure gazets, which is something lesse then a groat. These merry fellowes doe most commonly continue two good howres upon the stage, and at last when they have fedde the audience with such passing variety of sport, that they are even cloyed with the superfluity of their conceits, and have sold as much ware as they can, they remove their trinkets and stage till the next meeting.

(Coryate, *Coryate's Crudities*, 1611, pp. 272–5)

ACTORS AND MOUNTEBANKS

Ottonelli on mountebanks performing plays

That mountebank stages provided more than mere short comic turns and sketches, and that they may well have been the breeding grounds of many of the first regular actors, seems clear from the following vivid account of a street performance by the cleric Ottonelli, an account the more interesting as he implies that what he describes was quite general practice.

But let us consider the practice of charlatan players. At times a company of these good fellows appears in a town: along with them are women experienced in the same profession, for they are convinced that without women they would make no impression and win little applause. They widely publicise their wish to serve the public by selling astonishing cures and performing excellent plays — and all this they claim to do free of charge, and from no more than a wish to please and entertain. They select a place in the public square where they set up their platform, and on this first the charlatan, then the actors perform. Each day at a convenient hour a Zanni or some similar entertainer steps onto the stage and begins to perform or sing in order to attract a crowd about him. A little later another player appears, and then another, and often a woman among them. Then all in a group, and with various kinds of trickery, they present a mixed bag of popular entertainment. Suddenly the key figure appears – he who is the arch charlatan, the guardian of the elixir – and in subtle ways he sets about extolling his wonderful cure-all in the most extravagant terms. After selling a great deal of it, and having gathered up all the money, he brings his principle business to an end. He is followed by another charlatan who, if the first has not managed to dispose of all his wares, peddles them once again. Then after him comes a woman who similarly tries to sell her lozenges or merchandise. When they are done they inform the public thus.

A play is about to begin – a play! Closing their boxes, removing their trunks, transforming the platform into a stage, each charlatan becomes a player and, just like actors, they act out a dramatic tale, entertaining the spectators with laughter, *lazzi* and diversion for nearly two hours.

(Ottonelli, *Della Christiana Moderatione del Theatro*, 1652, Bk.V, p. 455–6)

PLATE 8 *Late sixteenth century drawing of a* Carnival Scene *by Lodewyk Toeput (but attributed to Louis de Caulery by M. A. Katritsky). Permission of the Fitzwilliam Museum, Cambridge*

Whetstone on Italian entertainers

But the performances of such small mountebank troupes, notwithstanding similarities in comic styles and strategies, were still in essentials distinct from those of the regular acting companies which had emerged by the middle decades of the sixteenth-century. As much seems clear from George Whetstone's description of entertainers performing in an Italian patrician villa during Christmas festivities. Whetstone had visited Italy in 1580, and while his Heptameron of Civill Discourses *(1582) was not a travelogue, but an attempt to imitate a then fashionable Italian narrative pattern which mingled stories and debates, his account may well be based on his own experience. He tells how guests in a noble household were entertained one evening by a mountebank and his support troupe:*

In the ende, when Supper was done, and Queene Aurelia, and the most Honourable of the companie had taken their places uppon a Scaffolde made for the nonce, there mounted a Mountebanke, his necke bechayned with live Adders, Snakes Eau'ts, and twentie sundrie kinde of venemous vermines, whose mortall stinges were taken away by Arte, & with him a Zanni, and other Actors of pleasure; who presented themselves onelie with a single desire, to recreate Segnior Philoxenus, and his worthie companie: and not with the intent of common Mountebanckers, to deceyve the people with some unprofitable Marchandize.

(Whetstone, *Heptameron of Civill Discourses,* 1582, p. liii verso)

On another evening, however, a company of players from Ravenna devised a play on the basis of suggestions thrown out to them by the dinner guests. It seems clear from Whetstone's description that improvisation was the stock-in-trade of these players and, further, that they and their performance were of rather a different order from that of the mountebank troupe and the kind of entertainment it had given.

By that time, Supper was done, certayne Comedians of Ravenna, presented their service to Segnior Philoxenus, & his honourable companie, who are not tide to a written device, as our English Players are, but having a certayne groundes or principles of their owne, will, Extempore, make a pleasaunt showe of other mens fantasies: so that to try the quicknes of the Gentlemen, & Gentlewomens wittes, to give the Comedians a Theame, Segnior Philoxenus, demanded the meaning of certain Questions.

(Whetstone, *Heptameron,* 1582, p. r ii)

The players then proceeded to improvise pieces around the questions and themes put to them by members of the audience. Whetstone leaves us in no doubt that the kinds of entertainment offered on the two evenings were distinct. It is unfortunate that he is not more specific, for the exact nature of the relationship, and the undeniable interconnections, between mountebank troupes and regular players in the mid and late sixteenth century is tantalizingly elusive. Mountebanks long remained active in the main Italian cities and they employed masked actors of the improvising tradition to help canvas their wares by acting out short playlets, a practice that continued well into the eighteenth century.

An eighteenth-century mountebank troupe

The eighteenth-century Venetian dramatist, Carlo Goldoni, described in his memoirs encountering in 1734 in Milan one of the most celebrated mountebanks of the age, Bonafede Vitali, and the small troupe of performers who worked with him. Vitali, known as the Anonymous, was, too, a company manager, engaged in theatre as well as practising his charlatan's trade; the players, it should be noted, were apparently not the same as the trestle stage performers. For a short time Goldoni wrote for him and his Compagnia dell'Anonimo and helped them to get established in Milan.

There came to this town in the beginning of Lent, a mountebank of a singular description, whose name deserves a place perhaps in the annals of the age.

His name was Bonafede Vitali; he was a native of Parma, and he styled himself the Anonymous. He was of a good family, had received an excellent education, and had been a Jesuit. Disgusted with the cloister, he applied to the study of medicine, and succeeded in obtaining a professor's chair at the University of Palermo.

This singular man, to whom no branch of science was unknown, possessed an inordinate ambition to display the extent of his knowledge; and as he was a better orator than a writer he quitted the honourable situation which he occupied, for the purpose of mounting the stage and haranguing the public; but as he was not rich enough to be satisfied with mere glory, he turned his talents to account by vending his medicines.

This was nothing more nor less than playing the mountebank; but his specific remedies were good, and his science and eloquence procured for him a reputation and a degree of consideration by no means common.

He resolved publicly all the most difficult questions which were proposed to him in every science and on the most abstruse subject. Problems, points of criticism, history, and literature, were handed up to him on his empirical stage, and he returned an immediate answer, and gave very satisfactory dissertations.

[. . .] When at Milan, the Anonymous had the satisfaction of seeing the place where he exhibited, always filled with crowds of people on foot and in carriages; but as the learned were far from being the best purchasers, he was obliged to furnish his scaffold with objects calculated to attract and entertain the ignorant multitude, and the new Hippocrates therefore vended his drugs and displayed his rhetoric, surrounded with the four masks of the Italian comedy.

M. Bonafede Vitali had also a passion for comedy, and kept up at his own expense a complete company of comedians, who, after assisting their master in receiving the money thrown up in handkerchiefs, and returning the same handkerchiefs filled with small pots or boxes, represented pieces in three acts, with the help of torches of white wax, in a style which might be called magnificent.

(Goldoni, *Memoirs*, trans. Black, 1814, vol. I, pp. 189–90)

The relationship between Carnival entertainers, buffoons and mountebank players on the one hand, and acting companies proper on the other, was a long and complicated one: from the first they and their styles and kinds of performance certainly contributed, albeit in obscure and complex ways, to the emergence of an altogether new theatrical formation: the formally constituted professional acting companies.

2

The Emergence of Professional Companies

Beginnings

THE EMERGENCE in the middle decades of the sixteenth century of the organized professional acting companies, and of the new dramaturgy they evolved, was the outcome of broad and far-ranging social changes. These changes are inevitably hard to pin down: they occurred gradually, at a different pace in different regions, and by no means had a uniform outcome; they were connected with the political and economic fortunes of individual states, the widespread reverberations of the Sack of Rome in 1527 by the troops of Charles V, the moral retrenchments and realignments which issued from the sessions of the Council of Trent (1545–63), and the cultural changes which came with the firm establishment by the 1550s of Spanish power in many parts of the peninsula.

By the early years of the century the aristocratic and neoplatonic culture of the High Renaissance was beginning to break up, and the initial impetus of Italian Humanism appeared to be spent. Many scholars have remarked an increasing mood of gloom and despondency in the literature of the early sixteenth century, most readily evident in the cynical view of human nature found in the writings of, say, Machiavelli and Guicciardini, Aretino and Bruno. The seminal influence of classical example was still felt, but in much writing, too, it now tended to harden into rigid dogma and arid academicism. It was, further, gradually being overlain, where it was not actually displaced, by the very kinds of emphasis and enquiry Humanism had itself helped to generate: by the new premium set on individualism and special talent, and by new 'arrangements of knowledge', to use Foucault's phrase, which offered a unity that was man-centred. In the particular field of drama and theatre these were increasingly apparent in the location of dramatic action, notably that of comedy, in contemporary life, in the development of perspective stage settings replicating the familiar, and in the search for new theatre forms appropriate to the accommodation of the new coherences perceived in social and spatial relationships. Andrea Palladio's Teatro Olimpico, completed in 1585, is a particularly striking instance of the extent to which change had taken place, for it can now be seen as essentially archaeological, a throw-back to the concerns of early Humanist enquiry, and not a pointer forward to what was to come.[1] The formation of the acting companies and their elaboration of a new kind of drama that exploited pre-existent skills were attempts, however unconscious, to respond to these changed and changing conditions; attempts made, furthermore, by many who were forced to find new outlets for their talents to replace opportunities gradually being closed to them as Humanism retreated from the exclusive, but socially rather heterogeneous courts, to the more rarefied intellectual and cultural atmosphere of the academies.

Precisely how and why individuals came to band together in legally constituted acting companies in order to make their livings by the regular performance of plays is far from clear. But professionals seem to have been involved in one capacity or another in late fifteenth- and early sixteenth-century court theatricals, whether as advisers, stage-managers or performers. As vernacular scripted drama, particularly comedy, flourished, it accommodated to its Latin formal models much from popular entertainment: not just elements from the *novelle*, but the jests, tricks, satires, pasquinades and 'business' of the low tradition.[2] The ability of comedy to root itself in immediate life, and to treat of the local and the seamy, gave it a directness and vitality which liberated it in part from slavish adherence to classical models. Some of Aretino's comedies for example, like *La cortigiana* (1525) and *Il marescalco* (1527), or the anonymous *La veniexiana* (c1540), reveal the underlying influence of popular entertainment materials. Indeed the classical example of Plautus licensed the incorporation of such elements.

Opportunities for professional entertainers to exercise their skills were considerable, not least because distinctions between amateur and professional cannot always have been clear. Talent in an art or craft, particularly those allied to theatre, like architecture or literature, and perhaps, too, certain kinds of performance, was always for the culturally and socially aspirant a possible springboard to patrician patronage or court notice and advancement. Unfortunately we know comparatively little of the early productions, from Pomponius Laetus's staging of Seneca's *Hippolytus* in

Rome in 1486, through to the mountings of vernacular drama, like Ariosto's *La Cassaria*, done at Ferrara in 1508, and Bibbiena's *La Calandria*, given at Urbino in 1513. Such cultural activities were largely the preserve of the patrician *cognoscenti*, but there were opportunities too for artisans to contribute.[3] Leone de' Sommi's *Quattro dialoghi in materia di rappresentazioni sceniche* indicate that amateur performers were by no means indifferent to, or uninfluenced by the skills of professional performers, nor to the contributions to play production of artificers. A member of a prosperous Jewish family in Mantua, de' Sommi's varied activities included playwriting (in Hebrew), stage-management and play direction, and the third of his *dialoghi*, written some time between 1556 and 1565, is the first systematic account of acting, staging and direction in the Western theatre.[4] De' Sommi himself was neither a professional nor an artisan, and he is concerned almost wholly with the staging of the literary drama, but what he writes is a pointer to many of the attitudes and practices those on the cultural fringes of the courts were at this time taking into the nascent professional theatre.

In the court sphere professionals seem to have been centrally involved in the production and performance of *intermezzi* – comic

PLATE 9 *Early seventeenth century painting by Sebastian Vrancx* A Festival in a Palace Garden. *Permission of the Statens Museum for Kunst, Copenhagen*

and often spectacular interludes presented between the acts of scripted plays. In the course of the sixteenth century these became increasingly elaborate, their scenic effects devised by professional painters and machinists whose artisan skills tended to underscore an increasing awareness of the need for, and the value of, specialist expertise. As far as performance is concerned, the professional contribution was perhaps earliest most evident in the activities of buffoons. Productions of the literary drama were not usually isolated events, but formed part of a complex of festival activities which included balls and banquets. Solo buffoon entertainment was a feature of the latter, as, too, was the performance of plays, with *intermezzi* interspersed between the acts.[5] In these *intermezzi* buffoons participated, sometimes as principal performers. As can be seen in the documents given above (see p. 24), Venetian buffoons like Zan Polo Lianpardi, Domenico Taiacalze and Cimador provided solo sketches, or acted along with other comedians and dancers. In fact it is in Venice and its adjacent territories, far more than elsewhere, that we find documentation which helps to chart the emergence of professional companies and the improvised drama.

Venetian Theatricals

Nowhere in Italy during the early decades of the sixteenth century was there such a rich coexistence of, and so many fruitful interconnections between, popular and aristocratic culture, as in Venice and the Venetian territories. Theatrical entertainment in particular was considerable and took a variety of forms, as the many entries in the *Diarii* of Marino Sanuto show.[6] It took place, too, in a range of performance places, including the houses of the nobility and in hired rooms and halls, as well as on fit-up street stages, and Carnival in particular provided the occasion for it. In these many kinds of entertainment, and in the confluence of popular and elite traditions, may lie the beginnings of organized professional theatre. Those beginnings appear to be intricately connected with the highly original achievements of dramatists and actor-dramatists who devised dialect and multilingual comedy, the activities of amateur and semi-professional acting companies, and of individual performers the actual status of whose work, whether amateur or professional, remains problematic.

Of the several Paduan and Venetian dramatists and actor-dramatists who flourished in the early and middle decades of the sixteenth century, the most celebrated are the Paduan playwright and amateur actor Angelo Beolco (*c*1502–42), better known under his stage-name, Il Ruzante, and the Venetian, Andrea Calmo (*c*1510–71), likewise a performer as well as a writer. In the plays of both, the farcical comic tone, recourse to dialect, use of rustic characters and knock-about stage 'business', as well as the presence of certain specific character types, have all been seen to presage aspects of the professional improvised comedy. In their functions as actor, playwright and deviser of productions they have been taken by many, too, to provide the link between street and festival entertainers and the more extensive and regular activities of the professional acting companies.

Beolco took his stage-name from the characteristic type he introduced into many of his plays and performed himself, a boisterous, clumsy and garrulous Paduan *villano* (peasant) whose antics imbue the otherwise simple plots with an engaging comic brio.[7] His plays, of which *La Moscheta, Il Parlamento* and *Bilora* (all of the 1520s) are perhaps the best, were devised for performance by himself and his friends, often at Carnival-time and before audiences of mainly prosperous friends and associates. They are rich in rustic mood and colour, are at times bawdy and scatological, and treat of comic incidents in the lives of peasants, whose hard lives and domestic imbroglios are handled with insight and compassion. In them Ruzante may have provided opportunities for extensive pantomime and improvisation. He is a figure of major importance, the most impressive writer of rustic and dialect drama in the period, and one who tapped an authentic vein of popular life in a simple, natural style unusual to most drama of the time. He was not indifferent to the example of classical comedy, and indeed in his later plays, like *La Fiorina*, conspicuously applied classical form to his peasant material. But he avoided academic pedantry and any slavish imitation of the ancients, turning the vigour of Plautine farce to his own very distinctive purposes. His links with the later improvised comedy, at least as far as his plays are concerned, are at once real and tenuous. He was not its precursor in the sense sometimes argued that characters in his plays manifestly anticipate figures of the improvised *commedia dell'arte*. In that regard he offers little to those seeking to establish the origins of the individual masks. In other respects, however, he was very much a precursor. The example of his work may well have offered much that was instructive to the later comedians: ways of organizing a sequence of farcical incidents in a low comedy plot line, methods of exploiting regional dialect for comic purposes, and strategies for turning scripted dialogue to the service of an essentially performer-oriented drama. For Beolco, it seems, from both the records which have come down to us and the dramaturgy of the plays themselves, was as much a practitioner as he was a writer. The illegitimate son of a well-to-do father, Ruzante had the time and resources to develop his interest in stage performance. He organized companies, stage-managed and took the lead roles in his own plays.[8] There is no evidence however that he ever was, or aspired to be, a professional actor, nor even that he saw his theatrical work as of semi-professional status. He was a mere eighteen when he first formed an acting company with a group of friends, and for many years with like-minded *dilettanti* he performed his plays before bourgeois and patrician audiences, including those who gathered at the villa of his patron, a wealthy Venetian patrician, Luigi Cornaro.

Another, although admittedly lesser, practitioner of the *commedia villanesca* was Beolco's younger contemporary, Calmo, a Venetian gondolier who was perhaps more regularly an actor than Beolco, and possibly worked on a semi-professional basis. Where Beolco wrote primarily in the Paduan dialect, Calmo very deliberately employed a variety of dialects in order to define certain recognizable regional types. A prominent character in some of his plays is a Venetian *vecchio*, whom some scholars again have taken to foreshadow a figure of the improvised *commedia dell'arte* – the Venetian Magnifico – although it is not an identification that has won general acceptance. Inevitably, most of what we know of Calmo, just as of Beolco, concerns his scripted work, and even allowing that this admitted possibilities for the development of character and business through improvisation, little in the texts themselves, nor in those of other sixteenth-century comic dramatists like Strascino and Alione, manifestly anticipates the peculiar spirit, constituents and characteristics of the improvised *commedia dell'arte*.[9] In the plays of these dramatists, as in those of Beolco, we find, not the *origins* of the *commedia dell'arte*, but a pre-history which contributed in complex ways to the emergence of professional theatre.

The Earliest Companies

Where Beolco and Calmo must be considered of particular additional significance is in their performance work, for although the companies they played with were not established on a regular acting basis, their activities do seem to presage the formation of organized professional acting troupes. So, too, and perhaps even more so, does the work of Francesco Nobili, known as Cherea. Nobili was a gifted actor who had probably acquired considerable stage experience in Mantua and Ferrara before appearing in Venice about the year 1507. A year later we know that he acted there in Italian translations of antique plays, like *Asinaria* and *Menaechmi*, subsequently peforming in both private halls and public rooms, and helping to excite sufficient public interest in play productions to arouse Venetian government suspicion of this new-fangled and potentially disruptive mode of entertainment. Cherea seems to have acted quite frequently in Venice through to 1526, after which no more is heard about him save for a brief reference some years later to his being in Hungary. It is primarily from Sanuto's diary entries that we know something of Cherea's work; although these are tantalizingly brief, they seem to suggest that he was more than a *dilettante*. It is at least conceivable that the companies he led were the first Italian professional acting troupes. But then it is conceivable too that other groups of players whose activities in Venice (and indeed in Rome and elsewhere) have left faint traces in extant records, may have equal claim to be considered the first professionals.[10] Whatever troupe merits that accolade, we can say with certainty that by the middle decades of the sixteenth century the Italian professional companies were in being: the first extant contract (see below p. 44) made by a group of players at Padua in 1545 provides a convenient *terminus a quo* for their operations.

How, when and why the first troupes came together are elusive matters; so too is the provenance of the performers who made up those troupes. To judge from the kinds of patronage he enjoyed and the material he performed, Cherea moved in elite circles and was a man of some culture. On the other hand, the players who signed the Paduan contract were apparently of fairly low social and cultural status. But as professional theatre evolved it tended to bridge social gaps. In so far as it is possible to generalize from the scraps of evidence which have come down we would hazard that the early professional players were in the main drawn from two spheres, which on occasions, and to a varying extent, overlapped: on the one hand, and perhaps particularly in the 1540s and 1550s, the world of popular street and Carnival entertainment; and on the other, more possibly from the 1560s and 1570s onwards, the cultural fringes of courts which were no longer as hospitable to aspirant talent as they had been in their *quattrocento* heyday.

PLATE 10 *Venetian Carnival figures from F. Bertarelli,* Il carnovale italiano mascherato *(1643). Permission of The British Library, C 43 a27*

What seems additionally to have occurred in the early and middle decades of the *cinquecento* to give further impetus to this confluence of talents from the popular and courtly spheres was the development of a public taste for play performances at various social levels. Why, is again hard to calculate. Perhaps Humanist experiment had quite unwittingly opened a Pandora's box. What entertained academies and courts perhaps came quickly to be seen as desirable by many beyond the courts, and such theatrical activity, accomodated to more popular tastes, became self-generating: the more of it there was, the more a market appeared for it. Quite how sophisticated the taste was of this early public is a moot point. One Venetian observer sourly noted: 'they wish to have on the stage nothing else but silly buffoons, an empty confusion of languages and little honest action.'[11] But an audience was there, and the temptation increased for some amateurs to capitalize on public interest by exercising their talents as a regular means of livelihood: the skilled amateur, given the right conditions, could be an incipient professional. Judging from the entries in Sanuto's *Diarii* something like that seems to have happened in Venice in the early decades of the sixteenth century. High and low culture came increasingly to interconnect, the distinction between amateur and professional became ever more blurred, opportunities opened up for the exploitation of entertainment as a business, and for the practice of acting as a career, not just on a solo performer basis, or through a random gathering of solo performer abilities (a musician, a rope dancer, a jester), but by the banding together of individuals in formally constituted acting companies. There would appear to be some connection too between the decline in the quality and vitality of *cinquecento* Humanist-inspired scripted drama by mid-century, and the emergence of professional acting companies performing both scripted drama and improvised plays, the plots and characters of which bear close resemblance to the materials of the Humanist drama but are pitched more broadly to meet professional needs and the disparate tastes of paying publics. The superior appeal at all levels of professional and regular over *dilettante* and occasional performance cannot be discounted. Altogether fortuitous, but symbolic of changing times, interests and attitudes, was the fact that 1565 in Venice saw the final performance of the amateur Compagnia della Calza, whose productions had been a feature of Venetian theatrical life for decades: the name of the company that acted *Antigono* was soon to be that of a *commedia dell'arte* troupe, the Accesi.[12]

The introduction of actresses in the 1560s, the first record of which is the appearance in a troupe list in 1564 of a certain Lucrezia Senese, may have marked a new phase in the development of the professional companies: an elaboration perhaps of the romantic plot lines to balance the low comedy, and a calculated bid for greater commercial appeal. The arrival of the actresses seems to coincide with, or to be quite rapidly followed by, the presence in professional companies of actors better educated and more socially sophisticated than was customary among popular street and Carnival entertainers. Both appear to have been crucial to the quite rapid development of the companies and their ability to open up and exploit a burgeoning market for theatrical entertainment. The Italian philosopher and theatre historian, Benedetto Croce, argued persuasively that one of the central characteristics of these acting companies was their immersion in the market; that the kind of drama they evolved was the product of an embryonic industrial system and a mode of production that was a response to market pressures and possibilities.[13] More recently, a very perceptive historian, Ferdinando Taviani, has observed that this industry developed, in effect, as theatre passed from being a species of entertainment within the economy of the *festa* to being an entertainment organized according to the economic dictates of the market.[14] What marks off the professional companies from the performers who had preceded them, and serves to distinguish them as a wholly new theatrical formation, is the fact that they earned their living by acting plays. By virtue of that alone they were a definable social group with a particular, if variable, social position.[15] Their activities were largely determined by the needs and possibilities of the market, and their status – economic, social and artistic – was conditional on the kind of place they were able to secure in it. Further, the sheer need for these professional companies to operate at different social levels, from the aristocracy of the courts, through less affluent private patrons, to the bourgeoisie and the broader populace drawn to performances in halls, rooms, streets or *piazze*, and to supply according to occasion and demand a wide variety of different kinds of theatrical entertainment, including comedies, tragi-comedies, pastorals, *intermezzi* and so on, impelled them to devise a species of production which could meet these different market opportunities and requirements without imposing impossible demands on their materials and resources – namely, the composition of their stock plays by improvisatory techniques. What emerged, then, in the middle decades of the sixteenth century was a professional theatre consisting of actors ultimately drawn from diverse social and educational backgrounds, who banded together to sell their product, plays in performance, wherever they could find paying audiences. They were the *commedia mercenaria*, and it is their economic motivation and their professionalism, that ultimately defines them.

Documents

The documents included below are fairly wide-ranging and illustrate various aspects of Italian sixteenth-century theatre, from formal stage-management, through rustic scripted dialect comedy and banquet entertainment, to evidence about actors and acting provided by early company contracts.

LEONE DE' SOMMI ON STAGE-MANAGEMENT AND COMEDY

Leone de' Sommi's Quattro dialoghi *are a descriptive and analytical account of Italian Renaissance theories of drama and theatre practice. What he has to say on the dramatic genres is little more than a precise of stock Renaissance literary theory, but his description of play preparation, acting and staging practice in the third dialogue is invaluable to our understanding of the production of scripted drama in the first half of the sixteenth century. Although it was not published until the twentieth century, and so was not a widely used contemporary handbook to practice, it indicates the kind of knowledge about approaches to staging that many on the fringes of court culture could easily have assimilated. As the title suggests, it is cast in the dialogue form, Veridico's here being the experienced, authoritative voice.*

Veridico: First I carefully copy out from the play all the parts and then, having chosen the most suitable actors (bearing in mind as far as possible those matters of which I shall speak later), I bring them all together and having given to each the part most suitable for him, I then have them read the whole play so that even the children who might have parts are familiar with the plot, or at least know what they themselves have to do. I try to impress on all of them the nature of the characters they have to interpret. Then I send them away and give them time to learn their parts.

Massimiano: This seems to me a good beginning. Now let us consider the selection of the actors and the distribution of roles, which I think is most important.

Veridico: It is, indeed, of cardinal importance, and in fact I would claim that it is more important to have good actors than a good play; and that this is the case is clear to all of us, for we have seen many times that an audience will respond more favourably to a bad play well acted, than to a fine play poorly executed. So when I am choosing the actors, assuming I have a number of capable, willing and obedient men, first I try to select those with a good accent, for this I consider the most important consideration. Then I try to ensure that they correspond in physical appearance as closely as possible to the roles they will perform. Thus I try to make sure that a lover is handsome, a soldier is robust, a parasite is fat, a servant is very agile, and so on. My next concern is the voice, for this I consider one of the actor's main assets, and naturally when I could avoid doing so I would not assign the part of an old man to one who had an immature voice, not give the role of a woman (especially that of a girl) to one with a very deep voice. Likewise, let us suppose I had to cast someone for the part of a ghost in a tragedy, then I would look for a voice naturally sharp and clear, or at least capable, with a trembling falsetto, of achieving the requisite impression. I should pay least attention to facial features, for a great deal can be supplied by artifice where nature was deficient: colouring a beard, simulating a scar, making a face pale or yellow or making it look more vigorous and ruddy, or whiter, or darker, or by similar other effects. But at no time would I use masks or false beards, because they are a hindrance to good acting. If necessity obliged me to give the role of an old man to a beardless actor, I would-paint his chin to make him appear shaven, and would show white hair under his cap; and his cheeks and forehead I would touch up with a brush so that he would appear not merely elderly, but, if I so wished, decrepit and wrinkled. [As far as acting is concerned it is important for the actor to convey the mood of the character at any given moment] [. . .] it is not enough for one playing the part of a miser just to keep his hand on his purse, as if checking that he still has the key to his money chest; he must also know how, at the appropriate moment, to imitate the frenzy he will undergo when he learns that his son has stolen his hoard. If an actor is playing the part of a servant then, at the right time, he must know how, in a moment of sudden joy, to leap about nimbly; or in a moment of grief how to tear a handkerchief with his teeth; or in a moment of despair to tear at his hair, and so on with other similar effects which give spirit to

PLATE 11 *A late sixteenth century comic stage setting. Woodcut to C. Gonzaga* Gli Inganni *(1592). Permission of The British Library, C 125 aa16*

the acting. If he is playing the role of a fool, then in addition to speaking off the point, as will be indicated for him by the author's dialogue, he must on occasions be able to appear even more of an idiot, by trying to catch flies or search for fleas and other similar such buffoonish antics. If he takes the role of a maid-servant coming out of a house, then he must know how, when appropriate, to toss his skirts vulgarly or to bite his thumb in anger, and other similar things which the author cannot explicitly indicate in his text.

(Leone de' Sommi, *Quattro dialoghi*. From Ms Cod. 2664, Biblioteca Palatina, Parma, in Rasi, *I Comici*, I, pp. 108–10; also in Marotti, 1968, pp. 39–42)

Among points of particular interest here are: the distribution to actors not of the play text, but only their individual parts; the emphasis on the entire cast reading together from their parts; the assumption that all performers are male; the relationship between the actors' physical appearance and type roles; the detailed attention paid to ways of expressing specific and basic passions and vices; and the over-riding importance accorded the actor.

THE RUSTIC COMEDY OF ANGELO BEOLCO (IL RUZANTE)

Some of the classical character types in the academic drama were taken over by Angelo Beolco in his commedia villanesca, *but when translated to Paduan dialect and locales, the colloquial idiom, earthy direction and rustic brio of Beolco's plays subsume literary character typology in a situation comedy that is scripted, but very performer-oriented. Beolco's dramaturgy, if not the specifics of his comic characterizations, helped to prepare the way for that of the later improvising players. In the following passage adapted from the dialogue usually called* Bilora, *the comic protagonist, an indigent peasant, has finally tracked down his wife, Dina, who in economic desperation has absconded with an elderly but prosperous bourgeois.*

(Dina has come out of Andronico's house to talk with her husband, Bilora)

Dina: Lord help me, I don't feel too good. If truth be told, I've had my fill of this old man (*meaning Andronico*).

Bilora: I can believe that. He's an old dodderer. Young and old never hit it off. You and I are a pair.

Dina: Oh Lord! he's on his last legs. He coughs all night like a sick sheep. He never goes to sleep. He's always on top of me, and kissing me, and he seems to think I like it. God help me, I'd like never to see him again, I'm so fed up with him.

Bilora: He stinks like a dung heap. You can sniff his rotten hide a thousand miles away, and he's such a leaky arse . . . but he got up somewhere didn't he?

Dina: Get off! – you do nothing but talk dirty.

Bilora: Look here . . . alright, I say . . . do you want to return to your own house with me, or leave me and stay here with the old man?

Dina: Well, personally I'd like to go with you, but he won't like it, and I don't think he wants me to go. If you could only see the way he feels me up, you'd never get over it! Mind you, he does love me, and I have a good time here.

Bilora: What do you mean, he doesn't want you to go? You're driving me nuts! He may want you, but what do *you* want? God!, I'll finish up doing something daft! . . . Come on, what do you want?

Dina: I'm not sure. I'd like to – but I'm not sure I'd like to.

Bilora: God give me patience! What time does he get back? Is he coming soon?

Dina: Quite soon – he'll be here all right. (Aside) And I don't want him to find us talking together. (*To Bilora:*) You'd better get going, love. Come back when he's here and see if you can agree something.

Bilora: In the arse we'll agree something! And you watch out if we don't. Bloody hell! I swear I'll . . . Christ! when I start I'm worse than a soldier . . . I think you're screwing me about. But don't you screw about with other people, you filthy bitch! (*He threatens to hit her*).

Dina: That's all I can hope to get from you! He can get just as angry as you, you know. Listen, I swear I'm serious. Come back later when he's here, knock on the door and say you want a word with the master. Tell him straight out you want me to go home with you, and let's see what he's got to say. If he goes along with it, fine. If not, I'll still go with you.

Bilora: Honest? You'll come with me anyway?

Dina: Yes, I've told you – I swear I will. Now get going – don't let him find you here.

Bilora: Look, do you have a bit of bread for me? I swear I'm starving to death. I've not had a bite since I left home last night.

Dina: I'd sooner give you some money, if it's alright with you, then you can go to the inn at the bottom of this road and eat and drink what you like. I don't want him to come back and find me giving you something from the house.

Bilora: Damn it all, give me the money. Where's this inn, very far?

Dina: No, just at the top there, turn that way. (*She points, and as he looks she goes into the house*)

Bilora: It'll be a damned nuisance if I can't find it. But look here . . . she's shut the door! I'm so famished I forgot to ask her how long I should wait before coming back. No matter, let's get some grub. By the time I've had my fill I expect he'll be back here. Now let's see how much she's given me. Blimey! What's this? I can't make out what this first one is. Got it! a two-mark piece. Didn't recognize it, but it's the very same one I blew when I first fell in love with her. This one's a *moragia*. This one? Pretty bloody big and weighty; bigger than the others. Shit, I can't think what it is. I've got it, a *cornacion*; and I fancy it's worth more than the rest. But let's get something to eat. Well, that's the door of the house, but will I recognize it when I get back? I don't want to make a mistake. Anyway, let's count up the money again: this one's worth two, a *moragia* makes four, then there's the *cornacion*, that's five, then one I'll keep, making six, and another I'll spend, so that makes seven, so I'm just nineteen marks short of a *tron*! (*Exits*)

Andronico: (*Entering, on the way to his house*) How very true it is, if you don't do childish things when you're young, you're bound to want to do them when you're old. It reminds me of how people long gone like Messers Nicoleto di Aliegri and Pantasileo da Ca' Bucentoro used to say to me, 'Why do you revel in this melancholy mood, Andronico? Why the devil don't you find a girl, and have some fun with her? When do you plan to have a good time? – when you can no longer manage it? You really are a chap who's in a trance. But you mark this, when you are old you'll make a fool of yourself for love.' And that's precisely what's happened. But still I think I'd sooner be in love now, than when I was young, except that a certain something isn't up to it – I mean knowing that *non respondent ultima primis*. Confound it, growing old is a grim business, *tamen* I still want it. But enough of that. Let's say no more. I'm not yet senile. Love can give you a lift. Consider the way I took this girl from her husband. Risked my life to get her – that's how much I love her and long for her. What's more, *breviter concludendo*, the girl's a Ganimede, with a little mouth hot for kisses! *In summa summario*, the only thing I'm afraid of, and it's a real worry, is that someone will come along and take her away from me. But if he does he'll get a rough welcome, because I intend to enjoy her myself.

(From *Ruzante; Tutte le opere*,
Second Dialogue, Vicenza, 1617, pp. 15–17)

Beolco had great confidence in his Paduan roots, and in his local dialect as the language most fitted for his peasant characters and subject matter, and his awareness of the vitality dialect could give to stage dialogue was similarly perceived by the early improvising players, the regional variety of whose stage language was an important feature of their performance.

EARLY PROFESSIONAL CONTRACTS

As we have remarked, a convenient start date for the formation of professional acting companies in Italy is the contract a group of eight artisans agreed in Padua in 1545. It bound them in a 'fraternal company', the future success of which was seen to depend on their mutual willingness to abide by its rigorous, but sensible stipulations. The company was to operate as a collective, sharing 'communal monies and earnings' even in sickness (save when that entailed departure from the group), but functioned under an elected leader whose business included the preparation and rehearsal of plays, deciding travelling itineraries, and entering into agreements on behalf of the group. The troupe's cash holdings were kept in a box to which three members held keys, and money could be dispensed from it only with the approval of the whole company. Presumably the signatories established from the start a communal fund to be augmented by earnings. Total assets were eventually to be divided equally between the companions. Precautions built into the contract to cover abscondment and severence were highly pertinent and indicate that from the beginning the likelihood of players being enticed away by more lucrative possibilities elsewhere had always to be taken into account. It is highly unlikely that the Paduan company was the first such to be formed. Interesting too is the oblique reference to 'such patrons as there may be'; the companions were evidently aware that if successful they might attract formal patronage. What this contract quite clearly indicates is that even before the middle of the century there was a market for organized professional company performance, and practitioners willing to band together to supply it: their intention, quite clearly, was to act comedies, although the nature of the comedies they gave, whether scripted, part-scripted, or improvised, is not known.

1545, Inditione 3, on the day of Mercury, 25th of the month of February in Padua, in the quarter of St Leonard, in the house of my solicitor, in the room on the ground floor.

Since the undersigned companions, namely Ser. Maphio called Zanini from Padua, Vincentio from Venice, Francesco de la Lira, Hieronimo from San Luca, Zuandomenego called Rizo, Zuane from Treviso, Tofano de Bastian, and Francesco Moschini, decided to form a fraternal company which should last until the first day of next Lent that will come in 1546, and which should commence in the octave of next Easter, together they have concluded and determined that in order that such a company shall survive in fraternal love until the above-mentioned time without any hatred, rancour and dissolution, to make and observe with love, as is customary among good and faithful companions, all the articles written hereunder which they promise to observe and abide by without cavil, under penalty and loss of the money written hereunder.

And first they have unanimously elected as their leader in the acting of their comedies from place to place wheresoever they may be the aforesaid Ser. Maphio, to whom all the aforesaid companions, in so far as concerns the acting of these comedies, must submit and give obedience to do all that he will order in things and to go acting through the country as he will order.

Item, that if by chance any of the companions during the life of the company shall fall ill, then in such a case the said companion will be helped and taken care of from the communal monies and earnings and be sustained until he has recovered, or be taken to his own home and until such time will receive his share, but on being returned to his own home will receive no more from the said company.

Item, that if the company is required to take to the road, all members are obliged to go and that any agreements made must be made by the said Zanino.

Item, in order that the said company may exist in complete harmony until the agreed time the aforesaid companions in agreement have established and determined that a cash box shall be made with three secure keys, one of which the said leader will have and keep, another Francesco de la Lira, the other Vincenzo from Venice, into which each day will be put the day's takings, now a ducat, now more or less, according to the takings made; and that this box should never be opened, nor any money taken from it, without the express consent and wish of the entire company. And if, during the life of the company, it enters the head of anyone of the companions, or two or more, to leave and abandon the others to their great harm and shame, then in such a case the person or persons who leave, in addition to the penalties written below, shall lose all use and profit from the money that may be in the said box, and that the portion which would have been allocated to those who have left shall be divided into equal parts and shared among those companions who find themselves fraternally united and not divorced from the company.

Item, that should any one of the said companions abscond from the company, then that person, in addition to foregoing the said portion that may be in the box, shall suffer a penalty of one hundred lire in cash of which a part shall be given to such patrons as there may be, a part to the poor, and a part to the company, and that such persons shall be summoned, tried and sentenced wherever the company shall think fit.

Item, that a horse shall be bought from the communal fund of the company, that shall carry the belongings of the brothers from place to place.

Item, than when the company reaches Padua, which should be in the month of June, then the money in the box shall be divided equally.

Item, that at the beginning of the month of September next the said company, subject to the afore-mentioned penalties, being all in agreement, shall go each his own way.

Item, that the said companions together shall not play cards with each other nor do anything else but take meals.

(From Cocco, 'Una compagnia comica della prima meta del secolo XVI', 1915, pp. 57–8)

Fours years later the players agreed another contract, no less fascinating and revealing for the detail it provides about the life of such itinerant actors. We may note both in this and in the previous contract the absence of any mention of actresses.

Thursday, 29 August 1549, in Padua, in the San Leonardo quarter, in the residence of myself, notary, and in the lower back room. Here Giovanni Trevisan, [son] of the late Antonio, resident of the Belle Parti quarter of Padua, as one party, and Maphio del Re, [son] of the late Giovanni, resident in the Borgo S. Croce quarter of Padua, as the other party, unanimously and harmoniously have formed an honest, firm and legal society, which is to last for the next six years, starting on the day they will begin to perform plays. They have formed such a society for the said reason of performing plays, and if in so far as they will be performed throughout the said time of six years and not otherwise. They promise each other, and their other associates, to go wherever the society will go, in whatever city, castle or country, for the purpose of staging the said plays, not only as they may be obliged by their other associates, but also if mutually obliged by each other – the above-mentioned Giovanni and Maphio. There is this proviso, however: when for the said purpose of staging plays they travel out of the city, they will not be permitted to take others into their society to perform the said plays, nor may they themselves go out of town with others without taking Giovanni Pietro, called Zambelloto, a Venetian, son of Ser Bartolomeo di Rossi, resident in Padua, the San Giovanni delle navi quarter, and Geronimo, son of Battista Bragati, resident of Padua, in the S. Luca quarter, and Francesco, called Moschin, son of the late Andrea di Catano, resident in the Volto del Lupo quarter in Padua. On the other hand, and in their turn, the said Giovanni Pietro Geronimo and Francesco here present, have pledged themselves to go with the said Giovanni Trevisano and Maphio during the whole of the above-said period, and in the same way these three will not be free to go with others except by the express agreement of the above-named two.

If any of them transgress always and at any time during the six above-mentioned years, and in any place, city, castle or villa, pay a fine of fifty gold ducats for the inconvenience, which sum shall be divided and asigned, half to the lord of that land, city, castle or villa, or even the place in whose jurisdiction the matter has taken place, and half to the members of the said society who had observed the said obligations of the said pact. They agree that in any place and at any time they shall be obligated as indicated above.

[Further] the three above-mentioned members of the said society shall obey the above-mentioned Giovanni and Maphio in all that is reasonable and honest, and this always and in any place, and throughout the period of the six years mentioned above. And whoever of the three does not wish to obey the said Giovanni and Maphio, that is in what pertains to the staging of any play, shall be penalized, and pay the said Giovanni and Maphio and the other members the whole sum of money the society would have gained from his, or their, portion. With the exception of such rights and obligations [. . .] on condition that the said Giovanni and Maphio and the other three mentioned above, feel obliged every year for fifteen days before or after the Day of S. Giustina the Virgin and Martyr, in the month of October, at the request of anyone in the said society, to go with the whole society to perform plays and observe the said articles until the first day of Lent each year. And in the event of failure to do so, he or they must pay the fine of the said fifty ducats to be divided and assigned as indicated above. The only exceptions are to be cases of illness, of just impediment, and honest and permissible accidental circumstances. In such cases of infirmity, and just and accidental impediment, each member of the

PLATE 12 *Early seventeenth century painting by Sebastian Vrancx* An Outdoor Banquet. *Szépmüvészeti Múzeum, Budapest*

said society can and should be excused, but not otherwise. Further, all the members shall follow the itineraries to be determined by the said Giovanni and Maphio, and whosoever transgresses shall be penalized as above. Further, all the afore-mentioned must keep the times arranged, and to be arranged, and be available in person to the said Giovanni and Maphio for the purpose of staging the said plays, and those who transgress in this shall be obliged to pay the above-mentioned penalty to be divided and asigned as indicated above.

(From Cocco, 'Una compagnia comica', 1915, pp. 66–7)

AN IMPROVISED COMEDY AT THE BAVARIAN COURT, 1568

The earliest surviving detailed description of an improvised performance is that by Massimo Troiano da Napoli, Master of Music at Castle Trausnitz in Bavaria. His account of what he and his colleagues performed is often referred to as a description of a commedia dell'arte *performance, but that is misleading, for it was given not by professionals but by court amateurs. During festivities at Trausnitz during February 1568, Duke William asked Troiano to supply a comedy for the entertainment of his guests. Much of the pleasure of the piece for the spectators, many of whom were ladies of the court, almost certainly lay in seeing well-known members of their own refined circle playing the fool. The gentlemen doubled parts, and the female parts were played by males. The description does not serve as a guide to professional performance, but clearly indicates that by 1568 acting* all'improvviso *was known beyond Italy, and was defined as performance 'in the Italian manner'.*

Fortunio: This evening a comedy was performed in the Italian manner *all'improvviso*, in the presence of all the most illustrious ladies, and notwithstanding that most who attended did not understand what was said, so accomplished and so delightful was the Venetian Magnifico, Messer Orlando di Lasso, together with his Zanni, that their jaws ached with laughter at all the antics.

Marino: Be so kind as to tell me what it was all about.

Fortunio: The day before the performance it had occurred to the illustrious Duke Wilhelm of Bavaria to hear a comedy the following evening. He ordered Messer Orlando to be called for, knowing him to be good at everything, and earnestly required this of him. Unwilling to disappoint his pleasant and considerate lord, by chance he happened to find Massimo Troiano in the antechamber of the illustrious Duke's wife, who was discussing the affairs of Spain with the noble Lodovico Welsepro [. . .] and referred the whole thing to him, inventing the delightful plot, and between the two of them they composed the dialogue. In the first act a peasant straight out of farce, so crudely dressed that he seemed a very ambassador of mirth . . .

Marino: Tell me how many characters were there?

Fortunio: Ten, and the comedy was in three acts.

Marino: I should like to know the names of all the actors.

Fortunio: The excellent Messer Orlando di Lasso was the magnificent Messer Pantalone dei Bisognosi; Messer Giovan Battista Scolari from Trento was the Zanni; Massimo Troiano played three roles: the clumsy peasant who delivered the Prologue, the love-sick Polidoro and the desperate Spaniard with the name of Don Diego di Mendozza; Don Carlo Livizzano was Polidoro's servant; Giorgio Dori from Trento was the Spaniard's servant; the Marquis of Malaspina was Camilla, the Courtesan in love with Polidoro; Ercole Terzo was her maid and a French manservant. To return to the comedy, after the delivery of the Prologue Messer Orlando had a sweet five-part madrigal sung, and in the meantime Massimo, who had played the role of the peasant, removed his rustic habit and, together with his servant, re-entered dressed entirely in crimson velvet finished with broad gold braid at top and bottom and wearing a black velvet coat lined with very beautiful sables. He is praising Fortune and boasting that he lives happily and contentedly in the realms of love, when the Frenchman, servant to his brother Fabrizio, suddenly arrives from the country bearing a letter full of dire news which Polidoro reads aloud. After reading the letter, with a deep sigh he summons Camilla, and having explained his need to depart, kisses her, takes his leave, and exits. From the opposite side of the stage Messer Orlando emerges, dressed as a Magnifico in a long surcoat of crimson satin and scarlet stockings in the Venetian style, with a long black coat reaching to the ground, wearing a mask the mere sight of which made people laugh, and with a lute in his hands, playing and singing:

> Who passes through this street
> And does not sigh, is a lucky one . . .

After repeating this twice he sets aside the lute and begins to bemoan Love, crying: 'Oh poor Pantalone, who cannot pass down this street without filling the air with sighs and watering the ground with his tears!' All roar with laughter, and for as long as Pantalone is on stage nothing is heard but uncontrollable laughter, all the greater my dear Marino, when, a little later, after a long set-piece by Pantalone, either alone or with his Camilla, the Zanni appears, and not having seen his Pantalone for many years, not recognizing him, and walking nonchalantly about, keeps pushing Pantalone roughly until the two begin to scuffle.

Finally they recognize each other, and in sheer joy there and then Zanni lifts Pantalone on to his shoulders, and rotating like a mill-wheel, whirls about for as long as he can, and then Pantalone does likewise with Zanni.

Finally they both fall to the ground. Then, after getting up and chatting together, Zanni asks his master about his old mistress, Pantalone's wife, and hears the news that she is now dead, at which both start to howl like wolves, and Zanni begins to weep, recalling the *maccaru e sbruffadei* that she used to make for them in the past. Brushing their tears aside they recover their good mood, the master arranging with Zanni that he take some chickens to his beloved Camilla. Zanni promises to intercede for him, but does the opposite. Pantalone leaves the stage and Zanni, all fearful, goes to Camilla's house. Camilla falls in love with Zanni (and this is not so odd, for women often leave what is good for something worse) and allows him into the house. At this point there was some music from five violas and a like number of voices. Now consider whether or not this act was funny, for, by God, I swear to you that for all the comedies I have attended I have never encountered so much hearty laughter.

Marino: Indeed one must conclude that it was most entertaining and pleasing. Tell me more, for I am very much enjoying it.

Fortunio: In the second act Pantalone appears wondering why Zanni is taking so long to give him an answer. During this Zanni enters with a letter from Camilla that says that if Pantalone wishes to enjoy the fruit of her love he must disguise himself in the manner and style Zanni will advise, and on this happy note Pantalone and Zanni go off to exchange clothes. At this point the Spaniard enters, 'his heart submerged in that sea of fury called jealousy', and holds forth to his servant about his great deeds and extraordinary feats, and of the many hundreds and hundreds he has sent to Charon's boat, but how a vile woman has now deprived him of his valorous heart. Spurned by love he goes to find his Camilla and begs her to let him in. Camilla, with flattering words, extracts a necklace from him and makes an assignation for that evening. The Spaniard departs, satisfied, and at this point Pantalone enters dressed in Zanni's clothes, with Zanni in his master's clothes, and they spend a long time instructing the magnifico in what he must say. Finally both enter Camilla's house.

At this point there was music for four voices, two lutes, a mandolin, a pipe and a bass viola da gamba.

In the third and final act Polidoro, who has maintained Camilla at his own expense, returns from the country, goes into the house and encounters Pantalone dressed in menial clothes. He asks who he is, and in reply is told that he is a porter and Donna Camilla wants him to transport a trunk full of drapes which she is sending to Sister Doralice at Santo Cataldo. Polidoro believes this, and tells him to take the trunk immediately. Pantalone, being old, is unable to do so. He protests for a while, finally insisting that he is a gentleman, and Polidoro, indignant at this, takes a stick and (in tune with the hearty laughter of the spectators) beats him so much that he will remember it far better than I.

Pantalone having fled, Polidoro returns and enters the house angry with Camilla, while Zanni, who has heard the beating, finds a sack and hides in it. Camilla's maid pushes him about the stage tied in the sack. Then the Spaniard appears, since it is the hour Camilla has arranged. He enters the house and the maid tells him Polidoro has returned from the country. The Spaniard, angry at this unwelcome news, departs, and raising his eyes heavenward, with a sigh, and while exclaiming 'Ahi, Margodemi!', trips over the sack containing the poor Zanni, and both he and his servant after him fall flat on the stage. Getting up, with great indignation, he unties the sack, drags out Zanni and wallops him with a stick. Then Zanni flees, the Spaniard and his servant pursue him, and all leave the stage.

Then Polidoro enters with his servant, and Camilla with her maid. He tells Camilla that she must make up her mind to marry because, for a very good reason, he no longer wants to maintain her. After much protest she decides to do what Polidoro commands, and so agrees to take Zanni as her lawful husband. While they are arguing Pantalone enters loaded with weapons, but unbuckled, together with Zanni, who carries two archebuses on his shoulders, eight daggers at his belt, a shield and sword in his hands, and a rusty helmet on his head. Both have been looking for the person who gave them the beatings. They pretend to fight, delivering blows of a kind they want people to think they will use to kill their enemies. During this, Camilla persuades Polidoro to speak to Pantalone who, recognizing him, points out Polidoro to Zanni, and Zanni, petrified, signals to his master that he should be the first to attack, while Pantalone signals the same to Zanni.

Polidoro, realising how afraid they both are, calls him by name: 'Oh Signor Pantalone!', and then drawing their swords (while Zanni is lost to know what weapon to use) they engage in a ridiculous skirmish that goes on for some time. Finally Camilla takes hold of Pantalone and the maid takes hold of Zanni, and with peace restored Camilla is given as wife to Zanni, and in honour of this wedding there is a dance in the Italian style. Then Massimo, on behalf of Messer Orlando, apologized if the said comedy was not worthy of such illustrious princes, and with all tokens of respect bade them goodnight, and everyone went to bed.

Marino: In hearing this *soggetto* I cannot but conclude that this fine work was both absurd and delightful.

(Troiano, *Discorsi delli trionfi, giostre, apparati*, 1568, pp. 183–8)

SOME NOTICES OF EARLY PERFORMANCES

Below is a selection of brief notices recording the activities of early professional groups and companies in Mantua in 1567. They are among the earliest records we possess, and are interesting in a number of respects: there are no specific references to masked actors; the performers acted in a wide variety of pieces, including comedies, tragi-comedies, tragedies and intermezzi; *by this time the performances of lead actresses constituted the particular attraction of some productions; such actresses were sometimes even leaders of their troupes; the professional rivalry of companies was already well established.*

His Excellency has today had a play performed by the Gratiani on the stage at the Castle, and he went to hear it with the most Illustrious Prince and, as far as I can judge, enjoyed it very much. [11 May 1567]

Yesterday in the palace of the Illustrious Signor Cesare was performed a comedy of the Gratiani. [18 May 1567]

Here one can see nothing new but the comedies of Gratiano. [18 May1567]

Today two comedies were acted in competition: one in the usual place by Signora Flaminia and Pantalone who were accompanied by Signora Angela, the one who leaps so well; the other at the Purgo in Lanzino's house by that Signora Vincenza whom Signor Federigo da Gazuolo adores. Both companies have attracted a great public and a huge following; but Flaminia more of the nobility, and she did the tragedy of Dido but transformed into a tragi-comedy, which was very successful. The others, according to report, turned out to be very clumsy. They will continue to compete, and with some rivalry, each doing its best to attract the largest audience, like lecturers in university towns who strive to get the most students. [July 1567]

(All from D'Ancona, *Origini del teatro italiano*, 1891, vol. II)

GRAZZINI ON STROLLING PLAYERS

Of course by no means all the early professional companies performed scripted as well as improvised pieces. Indeed in all probability the earliest professionals not only specialized in the last, but were anxious to assert the liveliness and popularity of their particular performance techniques and the comic sketches they offered by comparison with the work of actors who performed serious scripted plays. The Florentine poet and dramatist Anton Francesco Grazzini, known as Il Lasca, wrote popular songs and quasi-dramatic duologues possibly performed by early strollers. The verses below were first printed in 1559, but may have been written some years earlier. They provide one among several pieces of evidence which seem to suggest that encounters between Zanni and Il Magnifico (Pantalone) were the nuclear comic situations out of which longer improvised dramas developed (see Apollonio, 'Il duetto di Magnifico e Zanni', 1971.

Canto di Zanni e di Magnifichi
We act the Bergamask and Venetian
And travel all over the place.
Performing plays is our business,
And today we're doing Florence,
As you can see, Messer Benedetti
Each of us is a Zanni,
All slick and smart performers.
Other notable players,
Lovers, Ladies, Soldiers and Hermits,
Remain on guard at the hall
Those tedious players of yours
Act out their rigmarole,
Long drawn-out gloomy stuff,
With little in it to laugh at
And decidedly less that will please.
And the end result of their efforts
Is that not just men and women,
But even the pillars are bored.
Today while we're doing our show,
We're happy to pose as Tuscans,
But when we're in our own hall
We'll be Bergamasks and Venetians:
Men so extremely bizarre,
And so quaint that with other people
They astound every person who hears them.
We've composed new plays in our style,
And when you hear them delivered
You will nearly die with laughter,
They're so brilliant, smart and witty.
And then again you will see
A dance done on the stage
With plenty of brand new jokes.
But because in this country
Ladies, you're not allowed to attend
Our performance in the hall,

Where we delight all those who see us,
If you care to offer an invite
We'll attend you at home, and may please you
With the sweetness and skill of our art.
So listen to this fine thing
Those scare-crow faces perform:
See how from under their clothes
Their little swords poke out,
See how some of their gestures
Rock the wise and foolish with laughter.
Finally we will show, beautiful and well-devised,
A new scene to please your eyes,
During which Cantinella
And Zanni perform and delight you.
So if you wish to enjoy
A jolly good laugh and some fun,
Seek us out in our hall tomorrow.

(Grazzini, *Tutti i trionfi, carri, mascherate o canti carnascialeschi*, vol. II, 1559, pp. 499–501)

3

The Major Companies

The Heyday of the Companies

TAKING a very broad view we can see that the history of the *commedia dell'arte* acting companies between the sixteenth and eighteenth centuries falls roughly into four periods. The first, covering the early and middle decades of the sixteenth century, saw the gradual emergence of organized troupes, initially perhaps of a fairly humble kind and often operating at a popular level. The second was that dominated by the major companies, like the Gelosi, the Confidenti and the Fedeli, and may be taken to run from the late 1560s through to the 1630s – a period that saw the introduction of actresses, the fruitful intermingling of popular entertainment forms with the styles and materials of the 'high' culture, and the elimination of verbal and stylistic crudities, all of which served to give wide audience appeal, artistic coherence and social and cultural status to the work of the professionals. The third, at least viewed from our perspective, seems to have been dominated by the activities of the companies abroad, particularly in France, and was possibly marked by a certain retrenchment, and accommodation to changing economic and cultural conditions, in Italy itself – a period that covered the decades from the 1640s to the end of the century. The fourth, from the turn of the century to the middle decades of the eighteenth century, saw the gradual decline in popular and artistic favour of the companies' improvising techniques, and their displacement by a drama scripted by professional playwrights, of whom certainly the most prolific and significant was Carlo Goldoni.

The later 1560s and the 1570s witnessed the formation of those companies which in a few decades were to give the Italian professional players a reputation far beyond the peninsula. Indeed, the emergence of distinguished troupes, rich in performing talent, flexible in the kinds of drama they could perform, and although dependent on noble patronage, able, too, in important respects to establish a profitable public market for their wares, was remarkably rapid. By the 1570s companies were not only firmly established in Italy, but were travelling abroad, to France, the German states and Spain. Increasingly in the final decades of the *cinquecento*, as the structure of the companies and their performance materials and techniques became settled, they drew away culturally, commercially and socially from the comparatively unorganized mass of low-life street entertainers. Inevitably some were more successful than others, and a certain hierarchy developed within the professional ranks, companies ranging in quality and status from the most sophisticated, like the Gelosi and the Confidenti, to those rough vagabond troupes of semi-indigent strollers particularly anathema to moralistic clerics. Across this range it is hard to categorize the companies, although three basic kinds have been identified: family led troupes, like the Gelosi when under the control of Francesco and Isabella Andreini, and the Fedeli, led by G. B. Andreini; the court companies, prominent in the middle decades of the seventeenth century, but important much earlier, most notably

PLATE 13 *Late sixteenth century painting of Italian players, probably at a French court, by Frans Porbus. Permission of the Musée Baron Gérard, Bayeux, with special authorization from the Town of Bayeux*

at Mantua from the 1580s where the Gonzaga were active patrons; and companies which were autonomous, although tied by the contractual obligations they entered into with theatre impresarios.[1]

In this period of the heyday of the great companies, from the late 1560s through to the 1630s, those we know most about are the major troupes, and for obvious reasons: they were the most successful in the struggle for upward social mobility, were admired by the aristocracy and *letterati*, and moved frequently in the ambience of the courts; it was they who were invited to perform on those special occasions – birthdays, weddings, and royal and diplomatic visits – most likely to be written up by the educated minority; it is the letters, reports and memoirs recording the interests and activities of the educated, and more particularly of the great, which have survived in print or in archives; and finally, but by no means least, it was cultivated members of those troupes who not only gave a degree of sophistication and distinction to their activities, making the companies the more acceptable within elite circles, but who consciously sought, by publishing plays and performance materials, to achieve social and cultural recognition and acceptance for their art.

Quite certainly, however, many lesser acting companies and groups of players toured at this time in Italy, and probably abroad too, of whose composition and activities little if any record has come down.[2] Valuable for the information they provide about strollers who operated on a social and cultural level far from that of the courts are the homiletic and denunciatory accounts of seventeenth-century clerics like Hurtado de Mendoza and Federico Borromeo (see chapter 9) who viewed bands of travelling players with a mixture of hostility, irony and contempt. From them we learn much, even allowing for prejudice and exaggeration, about the characteristics and practices of the lower levels of the profession: but their comments tend to the general, and when troupes or individual players are mentioned by name, it is nearly always the major companies, or the leading actors and actresses, whose names are invoked, usually for the express purpose of castigating strollers by comparison with the excellence of the elite.

All the companies, however, whether rich or poor, were dependent on the vagaries of patronage and the market. The extent to which what social historians have called the economic crisis of *seicento* Italy impinged on the work and livelihood of the later seventeenth-century acting troupes is elusive in the extreme, and there is an obvious danger in making too much of what evidence there is. However, that the general economy of Italy suffered severely in the course of the century, and particularly perhaps in the early and middle decades, seems well established: patterns of trade shifted radically to the disadvantage of many of the city states; much mercantile and banking wealth was displaced to the English, the Germans and the Dutch; on several occasions plague and famine ravaged the peninsula to a nigh unprecedented extent, decimating the artisan populations of many major towns and undermining economies in both the short and long term.[3] It would seem scarcely likely that so social an art as theatre, and an art which, for the livelihood of the professionals practising it, was so dependent on social stability and economic prosperity, would not have been significantly affected by these upheavals and changes. They may in part have contributed to the decline and eventually the disappearance of the great companies, to a slow waning in aristocratic patronage, and to the apparent tendency for some troupes to look increasingly, and for longer periods of time, to foreign touring. They possibly contributed as well to the emergence of Paris as an ever more important focus for the activities of many of the most accomplished companies and players.

Unfortunately, too little is known about the economy of the troupes to permit documentation of their fortunes with any precision. Many other factors too must be taken into account: on a more general plane, dynastic shifts and realignments, the activities in Italy of foreign powers fostering revolts and civil war, as in Naples and Piedmont, and the effects in Italy of the Thirty Years' War; and on the more specifically theatrical plane, the emergence of new dramatic forms, styles and tastes, like the growth in public favour of *melodramma*, to the disadvantage of the acting companies – a development in the middle decades of the seventeenth century perhaps most conspicuous in Venice. Nonetheless, by the 1640s conditions in the peninsula seem to have been economically less propitious for the *commedia dell'arte* troupes than they had been two or three decades before. Harder times coincided, too, with the passing of the great generation of the profession's standard bearers: Scala died about 1620, Francesco Andreini in 1624, Francesco Gabrielli in 1636, Silvio Fiorillo probably sometime in the 1630s, Barbieri in 1641 and Cecchini in 1645. Perhaps it is a result of mere historical accident, but the extant records tell us more about the activities in Italy of these players and their contemporaries than later records do about the Italian careers of most of the generation of players who followed them. With the exception of Riccoboni's very general history of the Italian theatre (1728), written in France,[4] and Francesco Bartoli's late eighteenth-century biographical compilation of actors' and actresses' lives, the *Notizie istoriche* (1782),[5] for many of the later seventeenth-century players it is foreign, and particularly French rather than Italian, documentation that speaks of their lives and work. It is with the troupes of the late sixteenth and early seventeenth centuries, however, that we are more immediately concerned.[6]

Some Major Troupes

Many of the major companies were in the service of, or had close ties with, aristocratic patrons. The nature and extent of noble patronage is elusive and complicated, and will be discussed in more detail in chapter 4. Suffice it to say here that as the professional companies sought to establish a firm economic base, and to acquire social status for themselves and cultural recognition for the kinds of theatre they practised, they necessarily looked to the courts for support. To some extent we can generalize and say that professional acting companies at first worked alongside *dilettanti* and academic performers, then came gradually to replace them, particularly in the sphere of comedy. The accomplished professionals organized their performance programmes according to the entertainment needs and the social calendars of the courts, and those in the regular service of a patron were, at least at first, very much subject to his whim and rule.

The extent to which the late sixteenth- and early seventeenth-century companies moved in the court ambience, and looked to the high culture to provide models for their activities can be seen both in the names they assumed, and in the way in which the rhetorical emphases and formal preoccupations of elite literary discourse permeated their work. Names like the Gelosi ('The Jealous Ones') and the Fedeli ('The Faithful Ones'), were consciously modelled on the titles assumed by the Renaissance Humanist academies, and were designed to give a patina of social, cultural and artistic authority and respectability to the work of professionals whose status in all other respects was ultimately defined by the fact that they were commercial and mercenary, and practised the *commedia mercenaria*.

Of course 'high' cultural emphases were probably not characteristic of all the companies in the period of which we have record. To judge from Garzoni's description cited below (p. 69), when some of the rough strolling troupes attempted to ape the sophisticated discourse of their professional betters the results were altogether abysmal. Crude buffoonery was probably more their stock in trade. But verbally rich and refined dialogue did not exclude vigorous physical playing; pantomimic performance was not *per se* trivial and oafish: hence the attempts of apologists like Niccolò Barbieri to distinguish firmly between the art of the comedian and the antics of the buffoon (below, p. 254). Amost certainly when the companies performed abroad the verbal, rhetorical and declamatory virtuosity of the most accomplished players would have made less impact on their audiences than when they acted in Italy, and thus physical 'business', musical and mimic skills, and emphases on the delicate, the pathetic and the sentimental, as well as on the balletic and farcical, were the more strongly underscored in performances given before foreign spectators. It was probably the vigorous and pantomimic, the kind of playing that exploited entertainer skills, that characterized the work of the first Italian actor of whose activities abroad we have some record: Alberto Naseli.

Naseli's stage-name, Zan Ganassa, indicates that he specialized in the role of the *zanni*. Although active in Italy probably as early as the 1560s, when he is known to have played before the Ferrarese court, traces of him in Italy are few and most records concern his work in France and Spain. We first find him in Paris in 1571 under the protection of Charles IX, who defended his troupe against attempts by the French Parliament to prevent it acting in public. That visit was successful enough to persuade Naseli to return, and he was in Paris again from 1572 until early 1574, several scholars surmising that his may have been the troupe of Italian players seen and admired by the English Earl of Lincoln, then visiting the French court.[7] There is no concrete evidence, however, to support Nicoll's suggestion that it was Ganassa's company that entertained Queen Elizabeth during her July progress to Windsor and Reading in 1574.[8] Nor are we justified in concluding, as some scholars have, that the Italian players depicted in a painting in the Musée de Bayeux (see plate 13) are those of the Ganassa troupe.[9] After leaving France in 1574 he is next found, in the same year, in Madrid, and thereafter a company, or several companies, run by him apparently performed in Spain for many years. In Madrid he erected a theatre in the Corral de la Pacheca and his company enjoyed great success, touring to other Spanish towns like Seville, Toledo and Guadalajara. In 1582 Ganassa was imprisoned, and although the reason is not known it may well have been for debt: he possibly had a cash flow problem, for it seems the Medici owed him a large sum of money.[10] How long Ganassa remained in Spain (let alone in prison) is not known, although Ottonelli remarks that he heard at third hand how Ganassa was still touring there as late as 1610 (see below p. 220). The few extant records indicate that Ganassa was a confident, flamboyant figure, and something of a theatrical entrepreneur. His work undoubtedly left a strong mark on the Spanish scripted drama of the day, and in this respect at least he was akin to many of his fellow Italian professionals, their example serving to stimulate the growth of national dramas in several lands far beyond the peninsula.

Records of the itineraries and fortunes of the leading Italian acting troupes are distinctly patchy, and we are quite heavily dependent on accounts of their court activities in Italy and in other countries for what little information we have: indeed, were we to eliminate reports of their activities in France, and of attempts to attract them there, for long periods we would have scant knowledge of their doings, particularly after the 1620s. However, the weight of evidence that has survived from Italian and foreign court and elite sources may well be misleading, and it is hazardous to conclude from it that the courts were their exclusive or even principal ambience. The players became increasingly aware of their professional strength, and the great companies and the most sought-after players seem to have pursued policies, for both personal and economic motives, often independent of, or recalcitrant to, the pressures exerted by noble patrons. The following brief *resumés* of the histories of some of the major troupes of the heyday indicate something of their dependence and independence, the internal disputes which often racked them, and the extent of their itinerancy (as too do many of the documents in chapter 4). They show that it is even more difficult to establish for them than it is for the English Elizabethan and Jacobean acting companies any adequate calendar of performances even in the sphere of the courts.[11] But they conspicuously demonstrate, too, that the bulk of the reports we possess of their work pertains to special and occasional events of a kind, and occurring in a place, likely to attract record – invariably, that is, the court environments. Little has survived that permits us to chart their day to day activities – those operations which gave many of them their regular livelihood.

THE GELOSI

This company was probably the most prestigious of those active in the second half of the sixteenth century. We first encounter it in Milan in 1568, and in the course of its nearly forty-year existence it is often found there, as well as in the other major towns of northern Italy, more particularly Florence, Ferrara, Genoa, Mantua and Venice. The company's skills covered all kinds of drama: comedies, tragi-comedies, tragedies, *intermezzi* and pastorals, both scripted and improvised. Indeed we know that from its early years the Gelosi interpreted the most sophisticated written texts of the literary drama, for together with court amateurs in 1573 it gave the first performance of Tasso's pastoral play *Aminta* on the Island of Belvedere, on the Po near Ferrara.[12]

In the 1570s, too, we have record of the company's visits to France. The first of these, in 1571, was probably made at the invitation of Luigi Gonzaga, Duke of Nevers, in whose house in Paris the Gelosi played before guests who included Charles IV. The English Ambassador mentioned the Gelosi players appreciatively in a report to London in September, but exactly how long they stayed is not known.[13] That they made a considerable impression at the French court is suggested by the fact that in 1575, while on his way back from a visit to Poland, Henry III passed through Venice, and sent a request ahead that the Gelosi be there to entertain him; the Signoria summoned the troupe urgently from Milan for that purpose. The company was in France again in 1577, its stay lasting probably until May, 1578. It was an eventful visit. Going at the invitation of Henry, on their way to Blois the players were taken prisoner by Huguenots, then in contention with the King, and were only released in January on royal intercession.[14] They played first at Blois, then in Paris where, under an arrangement with the Confrérie de la Passion, they acted publicly at the Salle de Bourbon, enjoying enormous success, despite the high cost of their four soldi entrance charge. Their public performances attracted the hostility of some members of the French Parliament, but they were protected by the King (see below, p. 269). Between this visit and their last in 1603 the Gelosi may have made other journeys to Paris and elsewhere, but no certain record is available. It seems unlikely that the company appeared in England, as some scholars have speculated.

Records show that the Gelosi players were active throughout the 1580s and 1590s, sometimes running into trouble: the Duke of Mantua banished them from his city in May 1579, for reasons unknown, and they again ran foul of him in July 1582 (see below, p. 76). Dissension within companies was common enough, as we have said, and the Gelosi troupe was no exception. In 1589 it appeared at the festivities mounted in Florence to celebrate the marriage of the princess Christine of Lorraine to the Grand Duke — one of the most splendid occasions of the period, the spectacular shows being prepared under the overall direction of the architect, engineer and stage designer Bernardo Buontalenti.[15] The Gelosi company presented *intermezzi* between the acts of plays, and its two lead actresses quarrelled over what to perform – whether Vittoria Piissimi's show-piece *Zingana*, or a piece that best displayed the skills of Isabella Andreini, *La pazzia d'Isabella*. The women were more or less placated when it was finally agreed that both should be given on separate nights (see below, p. 74).

From the mid-1590s to 1603 records are sparse, but in the summer of that year the agent of Henry IV of France initiated arrangements for the company to pay a further visit to the French court, which it did in the following winter and spring of 1603–4. It was a successful, but a fateful visit. While returning to Italy, bearing with them gifts and letters of passage from Henry, and a letter commending their skill from Catherine de' Medici, the players stopped at Lyons, and there the troupe's celebrated lead actress, Isabella Andreini, fell ill and died on 11 June 1604. Her husband, Francesco Andreini, the company's director, disbanded the Gelosi. The players of this, perhaps the most admired company of the late sixteenth century, dispersed to other troupes. Andreini himself retired from the stage, devoting much of his later life to the publication of his own writings for the theatre, and to editing and publishing his wife's literary remains.

PLATE 14 *Portrait of the actress Isabella Andreini. The frontispiece to her* Lettere *(1607). Permission of The British Library, 1085 m11*

The high standing of the Gelosi is well attested in contemporary letters and panegyric. The late sixteenth-century writer, Tommaso Garzoni, linked the Gelosi with the Confidenti as one of the two most distinguished troupes of the day, and the extent to which the company was sought after by nobility and royalty, at home and abroad, is witness to its quality. Precisely in what that quality consisted, however, few records bear detailed witness, notwithstanding that we have more information about it than about any other company: all too frequently the descriptions and comments which have come down to us are cast in general rather than specific terms, whether they are lauding the virtues of the troupe as a whole, or those of individual players. We may assume a high degree of professionalism in scenic decoration, costuming, stage orchestration and ensemble work, for these would have been crucial for success in the theatrically sophisticated circles in which the company often moved. Individual performer expertise and versatility we can likewise assume, for they were qualities essential to the players' ability to move easily between scripted and improvised performance. We can draw certain tentative conclusions too about the kinds and styles of their performance in the 1580s and 1590s from contemporary printed materials, like the Scala *scenarii*, Francesco Andreini's collection of *bravure*, and Isabella Andreini's various writings (see chapter 8). Notwithstanding the great reputation this company enjoyed in its own day, however, for long periods it may have had no greater stability in its acting complement than did other companies of the age: players came and went; the troupe was several times reorganized; at times, particularly in the 1580s, there may have been temporary amalgamations between it and other companies, particularly the Uniti; and there are indications than once or twice it splintered, some members acting in one place, some in another. Strictly speaking, we should perhaps identify several reconstituted Gelosi companies between 1568 and 1604.

The players most frequently associated with the Gelosi are Francesco and Isabella Andreini (see also below, pp. 223–5). When they joined is not known, although it may have been in the mid to late 1570s. On occasions, however, after 1580 Isabella appears to have been in other troupes: perhaps with the Confidenti in 1589, and the Uniti in 1601. Again, although Francesco was for long the Gelosi's company director, exactly when he first assumed that function, and for how long he did so on a continuous basis, are details which remain uncertain. Some scholars have argued that the company's great reputation was essentially established by the Andreini. They certainly helped to enhance its repute, but nonetheless the troupe seems to have been held in high regard virtually from its foundation: it is most unlikely, for example, that Francesco Andreini was with the Gelosi on its first and successful visit to France. At various times the company included, in addition to the

Andreini, some of the leading performers of the day, like the *prime donne* Vittoria Piissimi and Aurelia Romana, the *Pantalone* Giulio Pasquati, Silvia Roncagli (Franceschina) and Simone da Bologna (Zanni). One of its early directors may have been the skilled Rinaldo Petignoni. Although the eighteenth-century theatre historian Francesco Bartoli says in his *Notizie istoriche* that Flaminio Scala was long associated with the Gelosi, and was for a while its first director, there is no other documentary evidence to confirm this, and his claim that Scala led the troupe seems very doubtful. In one of his *bravure* (see below, p. 72) Andreini gives a valuable list of the members of the company, but unfortunately does not say in precisely which year this was its complement. His encomium to its unrivalled skills should not be taken as merely the pride of one long associated with it. Travelling under its motto 'Virtù, fama ed onor ne fer Gelosi', more than any other troupe in its age the Gelosi, within a few decades of the first formation of acting companies, carried the fame of the Italian players abroad and helped to establish their European-wide prestige. The company's posthumous reputation for skill and excellence was certainly unrivalled.

THE CONFIDENTI

Linked by Garzoni with the Gelosi as the most impressive of the early troupes, this company is first encountered touring through Cremona, Pavia and Milan in 1574, and sporadic notices of its performances and affairs are found up to 1639, when it went to France at the invitation of Louis XIII. Its main Italian touring territory was again the large northern towns, and from time to time in the late 1570s and 1580s it had some ties with the Duke of Mantua. It was certainly in Mantua and Bologna in the spring of 1581 for the entertainments which celebrated the marriage of Vicenzo Gonzaga to Margherita Farnese. Two years later the company was apparently reorganized: it seems for a while to have splintered, one group playing at Mantua under the name of the Confidenti, another at Genoa. The assemblage of talent that emerged at Genoa was possibly in union with members of the Uniti, for it called itself the Uniti Confidenti – but the details of these possible realignments remain obscure.[16]

In any event, the main Confidenti troupe is found the following year once more in Turin and Milan, from whence it went to France for several months, staying well into 1585. In 1587 it travelled even further afield, and under the leadership of the brothers Tristano and Drusiano Martinelli spent over a year in Spain. Although back in Italy in 1589 next to nothing is known of its fortunes until after the accession of Don Giovanni de' Medici, when about 1612 the company entered his service. From then until 1620 it was probably led by Flaminio Scala.[17] An extant letter of Don Giovanni, dated 21

March 1620 (see below p. 76), suggests that Scala was director of the troupe, and among the leading players were the Pantalone, Marc' Antonio Romagnesi, Francesco Gabrielli (Scapino), Domenico Bruni (Fulvio), Niccolò Barbieri (Beltrame), and a number of actresses, including Marina Dorotea Antonazzoni (Lavinia) and Maria Malloni (Celia). The letter also suggests that the composition of the company had been relatively stable for some years, although other correspondence between the players and the Duke indicates frequent and bitter internal squabbling, much of it domestic, but some issuing from changes in company personnel. This important and illuminating letter seems to be the Duke's final exhausted response to many years of listening to the players' internal bickerings, rivalry and complaints. It speaks volumes for his patrician patience, and throws a grim light on the hazards of offering patronage and protection to a *commedia dell'arte* troupe. It is also one of the last reports we have of the Confidenti until that troupe emerges briefly again in extant records, performing in Milan in 1639. In that same year it was invited by Louis XIII to Paris, but of its fortunes there, and elsewhere later, there is no further evidence.

THE ACCESI

Although it is not known when this company was formed it was certainly in existence by 1590, receiving permission in that year to give a play at Brescia. In 1600 it was in France, Vincenzo Gonzaga having recommended it to Henry IV, before whom it gave several performances in August at Lyons. It remained in France a long time, being included in the entertainments prepared to celebrate the marriage of Henry to Maria de' Medici on 17 December 1600, and playing frequently before the Parisian court through to the end of October 1601. At that time the company was probably led by Pier Maria Cecchini (Fritellino), an experienced but apparently irascible and devious manager (see for example Francesco Gabrielli's letter below, p. 123).

For a brief period in 1606 the Accesi joined forces with a new company, the Fedeli, led by Giovan Battista Andreini and his wife Virginia Ramponi (Florinda), but by late 1607 was independent again, travelling once more to Paris where it performed from early February 1608 at the Hôtel de Bourbon before the French King and court, and then gave public performances to paying spectators. (For G. B. Andreini, see also below, p. 228). This visit was the final outcome of a lengthy correspondence between Paris and Mantua in which Maria de' Medici and Henry IV tried to secure the return to Paris of the popular Arlecchino, Tristano Martinelli, who had so pleased the French court on the company's first visit (see chapter 10). Although Martinelli remained in Italy, the company nonetheless enjoyed great success in Paris, both at court and with a paying public. Shortly after its return to Italy, in 1609, the company amalgamated with the Fedeli, but once more the union was brief. The two company leaders, Cecchini and G. B. Andreini, were rarely in agreement, while between Cecchini and at least one of his fellow players, Tristano Martinelli, there was often bitter discord (see below p. 222). By the following year, 1610, the Accesi was again an independent company touring the northern Italian cities, and even further abroad, as it was in 1613 and 1614 when it performed in Vienna and Linz. Later records of its activities are sparse, and it is last heard of in Parma in 1628.[18]

Notwithstanding the frequent professional jealousies and antipathies, and the troublesome web of internal amatory entanglements which seem often to have disrupted this company, the Accesi was a troupe of high standing, and at various times in its existence it included, other than the players already mentioned, such notable performers as Flaminio Scala (Flavio), Drusiano Martinelli, the elder brother of Tristano, and his wife Angelica (both of whom performed in England in the 1570s), Girolamo Garavini (Capitano Rinoceronte), Girolamo Salimbeni (Piombino) and the brilliant actor Silvio Fiorillo (Capitan Matamoros). Several players, like Cecchini and Fiorillo, when they published work of their own, were proud to describe themselves as *Comici Accesi*.

THE UNITI

This early troupe was long under the protection and patronage of the theatre-loving Dukes of Mantua – so much so that for a time it was also known as The Company of His Excellency the Duke of Mantua. When it was formed is uncertain, but it was in existence by 1578, playing at Ferrara.[19] What evidence has survived indicates that like the other major companies it toured the northern Italian cities, but records of its later activities are few: after an appearance in Genoa in 1614, nothing more is heard of it until it shows up in Florence in 1640. There is no indication that it toured abroad, although it probably did so. Conceivably in 1583, as remarked above, it was joined by members of a break-away group from the Confidenti. Possibly it broke and reformed more than once, and certainly in the course of its long history it saw frequent changes of personnel. Members at various times included some of the most distinguished players of the age, like Isabella Andreini (in 1584), Diana Ponti, Vittoria Piissimi, the *Arlecchino*, Drusiano Martinelli, and Silvio Fiorillo (Capitan Matamoros).[20] A company list of 1614 includes one Ottavio Bernardino, described as 'Romano Franceschina': assuming there is no mistake in the spelling of the name, we have here the *servetta* role played by a male. Given that actresses were not always welcome in the Papal States, the actor's Roman origin may conceivably account for the role specialization.

THE DESIOSI

The first reference we have to this company occurs in Montaigne's *Voyage en Italie*: he saw it perform in Pisa in 1581, and went backstage to visit the actresses. In addition to the usual circuit of northern Italian towns there are records that the Desiosi performed at least twice in Rome (in 1588 and 1590), where they acted in the Papal Palace and were expressly forbidden to bring actresses with them on the visit.[21] The Desiosi were sometimes known as the Company of Diana, by virtue of the occasional presence in the troupe, possibly as its director, of the actress Diana Ponti (Lavinia). A celebrated player, she is found in a number of companies in the 1580s and 1590s, and obviously could not have led it all the time.[22] The company seems to have played quite frequently in the Papal States; conceivably, when playing elsewhere, and when Diana was with the troupe, it used her name specifically to advertise the presence of actresses in its performances.

The Desiosi are last mentioned as playing in Verona in 1599. In 1597 Flaminio Scala was perhaps the company director, and for a time the *Arlecchino*, Tristano Martinelli, was one of its members. It was, then, a not undistinguished troupe, yet in the eighteen years of its existence we know of only a handful of places it visited – a measure of how elusive is the history of the early Italian acting companies.

THE AFFEZIONATI

Very little is known of this troupe, active in the early decades of the seventeenth century. In 1632 it was seen in Venice by an English traveller, Sir Aston Cockain, who subsequently wrote a play, *Trappolin creduto principe*, on the basis of the *scenario* the company performed. The troupe is later found in Bologna, playing during the Carnival of 1634, and included in its complement Isabella Chiesa, an actress versatile in both comedy and tragedy, and the celebrated Capitan Matamoros, Silvio Fiorillo.

THE FEDELI

Perhaps the major seventeenth-century troupe, the Fedeli was formed in 1601 by Giovan Battista Andreini (Lelio), the son of Francesco and Isabella Andreini, and it was for long in the service, and under the patronage, of the Dukes of Mantua. As already remarked, it several times amalgamated with, and broke away from, the Accesi company, union between the two troupes being frustrated by ill-feeling between their leaders. The Fedeli made a notable contribution to the 1608 entertainments in Mantua held to celebrate the marriage of Francesco Gonzaga and Margherita of Savoy: its lead actress, Virginia Andreini, made a powerful impression as a singer when at short notice she took over the lead role in the Rinuccini–Monteverdi opera *Arianna* – a good example of the diverse performance skills of some of the *commedia dell'arte* players.[23]

The members of the Fedeli seem to have made their first visit to France in 1613, where from September onwards they acted first at Lyons, then in Paris, at the Louvre and the Hotel de Bourgogne, continuing to entertain the French court regularly at Fountainebleau and Saint-Germain through to July 1614. Tristano Martinelli, who had refused to go to Paris with the Accesi in 1608, went with the Fedeli on this trip, and indeed was one of the company's main attractions in the eyes of patrons like Maria de' Medici. Between 1614 and 1620 there are scattered records of the company playing in the northern Italian towns; at the end of that year it left again for France, arriving in Paris on 12 January 1621.[24] The journey to Paris was always a long and hard one, notwithstanding possibilities for companies to earn money by performing in towns *en route*, and long-distance travelling carried its hazards as we have seen with the Gelosi: this time the Fedeli troupe was disrupted, and its journey delayed, by the death of the actor, Leandro. G. B. Andreini was in Paris and elsewhere in the 1640s, but whether with the Fedeli is not known.

LATER SEVENTEENTH-CENTURY COMPANIES

About the later seventeenth-century companies we know comparatively little, for although a fair amount of players' correspondence has survived, it tends to the local and particular.[25] Where the earlier troupes had carried names rather like those of the learned academies, increasingly the later companies came to be known by the name either of their leader or their patron. The importance of 'star' performers became more pronounced. Patronage remained important, the 'stars' being particularly sought after. Mantua, for example, maintained its traditional support of companies, and patrons continued to send not just individual players, but whole troupes abroad to visit foreign courts as gestures of goodwill or political strategy. The visit of the Duke of Modena's troupe to England in 1678 is a case in point (see chapter 10). Nonetheless, as has been suggested above, the seventeenth-century economic decline of some of the major Italian cities, and the competition offered by new forms like *melodramma*, and later by *opera buffa*, may adversely have affected the players and encouraged more foreign touring. The players' very success, too, at the turn of the century, in establishing their professional credentials may have begun to be counter-productive, bringing an influx of the less talented, debasing skills, fostering knock-about buffoonery and encouraging an eventually self-defeating tendency to play to the gallery. Riccoboni, as a reluctant actor and would-be reformer, perhaps took an overly jaundiced view of the profession in the final decades of the century, but he judged there to be then few good players around, and fewer still of education or refinement.[26]

Perhaps a not untypical late *seicento* autonomous troupe of this time was that led by Francesco Calderoni (*c*1645–1705), stage-name Silvio. Few records of its activities survive, but those which do suggest considerable dependence, particularly in the last decades of the century, on foreign touring, to Bavaria and elsewhere. Riccoboni praises the attempts of another actor and troupe leader of this time, Pietro Cotta (*fl.* late seventeenth century), to reform comedy and re-establish tragedy and pastoral in the performed repertoire; but little is known of Cotta's activities, and Riccoboni's view may well be coloured by his own concern to reform the stage.[27] The history of the companies in the late seventeenth century, however, as in the *settecento*, has received little detailed examination, and there may have been much more and more interesting work done outside the Italian and foreign court spheres than currently available evidence suggests.

Documents

GARZONI ON A TRAVELLING COMPANY

Many commedia dell'arte *companies, as we have said, probably made no more than a subsistence living, and were made up of players of very modest talent. Denounced by clerical opponents of the theatre, and treated with suspicion and often downright hostility by village and town officials, these poor professionals may occasionally have performed for provincial nobility and dignitaries, but largely depended for their livelihoods on entertaining more popular audiences. Tommaso Garzoni, writing before the mid-1580s, delivers more than one diatribe against such strollers in his* La piazza universale *(1585). Characteristic of much clerical diatribe against theatre is the distinction he makes between humble actors such as these and those 'fine players' of the great troupes who enjoyed the support of the* letterati *and nobility. What makes his description considerably more engaging than most is its witty and satirical tone. While no doubt exaggerated for effect, some of the detail of his account is probably close enough to fact to make the ridicule entertaining to his educated readers: the pattern of activity he describes was common enough, like the initial parade through the town to drum up an audience and the simple fitting up of a hired hall for performance.*

But those profane players who pervert the ancient art, introducing into plays only untruths and scurrilities, cannot be allowed to escape blame for bringing shame on themselves and the art of acting with the dirty rubbish that flows from their mouths with every word. To the extent that the art of comedy has benefited from the afore-mentioned [Isabella Andreini, Vittoria Piissimi etc.] to an even greater extent has it been besmirched by these people who, along with Aretino or Franco, have perverted the language in order to argue in a way as dirty and offensive as they are themselves. In their actions they have less civility than asses, in their gestures they are unmitigated ruffians, in their language they display all the effrontery of common prostitutes, in their inventions they are wholly villanous and in everything they do you can smell the scoundrel; and where occasionally they could handle the subject in an appropriate manner, they seem to think it better to express things in a distorted way, or to twist everything to their own style. Thus, thanks to them, the art of comedy lies buried in mud: lords banish them from their lands, the law holds them in contempt, different nations scorn them in a variety of ways and the whole world, as if to punish them for their improper conduct, rightly rejects them. Thus you find the companies split up: the Signora is in Parma, the Magnifico in Venice, the Courtesan in Padua, the Zanni in Bergamo, Gratiano in Bologna, and licences and permits have to be sought on every side if they wish to act and earn their living, because everyone is sickened by this vile race that spreads disarray everywhere and introduces a thousand scandals wherever it goes. This is the reason, according to Valerio, why the city of Marseilles never wishes to suffer the presence of strollers and buffoons. When these enter a city, immediately a drum makes it known that the gentlemen players have arrived. The Signora, dressed as a man and with sword in hand, advances to survey the field, inviting the public to a comedy or a tragedy or a pastoral in a palace or at the Pilgrim Inn, to which the mob, by nature eager for novelties and curiosities, immediately rushes to get seats and, paying its entrance money, enters the hall that has been prepared. Here you find a fit-up stage and a scene crudely depicted in charcoal; you put up with an opening concert like that of asses and hornets; you hear a prologue from a charlatan; a clumsy tune like Brother Stopino's; an action as painful as a malady, and murderous interludes; a Magnifico not worth a toss; a Zanni who's a goose; a Graziano who squitters words; a daft, witless Courtesan; a Lover who saws his arms at every speech; a Spaniard who can say nothing but 'Mi vida' and 'Mi corazon'; a Pedant who drops into Tuscan at every line; a Burattino who knows no other gesture but to put his cap on his head; a Signora like a monster in her speech, dead in her delivery, soporific in her gestures, at perpetual war with the Graces and locked in a major altercation with Beauty. So the spectators depart from them scandalized and dissatisfied, carrying away a memory of their ghastly speeches, and on the following evening they will not

spend a penny to hear again such absurdities, which have everywhere been displayed and exposed to universal scorn. Thus thanks to the abuses of such people even fine players come to be despised and suffer affronts which they do not deserve.

(Garzoni, *La piazza universale*, 1595 ed., pp. 739–40)

PLATE 15 *A seventeenth century drawing of travelling players in a street or square. Permission of the Bibliothèque Nationale, Paris*

FRANCESCO ANDREINI ON THE GELOSI COMPANY

The composition of the Gelosi troupe was described by Francesco Andreini in the fourteenth dialogue of his Le bravure del Capitano Spavento *(1607). Andreini himself played the role of the Capitano for whom these* bravure, *or boasting dialogues, were written. In the following passage he recollects members of the troupe he once knew, although when exactly these particular players were in the Gelosi is uncertain: it was probably some time in the 1590s. We learn that the Gelosi Company had an emblem and motto, and gather too that an actor could take on a number of very distinctive parts, including characters in pastoral plays, and might possess in addition a useful command of languages and considerable musical skill.*

Andreini's estimate of the company's quality is of course coloured by the fact that he was its troupe leader, but many tributes of the period bear witness to its pre-eminence.

Trappola: You're laughing a lot, master. That must surely be one of those letters from Dottor Graziano I told you about before. Yes, it certainly is, and it must be from that famous Graziano of the Comici Gelosi.

Capitano: The letter's not from him, but I knew him. In fact I knew not only him – his real name was Lodovico da Bologna – but in addition to him I knew Giulio Pasquati of Padua, who played Pantalone; Simone da Bologna, the Zanni; Gabrielle da Bologna, who played Francatrippa; Orazio Padovano, who played an Innamorato, Adriano Valerini of Verona, who played the same role; Girolamo Salimbeni from Florence, who played the old Florentine Zanobio, and Piombino; Signora Isabella Andreini, a Paduan, who played the first Innamorata; Signora Prudenzia, a Veronese, who was the second Innamorata; Signora Silvia Roncagli from Bergamo, who was Franceschina; and a certain Francesco Andreini, husband of the Isabella I mentioned, who acted the role of a vain and boastful Capitano, called, as my own name reminds me, Capitano Spavento da Vall' Inferna.

Trappola: I too remember him, master, and would swear I've heard him act in Milan, at Porta Tosa, in the house of the Incarnatini, together with all those other people. What's more I remember he acted the role of a very comic Sicilian Doctor, as well as the part of a Magician (called Falsirone) – astonishing for the many languages at his command, like French, Spanish, Slav, Greek and Turkish. In pastoral plays he acted too the part of a shepherd called Corinto, performing on many different wind instruments made from flutes, and singing bucolic and iambic verses in imitation of Sannazzaro, known as Azio Sincero, a Neapolitan pastoral poet.

Capitano: That's true, I remember that; and these same players were collectively known as the Gelosi Company, which had as its emblem the two-faced Janus, and a motto that went 'Virtue, fame and honour made them Gelosi.' My dear Trappola, you can't find such companies any longer, and I say that without disrespect to those around today. Even if there are similar companies, they have only three or four good roles, while the rest are of little distinction and not up to the standard of the principals. In that famous company, though, all the parts were played by actors who were all outstanding. In short, that company was the ultimate in dramatic art, and no modern company can compare with it.

(Andreini, *Le Bravure del Capitano Spavento*, 1607, Fourteenth Dialogue)

THE GELOSI

The following documents record appearance by the Gelosi troupe in Venice, Florence and Mantua. They indicate the high standing of that company, how it could be summoned to play before royalty and, in the account of Isabella Andreini's main piece, La pazzia d'Isabella (The Madness of Isabella)*, something of the kind of material it performed and the acting skills it possessed. They show too, however, that even a major company was not above the wrath of the powerful.*

The Gelosi company in Venice, 1574

To the Secretary, Milan:
We understand the Comici Gelosi are in that city (Milan), and that among them is the woman named Vittoria. We wish to employ them to entertain the Very Christian King, who will be here in about four days. We request that on receipt of this letter you inform them they should come here with all possible speed in order to make the necessary preparations. We shall not fail to bestow on these players the appropriate courtesies. [Not dated, but 10 July, 1574]

To the Prince and Most Excellent Alvisio Mocenigo:
These Gelosi players have requested that on their journey to Venice they should carry letters from me addressed to Your Lordship so that, should they pass through Modena, they will not be restrained there by the Duke, but be allowed to proceed to Venice to serve Your Lordship. Thus to satisfy them I could not avoid writing these few lines. Then they begged me to mention to Your Lordship that here, much to their advantage, they enjoyed a great audience, and requested I commend them to your singular generosity. I have said that Your Lordship will not fail to treat them with due courtesy, and they will be aware of how much profit they make at other times in the city of Venice, as well as in the other cities of your dominions. Milan, 13 July, 1574.

(Both the above from Nolhac and Solerti,
Il viaggio in Italia di Enrico III, 1890, pp. 232–3)

Meanwhile the Signoria had brought the Gelosi players to Venice [to entertain Henry III of France], and you know how unique that company is in acting tragedies, comedies and other stage pieces, Simon Bolognese being a member, and most outstanding at playing the person of the Bergamask porter, but even more outstanding in witticisms and spirited inventions which entertain and instruct; another is Giulio Vinitiano, excellent in plays requiring Il Magnifico, and in performing that role I don't know which is finer in him, his grace, or the brilliance with which he displays moods both at the right moment and with the appropriate pedantic weight. Rinaldo, too, is in the company, and he is excellent at arranging new subjects and in adapting them to the tragic and comic stage, with costumes, fashions and noble presentations. I could go on about all of them in the same way one by one, and especially about the Woman who is unique, but if by chance anyone heard me, he would condemn me.

(T. Porcacchi, *Le attioni d'Arrigo terzo Re di Francia*, 1574, 27v.)

The Gelosi perform Cingana *and* La pazzia d'Isabella *in Florence, 1589*

Saturday, which fell on the 6th [May 1589], the Comici Gelosi being in Florence with those two most famous women Vittoria and Isabella, it seemed to the Grand Duke that as entertainment it would be an excellent idea if they were to act a comedy of their own choice. The two women nearly came to blows, for Vittoria wanted to act *Cingana* and the other wished to perform her Pazzia, entitled *La Pazzia d'Isabella* [*The Madness of Isabella*] – given that Vittoria's favourite part is Cingana and Isabella's is La Pazzia. However they finally agreed that the first piece to be acted would be *Cingana*, and that *La Pazzia* would be given another time. And so they performed the said *Cingana* with the same *Intermezzi* as were prepared for the great play; and indeed whoever has not heard Vittoria perform Cingana has neither seen nor heard something rare and marvellous, and certainly all were very satisfied with the play. They will do *La Pazzia* at another time, and it will be Isabella's turn to be the mad woman. There is no need now to speak of Isabella's quality, nor of the grace with which she expresses her conceits, for her virtues are well known and manifest throughout Italy.

(Pavoni, *Diario*, 1589, pp. 29–30)

[. . .] On Saturday, which was the 13th, the Grand Duke wanted *La Pazzia d'Isabella* [*The Madness of Isabella*] to be acted, having been much delighted by the splendid improvisations in the character of Cingana performed by Vittoria, whom he thought a woman of intellect and altogether outstanding. The Grand Duke advised the Comedians of the Gelosi of his wish, and at about ten o'clock, on the same stage where *La Pellegrina* was acted, they also performed *La Pazzia* with the same *Intermezzi* we have referred to before. The main argument of this play was as follows: Isabella, the only daughter of M. Pantalone de' Bisognosi, fell in love with Fileno, a most virtuous gentleman, and he with her. Isabella's maidservant too fell in love with the servant of Signor Fileno, and the servant with her, and thanks to them their master and mistress were able to send each other messages. Meanwhile Flavio, a student in the city called Padua, falls in love with Isabella, but does not find his love requited, she already being in love with Fileno. It so happened that this very gentleman, via a friend of his, asked Isabella's father for her hand in marriage, but the old man rejected him thinking Fileno too young. His friends made many intercessions on his behalf, but to no avail. Therefore the young lovers, seeing their business making no progress, became so desperate that they did not know which way to turn. Things being in this stage, Isabella finally decided to leave her father's house one night and elope with Fileno abroad. They planned the flight for the evening, agreeing between them signs which would make each known to the other; and similarly their two servants decided to abscond together and to share the fortunes of their master and mistress.

It so happened that while they were planning their flight Flavio, who was concealed nearby, overheard all the exchanges between his beloved and his rival, and was as much wounded by this as can possibly be imagined by anyone who has suffered in a similar way. Therefore he decided to take advantage of the opportunity and to try to obtain his beloved Isabella by the same means, and that he succeeded in doing. At the agreed time, or rather shortly before it, Flavio appeared and made his presence known by way of the signs Fileno was due to give to Isabella. Isabella immediately came out of the house and was met by Flavio with a delight beyond imagining. And so they departed together without a word being spoken. No sooner had they left than Fileno appeared with his servant, but when he gave the agreed signs there was no response. Finally the maid came out by the door and told Fileno she was unable to find her mistress, and after searching again in the house still could not find her. At this the unfortunate Fileno fell into such grief that he began to rave, demanding of himself where she might be; and so overwhelmed was he by such thoughts that he became like a man possessed or demented and quite out of his mind. Meanwhile Isabella, finding herself deceived by Flavio's snare, and not knowing how to remedy her misfortune, became wholly possessed by her grief, and thus dominated by her passion, and allowing herself to be consumed by rage and fury, was beside herself, and like a madwoman wandered through the city stopping now one person, now another, and speaking now in Spanish, now in Greek, now in Italian, and in many other languages, but always quite without sense. Among other things she began to speak in French, and also to sing songs in the French manner, which gave such pleasure to the Most Serene Bride [the Duke's wife] that no one could have been more delighted. Then she began to imitate the ways of speaking of her fellow-actors – the way, that is, of Pantalone, Gratiano, Zanni, Pedrolino, Francatrippe, Burattino, Capitan Cardone and Franceschina – in such a natural manner, and with so many fine emphases, that no words can express the quality and skill of this woman. Finally, by means of magic arts, and with the aid of certain waters she was given to drink, she was restored to her true self, and expressed at this point, in an elegant and learned style, the passions of love and the pains suffered by those caught in its net, thus concluding the comedy. In acting out this madness Isabella demonstrated her wise and rich intellect, prompting so many murmurs of astonishment among her auditors that for as long as the world survives her beautiful eloquence and her worth will ever be praised.

(Pavoni, *Diario*, 1589, pp. 43–6)

The Gelosi in Mantua, 1582

Although I have not heard this from Mantua, nonetheless it is said here [letter from Rome, 28 July 1582] that the Duke desired to see a comedy by the Gelosi that was altogether ridiculous and farcical. So the players obeyed him by staging a very absurd and ingenious one in which all the performers were hunchbacks. His Highness laughed enormously at it, and was altogether delighted by it. When the entertainment was over he summoned the leading players and asked which of them devised it. Zanni said, I did, I did; the Magnifico claimed he had; and Gratiano too sought the palm; each assumed he would get a rich reward. But the Duke had the three arrested, and they were condemned to be hanged. All the gentlewomen of Mantua banded together and begged for the players to be pardoned, but without success. The most they obtained was permission to make the ropes in their own fashion. These ropes were made of such rotten cord that all three players fell to the ground, and the city cried out pardon, pardon. But although the poor wretches were taken to prison half naked, and were shaven and bloody, nonetheless the Duke was still determined they should be hanged once more. And this story I have from a good source, although not from those regions.

(From Rasi, *I Comici*, III, 1905, p. 228)

A PATRON'S DIFFICULTIES WITH A TROUPE, 1620

If the power of patrons was considerable, however, so too were the problems which could accumulate when a patron took a company under his wing. The following letter, which speaks of Flaminio Scala and the Confidenti (see above p. 64), is particularly illuminating of the innumerable complications which could bedevil patronage.[28]

Illustr. Signore,

Our Signor Flaminio Scala came to me seeking permission to take his leave, and I was about to give him some oysters for Her Highness, but even as the barrels were being prepared, as I had asked him his reasons for leaving, he showed me a letter from Your Lordship, dated 11 March and written about six o'clock, reading which made me tell him immediately that there was no point in his going, neither by sea nor by land, if he had other business in which to serve His Highness than that of forming a company to take into France, because the arrangement made with him I knew could in no way be put into effect, it having bearing on the Company of the Confidenti, which is still under my protection, having been most amiably reconstituted, and of which company he is still a member. With regard to the other comedians which His Highness is maintaining there, I replied that I could not see what business he might have with them, and added further that as he was well aware of the very firm resolve and determination of his colleagues, I was surprised he could think of going there with nothing to offer. As he objected that he was doing so out of a sense of duty, I begged him, given that he now knew he could do nothing in this arrangement with His Highness, to allow me first to write to Your Lordship about the matter so that he would not make a fruitless journey; and so I succeeded in restraining him. I therefore advise Your Lordship that on the said Scala's return from Monferrato with His Highness's letter, I replied to His Highness, as he knows, that for the time being the Company should satisfy its obligations here in Venice, and that in Lent I would then do what I could to serve His Highness. And in truth I thought I could do so, for I saw that almost all of them were restless and had great difficulty in keeping together, as is usually the case with players. And I let them (as they say) stew in their own juice. But by the time of Lent, when belts are tighter, first one then another started to come to me and berate my ears, every one of them demanding unity, unity. And then all of them came to me together, not once but four times, to declare and insist that under no circumstances did they want to be disbanded. And after I had repeatedly told them that I had no wish to be involved in this business, but that I would let them know what seemed to me best both for their good and my desire, they all returned to beg me, with very humble prayers, not to abandon them, for they were absolutely resolute in their wish not to be broken up, nor divided in any way, and that therefore if in that respect I chose to give them orders they were very ready to obey, but if I ordered them in some other way they would prefer to be divided – for they foresaw the manifest disaster that would befall them, and recognizing that they would be ruined if they were disbanded, they preferred to do any humble task rather than acting. As I see it, all this is rooted in the fact that they realize how much money they have made this year. Now, my dear Signor Ercole, if I may speak freely with Your Lordship, seeing in what their decision consisted, and on what it depended, I did not know how, nor (to tell the truth) did I wish, to put pressure on them, for as a poor *Cav.*[re] *di spada et cappa* I do not have the means to give each of them 500 scudi, together with food and clothing for them and their families the whole year round, which is what each of them has earned this year – and Your Lordship must believe that before I wrote this I made certain of the facts. I beg you to tell me on your life, how could I possibly say to them: you must leave, you must stay, you who are first will have to be second; and how could I impose hierarchy and dependence upon men accustomed to liberty and free association? What Christian charity would I have bestowed on these poor men and their families? What courtesy or gratitude would I have shown to these people who for seven years continuously have obeyed my every wish, if I had ruined and sunk them, as they are convinced would have been the outcome if they had been disbanded? My dear Sir, I am poor but generous, and to tell truth, I am a compassionate person and cannot harm those who respect me. Your Lordship knows that the world is ruled by opinion; these poor men believe that ruin will follow if they are disbanded, therefore for the reasons I have given I could not find the words to tell them, let alone persuade them, otherwise. So I told them to do their best and that I would always help them; and so I allowed them to go their way. I asked each of them separately to promise that if by any chance they did split up, then each of them should do what I wished.

[. . .] Believe me, Your Lordship, if these players are divided they will please neither Man nor God. Indeed, if His Highness were to divide these players, mixing some with others, he would send to France not so much a company of players as the Tower of Babel [. . .] My dear Sir, the Lelij, the Florinde, the Flamminie, the Frittelini and the Arlichini, are all very famous and celebrated as people eager and ambitious for power and control. These other poor players, accustomed to fraternal association among themselves, would never submit to a peaceful and quiet subservience. The former, however, could never be weaned from their wish to dominate and give orders, for they are too accustomed to so doing, and have been for too long a time. In this I cannot blame them, for I too give orders more readily than I obey, and such an inclination is innate in every man, and therefore I dare say is unchangeable – indeed it grows with the years. Thus Your Lordship must believe that I think it advantageous to His Highness this business not be pursued, for it would not accord with his Greatness that a few comedians should fall short of his desire, and failing to show due respect should quarrel among themselves, as they certainly would — and all the more so in France, in the Theatre of such a great Court. Your Lordship may be sure I speak with confidence, as I recall instances which occurred at the time of Duke Vincenzo, of happy memory, the father of His Highness.

[. . .] I have no wish to disband a company that depends upon me in order to satisfy players who have enviously schemed against it, and who wish to batter, buffet and break it. The Confidenti Company in truth (although those others despise it) has a great reputation, and until now has been thought finer than any other; to disband it would indeed be (as they say) virtually a sin, the more so if the return that is hoped for is not forthcoming [. . .]

From Venice, 21 March, 1620
Don Gio Medici.

(From Rasi, *I Comici*, III, 1905, p. 517–9)

THE CONFIDENTI TROUPE PLAYING AT BOLOGNA IN 1615

The extent to which companies were able to exercise independence of noble patronage by virtue of their popularity and the level of fees and box-office returns they were able to command, particularly at Carnival time, is evident from the following letter.[29]

Today [11 November 1615] the San Martino palio was run in the presence of Sig. Cardinal Bevilaqua and numerous noblemen and ladies of Ferrara, and after the race these illustrious ones had the actors perform again their most beautiful comedy entitled *The Two Mezettini*, which has finished only now, and as I was there I have only just got back from it. I would have given much for your Lordship to have been present, for it turned out to be something quite marvellous, both in itself and for the host of eminent lords and ladies of Bologna and Ferrara who attended, in addition to the prelates already mentioned [. . .] I want to answer your Lordship tonight while I have time [. . .] regarding what your Excellency in a letter asked me about these players. First, as to my enquiring about their coming to Pesaro and what they would expect, I must confess I have done no more than broach the subject, but in any case I shall soon clarify things through a friend of mine, though to tell the truth I do not think they will be attracted, for this is perhaps the best company currently on tour, and they are always booked up from one carnival to the next, and when they leave here will go to Venice where they can command what they wish. As for the characters, first there are two *Zanni*, a clever one who develops the intrigue, and is called *Scappino*, the other so accomplished he has no equal, *Mezzetino*. There are four women: one *Lavinia*, who is the most beautiful, is the youngest, and acts better than the rest; another *Valeria*; and two others who play maidservants: *Nespole*, and *Spinetta*, *Scappino*'s wife. There are two lovers: one *Fulvio*, who acts better than the other, and who told me he once played at Pesaro in the house of Signor Federigo – he is the brother of *Valeria*, who is getting on a bit; the other is *Ortensio*, *Lavinia*'s husband. A *Pantalone*, a *Beltrammo* from Bergamo, a *Capitano spagnuolo*, an Italianate Frenchman called *Claudione* – these complete the characters. *Fulvio* also acts a *Romagnuolo* and a *Graziano*; the *Capitano* often acts the *Capitano italiano*, and so all occasionally double up parts.

(From A. Saviotti, 'Feste e spettacoli nel seicento', *Giornale Storico della Letteratura Italiana*, XLI, 1914, pp. 63–4)

4

Patronage, Performance Places and Repertories

Audiences

Commedia dell'arte companies enjoyed many different kinds of patronage. The patrons of performances in the streets and market places were certainly drawn from all levels of society, and some of them were neither able nor willing to contribute financially to the entertainment they were offered. Hence the preference of the troupes for rooms and halls where spectator payment could be fixed and controlled. How socially heterogenous the audiences were who attended the *stanze* of the major cities on the touring circuits is now hard to calculate. In the 1560s and 1570s, when the professional companies were in the process of displacing the drama of the academic *dilettanti*, audiences at plays may largely have been drawn from the courts and the economically-prosperous educated and professional classes, like those a contemporary observer noted at a play given by the Roman actress Flaminia and her troupe in 1567: 'Last Sunday the Company of Flaminia performed a beautiful play; it was well attended by many gentlefolk, judges, lawyers, doctors etc.'[1]

As the companies became established this, in addition to that of the courts, was probably the kind of audience they particularly sought: one able to afford the entrance charge and, if satisfied, willing to patronize a company on a fairly regular basis, educated enough to catch and delight in reference to, and parody or misuse of, classical and learned materials, and likely to set a premium on the formal sophistication of the plays they watched – on organizational coherence, verbal and visual decorum, and performer expertise. Although this audience might include those who fancied themselves connoisseurs of drama – like the Stranger who disputes with the Player in the Prologue to Flaminio Scala's *Il finto marito* (see below, pp. 197) – its preference was probably more for the relaxed and relaxing pleasures of comedy than for the intellectually heavier and more serious dramatic kinds. The support of this well-to-do audience, together with that of the aristocracy, probably accounts for the willingness of some clerical critics of theatre to direct their hostility mainly against the activities of those actors whose livelihoods were made primarily or exclusively by the broader mass of the people.

Regular professional theatre appealed to most social groups, and to both male and female. Grazzini's verses of the 1550s cited above suggest that *zanni* entertainment was then too socially and morally suspect for gentlewomen to attend in public, although more acceptable when performed for them in their own houses – further evidence perhaps that the players modified their material according to the audience they were playing to. According to Fynes Moryson, in Florence 'at publique Comedies Courtesans and Torch bearers enter freely, and pay nothing' – a remark that implies that male spectators made up the larger part of the audience.[2] By the early decades of the seventeenth century enthusiasm for the public performance of plays seems to have been sufficiently pronounced among both sexes to make it an object of concern to moralists: the young were keen patrons, to the consternation of employers and parents; married men, it was said, found in the ambience of theatre a fantasy and excitement wanting in their domestic lives; even otherwise sober matrons it seems were not immune, abandoning household duties for the lure of stage fictions, save perhaps in Rome (see below, p. 252).

The market for regular theatrical entertainment by the late sixteenth century was probably substantial at most social levels, particularly at Carnival time when major companies could command a high price for their wares, giving them some independence of the patronage and blandishments of the nobility. Records primarily report on players' activities in the cities and major towns, but the iconography, as well as the more general satirical accounts of clerics like Garzoni, indicate that itinerant troupes may have been equally popular in remoter villages and hamlets (see plate 15). Fynes Moryson describes how English actors touring in the Netherlands and Germany, and playing in a language unknown to the vast majority of the spectators, were followed from town to town by fascinated admirers, and how even 'marchants at Fayres bragged more to have seene them, then of the good marketts they made.'[3] The appeal of the Italian players was doubtless similar, whether they were touring in Italy or abroad.

Noble Patrons and Impresarios

The evolution of aristocratic patronage of the professional companies, as well as the nature and extent of that patronage, is particularly difficult to chart. It was decidedly uneven, some great families, like the Medici and the Gonzaga, being more supportive than others; it was variable, in that some members of a noble family were more enthusiastic than their fellows, and dynastic change could lead to a severance of patronage, as seems to have happened to the Fedeli company in the mid 1620s; it was capricious, in that favour and support bestowed could quickly and easily be withdrawn, with little redress for the players, on the whim of a patron, or a shift in aristocratic entertainment fashion; and although noble patronage continued throughout the seventeenth century, it seems to have been less widespread in the final decades. As remarked above, the economic decline of Italy in the seventeenth century possibly led to a contraction in patronage, and some former centres of cultural activity conspicuously declined as a result of annexation or natural disasters like famine and plague.[4]

However, where and when aristocratic support was available, the advantages to the players could be considerable. Many patrons attempted to assemble or exchange the best troupes; thus membership of such troupes, particularly for rising players, gave professional and social status. Noble interest could bring with it financial reward and favour and, at least for a time, a degree of economic security. We have cited Francesco Gabrielli's letter to the Duke of Mantua (see below, p. 123) as an instance of the difficulties involved in forming a company and of maintaining a balance of roles within it; but the tone of Gabrielli's letter suggests, further, that in writing to the Duke the old actor was less interested in artistic than in economic considerations. Behind his reminder of faithful service given, and of patronage now hopefully to be received again, lies surely the anxiety of one hoping to obtain a secure place for himself and his dependents within the Duke's retinue. More than one distinguished player at the end of his career looked, sometimes in desperation, to aristocratic beneficence. Scala turned to the Duke of Mantua, as too did Francesco Andreini. One of the last records we have of the versatile and indefatigable Gian Battista Andreini is a letter to a later Duke requesting, in vain it seems, rescue from the poverty into which he had fallen.[5] Noble patronage could be valuable of course to companies as well as to individual players. It bestowed a degree of social and cultural approval; it could protect a company against the suspicion, disdain or bureaucratic intransigence of officialdom, or the vigorous hostility, and often devious machinations, of clerical opponents. It could smooth passage across territorial boundaries, and simplify travel through foreign states. It could ensure, if not always a welcome, then at least a minimum of hindrance in towns and cities. Noble intervention was sought by companies to ease not only travel, but performance problems: the booking and cancellation of halls, approval of plays, and recruitment to companies. The patron could use his influence in a variety of ways towards a troupe's well-being.

But patronage brought with it, too, for individual players and companies alike, a dependence that could be tyrannous. Aristocratic patrons were not disinterested champions of theatre: they formed and supported companies for their own purposes. They were of course keen to secure regular entertainment for their courts. But court theatre in the sixteenth and seventeenth centuries was more than a mere occasional entertainment provided by a wealthy and beneficent ruler for the delight of his entourage and guests. Nearly all such theatre had a certain political dimension, and was in one way or another an extension of diplomacy: a means of demonstrating locally, or on a more Europe-wide plane, the power and prosperity of a ruler through festivity and emblematic display. Such a political dimension is of course most conspicuous in the great court *feste*, mounted to celebrate dynastic occasions, and which often used visual means to point current or future power relationships.[6] It would be extravagant to claim that aristocratic patronage of the professional acting companies was expressly intended to serve these purposes, but nor was it wholly unconnected with them, for the companies, too, performed at court on the great festival occasions, and were a part of the overall purposes of such festival display. That a troupe was a ducal company, or was employed by a duke, bespoke the munificence of the dukedom. Both companies and players could be used, too, as pawns in a broad game of dynastic relationships which was ultimately political. Noble patrons not only formed companies for their own court entertainment but exchanged or loaned players, put together companies to send to foreign courts as gestures of friendship or familial generosity, and despatched players abroad at the request of a foreign ruler. Direct and specific political purposes did not necessarily underlie these favours, but they served in their own way to cement links which were based ultimately on political considerations. If the fame of the *commedia dell'arte* spread so rapidly throughout Europe in the late sixteenth and seventeenth centuries, and more particularly in France, Spain and the German states, this was in no small measure due to the influence exercised, and the patronage dispensed, by a network of great aristocratic houses interconnected by familial and political ties.

In Italy itself court fashions and tastes, as well as the calendar of court summer and winter activities, determined many major company programmes and the range and kinds of dramatic pieces they prepared and presented. Patrons made repertory demands, changed the composition of troupes and banished or punished players who proved recalcitrant to aristocratic whim. Extant letters of companies and players to noble patrons (often addressed indirectly to the patron via one of his household officials) are of course couched in the obsequious terms conventional to correspondence in the age. But the convention usefully underscores the enormity of the gulf which lay between the players and their patrons both at home and abroad. Some scholars have marvelled at the familiarity of Tristano Martinelli's letters to Maria de' Medici, and have seen them as evidence that some highly talented and sought after performers were able to assert their independence, speak bluntly to the great, and dictate their own terms.[7] But Martinelli's familiarity was simply a licence granted the court fool: it was part of a game, the very playing of which defined his place in the social scheme of things. In that scheme actors ultimately were of little importance, and retribution could be swift and severe for any, however apparently favoured, who forgot their true place.

Of course the players were not wholly subservient, and it would seem that the more firmly they came to secure commercial markets, the more independence they were able to exercise. Absolutist political power was hard to gainsay, but they had resort to a variety of indirect means for resisting the pressures of authoritarian or paternalistic patronage. They could plead the commercial demands of the public market and its importance to their collective and individual economy; they could advance obligations to their fellow professionals for reluctance to leave one troupe for another; they could urge the complications implicit in familial and amatory ties; and in any proposed composition of a new ducal troupe could stress the need to accommodate, without duplication of skills and role specializations, the talents of groups of performers (see below, pp. 124). Increasingly, by the turn of the century, tensions within troupes seem to have been complemented by tensions between companies and their noble patrons as individuals or groups sought greater freedom for themselves or greater control over a company's affairs.

The extent of a company's autonomy, and the kind and degree of its relationship with a patron, were further complicated by the emergence, certainly before the turn of the century, of theatre impresarios. Product of the commercialization of theatre, they are important well before the end of the *cinquecento*. If it is to Venice that we look for the beginnings of organized professional acting companies, it is there too that we find clear evidence of early appropriation of commercial theatre by patrician impresarial interests. In the 1580s two noblemen, Alvise Michiel and Ettore Tron, erected theatres in Venice, hiring them out on contractual bases to the professional companies. The power of these patrician impresarios flourished, and they established what were in effect profitable family businesses, some of which survived for many generations. One of the most important Venetian theatres of the *seicento* was the San Cassiano, first opened for the public showing of *melodramma* in 1637. Other theatres often housed the non-musical drama, like Alvise Giustinian's San Moisé, and the Vendramin family's San Luca.[8] By the end of the seventeenth century it is estimated that there were no fewer then sixteen theatres active in Venice.[9]

The contracts acting companies entered into with impresarios initially were for short periods, but by the early seventeenth century longer-term arrangements of one, two or more seasons were quite common. Other cities were not slow to follow the Venetian example; indeed the first recorded attempt to set up as a commercial theatre impresario, that by Leone de' Sommi in 1567, is found not in Venice, but in Mantua (see below, p. 100). The emergence of *impresarii* is itself eloquent witness to the extent to which the market for regular commercial theatre had burgeoned by the end of the sixteenth century. This commercial success necessarily strengthened somewhat the position of the acting companies in their dealings with noble patrons. Advance booking became a feature of the seasonal programmes of the major troupes, Particularly at Carnival time the actors could command large sums of money, and thus were not as readily available as perhaps they had once been to service aristocratic occasions (see below, p. 98).

Outdoor Playing

PLATE 16 *Engraving of mountebanks in Piazza San Marco, Venice. Giacomo Franco,* Habiti d'huomini et donne venetiane *(1609). Permission of The British Library, C 48 h11*

While we possess an abundance of literary and visual matter illustrative of many aspects of the *commedia dell'arte*, a fair amount of that material is of later seventeenth- or eighteenth-century origin, and nearly all the iconographic evidence dating from before the mid-seventeenth century bears on performance *al fresco*. Performance in streets and squares remained a characteristic activity of the companies throughout both centuries and for a number of obvious reasons: gathering out of doors was a feature of social life, the Italian climate lent itself to open air playing, and companies were able to avoid the rents payable for the hire of theatres and halls. If the pictorial evidence is to be trusted, the scenic elements of street performance changed very little over two centuries or more. An early seventeenth-century engraving of charlatans performing in the Piazza San Marco in Venice (plate 16) shows three examples of the basic trestle stage that was to remain a constant for many of the lesser troupes: a simple, portable structure the prime function of which was to elevate performers well above spectators on a platform large enough to permit a degree of movement. The comparatively small size of the stages in this engraving may reflect pictorial distortion, but may indicate, too, that the dramatic element of the performance was embryonic, consisting of verbal duologues or triolets, the kind of entertainment provided by singers, jugglers and mimes. Music was obviously a feature of these shows: female instrumental (and probably vocal) performers are to be seen on two of the stages. On the stage in the foreground of the picture the two figures are very obviously of the *commedia dell'arte*: a Pantalone and a Zanni.

The detail of this engraving is interestingly corroborated by Thomas Coryate's description of Venetian charlatans (see above, p. 26). His account suggests that the function of the performers was principally to supply musical accompaniment to the charlatan's oratory, act as his foils in comic and scurrilous badinage, and serve as his assistants in passing out medicines, perfume and nostrums, and collecting monies. According to several contemporary witnesses the charms of female assistants, like those mentioned by Coryate, were freely exploited in the business of selling goods (see below, p. 245). Coryate's account includes reference to a charlatan playing with a viper; this detail we likewise see in the engraving, where a figure on the stage in the foreground holds a snake in his right hand. Important too, however, is that nowhere in his account does Coryate suggest that the entertainers performed plays or playlets, nor does he describe them as actors or actresses. Indeed he expressly says that 'some weare visards being disguised *like* fooles in a play' (our italics).[10] In a later account of charlatans in the Piazza Navona in Rome, John Evelyn, who visited Italy in the 1640s, refers specifically to their attracting spectators by 'Jack-puddings and *Pantomimes*', but how elaborate the latter were he does not say.[11]

Stage players, however, as well as mountebanks, performed in the great squares. A company of comedians, and not a charlatan group, is depicted in a seventeenth-century painting of performers in Piazza San Marco (in the Hermitage, Leningrad, but reproduced in Nicoll, *Masks, Mimes and Miracles*). In this the trestle stage is a more substantial platform – measuring, on a very rough estimate, something like eight-foot by twelve-foot, and elevated well above the head-height of the spectators. The performance was given at Carnival time, as is clear from the masked and costumed figures passing by or gathered about the stage. On the platform itself there is a structure distinctly more substantial than a mere painted backcloth: house facades are sketched in rough perspective, and slits serve for entry and exit; however, the structure also has a back and sides, so the players were evidently concealed from the spectators when not actually involved in the performance. The players are grouped in a fairly typical stage scene: an actress addresses the audience; an *arlecchino* addresses it too, or looks on; a third figure has turned away back-stage, perhaps on the point of exiting; a fourth conspicuously eavesdrops on the action. Such platform stages were regularly set up in streets and *piazze* throughout the seventeenth and eighteenth centuries (and indeed later), although not all employed the boxed-in scenic apparatus depicted in this painting.

Well illustrative of the continuity maintained in the basics of open-air stages and *mise-en-scène* are the stages of somewhat similar size seen in many eighteenth-century engravings of players performing in the Piazza Navona in Rome or in the Venetian *piazze*. Nearly all these stages are simple and utilitarian: large enough to permit considerable movement, comic 'business' and a conventionalized identification of 'houses'; with scenic areas backed by a simple cloth, with slits on it for exits and entries, and with no attempt been made to paint streets or houses in perspective.[12] Interestingly, nearly all the illustrations of trestle stages indicate that the players made little or no attempt to conceal the scaffold supports by cloths or hangings, surely a clear indication not that the players were too poor to dress their performance place, but that they and the spec-

PLATE 17 *Eighteenth century players in Piazza San Marco, Venice. Engraving in* Le Fabriche e vedute di Venetia *(1703). Permission of The British Library, 746 d22*

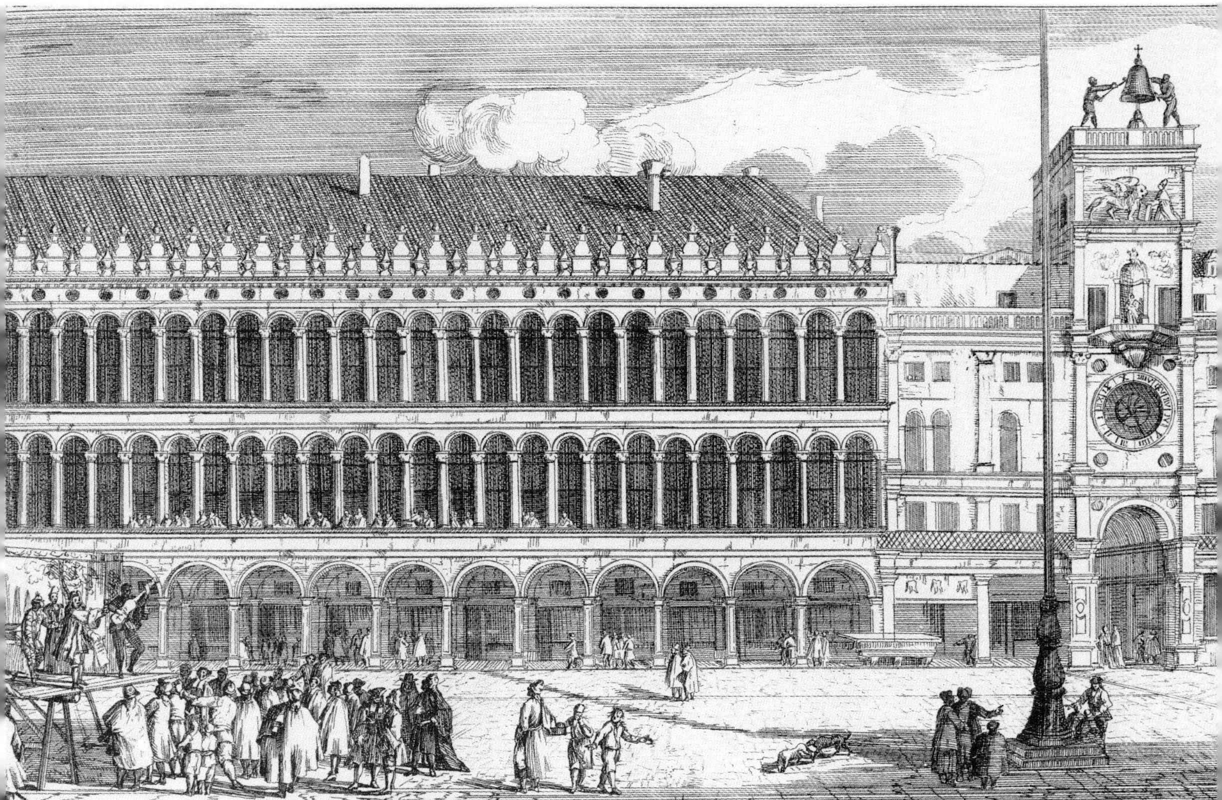

tators recognized that the stage was indeed a stage, and that it was the action not the scenic structure which created the world of the play.

Stanze and Halls

Such was probably the case, too, when players performed indoors. Unfortunately, very little illustrative material has survived of early indoor performances, and to that extent the iconography may well be rather misleading, for indoor performance was common and favoured. Verbal accounts suggest however that travelling players who hired a hall or room for performance set up their trestle stages much as they would if performing '*al fresco*'. There is no reason to suppose that the rooms, or *stanze*, were anything other than modest: as we have seen, Garzoni's generalized account of an itinerant troupe arriving in a town and performing in the room of a palace or an inn disparagingly emphasizes the players' crudity of staging means (see above, p. 69). Even setting aside his satiric and polemical intent, it is probably a not inaccurate description, for some of the travelling troupes, including in all likelihood those depicted in the illustrations discussed above, were small companies, as modest perhaps in ability as in scenic accoutrements.

Whether or not major troupes performed at all regularly open-air and in the streets and *piazze*, is another matter. They would do so, of course, if such were the whim of a noble patron who wanted an entertainment to be given in his courtyard or gardens, or if some other particular occasion required it. But performance in rooms, halls or theatres was to some extent, and became increasingly, a mark of success and status which the major companies would have been reluctant to compromise. To what extent they were prepared to do so when they travelled abroad, en route say to Paris or Vienna, is uncertain. Nor is the situation at all clear with regard to their performance in the Italian states. On the one hand, economic considerations were always a determining factor for professionals; but on the other, the quality, even exclusivity, of the product being marketed called for careful exploitation. Much must have depended on the conditions and imperatives of the moment. The most famous companies, as is amply evident, acted quite regularly in native and foreign courts, like those of Mantua or Turin, Paris or Vienna, and in grand surroundings on elaborately fit-up or purpose-built stages: at the Louvre, the Palazzo Mocenigo, or the theatre in the Uffizi.[13] But patronage by the wealthy was not always available, and even when a company enjoyed the special support of a patron its services would not always be required by him. Many major companies depended too for their livelihood on a less elite paying public: hence the importance of travelling at home and abroad, and of booking engagements ahead on the various circuits; hence too the insistence of some troupes when invited to play at foreign courts – like the Fiorilli company when invited to London in 1676 – that they be given permission to act in public as well as at court. The possibility then that even the most important troupes at times gave public performances to paying spectators in city squares cannot be discounted.

Their preference, however, would almost certainly have been for indoor venues and securing these was competitive, and a prime concern of a company's business manager. In fact the use of *stanze* for play performances seems to have preceeded the establishment of the professional companies and their touring circuits: *dilettanti* productions were given in halls and rooms, and *stanze* or *sale* were quite regularly used in Venice in the early decades of the sixteenth century. By the turn of the century the boundary between *stanze* adapted for theatrical performances and regular playhouses was probably a fine one. Apart from some spaces expressly prepared for special court activities, the accoutrements of most seem to have been modest. Thomas Coryate has left a description of a Venetian playhouse he visited in 1608, and he compares it unfavourably in the main with the theatres he was familiar with in England (see below, p. 100). The facilities at the 'osteria' del Falcone in Genoa, where a troupe played as early as 1566 (by 1640 it had become the Teatro del Falcone), were almost certainly austere; but even those at the celebrated Baldracca theatre in a rough quarter of Florence were probably modest, for all that the Medici dukes and their entourages visited it, watching performances from a private gallery linked to the palace by a private passage-way.[14]

Despite the rents companies had to pay for hire of rooms, halls and, eventually, theatres proper, indoor performance was advantageous to the players. Money paid by spectators for performances in the squares and streets was variable, and when given was more in the nature of a gratuity; the closed room or hall gave control over entrance and allowed the price of entry to be fixed. It opened the way gradually to the graded arrangement of seating by price, from the simple stools remarked by Coryate, to the later tiered balconies and boxes of the mid and late seventeenth- and the eighteenth-century theatres.[15] Charges could be flexible according to the nature of the entertainment offered, and to the occasion and time of year, and the extent of audience demand. It made theatre, in short, a much more organized business activity. Along with disciplined commercialization came the need for tighter forward planning of a company's activities. Likely returns had to be calculated over a long period to offset the rents to which companies were liable by the legally binding contracts they entered into, bookings had to be made well in advance of the performance season, and publicity became an important factor.

The use of rooms, halls and theatres on a regular basis meant much more to a company, however, than just tighter control over box office returns, and the need carefully to manage seasonal commitments. It had implications for all aspects of a company's work. In an important respect it helped further to mark off acting companies from troupes of street performers. For the spectator who attended the activities of the latter, no matter how carefully they were prepared and timed, was perforce casual. The audience was floating not captive, might or might not stay out the performance and pay for the entertainment, and could easily be drawn away by other attractions. But the spectator who went to a performance in a room, hall or theatre, even to leave dissatisfied before the end, had made a deliberate decision to attend that event and had paid for it in advance. The event, then, became a special, organized occasion, and the wise company treated it as such. In a room or hall it had considerable authority over the whole performance environment, and was in a better position to control not just box office, but the mood and tone of the performance itself. Ways in which lighting, sound and music, for example, were employed could be more precisely calculated in the service of the show, and likely audience response more accurately judged in advance. The show became even more the focus of attention, because it was the show the spectator had paid to see. Thus a premium was put on the preparation of material, and on the disciplined orchestration of performance and presentation.

Repertories

The companies we probably know most about are the Gelosi and the Confidenti, and it will have been clear from the brief histories of these above that our knowledge is distinctly patchy. It is impossible to establish clear chronologies of their comings and goings, and difficult to get a firm impression of the range of their activities. Such evidence as there is, however, suggests that both companies acted a wide range of dramatic kinds, as did certain other troupes like the Fedeli. But just as not all players could move easily between improvised and premeditated playing, so some companies appear to have confined their performance to improvised plays. Doubtless repertories depended on the frequency with which any particular troupe might be called upon to perform different dramatic kinds, and that itself could depend on the extent to which it enjoyed court or noble patronage. On the work of companies so patronized, the influence of courtly tastes, and the styles and materials of the high culture were understandably pronounced.

Courts seem to have had their preferences. At Ferrara, for example, in the 1570s, not only improvised pieces but pastoral plays appear to have been much in vogue. It was under the patronage of Alfonso II of Ferrara that in 1573, as we have remarked, members of the Gelosi joined with court amateurs to act Tasso's *Aminta*. Florence seems to have preferred the professionals in comedy and *intermezzi*, the more formal drama being done there by court amateurs. Mantua on the other hand looked to the professional troupes to supply both improvised and scripted plays, and probably in a variety of dramatic kinds.[16] But notwithstanding the different tastes of the courts, flexibility across a range of genres was clearly useful for a company, helping it to get bookings for special occasions. In this respect the Gelosi and Confidenti were well placed. When the Gelosi were engaged to entertain Henry III of France at Venice in July 1574 (see chapter 10), they offered 'Tragedies, Comedies and other stage shows', including a musical allegory *Tragedia* by Frangipane and Merulo: 'All the actors sang in very smooth tones, sometimes solo, at other times accompanied, and in the finale the Chorus of Mercury consisted of players who used as many diverse instruments as ever were played.'[17] The Confidenti were equally versatile: a request to the Grand Duke for permission to act in Florence boasted that in addition to 'comedies, and new works', they could perform 'Spanish and Italian dances to music'.[18]

Only a scattering of records survive to indicate the range of the different dramatic kinds performed by the *commedia dell'arte* companies. It does not follow, however, that performance of scripted rather than improvised pieces was a very rare occurrence. Information about any of the plays the companies performed, whether scripted or improvised, is sparse – to such an extent indeed that even when we have specific record of a performance by a major troupe very rarely is the title of the piece recorded: we know of few improvised plays done by the Gelosi troupe other than the *Cingana* and *La Pazzia d'Isabella* acted in Florence in 1589. Nonetheless some indication of the range of work done can be traced through the history of the great companies in their heyday. As early as 1567 a company led by the actress Flaminia performed a tragedy taken from Canto XXXVI of Ariosto's *Orlando Furioso*, although whether this was improvised or scripted is difficult to tell from the extant account of it (see below, p. 98). In the same year, and again in Mantua, Vincenza Armani acted in a tragedy based on Virgil's story of Dido, Queen of Carthage (see above, p. 52). In 1573, as we have already noted, the Gelosi acted in Tasso's *Aminta*. In 1586 Piccolomini's *L'Amor costante*, certainly a scripted piece, was done by the Gelosi in the Casa Rucellai in Florence. Virginia Ramponi, wife of the Fedeli company's leader, Giovan Battista Andreini, in 1608 took over at the last moment the lead role in Rinuccini's *melodramma, Arianna,* set by Monteverdi; the piece remained in the repertory of the Fedeli after 1608, although in what form is uncertain. A celebrated pastoral play of the early seventeenth century, widely admired beyond Italy, in England and elsewhere, Bonarelli's *Filli in Sciro*, was performed by the Accesi in 1614. Pastorals enjoyed a particular vogue in the early seventeenth century, and several others were done by the professional companies, including the most celebrated pastoral of the period, Guarini's *Il Pastor Fido*, acted by a troupe that included Pier Maria Cecchini in May, 1618, in the royal palace at Naples.[19]

Call for performance of scripted plays abroad was probably limited because of the language barrier. However, we should not ignore the fact that in many European courts there was a considerable Italian presence and a taste for things Italian, and there may have been performances of which we have no record. Some of the first Italian plays performed in Spanish courts for example were of the literary drama and were probably done in Italian (see below, p. 258). Naturally *melodramma libretti* in Italian were more readily acceptable to most courts, Here we may note that the first opera given at the Petit Bourbon, the Strozzi and Sacrati *La finta pazza*, mounted by Giacomo Torelli in 1645, was part acted and part sung in Italian by Italian professional players.[20] Whether or not the professional players occasionally performed in Italy or abroad vernacular versions of classical comedy and tragedy is not known, although a reference to the actor Francesco Gabrielli remarks that he played Oedipus.[21]

Such notices of performances are few and scattered, but they clearly indicate that at least some of the players and companies performed comedies, tragedies, pastorals, *melodramma* and *intermezzi* in addition to improvised plays. The stock in trade of the troupes, however, was improvised drama, and for sound economic reasons (see chapter 5). The preparation of new *scenarii* for these seems to have been the responsibility of particular individuals in the companies. There may indeed be some connection between the quasi-literary activity of writing *scenarii*, and the inclination of some actors to write and publish fully scripted plays. Flaminio Scala, who published an important collection of *scenarii* in 1611, *Il Teatro delle Favole rappresentative*, also wrote a play, *Il finto marito* (see chapter 9). Similarly, others who published plays, like P. M. Cecchini and Niccolò Barbieri, may have prepared *scenarii*. Many *scenarii* were taken from scripted plays, the motives, plot-lines and incidents being plundered not only from Italian, but from French, Spanish and classical drama, and many were drawn too from other, earlier *scenarii*. Some players certainly translated plays into Italian from other languages, although whether any saw the stage in scripted rather than in scenario form is uncertain. The nature and range of the *scenarii* are discussed in more detail in chapter 6, but here we can usefully note their catholicity, from the comic, through the pastoral to the tragic and quasi-operatic. By the major troupes at least some pieces were certainly mounted – if not regularly, then on

PLATE 18 *Figures depicted in C. Gonzaga* Gli Inganni *(1592). Permission of The British Library, C 125 aa16*

special celebratory occasions – with all the spectacular setting out that Renaissance scenic designers and machinists could devise.[22] *Scenarii* circulated, too, it seems, in manuscript, usefully augmenting the stock of plays a company could put on according to the predilections and performance emphases of its players. The richness of the repertories of the major troupes was a governing factor in their success, for *commedia dell'arte* actors and actresses were traders in plays.

Documents

Travelling companies of course needed official permission to perform plays in public in the cities they visited, and officials sought to keep a firm control on the kinds of performance they gave, and where and when they performed. Regulation affected all kinds of performer, from street entertainers to organised professional companies.

AN ORDER OF THE STATE GOVERNOR OF MILAN, MAY 1566

And it is further ordered that the Leaders and Performers of plays, Herbalists, Charlatans, Buffoons, Zani, Trestle singers, and others of similar profession who are in the habit of mounting a trestle stage and gathering people about them, are forbidden, and should neither dare nor presume, to mount their stages at certain times of the year, and particularly throughout Lent, and on those festive days proclaimed by Holy Mother Church. Nor *etiam* should they, either off stage or in any other way, engage in their activity other than between the centre and the rear of the *piazza*, it being decreed that this *piazza* starts where the steps end. Nor are they permitted to perform near other churches during divine services, under penalty of two lashes of the rope or such other punishment as His Excellency shall determine.
(From Castiglione, *Sentimenti de S. Carlo Borromeo*, 1759, pp. 22–3)

THE INFLUENCE OF THE PATRON

The following short notes and letters indicate the kinds of influence discussed above that a noble patron could exercise on behalf of players and companies.

The Confidenti wish to perform in Verona, 30 May 1580

The Company of the Confidenti players, currently in this city, wishes when it leaves here [Mantua] to come there [Verona] to perform its comedies for the public entertainment of that city, and has therefore asked me to intercede with Your Highness on its behalf so that you will grant it a licence to do so.

(From D'Ancona, *Origini del teatro italiano*, 1891, II, p. 474)

The Company of Vittoria wishes to perform in Padua, 27 April 1580

Vittoria and her company of players[23] wish to be free to act their plays in the city of Padua, and therefore have begged me to intervene with your Illustrious Lordship and request that you show favour to her and her companions, so that by the authority of your Illustrious Lordship they can obtain their wish.

(From D'Ancona, II, p. 475)

Aurelia seeks an acting post, 27 March 1593

The actress Aurelia most earnestly desires to have a position with, and to be part of, the company of Vittoria, hoping that under the guidance of such a great woman she will be able to advance in her profession. As she is aware that the slightest sign from your Serene Highness can make her merit such a favour, she came to beg me with all the entreaty in the world to plead for the favour of Your Highness on whose benevolence she has based all her hopes, and she calculates that my intercession, being that of a most faithful and dedicated servant, will help her to no small extent. I would very much like this woman's earnest wish to have the support of my respectful affection. With all my soul I therefore beg that Your Highness deign to satisfy such a just and virtuous request, for by it not only will the company of Vittoria itself be enhanced, but our city in particular, where they hope to perform their plays, will hear something altogether delightful, for Aurelia is generally well liked by everyone. I respectfully salute your Highness.

(From D'Ancona, II, p. 511)

A patron intervenes on behalf of a company, 29 May 1609

Illustrious and most Excellent Sir,

These actors of mine have told me of their wish to act in that city [Florence] for the coming San Martino until Christmas, but they fear they had been forestalled in obtaining permission by an actor called Nobili of another company who has deliberately occupied in advance the halls of the main cities. Therefore, being begged by them, I come with this letter to beseech Your Excellency that Your Excellency be good enough to obtain a licence for them by removing it from the others for, aside from my own concern, it is better suited to the above-mentioned as they have acted in it before and their company is better. I shall remain obliged to your Excellency and promise to serve Your Excellency in some way that will please you more. Meanwhile I kiss your hand and wish you happiness. From Mantua, 29 May, 1609.

Sent to Your Excellency from your brother-in-law and servant, the Duke of Mantua.

(From Mamone, *Il teatro nella Firenze medicea*, 1981, pp. 127–8)

The Gelosi seek financial help, 3 November 1590

The *comici Gelosi*, who are currently here in Milan, having heard of my devotion to Your Serene Highness, have begged me to intercede, so that by my assistance they may be granted the favour of being relieved from payment of the rent they owe on the hall in which they are accustomed to act their plays, for the period their contract lasts – which I understand to be about two months. They themselves cannot come at present (Your Highness willing), being forced by the current famine to avoid the expense of such a long journey, and because they doubt too, for that same reason, that they would be much welcomed in that city. Trusting in the infinite kindness and affection Your Highness has ever designed to show me, and wishing these Gelosi to be well treated, I seek with this letter to beg Your Highness that for my sake you condescend to give the appropriate order to relieve them of the rent, and for this not only they, but I too, will be much obliged to Your Highness, as if it were a favour done to me personally, and I humbly bow to Your Highness, and pray that Our Lord give you a happy and long life.

Milan, 3 November 1590. From Pirro Visconte Borromeo.

(From Evangelista, 'Il teatro della commedia dell'arte a Firenze', 1980, p. 174)

The Duke of Mantua praises the Desiosi to the Duchess of Ferrara, 6 January 1596

On the occasion the actors of the Desiosi passed through [Mantua] I saw some of their plays, which indeed gave me no little pleasure. Therefore when they told me they would willingly come here this Carnival time, provided they could obtain permission from the Most Serene Duke, I did not wish to lose the chance to beg Your Highness on their behalf that you condescend to give it them, for I assure you they are well behaved people and so amusing that believe me you will be particularly well pleased any time during these days of Carnival you condescend to hear them.

(From D'Ancona, *Origini del teatro italiano*, 1891, II, p. 520)

Players receive a patron's aid to travel abroad, 30 April 1635

As the players Diana and Buffetto[24] must go to Paris to perform at Court there, and finding it necessary to pass through this state, we wish them to carry the present document. According to this we grant them free and ample passage for their persons, and those of four or five others they will take with them, together with their belongings, notwithstanding any contrary order. We therefore instruct all ministers and officials, both of justice and war, customs officers, tax officials and gate-keepers, and all others it may concern, not only that they should neither harass nor impede them in any way during their journey, but rather should lend them all possible help, observing the present document, and ensuring its observance, for the next thirty days.

Issued in Milan, 30 April, 1635.

(From Rasi, *I Comici,* pp. 571–2)

PRESSURES EXERCISED BY NOBLE PATRONS

Patrons were not only beneficent, however; they could put considerable pressure on individual players and companies. Sometimes players were able to resist, sometimes not, as the following short pieces show.

Players performing in Mantua without permission, May 1585

Our very Serene Duke has heard that certain players are acting in Mantua without either the permission or knowledge of his Serene Highness. He has thus asked me to write to Your Highness to point out that, as far as he is aware they are not here at the request of the Most Serene Prince. He assumes they came in order to perform for his Serene Highness' entertainment, not to act in Mantua without permision of the most Serene Duke, my master. I therefore beg Your Lordship to be so good as to advise me how things stand, that I may inform His Most Serene Highness accordingly.

Our Most Serene Lord commands Your Lordship to order the players acting in the city to leave there immediately, without stopping anywhere. Indeed, they merit much worse punishment than this, for it is untrue that they have been given permission by His Highness to stop in Mantua and perform there. Your Lordship should reprimand them by demanding why they have presumed so falsely to use the protection of the Most Serene person of His Highness.

(From D'Ancona, *Origini del teatro italiano,* 1891, II, pp. 488–9)

Vittoria runs foul of patrician authority, 22 June 1580

After the departure of His Gracious Highness the Prince, I went to Signora Vittoria to wish her good day and found her in such despondency that she nearly reduced me to tears by telling me that his Most Gracious Highness has instructed some members of her company, on pain of his disfavour, to transfer to the troupe of that woman [. . .] and the said lady [Vittoria] complained, saying that she did not understand why His Most Gracious Highness the Prince should wish to wreak havoc by dismembering her company since she had never ceased to serve him by day or by night or at any time, yet as reward for this had received such treatment. Confident that His Highness could reverse this decision, I have thought it appropriate to write a few words to your lordship so that you can do the Signora and me the favour of begging His Highness not to injure this company in such a way since they have been His servants and will make themselves available at a moment's notice, as has ever been the case until now.

(From D'Ancona, II, p. 475)

An actor apologizes for not responding to a patrician's request, 12 February 1574

Rinaldo,[25] otherwise known as *Fortunio*, in his name and in that of the Company of players called the Gelosi, in all humility and with due reverence, appeals at the feet of Your Highness begging you to believe nothing save what will transpire to be merely the truth concerning the regret expressed to the said Rinaldo and his companions by Sig. Agosto Trissino that they did not come to Mantua this Carnival to perform their plays. The truth is the said Rinaldo repeatedly asked Sig. Agosto if he should go with the Company to Mantua for Carnival, but was invariably told by him that he knew nothing, and had received no instructions whatsoever concerning the matter. At the end of Carnival the said Rinaldo and his companions were suddenly told they should go to Mantua for this purpose, but he begs His Highness to have regard for his and his companions' poverty, for being mercenary men they have already taken on obligations in Venice, and cannot leave without suffering great loss and shame. Had they been free they would have come, as they often have in the past, without regard to their expense or loss. You will be informed of all this, and receive confirmation of my reasons and those of my companions, if you write a letter now to the said Sig. Agosto. When you are clear as to the truth, and of our innocence, I beseech you to defend us from the said Sig. Agosto's wholly unwarranted anger, as displayed in a letter to me in the recent mail. This can be done by forcing him to say no more about it, particularly as you have now been advised of my prompt willingness always to serve His Highness, for whom I pray eternal happiness and contentment and whose hands I humbly kiss.

Most humble servant, Rinaldo Petignoni.

(From D'Ancona, II, p. 463)

Francesco Andreini resists a patron, 13 April 1583

I heard through Sig. Antonio, musician to Your Serene Highness, of your decision regarding, and good intentions towards, the new Company you wish to form. As I am deeply indebted to Your Serene Highness very generous favour, it is with the greatest respect that I thank you for his most kind decision to consider me, together with my wife, worthy to be included in such a notable Company. However, I find myself obligated and formally bound to the Gelosi Company, and in particular to the illustrious Sig. Alvise Michiel, proprietor of the hall in Venice, and am in no position to respond to Your Serene Highness' wish and command, for in order to form this Company it would be necessary to break up three others, and it is difficult to do that, although for Your Serene Highness even the most difficult thing is very easy. Further, finding myself alone in Ferrara, and unable to consult with my companions, I cannot offer the services of the Gelosi Company to Your Serene Highness. Begging you to hold my wife and me among your most humble servants, etc,

Francesco Andreini, *comico geloso.*

(From D'Ancona, II, pp. 484–5)

THE INTERESTS OF SPECTATORS

Next to nothing is known about the Roman actress Flaminia, but the following description of a tragedy she performed in 1567 indicates the kind of material that particularly appealed to educated audiences. Her troupe was clearly in competition with that led by the rival actress Vincenza Armani, the kind of contest audiences delighted in, and one that in this case continued for much of July and was carried on elsewhere.

Only the day before yesterday [4 July 1567] Flaminia was praised for her delivery of certain laments in a tragedy taken from Ariosto's tale of Marganorre that was acted by her troupe. Flaminia played the bride of Marganorre's son, to whom in revenge she gave some poison to drink over the corpse of her first husband, who shortly before had been killed on stage. As she herself had already taken poison, bride and bridegroom died together over the first husband's corpse. Marganorre then attempted to kill all the other women, but instead the women stoned him to death.

Vincenza, on the other hand, was praised for her music, for the beauty of her costumes, and for much more besides, although the

PLATE 19 *Figures with trestle stage in background. Jacques Callot,* Balli di Sfessania. *Permission of The British Library, 1295 h29*

subject of her tragedy was neither so fine nor so well received. Yesterday, then, the competition was between the *intermezzi*. In Vincenza's tragedy Cupid was brought on stage to rescue Clori, a nymph who had been transformed into a tree; Jupiter appeared and hurled lightning from above, destroying the tower of a giant who had imprisoned some shepherds; a sacrifice was enacted; Ca[d]mus sowed his teeth and saw warriors spring up and fight; the replies he received from Phoebus, and then from Pallas armed, were portrayed, and finally he began to build the city. Flaminia not only prepared her stage magnificently with gilt decor, and chose beautiful costumes for the nymphs, and recreated in Mantua those woods, mountains, meadows, rivers and fountains appropriate to Arcadia, but introduced to the *intermezzi* of the play, first satyrs, then certain magicians, and then executed some *moresche*. Thus there is now nothing else but talk of such things: some praise the gracefulness of the one, some the ingenuity of the other, and that is how we pass the time in Mantua.

(From D'Ancona, *Origini del teatro italiano*, 1891, II, p. 451)

Niccolò Barbieri has left an interesting account of the reasons for spectators attending theatre; it may be compared with Ottonelli's rather ironic account (below, p. 246), written with Barbieri's in mind.

If I am not wrong, the reasons people attend plays are the following: many are curious to see how good the actors are, and many are inclined to any new attraction; this one goes out of boredom, because he does not know what to do with himself; many go to hear original turns of phrase and fine discourses, and others to hear the comic roles; an individual thinking of becoming a player himself may go to learn, someone else for the conversation of his friends; another in the hope of cadging from an acquaintance; yet another to avoid an hour gambling, another to banish dull spirits, another to observe behaviour, or not to seem miserly or ignorant, another out of habit, and another because he sees that others go.

(Barbieri, *La Supplica*, 1634, chapter XV)

STANZE AND THEATRES

Within a decade or so of the formation of the first professional companies one of the most active and original theatre practitioners of the mid-sixteenth century, Leone de' Sommi, petitioned the Duke of Mantua for the exclusive right to hire out a hall as a performance place for professional actors. His petition was probably unsuccessful, but is intriguing in that it seems to have been an attempt by an astute operator to set himself up as an impresario with a monopoly holding over public theatre performances in Mantua. It is witness to the rapidity with which halls and large rooms became sought after as convenient performance places to which the acting companies could attract paying spectators.

Most Illustrious and Excellent Sir,

The most devout, although humble and unworthy servant of your Excellency, Leone de' Sommi the Jew, certain of the beneficence of Your Excellency, is moved to request as a singular grace and favour, authority from you that he alone, for ten years, may provide a hall in Mantua where those who charge for performing plays may represent them. He offers to give every year to the poor of the Misericordia two sacks of grain in order to show that in a small way he is grateful for the favour received; alternatively, the equivalent in money to whomsoever Your Excellency may decide. This (although he is altogether without personal merit) he begs as a favour, reverentially bowing at the feet of Your Excellency.

This applicant wrote on 15th April, 1567.

(Leone de' Sommi, *Quattro dialoghi*, ed. Marotti, 1968, p. XLIV)

During his visit to Italy in 1608 Thomas Coryate visited the theatres of Venice, and in his Coryate's Crudities *(1611) briefly described what he saw, although unfortunately he tells us more about the exotic female members of the audience than about the theatre buildings, the players or the pieces he saw performed.*

I was at one of their Play-houses where I saw a Comedie acted. The house is very beggarly and base in comparison with our stately Play-houses in England: neyther can their Actors compare with us for apparell, shewes and musicke. Here I observed certaine things that I never saw before. For I saw women acte, a thing that I never saw before, though I have heard that it hath beene sometimes used in London, and they performed it with as good a grace, action, gesture, and whatsoever convenient for a Player, as ever I saw any masculine Actor. Also their noble and famous Cortezans came to this Comedy, but so disguised, that a man cannot perceive them. For they wore double maskes upon their faces, to the end that they might not be seene [. . .] They were so graced that they sate on high alone by themselves in the best roome of all the Play-house. [. . .] I saw some men also in the Play-house, disguised in the same manner with double vizards, those were said to be the favourites of the same Cortezans: they sit not here in galleries as we doe in London. For there is but one or two little galleries in the house, wherein the Cortezans only sit. But all the men doe sit beneath in the yard or court, every man upon is severall stoole, for which he payeth a gazet.

(Coryate, *Coryate's Crudities*, 1611, pp. 247–8)

Riccoboni gives a brief but interesting account of the theatres in Italy which probably holds good for much of the later seventeenth, as for the early eighteenth century.

In *Italy* they are entirely Strangers to the Custom of exhibiting Theatrical Entertainment thro' the whole Year, the Towns where they are at all established having their stated Times for Playing, which do not happen always at one Time of the Year: the Comedians, during the Space of twelve Months, visit a good Part of *Italy*. The Theatres of *Venice* are open from the Month of *October* to the first day of *Lent*. In many Cities of the two *Lombardis*, the Spring of the Year is allotted for Comedies; and they are represented in the Day-time without any lights, because the Play-houses are built in such a manner as to be sufficiently enlightened by the Sun. These Play-houses or rather Halls, are sometimes a plain Booth erected in large *Areas*, almost like that of *Verona*, where every Year such Booths are built in the *Arena* of the great Amphitheatre [. . .] The Theatres are open in *Rome* only the last eight Days of the *Carnaval*. And ever since *Innocent the Eleventh* prohibited Women from acting on the Stage, young Men supply their Place in the Habit of Women.

(Riccoboni, *A General History of the Stage*, 1741, pp. 54–5)

BOOKINGS AND CONTRACTS

The documents included here give an indication of the extent to which the companies regularised their affairs. The players had often to book a stanza *six months or more in advance of their appearance, particularly if they wished to secure a hall they were familiar with. To delay booking meant to run the risk of losing a prime performance place to a rival troupe, for the development of theatre as a market commodity bred intense competition. The contracts below show how increasingly sophisticated hiring arrangements became. The Naples contract of 1618 indicates that a hall was expressly prepared for the players, and their financial liabilities began immediately on the completion of building work. The Venetian contract of 1623 ran for two years and bound the players in a number of ways, including making them responsible for the maintenance of all the theatre lighting during their stays, and requiring them to supply an alternative company of stature equal to their own, and acceptable to the theatre management, should they for some reason be unable to fulfil their engagement. The details of the penalties exactable for failure to comply with contract terms indicate how heavily companies became committed. Whether or not such contracts could always be enforced on a defaulting company when it was outside the territories of the state concerned is a moot point, but as most were prime touring places no company would casually have risked losing its ability to play in them.*

The Uniti hire a hall in Florence, 1594

2 April, 1594

By this it is declared that the Company of the Uniti, as can be seen by their application, and on behalf of the company Signor Valentino, called Il Capitano Cardone, agree to rent from the Dogana of Florence, and on behalf of the said Dogana, from Signor Francesco Bilfoli, *proveditore*, the hall which is invariably let, together with the customary and usual rooms, and promises to pay a scudo and a half per day, beginning on 1 November and continuing to the first day of Lent, 1594. And Girolamo di Domenico Salimbeni, called Piombino, equally promises and pledges himself to be the principal guarantor that what is stated above will be observed and that this rent will run as above. In addition to this, however, should they be unable to act they will be obligated to pay at the agreed time one hundred florins in cash, and the said *proveditore* will be free to let to others as he thinks appropriate, notwithstanding the said penalty to the above. To what is above the afore-mentioned Cardone and Girolamo pledge themselves, and each of them will sign agreeing to the articles written above.

I, Valentino Cortesei, called Capitano Cardone, subscribe to the above. And I, Girolamo di Domenico, the above-mentioned, agree to the above, and in good faith have signed below in my own hand.

(From Evangelista, 'Le compagnie del Comici dell'Arte nel teatrino di Baldracca a Firenze', 1984, p. 68)

The Desiosi arrange for a new stage design, 1603

On 9 December, 1603, the Desiosi Company signed a contract with the Neapolitan actor, Lutio Fedele, for temporary occupancy of the Stanza di

San Giorgio de'Genovesi in Naples. An item in this indicates something of the arrangements involved when a company wished to change the design of the stage to suit its own repertory.

Item. As the Desiosi of Viterbo wish to make a new stage design, and this will require the removal of the one currently in Lutio's *stanza*, once their performances are over the Desiosi of Viterbo shall make one similar to it at joint expense including the cost of the wood and painting. As Lutio wants the former design and machines restored, everything will be entrusted to two mutual friends with authority to arrange the business and advise on the costs incurred for the new stage design. The expense of making the *intermedii* and the properties shall be met from joint funds, and being jointly made they will belong to both. When the Company is finished everything must be divided equally, one half going to Lutio and the other to those from Viterbo.

(From Prota-Giurleo, *I teatri di Napoli nel '600*, 1962, pp. 15–16)

Contract for hire of a newly equipped hall for performance in Naples, July 1618

[. . .] Vincentius Capete of Naples and Octavius Sgambato of Naples have jointly in our presence freely hired and let to Petro Maria Cecchini, called Frittellino, and Jacobo Antonio Fedenzi, called Cinthio, and to Antonio de Melo, called Capitano on the stage, also being there, a hall belonging to the said Vincenzo and Ottavio located near the Church of San Giovanni de' Fiorentini, that is already in preparation, and the said Capece and Sgambato promise to finish not only the building, but the stage, the boxes, the *corritori* and seats by the first of September next of the present year 1618, at the expense of the said Capece and Sgambato. And this [to hold] from the first of September 1618 until the last day of the second Carnival to come, in the year 1620, for the consideration of three hundred ducats a year, and in addition one eighth of the income from boxes, *corritori* and seats in the said hall [. . .] [The actors] promise to pay to the said Capece and Sgambato each month an instalment of the said rent of three hundred ducats, and of said half of said quarter in the following way: that is, two-thirds of said rent, and of said half of said quarter, to the said Ottavio, and similarly each month for the purpose of continuing the said payment and not failing for any reason whatsoever [. . .]

With the proviso that if said hall is finished before said 1st September, or after said 1st September, then in such case the rent and half of said quarter shall commence from the day that the said hall will be finished.

(From Prota-Giurleo, *I teatri di Napoli nel '600,* 1962, p. 159)

Contract for hire of the San Luca theatre in Venice, 1622–4

By the present contract the undersigned illustrious Signori Vendramin[26] agree to give and consign their Theatre, situated in the S. Salvadore quarter of this City, to the acting Company of the Accesi, who will also here undersign, for them to act therein their respectable comedies, these undersigned players being obliged to come and perform by S. Martino next, or a little later, as circumstances permit. They will stay for the whole of next Carnival, which will be the last day of February 1623 *More Imperii*, will be entitled to all the box office takings and then at Christmas will be given a gift of three hundred Venetian ducats in cash with the proviso that as long as the players perform they must maintain the lighting, not only on the stage, but throughout the theatre. If it does not suit them to start by the Easter following the undersigned are further obliged to arrive at least by S. Martino, and to remain for the whole of Carnival as before, and if circumstances prevent them from coming, then in the owners' interest they must provide another good company in their place to the satisfaction of the illustrious Signori, and this company, on the same conditions afore-mentioned during the present lease, will occupy and work in the Theatre that for these two years the Signori Vendramin wish to put at the disposal of the undersigned players.

And because at least four *palchi* must be constructed for the theatre's facilities to which there is no access from the main door where the public pay entrance, the Signori promise to give the company one *palcho* for their own use; and in order that each party can have confidence in what is now promised by both, every player is obliged during these two years to pay a fine of two hundred scudi if he fails to honour and observe the present contract, half of this going to the afore-mentioned Signori and half to the company, while on their side the illustrious Vendramini are pledged to abide by this contract or pay compensation of one thousand scudi to the company, and therefore they offer their possessions for security to the said sum of the said one thousand scudi, as in their turn the afore-mentioned gentlemen players undertake to observe what has been set out above on the security of their possessions and lives, and this shall be legally binding everywhere and all will undersign in good faith.

(From Mangini, *I Teatri di Venezia*, 1974, pp. 49–50)

5

Masks and Roles

The Recourse to Improvisation

THE FACT that the Italian professional companies performed much of the time *all'improvviso* is a feature of their work that sets them apart from their fellow professionals elsewhere in Europe. Why that particular technique of making and performing plays should have evolved under the aegis of the companies continues to fascinate and perplex theatre historians. We shall consider in more detail below (see chapter 7) the nature and techniques of improvised composition, but would remark here the economic and logistical advantages to the troupes of that method of production. It gave flexibility and wide scope to company repertories at comparatively little cost, for composition often entailed no more than ringing changes on familiar materials, and pieces could be prepared rapidly as and when they were needed. A good witness to the truth of its convenience and economy is the Spanish actor, cited by Perrucci, who marvelled at the way an Italian company newly landed at Naples was able to mount a play within a mere hour of its arrival.[1]

Improvised playing enabled the troupes to accommodate within their performances very diverse entertainer skills, including those of erstwhile street performers like buffoons, tumblers and dancers, and it licensed, too, performer expertise to the advantage of the theatrical variety of the shows the companies purveyed. Above all, however, as a mode of production it is perhaps best seen as a calculated response to market pressures and possibilities. Economic factors were crucial to the emergence and development of the *com-*

media dell'arte, for the livelihoods not only of the players themselves, but of their families and dependents, turned ultimately on their ability to achieve and maintain market appeal, and in as financially modest a way as was possible. For these reasons the players were itinerant, versatile and flexible in their skills and repertories. Many of the companies operated at different social levels, from the aristocracy of the courts, through the bourgeoisie to the broader populace, according to occasion and demand. The most prestigious offered a wide variety of different kinds of theatrical entertainment. This impelled them to devise a species of production which could meet these different market opportunities and requirements without imposing impossible demands on their time, materials and resources. Improvisation was a mode of production, a way of composing and presenting plays on a bread-and-butter basis, and one admirably suited to the needs of travelling players, but convenient too for audiences at all social levels for it made theatrical entertainment more readily and widely available than it had been hitherto, and was welcome even in the court sphere, where royalty could now provide regular entertainment at a fraction of the outlay involved in mounting the scripted drama of the *letterati*.[2] The improvisation of mainstream entertainments on the basis of *soggetti* was the professional actors' response to the market situation.

What this does not appear to explain, however, is why the acting companies were unable to find dramatists capable of meeting their needs, and therefore turned to generating their own 'texts'. The amount and variety of material they required cannot alone account for this. About the same time that acting companies emerged in Italy, so too they did in England, and on somewhat similar professional and economically independent bases. In England, as in Italy, they quickly became established as business enterprises with broad social appeal, from the courts to the populace. The English companies similarly performed vast repertories, some plays receiving only one performance, few enjoying runs of more than two or three days, while the plays themselves embraced many different dramatic kinds and were sometimes pitched to appeal to distinctly different levels of patronage.[3] The turn-over of such plays, which were of course scripted and not improvised, was considerable, and troupes jealously accumulated their stock. On the closure of the theatres in 1642 the King's Men is estimated to have owned about 400 plays, nearly half of them unprinted;[4] it is a figure that surely compares favourably with the stock of *scenarii* and scripted plays likely to have been held by any *commedia dell'arte* company of the same period or earlier. Why then were the English companies able to find dramatists to supply their production needs, while the Italian companies apparently could not?

The reasons lie perhaps in very different socio-cultural and linguistic conditions, and in rather different attitudes, in England on the one hand and the northern Italian states on the other, to drama and theatre, and to the literary and social status and the expectations of the playwright. The absence of a unified national language in the Italian peninsula and the plethora of very distinct dialects, virtually enjoying the status of individual languages, made easy and universal communication through scripted drama the more difficult, and that difficulty was not significantly reduced by understandable but somewhat self-conscious attempts by the *letterati* to devise an agreed language for literary discourse. Many like Beolco, as we have seen in chapter 2, initially resisted this move to uniformity, recognizing the extent to which it would tend to displace the local, colloquial and idiomatic from dramatic dialogue.

Again, the earlier Italian *cinquecento* cultivation of drama at the courts, before the emergence of the professional companies, seems in one sense to have had a negative effect on the practice of playwriting. The decline in the quality of late *cinquecento* drama cannot wholly be explained by the restricting effects on drama of neoclassical theoretical prescriptions; those in any case gave comedy considerable licence. Nor can it altogether be put down to the increasing subordination of scripted drama to stage spectacle. The nature of early Italian court patronage of playwrights, and the manner in which stage plays were mounted on these occasions – as special events on which considerable time, energy and money were expended – may in the long run have had distinctly negative effects. They made the production of scripted drama an occasional rather than a regular activity, made it essentially the concern of an elite, distanced it from its popular roots, and made it overly responsive to literary fads and fashions.

Not least important too was the manner in which the court orientation of scripted drama undermined, by virtue of establishing playwriting as a status activity, the possibility for writers to develop playwriting as a professional pursuit comparable to, and complementary with, that of acting. When we find a court playwright like Giovan Battista Guarini, for example, protesting that his tragi-comic pastoral play, *Il pastor fido*, cannot be made ready for performance in a mere three months, we enter an ambience of high culture, in which dramatists' attitudes, expectations and assumptions were surely quite remote from those of the workaday Elizabethan dramatist.[5] They were equally remote much of the time from the workaday situation of many of the Italian professional acting companies. Again, operating conditions for acting companies in England and Italy were radically different. London was the English focus of theatrical activity and, certainly after 1593, the London acting companies were invariably playhouse-based for considerable periods of time. In Italy there was no comparable national centre, but rather a number of lesser centres, each with its own cultural and theatrical predilections and emphases. The Italian companies were not playhouse-based but itinerant, and were necessarily under a market obligation to supply different centres with the fare of their preference. It is hard to see how Italian professional dramatists, even had they been available in droves, could have supplied the acting companies with material of such flexible application as was required by the peculiar conditions of the Italian market.

In certain fundamental respects, then, the companies and players had to accommodate their activities to the nature and requirements of the working situation in which they functioned, although inevitably in the course of provisioning the market they were able themselves to create tastes, expectations and preferences in their audiences. At base, improvised drama was so structured, and company personnel so carefully organized, as to permit easy adjustment to different kinds and social levels of theatrical entertainment. The drama the companies presented was invariably improvised, for this was the routine way of working, but for some troupes it could, too, be scripted. The actual role composition of the companies, to which we shall now turn, was peculiarly subtle. It reflected what might be called an archetypal Renaissance dramaturgy which allowed the troupes to embrace in their repertories a wide range of dramatic kinds, both improvised and scripted.

PLATE 20 *Watercolour illustration to the* scenario La trappolaria. *Corsini MS. Permission of the Accademia dei Lincei, Rome*

The Role Composition of Companies

The companies strove as best they could to satisfy the market's disparate tastes – for comedy, tragi-comedy, tragedy, pastoral, *intermezzo* and *melodramma*. This they did by covering the field in as economic a way as was possible by forming acting troupes of about ten members, each of whom ideally was capable of performing in diverse dramatic kinds. Of course not all companies performed both scripted and improvised plays, and not all players could manage with ease the transition from premeditated to improvised, or from improvised to premeditiated performance, as is clear enough from Francesco Gabrielli's rather snide comment on the actress Lavinia (see below, p. 124). But the more versatile the individual members of a company, and the greater their range within their role specializations, the more readily could a company supply the market. Those basic truths about the working situation were not lost on the players, and underpinned the disposition of roles within the acting companies.

The very earliest troupes, which may have consisted of no more than half-a-dozen performers, appear to have been democratic cooperatives, working to some extent under a group-appointed leader but maintaining a basic equality among the membership, and largely, if of necessity rather than choice, free of any dependence on, and obligation to an aristocratic patron. In the course of developing markets for their wares, however, the more successful companies were those able gradually to accommodate their skills, materials and performance programmes to the interests of the courts, and their playing schedules to court seasons and festivities, while cultivating, too, paying audiences at other social levels. By the 1560s the average size of such companies seems to have increased to about ten. This complement was made up of what became the fairly standard pattern of role specializations within a troupe: at least two *vecchi*, in improvised plays often taking the roles of Il Magnifico (Pantalone) and the *Dottore*, two or more *servi* or *zanni*, two or more pairs of *innamorati*, a more free ranging male role, in improvised pieces the Capitano, a *servetta*, and possibly one or two support players, taking parts for children, constables and huntsmen, parts which may in all probability have been filled from among the actors' families. Doubling of small parts was also possible. The basic pattern of *vecchi, servi* and *innamorati* was characterized by a very careful balancing of roles within a troupe: thus we invariably find each player within a pair of *servi* (of which there could be two or even three pairs) complementing the other in performance skills, emphasizing respectively perhaps the acrobatic or the ingenious; similarly, pairs of lovers sought distinctive stage *personae*, often worked up by frequent playing together.[6]

This carefully organized balance of performer skills and specializations was both a strength and a weakness. Successful performance, more particularly in improvised plays, was heavily dependent not just on a troupe being at full complement, but on the harmonious intermeshing of the expertise and the personalities of individual players. Such equilibrium was difficult to achieve, and even harder to maintain. Putting together a company was an intricate and problematic business, for it entailed blending talents and temperaments in a subtle and delicate mix. Personal as well as professional considerations dictated suitability and availability: familial connections and amatory entaglements were often crucial, and assembling a troupe entailed not just selecting from among available individual talent, but blending small groups (a husband, wife and daughter, or a lover and his mistress), each member of which had his or her specialist role which needed to be accommodated within the role structure of the company. Francesco Gabrielli's letter (below, p. 123) is an eloquent witness to the difficulties involved in assembling a troupe. Naturally, when a player left a company, or a new player joined, the ensuing problems could be equally difficult, for all disruption affected the nature of the material the remaining players were able to perform, or the way they performed it.[7] Needless to say, similar adjustments and accommodations had to be made when a new player or group of players joined a troupe.

It has often been remarked that the influence of the learned scripted comedy on the improvised comic drama of the professionals was substantial. Many of the *scenarii* performed by the *commedia dell'arte* companies trafficked in the same stories of intrigue and confusion, in conflicts between young and old, and in the misunderstandings of lovers and friends, as recur in the learned drama, and which that drama had in its turn partly taken over from Latin comedy. In the improvised drama these plots and situations, as well as some of the 'business' and language, were in many respects a popularization of the learned comedy in a bid to capture an audience more socially heterogeneous than that of the courts, and yet at the same time flexible enough to retain appeal at the courts. The basic role pattern remarked above of *vecchi, servi* or *zanni, innamorati* and two or three other stage figures, corresponds closely to the character typology of the literary comedy.[8] But the role composition of the professional acting companies does not simply duplicate in the improvised drama the character typology of the literary comedy. The role balances of the professional players not only accommodated the type of characters of the learned comedy, they could, and did, accommodate, too, the characters of tragedy, tragi-comedy, *intermezzo* and pastoral, both scripted and improvised – in short, they reflect a broad pattern of roles applicable to a very wide variety of Renaissance dramatic forms.

The nature of the roles, then, warrants brief investigation, for although they were clearly 'types', that word can be misleading. A number of modern scholars (Duchartre, Mic, Lea, Nicoll among them) have in various ways seen the roles of the improvised drama as being at once specific and general, imbued by the actor in performance with individual traits, but at the same time rooted in tradition, regionally distinctive and embodying the essential features of groups recognizable in society: the prosperous, self-assured citizen or well-to-do merchant, the fussy, garrulous pedant or professional man, the ingenious and scheming or obtuse and bumbling servant; sufficiently catholic in short to permit the players to exploit their different performer characteristics, idiosyncracies and skills, but sufficiently defined to be stable and recurring through the history of the *commedia dell'arte*. There is much in this view that is very pertinent, but it rather implies that from the beginning the players' stage *personae* were more determined by criteria laid down by social patterning and tradition – 'literary', 'theatrical' or 'popular' – than was perhaps the case. Further, it tends to invite a reading of the 'types' that makes them comparable to characters in a scripted play.

Two seventeenth-century commentators, Pier Maria Cecchini and Andrea Perrucci, provide us with valuable if at times rather elusive information about the role composition of the companies. Both writers must be considered as authoritative, although in slightly different ways. The first, Cecchini, was himself an actor, dramatist and troupe leader, and his account, *Frutti delle moderne comedie et avisi a chi le recita* (Padua, 1628), represents the first attempt to provide a systematic if brief examination and codification of the *teatro dell'arte*. Written by Cecchini after some thirty years' experience in the theatre, to the extent that it is critical of contemporary players, and of the directions more recent performance had taken, it may be seen to have a certain polemical intent. Perrucci's *Dell' Arte rappresentativa premeditata ed all'improvviso* (Naples, 1699) is a much more detailed discussion. It includes a compendium of improvised performance materials, and was the work of a man of letters more a *dilettante* than a regular practitioner, but whose knowledge of professional practice was considerable.

Readily identifiable in the writings of these commentators, and in the bulk of the *scenarii*, is the basic role composition remarked above of *vecchi, servi* (or *zanni*'), *innamorati*, and other *parti*, or 'parts', which are either particularized, like the Captains and *servette*, or include more general 'utilities' like mothers, huntsmen, constables and courtesans. But although both Cecchini and Perrucci attempt to describe the improvised theatre in a systematic way, their accounts are often confusing. Both give the impression of seeking to impose firm classification on roles and materials which are far less readily classifiable than they allow, and the terminology of neither (but more particularly that of Cecchini), has quite the precision we might wish. Both use the word *parti*, for example, very loosely indeed, sometimes of broad groups, like the *parti ridicole* (comic parts), in which they include both the *vecchi* and the *zanni*, and sometimes of particular figures within such a group, like Pantalone. However, in the usage of neither does the word *parti*, in whatever way applied, appear to mean 'parts', in the modern sense of the part of a character assumed by an actor in a play.[9] Rather, *parti* are something more comparable to what old English actors called 'lines': fields of performer specialization, a balanced combination of which would make up an acting company capable of undertaking all types of drama from tragedy and tragi-comedy to farce and afterpiece. This analogy with the make-up of an early English troupe is only approximate, but it may serve to underscore the extent to which the composition of an Italian professional acting company was play-orientated, broadly-based and needed to be well-balanced – all the more so perhaps as it might perform not only improvised, but scripted plays. *Parti ridicole, parti dell' innamorato* (the parts of the Lover), and various other *parti*, then, notwithstanding that neither Cecchini nor Perrucci is always consistent in his use of the word *parti*, appear to be umbrella terms covering a wide range of possible character parts in plays which all fell within a performer's 'line' of specialization.

The Masks

It is clear from both the early writings and the iconography that improvised performance mingled masked and unmasked players. However, the use of masked figures in Renaissance plays was not in itself novel. We find masked characters in Renaissance scripted drama and in the *intermezzi*. Masks were used too in the medieval *sacre rappresentazioni* which survived well into the sixteenth century, and were a feature of figures in Carnival and banquet entertainment. What seems to be more distinctive in the improvised drama was the fairly regular use of facial half or partial masks, and the fact that for the most part they were confined to certain roles or 'lines'. In the iconography at least, the *vecchi* and *zanni* were invariably masked; the other stage figures did not usually use the mask unless masking was specifically required by the action of a particular improvised play (a pastoral, for example).[10]

Face masks have of course long been used in theatre, and resort to them has generated much speculation about the psychological and philosophical properties of masks, their power to transform and liberate the creative imagination of the player donning one, and to shift focus from the player's physiognomy to the expressiveness of the totality of the actor's body moving in stage space. The face masks of the Italian players, however, were significantly different from those of, say, the Greek, Egyptian, Roman, Chinese or Japanese theatres, or from the ceremonial devil masks of regions like Tibet and Andhra Pradesh, which were mainly either full face or even more encompassing headpieces. The Italian actors employed half or partial leather masks, covering no more than forehead, eyes, nose and cheeks, leaving the mouth, jaw and other parts of the head free. They were, then, at once striking and yet discrete: the stage figure was manifestly masked, yet not to the extent that the personality of the player was absorbed wholly by the assumed *persona*; the mask did not dehumanize the actor, it lent mystery without detracting from the live actuality of the stage figure. *Zanni* masks were perhaps the most various, ranging from the smooth moulded and close-fitting, to vizards made rather more elaborate by the addition of bushy facial hair on brows and cheeks. The masks of the Magnificos emphasized a beaked nose and hollow cheeks; those of the Doctors were generally much simpler flat black forehead and eye covers. Conspicuous of course is the fact that the only improvising players to wear these half-masks at all regularly were the *parti ridicole*, the comic roles of the *vecchi* and *servi*, which may lend some credence to the view that it was they who early provided the nuclear trestle stage master-servant sketches which were elaborated into fully-developed dramatic narratives by the accretion of the serious roles of the *innamorati* and the other *parti,* like the Capitano and the *servetta*.

Why, however, did the players use masks and, equally important, mingle masked and unmasked figures? Certainly use of masks both signalled and licensed revelry and extravagant stage activity, as traditionally it had done for classical *gesticulatores*, devil figures in Medieval and Renaissance spectacle, and Carnival and banquet buffoons. Masks underscored too the highly stylized, pre-eminently theatrical world of the performed play; they served to distance, without divorcing, the traffic of the stage from that of everyday life, and by establishing distinctly non-naturalistic performance conventions which aesthetically complemented the extravagances of the *favole*, gave credence to the improbable. Yet the use of the face masks served, too, a further purpose. In the iconography the 'masks' are very obviously privileged, and it was their striking and idiosyncratic figures which artists delighted to depict. In the play in performance, however, the case was rather different. Curiously, notwithstanding their powerful visual presence, the effect of the 'masks' was to highlight those figures who did not wear masks by pointing the greater kinship of the unmasked to the spectators. In the theatrical event there were three planes of reality: that of the 'masks', that of the unmasked, and that of the audience.

PLATE 21 *Late sixteenth century engraving by J. Honervogt of Pantalone, Dottore and Zanni. Permission of the National Museum, Stockholm (photograph: Stateus Konstmuseer)*

The Masked Roles

Whether or not use of masks by *vecchi* and *zanni* was from the beginning as ubiquitous as the iconographic tradition suggests is hard to determine with certainty. As we have noted, early writings on the *commedia dell'arte* make little reference to them, and the iconography may itself gradually have contributed to making them more and more standard. Early notices (like those given above, p. 52) refer not to a comedy of 'masks' or of masked actors, but to the drama of 'Gratiani' or 'Zanni', or define the performance as *commedia all'improvviso*. As is clear from Francesco Gabrielli's letter (see below, p. 123), practitioners themselves apparently gave no special significance to masks, nor to the masked roles. Again, Cecchini and Perrucci neither refer to the stage figures as 'masks', nor distinguish between masked and unmasked roles, save when Cecchini refers to Neapolitan *zanni* dispensing with the face mask. It is striking in fact how rarely references to masked actors and to the physical artefact, the face mask, are encountered in the early written materials, for all that they bulk large in the iconography.[11] This would suggest that the use of masked figures was not in itself a crucial and defining characteristic of the *commedia dell'arte*.

In fact it is only much later, at the end of the seventeenth century and in the eighteenth century, that particular emphasis is placed on the 'masks' and on masked actors, as when we find Luigi Riccoboni in *Le théâtre italien* (1728) writing of 'the four masked actors' of the Italian theatre – those playing the *vecchi* and *zanni*. But the identification of the *commedia dell'arte* with masked playing, and more particularly with four 'mask' types, had evolved gradually in the course of the previous century, in part through a complex process of selection and elimination, accretion and simplication, in part from an appropriation by *dilettanti* in the later seveteenth-century academies of the professionals' way of making theatre, in part from a neo-classical predilection for formal clarity and symmetry, and in part too from the simplification of communicative codes brought about by performance abroad.[12] By the mid-eighteenth century the Venetian dramatist Carlo Goldoni was writing confidently of 'the four masks of the Italian theatre', and describing them, furthermore, much as if they were specific dramatic characters (see below, p. 137), as does his contemporary, Carlo Gozzi.[13] Such conceptions have tended to underpin much modern interpretation since Maurice Sand published his *Masques et Bouffons* in 1862. Recent seminal work by Italian theatre historians, however, has pointed up the possible misunderstandings which can easily be generated as we perceive the *commedia dell'arte* of the late sixteenth and early seventeenth century through the eyes of its *settecento* and later commentators.[14]

The widespread modern notion, in some measure inherited from seventeenth- and eighteenth-century views, but coloured too by late nineteenth- and early twentieth-century assumptions, that the *commedia dell'arte* was a single entity, and a 'popular' theatrical art form rooted in the presentation of 'type' figures, has particularly encouraged speculation about the origins of the 'masks'.[15] We may briefly take as examples of this kind of investigation something of the prehistories which have been proposed for the two *vecchi*, Il Magnifico (or Pantalone) and the Dottore. Thus it has been argued that the name 'Pantalone' was derived from that of a Venetian patron saint, Saint Pantaleone, or from the imperial ambition of Venice to 'plant the lion' (*pianta leone*) in territories beyond the Republic, or from the long hose or trousers (*pantalons*) the stage figures invariably wore. It has been remarked too that in the early to mid *cinquecento* we find characters in macaronic dramatic dialogues who are called Pantalone. Others have argued that this role may have evolved gradually from the folk tradition in the performances of individual players, each of whom contributed elements to it, modifying and augmenting it, according to whatever met with public favour. Again, Il Magnifico has been seen to have certain features in common with the *senes* of Latin comedy and the old men of Renaissance learned comedy, and to share certain characteristics too with the libidinous, tricked and often cuckolded ancients of the *novelle*, and with the amorous old men encountered in the plays of Beolco and Calmo.

Pursuit of the origins of the Dottore 'mask' has been as assiduous as for those of Il Magnifico. Some scholars have argued that it was developed not from an earlier stage or dramatic type, but from a character sketch of an individual in real life. A case has been pressed for the prototype being the famous and learned twelfth-century jurist Gratiano: in early references to actors, and in some *scenarii*, the Dottore appears under that name, often without a title. Others have sought as ancestor the distinguished fourteenth-century Dante scholar, Graziano de' Bambagioli. One proposed identification links a real life figure, a barber in Francolino, with a stage actor, on the basis of a reference in the work of a sixteenth-century Franciscan preacher, Panigarola.[16] But that the 'mask' actually derived from the dress and manners of a real barber remains unproven. So too do those much more general claims that the Dottore is essentially a development of the Dossenus figure of Atellan farce, or of the learned man often found in macaronic verse, or of the pedant of the literary dramatic tradition.

The origins of other 'masks' like those of the *zanni* and Arlecchino, have similarly been exhaustively investigated, and numerous suggestions have been made regarding their possible prehistory and the etymology of the names. Thus the origins of the *zanni* have been sought in the *servi* of Plautus, in the *sannio* or buffoon of the Roman popular stage, in the figure of a comic devil found in Dante, or in peasant types of the mountain region of Bergamo who were familiar *facchini*, or porters, in Venice and other northern Italian cities, and whose common name Giovanni, contracted to Gianni, in its dialect form provided the stage name *zanni*. Arlecchino has been traced to a comic devil character in French mystery plays, and linked to figures in Scandinavian mythology.[17] Similar enquiry has been pursued for the role of the unmasked Capitano. Investigation and speculation of this kind is not gratuitous; there may indeed be elements of truth in some, if not all, of the suggestions made, for the influence of the many traditions levied on was deep and ubiquitous.

However, what comes across very strongly in Gabrielli's letter, as it does in other documents, is the identification of the roles with the actors who played them, and this applies as much for the masked as for the unmasked players. In many of the early letters and documents the actors' given names and their stage names are often interchangeable. Some players assumed the names of the roles they performed, while others, like Isabella Andreini, gave their own names to their roles. Many were better known by their stage

PLATE 22 *J. Goltius, Venetian Costumes 1581. Permission of the Bibliothèque de l'Opera, Paris*

than by their actual names – by virtue of his publications we know Pier Maria Cecchini by his baptismal name, but to his contempories he was equally well-known by his stage name, Frittellino (although he himself preferred to distance himself from his stage name in ordinary life). Who exactly was the brilliant actress Flaminia, of whom a number of records speak (see above, p. 98)? What, in short, the early written documentation tends to foreground is not the four 'masks' of the *commedia dell'arte*, so familiar from the iconographic materials, but the actors. In modern histories of the *commedia dell'arte* the 'masks' have displaced the actors; but it was probably the actors who preceded the 'masks', not the other way about.[18] The actors did not simply inherit the 'masks', in all their essential lineaments, from pre-existent embryonic types already available in literature, folklore or Carnival figures. The players themselves often created the 'masks' for their professional purposes. In doing so they drew no doubt, consciously or unconsciously, on oral, literary and iconographic traditions, and on social observation, but they took according to the bent of their temperaments and their performance skills and needs.

If we allow that the actor often preceded the 'mask', then the origins of a particular 'mask' are in most cases virtually unfathomable, for such an actor's 'mask' would have been rooted in his conscious or instinctive awareness of his own performance skills and personal idiosyncracies, and in what he felt he could best exploit for stage purposes – particular ways of moving or speaking, a particular repertoire of language or gestures, particular emphases in costuming and 'business'. On such particulars the actor based his 'mask', and they and it defined him in his stage *persona*. Further, that *persona* did not become a recurring *character* in the plays in which the actor appeared, nor was it imposed on characters in particular plays; rather it both absorbed and accommodated to the requirements of the various characters in the many different plays in which the actor performed. *Commedia dell'arte* company performances consisted of individual actors playing ensemble in many different plays which could embrace a wide range of dramatic kinds, scripted and improvised. Nor, of course, did the 'mask' preclude flexibility. When need be the actor dispensed with his 'mask': Arlecchino, as Riccoboni tells us, 'set aside his mask' when occasion required (see below, p. 122). The 'masks' were but an element in the design of the improvised plays which were performed; roles balanced against other roles in that equilibrium of performer 'lines' which determined the composition of the companies.

The Flexibility of the Roles

Seen from an historical perspective it is clear that in individual actors' interpretations some of the 'masks' were more circumscribed than others with regard to visual attributes. Pantalone was fairly concretely perceived: a Venetian merchant, middle-aged or elderly, a father and housekeeper, and probably, if the evidence of the iconography is reliable, clad basically in the colours red and black.[19] But if such external lineaments early came to be 'given', a glance at the *scenarii* in the Scala collection and elsewhere will indicate the wide range of parts covered by an actor playing the Pantalone 'mask', and the numerous possibilities offered for diverse interpretative emphases. The costume of the Dottore was less 'settled', allowing a variety of ways to point the ridiculous in the academic mode, as too did the verbal extravagances and distortions which were a feature of the stage speech of the 'mask'. But again, in performance the actor playing it embraced numerous and different parts, and enjoyed much free play in interpretation.

This is even more manifestly the case as far as the 'masks' of the *zanni* were concerned, the very plurality of which defeats classification.[20] So various are the *zanni* and the parts they undertook in different plays that, although both the requirements of effective dramaturgy and the habit of frequent performance together of pairs of players may well have encouraged the pointing of differences between them of the kind Cecchini and Perrucci suggest, between the intriguing, quick-witted coiner of plot imbroglios and a duller, more clownish foil, nonetheless the neat classifications of the theorists seem all too frequently to be belied by the sheer diversity of the different kinds of part *zanni* are actually called on to play by the *scenarii*. Unfortunately we know little about the specific performance abilities and emphases of the many players who acted these roles, but that those performers include players as apparently diverse in skills and temperaments as Zuan Ganassa, Simone da Bologna, Pier Maria Cecchini, Niccolò Barbieri and Francesco Gabrielli would suggest that interpretation was as various as the plays in which the actors performed. Variety of costuming, too, may have been more marked than the frequently recurring loose white blouse and baggy trousers much of the iconography suggests.

The most familiar of the servant roles is of course the quasi-independent figure, Arlecchino, possibly first established on the Italians' stage by Tristano Martinelli, and apparently from the beginning more popular and distinctive a stage figure in France and elsewhere than in Italy. The traditional patched costuming seems to have reflected poverty, and came early to harden into the familiar chequer-patterned dress of the illustrations. In the course of the seventeenth century beyond Italy the role came to symbolize the very nature and spirit of the improvised drama and to bespeak the *commedia dell'arte*. In the course of the seventeenth century, too, the lozenge scheme of the dress seems to have become increasingly regular, refined and decorative, and the movements and gestures more stylized and balletic, particularly in the interpretations of Domenico Biancolelli and his successors in France. Its very popularity abroad may indicate how foreign touring led to an increasing reliance on visually striking and immediately recognizable stage figures whose dramatic functions were both pantomimic and firmly defined. Nonetheless, as with the other 'masks', in the hands of the numerous actors who played it, and under their many stage names, the role admitted various emphases. Striking too, particularly in the eighteenth century, are the number of references to players who could set the face mask aside and assume other, including scripted, parts (see below, p. 123).

The richness of opportunity actors had to interpret in different

PLATE 23 *Tristano Martinelli(?).* Compositions de Rhetorique, *Lyons, 1601, possibly showing Martinelli himself as Arlecchino. Permission of the Bibliothèque Nationale, Paris*

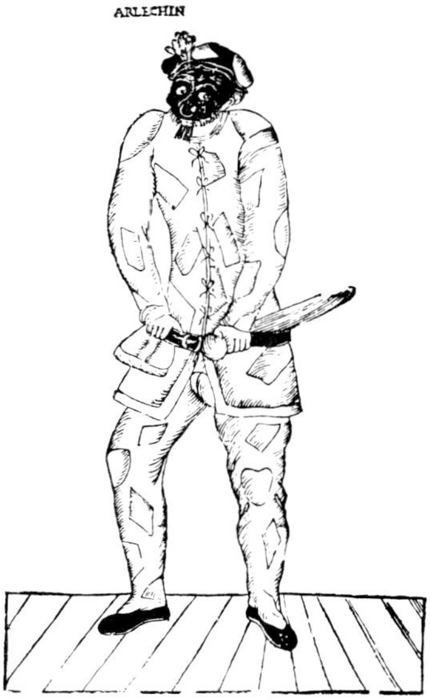

ways holds equally for the unmasked roles. There were numerous Captains, as the plethora of names indicates – Spavento, Fracassa, Spezzaferro, Terremoto, Rinoceronte, Coccodrillo. But this was not an enduring role and was easily subsumed later into that of a male Lover, with which it had certain affinities. Elements of this role perhaps shaded too into others distinctive in their own right by virtue of the expertise of an outstanding player: the Scaramouche of the great seventeenth-century actor Tiberio Fiorilli seems to have crossed various 'lines' including that of the Capitano. Comparatively few Captains are encountered in the improvised drama after the early decades of the *seicento*. Changed social conditions and the decline of Spanish power in northern Italy have been given as reasons for this, for ridicule of flamboyant Spanish soldiery is seen by some to have underpinned its early popularity. But the credibility of the role may have been undermined by the tendency of some players to pitch it too much on the level of low comedy, rather than to look for that element of the bizarre yet chivalric recommended by Cecchini. In a sense, too, the role was eclipsed by the taste of the baroque operatic and tragic theatre for superlative heroes. The captain ceased to be an apt role for the comic stage when the strutting and posturing demi-gods of the serious theatre traded rhodomontade as normal conversation.

Lovers and *servette* too were as numerous as their names. Although the iconographic tradition has focused attention on the 'masks', that should not be allowed to conceal the crucial dramaturgical function of the Lovers' roles.[21] Many of the plot lines of the *scenarii* turn on love entanglements, and it is often Lovers, both male and female, who directly or indirectly draw the other figures into intrigue and confusions. Indeed, it is scarcely an exaggeration to say that the introduction and elaboration of the *parti dell'innamorato* really marks the beginning of sophisticated play performances; hence the crucial contribution to the development of the companies and the improvised drama of actresses. It is no accident that many of the players who performed Lovers' roles were major box office attractions, and many actually led companies, an indication in itself perhaps of audience popularity. Such leaders of companies included the early Gelosi *capo comico*, Rinaldo Petignoni (Fortunio), the Confidenti troupe leader Flaminio Scala (Flavio), and the Fedeli company's G. B. Andreini (Lelio), female troupe leaders like Flaminia, Virginia Armani and Diana da Ponti, and actress-writers like Isabella Andreini, Orsola Cortese and Brigida Bianchi. It was, after all, perhaps most frequently the Lovers with whom many spectators tended to identify. Their stage costuming may not have been idiosyncratic enough to attract the attention of illustrators, but the rich, fashionable dress they wore would have pleased many spectators, as too would their highly formal and figurative stage discourse, often trafficking in extravagant *concetti*, witty repartee, and amorous 'flightings', reflective of modish poetic styles, and often cast in extravagantly sophisticated Tuscan. *Servette*, if less celebrated than the *innamorate*, were invariably important figures in the comic action, and increasingly so in the seventeenth century. They ranged from the young, pert and coquettish *ingénue*, through the vulgar and provocative woman of the world, to the stolid, elderly matron. It was often their sexuality that was exploited in the plots of the *scenarii*, and it is they who most usually appear in states of undress or change clothes on stage: some actresses interpretations of the role were akin to the antics of the female assistants of the mountebank stages, and stand firmly in the 'popular' tradition from which the brazenly co-operative house sevants of the *novelle* were drawn. The costuming of *servette*, if not distinctive in itself, was role defining. As with the Lovers, the many plays in which *servette* appeared provided many different kinds of part, again all open to interpretation by different players in quite different ways. Lovers and *servette* had a special dramaturgical importance too in that they served to bridge the imagined world of the play and the actual world of the spectators. Nowhere is that bridging better encapsulated than in the relationships between masked *zanni* and unmasked *servette*: numerous comic *scenarii* end not just with the marriage of Lovers, their unions invariably resolving plot complications and restoring domestic and social order, but with the wedding of *zanni* and *servette*, the union of the masked and the unmasked and, by implication, the world of the play and that of the spectators.

It is precisely the flexibility of the roles, the fact that they could embrace many parts in many kinds of play, than enabled the companies to work broad repertories. Allardyce Nicoll has remarked a problem for improvising players in effectively handling plays like *Avocato criminale*, which ran against the 'basis of the commedia dell'arte characteristic, and indeed unique, style in the presentation of dramatic figures', and he argues that many of the tragedies, *opere reali* and the like, were 'unfitted by their very nature for adequate presentation of the commedia dell'arte style'.[22] But this does not take into account the flexibility of the roles, the ability of the players to dispense with the mask when necessary, and their skill at turning their talents to a wide variety of dramatic styles and genres. Indeed, it assumes that there was a unique and definable *commedia dell'arte* style; that there was such a style is less than clear. The *commedia dell'arte* was not a single entity characterized by a single performance style. Rather, it consisted of companies of professional actors and actresses, some of whom were often masked, but in some pieces might be unmasked, who performed plays of all kinds, occasionally scripted, but invariably improvised, according to the scope of their talents and the possibilities of the markets. The role composition of their troupes enabled them to do so. The style of their performances depended on the stylistic requirements of the many different kinds of play they performed.

Documents

The documents below bear primarily upon the masks and roles, improvisation being examined in more detail in chapter 7. Improvised performances were given by amateurs as well as by the commedia mercenaria, *as we have seen above in the description of the entertainment devised by Massimo Troiano (chapter 2, documents), but it was peculiarly convenient for the working situation of the professionals, many of whom performed in both improvised and scripted pieces according to occasion and demand.*

IMPROVISED AND SCRIPTED DRAMA

As Riccoboni's comments below indicate, the reputation Italian players enjoyed for performing only by improvisation was largely based on an assumption about their mode of performance prevalent in countries beyond Italy, where for obvious reasons Italian scripted drama was of less appeal to audiences ignorant of the Italian language.

The *Italian* players dont always use to play their parts *extempore*; they have, as I shall shew by and by, sometimes learned it by heart, according to the different Ages in which they lived. But in those Courts in *Europe* who are not so well acquainted with the *Italian* Language, and where the *Italian* Players are sought after and encouraged, they have gone entirely to the *extempore* Manner, and it is under this Character that they are known over all *Germany*, and particularly in *France*. Hence arose the Mistakes into which the *French* Authors I have named were led, in supposing that the *Italian* Drama consisted *formerly* entirely in those Sorts of Buffooneries; and upon this Supposition, without examining further, they have pronounced the *French* Theatre to be superior both in Tragedy and Comedy, to all the other Theatres in *Europe*.

[. . .] The *French* Authors have run into another Mistake with regard to *Italian* Players, in maintaining that as they only excel in the Mimic Way, they are incapable of doing Justice to any thing that is great and pathetic. But this Notion is effectually destroyed, not only by the *Italian* Company established at Paris in the year 1716, but by other Players of that Nation, who at different Times have studied their Parts both in true Tragedy and Comedy . . .

[. . .] Besides we find in *Italy* an Excellence not easily to be met with amongst other Nations. No *Italian* company ever contains more than eleven Actors or Actresses; of whom five, including the

Scaramouch, speak only the *Bolognese, Venetian, Lombard* and *Neapolitan* Dialects. Yet when they are to act a Tragedy which requires a large Number of Players, every one of them is employed; even *Harlequin* lays aside his Masque, and they all declaim in Verse as properly as if they were Natives of *Rome*. This Practice renders them capable of doing Justice to the most Sublime Sentiments of Dramatic Writing, and at the same time of agreeably imitating the most ridiculous Oddities of Nature.

(Riccoboni, *An Historical and Critical Account of the Theatres in Europe*, English trans. 1744, pp. 66–8)

It is Riccoboni too who neatly, if indirectly, explains why the players in Italy could not readily assume the availability of dramatists to write pieces for them in the way Elizabethan actors were able to rely on dramatists to provision their repertories.

Since the year 1500 no *Italian* poet has professed to write for the Theatre, in order to pick up Money; Dramatic Poetry having since that Time been an Art, but not a Trade. The Dukes of *Ferrara, Florence, Urbin* and *Mantua*, suffered Plays to be acted only within their own Palaces. The Academy of *Sienna* was the first that, by its own Example, encouraged other Learned Bodies to compose and represent correct Comedies. Their Example was followed during the XVIIth Century; and the hired Actors, who till that Time had always acted extempore, never acted any Piece that had not before been printed.

(Riccoboni, p. 53)

FRANCESCO GABRIELLI ON FORMING A COURT COMPANY

Francesco Gabrielli (1588–1636), son of Giovanni (see below, p. 220), performed at various times in the Confidenti Company, under the direction of Flaminio Scala, and in G. B. Andreini's Fedeli troupe. He played under the stage name Scapino, and was noted for his musical as well as his acting gifts. In 1627, learning that the Duke of Mantua was trying to form a company, he wrote from Ferrara to the Duke's aide offering his own services and that of his family and companions. He illuminatingly, too, criticizes some other professional colleagues whose names had been proposed to the Duke. Of the many letters we possess written by commedia dell'arte *actors to patrons or potential patrons this is one of the most revealing. It well indicates the problems involved in attempting to assemble a well-balanced company of players. Gabrielli is here seeking patronage for his own troupe and support for his family, so of course his waspish comments on other players are self-interested, but they are not untypical of what comes through quite a lot of the actors' correspondence: economic competition combined with artistic rivalries and personal antipathies generated much dissension between and within the troupes. The accuracy of his judgements of his own troupe members, and of the rival players, cannot in many instances be verified, but some detail is corroborated elsewhere: Frittellino, stage-name of the actor Pier Maria Cecchini, seems to have had something of a reputation for being selfish and difficult to work with. Gabrielli's remark that Lavinia (Marina Antonazzoni) was distinctly better in scripted than in improvised plays indicates, as we might expect, that not all the players were equally adept in both kinds of performance techniques, although it also suggests that in this respect Lavinia was something of an exception. It seems, however, that performance in scripted drama was sufficiently common for a player to be primarily accomplished in that area, and the ability to assimilate the plot lines and performance possibilities of a* soggetto *could not be mastered by all with equal rapidity. Again, the implication of Gabrielli's letter is that the Duke looked to his intended troupe members to have skill in both techniques. Lavinia's husband (Francesco Antonazzoni) was certainly not the only actor to switch roles and his reason for changing interestingly indicates that the Capitano role was for some players at least a softer option for study than that of a Lover.*[23]

My Illustrious Lord,

On Sunday at the fourth hour of the evening whilst I was acting the Illustrious Signor Marchese Nicolo Tassone gave me your letter, and when I opened it at home and saw the favour in which His Highness holds me tears of happiness nearly came to my eyes. I am delighted His Highness is so well disposed to me, my wife, the Dottore, the Capitano, Citrullo and Flavia, just as I regret that Frittellino, his wife, Cintio, Lavinia, Ortensio, Pantalone della Podagra, and finally Mezzettino, are being recommended to His Highness. The reason for this I shall make plain to Your Excellency as briefly as I can in this letter, and you may show it to His Highness as I would not commit to paper something that was untrue. If we may begin by discussing Signora Lavinia, I think he will find it difficult to get her without Beltrame, which is what his late Highness of happy memory desired, for he is her associate and creditor for 500 scudi, and they were unwilling to come unless beforehand the debt was paid off and they were given a present: to this Signor Ercole Marliani and Luchesino can bear witness. Further, Signor Antonio, Lavinia is not much good in improvised pieces, so the company could not use her in other than scripted plays. Her husband was once a *secondo innamorato*, but as he detested study he switched over to play the part of *Capitano Italiano* in which he is not very good. Cintio, for reasons of his own, will not detach himself from Franceschina and her husband, thus together they fill three parts and are wanting a fourth, but where there is already a *serva* there is nothing for my wife to do, and thus nothing for me either. Mezzettino does not tumble and, more important, will not leave Olivetta who would make yet another *serva*. Frittellino is good at making himself detested, not just by actors but by everyone, and how true that is can be seen from the fact that when he wants companions he can get them only by the influence of princes or money. I say nothing of the fact that he always wants a better part than the rest. As to his wife, it is inconvenient that at her age she should want to pass as an innocent young girl, for what the stage wants today is youth. The Pantalone della Podagra is so maltreated by his affliction that last year when with us in Venice he could neither dress himself nor tie his mask, and I don't think it a good idea to put a statue on the stage who can do nothing but wag his tongue. I doubt that His Highness will believe my letter, but let him write and he will find it impossible to get Cintio without many others, nor Lavinia and Ortensio without settling debts and giving presents, nor Mezzettino without Olivetta. Whoever takes Frittellino will have to pay . . . and will bring discord itself into a company, while whoever employs Pantalone della Podagra will get a solid log of wood. However, if His Highness could hear the company Your Excellency heard here in Ferrara, even if only in one play, His Highness would come to appreciate that Celia is the leading *prima donna* of the stage both in scripted and improvised plays, for if the Company or others bring out devised pieces of new comedies she will perform them immediately, which Lavinia and other actreses would not until they had thought through the content of the *soggetto* for a month beforehand. I will say nothing about Flavia, for she is the best *seconda donna* now acting, whether in scripted or improvised plays. His Highness would find our Pantalone good too, both in the use of the native language and in the performance of ancient and modern *soggetti*. Bagattino, our second *zanni*, whom Your Excellency did not hear as he was ill, does not tumble but performs on the wire, and His Highness would find him a second Arlecchino. I will say nothing of myself, my wife, the Dottore, the Capitano and Citrullo, for thanks to His Highness we are considered good. It is indeed true that the *innamorato* is neither Cintio nor the *Dead Aurelio*, but he could easily search among the young and diligent who have won acclaim in Florence, the school of the Tuscan language, for one who might succeed by study as well as any other who has set foot on the stage, and, above all, without pretentiousness and other distortions. Do remember, Signor Antonio, that His Highness Duke Vincenzo of blessed memory, the father of his present Highness, had the same idea as His Highness has in mind, namely to assemble the best troupe of comedians, but he ran into infinite problems because of their self-interest and discord. Therefore Your Excellency, do me the favour of reading my letter to His Highness in some place where Your Excellency will be alone with His Highness, and assure him that I speak not as Scapino, but as Francesco, who will undertake anything His Highness wishes, and I, my wife, my mother, children and servant, making fourteen people in all, will come to serve him with the utmost humility. Forgive me Your Excellency if this of mine has been more a judicial report than a letter, but allow that what I have done has been done for the best, and in order to warn His Highness of all the interests of the players. So far I have had no letter from Signor Marliani, but if I do I shall undertake anything His Highness asks of me by letter. With this I conclude, recommending myself to him with all my heart. From Ferrara, 6 January, 1627.

Always a servant to Your Illustrious Excellency,
Francesco Gabrielli, called Scapino.

(From Rasi, *I Comici*, II, 1897, pp. 964–5)

CECCHINI ON THE ROLES

The Frittellino mentioned in Gabrielli's letter was Pier Maria Cecchini (see below, p. 227), who wrote the first systematic commentary on the teatro d'arte, Frutti delle moderne comedie *(1628), from which the following passages descriptive of the role composition of companies are taken.*

The role of the Lover (La parte dell'innamorato)

Those who delight in acting the difficult role of the lover enrich their minds beforehand with a pleasant quantity of noble speeches pertinent to the variety of subjects the stage requires. But I must caution that the words which follow on from what has been memorized should be so uniform with what has preceded them that the borrowing will seem more like a patrimony than a robbery. Therefore to ensure this I think it in no way contemptible to advise the frequent reading of thoroughly elegant books for the most beautiful phrases leave a deep impression on those who read, deceiving whoever hears them into thinking them the mental progeny of the speaker.

At the same time the actor who reads must ensure that his memory is controlled by his intellect (which distributes the treasure of memorized material across the vast field of opportunities constantly provided by the play) in such a way that he may hope to win approval and not meet with opprobium, as some do who address a stupid servant or a base woman with those forms and concepts which should only be used with wise men and men of high standing. Thus actors should be aware of the differences between men, and the nature of the cases they have to deal with, for they will surely appreciate that things which are different cannot be dealt with in the same way, by virtue of the fact that they are different, and that whatever accidents may befall, they need to tread the stage in the same way as they travel through the world.

(Cecchini, *Frutti*, 1628, pp. 18–19)

Ridiculous roles (Parti ridicole)

Some ridiculous roles have been devised, so lacking in verisimilitude that I cannot treat of their absurdities without resorting to the same absurdities myself. However, let us consider them without any attempt at reform, for that would have to start with the brains [of those who play them] and actors seem to be under the impression that each one of them has inherited the brains of Aristotle. Let us however consider their limitations, that they may know we are aware of them, even though we tolerate them.

(Cecchini, *Frutti*, 1628, p. 20)

Gratiano

The role of Doctor Gratiano, that so pleases audiences when performed by one who understands it, is today so much distorted by those of little understanding that nothing is left but the mere name.

Tell me, is it possible to have anything but contempt for an actor who, if you are Pantalone, addresses you as '*Piantalimon, Petulon, Pultrunzo*' or worse, and could you then, after a thousand insults, eventually give him your daughter in marriage?

PLATE 24 *Watercolour illustration to the* scenario Il Gratiano innamorato. *Corsini MS. Permission of the Accademia dei Lincei, Rome*

Another kind of Gratiano can be identified: this is the one who, intending to correct these abuses of speech, is so inclined to use Latin words, tirades and feats of memory, that he never allows anyone else to speak, confusing and undermining the plot line and the attention of the listener until it becomes impossible to follow, let alone understand, the transactions on the stage [. . .]

In order then to perform this most attractive role as I think it ought to be done, I would argue that an actor preparing it for the stage should first form a clear impression of that kind of man who is anxious to be modern despite his advanced age, and then, at the right time, he should come out with sentences appropriate to the subject, but inappropriate to the given moment. He should season his sentences with the Bolognese dialect as it is spoken by someone confident there is no finer way of speaking, but then occasionally, although without exaggeration, he should introduce words he thinks highly sophisticated, but which are in fact as ridiculous as anything you are likely to hear, like *interpretare* for *impetrare, urore* for *errore, secolare* (fancying it to be Tuscan) instead of *scholari*, and so on, without giving insult to the region or the individual.

It is sometimes worthwhile too for him to treat of some foolish trivial and very familiar subject by giving the impression that it is, or acting as if he believed it to be, the most strange, the most novel, and the least familiar thing in the world, and then, without even the hint of a smile, behave as if he thinks he has astounded everyone [. . .]

(Cecchini, *Frutti*, 1628, pp. 21–2)

The first and second servants

It is essential, and indeed particularly appropriate in comedy, that the part of the astute and ingenious servant, whose business it is to develop the plot-line by the exercise of wit rather than buffoonery, be balanced by another altogether different. This [servant] should be presented as a clumsy and ignorant person, and he should give every impression of being just that by pretending neither to appreciate nor comprehend what he is told to do. Hence arise comic misunderstandings, absurd errors, and similar contrived confusions which, if they are carried through by one able to interpret such a role, provide a very delightful part [. . .]

But today I see that in the practice of many [actors] that 'line' has been so modified, that to restore it to something more credible it would be necessary to give a great deal of measured instruction if what I am driving at is to be understood. Thus the costume of this [servant] needs to be restrained, for it has diverged too much from that appropriate to it: instead of patches (appropriate to a poor man) [these actors] adopt a virtual embroidery of lozenges all harmoniously composed, which gives them an air of amorousness and lasciviousness, rather than of the ignorance befitting a servant [. . .]

[These players . . .] have the habit of appearing on stage without regard for the requirements of the play, just at a moment when one or two of the serious characters are in conversation, pursuing some witty or demanding subject; and they interject with 'Dont make too much noise because the hen's laying an egg', or 'The pot's not boiling'. With comic interpolations such as these and others like them they undermine the seriousness and the acclaim due to those who quite certainly were deep in study when they themselves were asleep.

(Cecchini, *I Frutti*, 1628, pp. 23–4)

Pantalone

The role of the old man who has the costume and name of Pantalone is always a serious one, yet it is allied to the comic roles by virtue of language and costume. But the actor who plays it must retain that element of gravity that is never far from one who has to reproach, persuade, instruct, advise and do a thousand things required of an astute man, because this character is never a low citizen type, or at least is never less than a prosperous merchant.

He may, however, drop some of his gravity when dealing with a servant about amatory matters, banquets, entertainments and similar pleasant diversions, for these are appropriate to all social conditions, even the most grave and eminent.

(Cecchini, *Frutti*, 1628, pp. 25–6)

Capitano

This hyperbolic role perhaps sounds better in Spanish than in the Italian language, the former being a language in which impossibilities strike us as more apt and plausible. Today the performance of this role in both languages is so undisciplined that to purge it of the superfluous would certainly render it speechless.

If a player in this role says that the Queen of N. languishes for him, such an absurd notion may derive from a kind glance that Majesty has chanced to bestow.

If he boasts of being a field commander in Flanders, others too have done this, and something obviously false has been put about as a joke. But when he refers to the Coliseum in Rome when he means a ball, and says the Asinelli Tower in Bologna is a place to chase donkeys, and diverts himself with such tomfoolery, then you can only conclude the man is mad, and if he is mad then why give him your sister or daughter in marriage?

(Cecchini, *Frutti*. 1628, pp. 26–7)

Pulcinella

This delightful figure[24] has introduced a disciplined clownery which, at his first appearance, appropriately banishes all melancholy, or at least keeps it at bay for a long time.

I said disciplined clownery, because he makes a very concerted effort to overstep the bounds of nature and show a clown who is little short of being a madman, and a madman moreover who comes close to being a wise man.

The creator of this very clownish role was Capitan Mattamores [Silvio Fiorillo], a man of exquisite ability in other comic dimensions, since no one was better than he, and few his equal, in the role of the Spanish Capitano.

In order to persuade the world that simple-mindedness can be found even among Neapolitans, he discovered this way of introducing it, and it was even further enriched by the ability and initiative of Francesco who did not wish to deprive his country of such pleasure.

(Cecchini, *Frutti*, 1628, pp. 34–5)

PLATE 25 (left) *Frontispiece to Silvio Fiorillo,* La Ghirlanda *(1608), probably showing Fiorillo in the role of Capitan Matamoros. Permission of The British Library, 1429 aaa40*

PLATE 26 (right) *Puricinella. Engraving in F. Bertarelli,* Il carnovale italiano mascherato *(1643). Permission of The British Library, C 43 a27*

PERRUCCI ON THE ROLES

Cecchini's descriptions of the roles are brief, at times elusive, and occasionally marked by the querulous carpings of one antipathetic to the role modifications introduced by a younger generation of players. Much more detailed is the commentary written by Andrea Perrucci at the end of the century, Dell'arte rappresentativa premeditata ed all'improvviso *(1699), from which the following passages are taken.*

The roles of the Lovers

One should choose lovers who are young and not old, for among players there is a well-known saying, 'Zanni old, lovers young'. Old age is not suited to love, and anyone in love in his old age attracts laughter and derision, not applause [. . .]

Again, as they need to be addressed with phrases like 'my life', 'my adorable', 'my handsome', any actor not so, or not appearing to be so, looks ridiculous, for women do not love old men. Moreover when their memory fails them they are unable to act. Youth is even more desirable in actresses, Publius saying

Anus cum ludit morti delitias facit

No matter if they paint their faces with wax, with vermilion, with Spanish rouge and whitening and though they try to appear young and beautiful, yet Juvenal will tell them:

Facies tibi computat annos.

Furthermore, those who act lovers' roles should be chosen for their beauty, for beauty is always a recommendation . . . They should be well-dressed and elegant, for it is said

Che spesso accresce una bella un bel manto

They must remember all the rules of movement, in voice and in action; they should master the very best Tuscan words in the Italian language, if not in their entirety, then at least those expressions most widely used, and the most convenient way to achieve this is by reading good Tuscan books like the *Onomastici, Crusca,* Pergamino's *Memoriale della lingua, Fabrica del mondo, Ricchezze della lingua,* and other Tuscan lexicons, together with the afore-mentioned *Prosodia italiana* by Father Spadafuora, in order to get the right accent and emphasis. Thus gradually the language will become familiar, fluent and flexible enough to express the ideas of the mind.

They also need to be familiar with the figures and tropes of rhetoric, for with these they will be able to make a great impression, as they may with metaphors (provided these are moderate and not excessive), with metonymy, sinecdoche, antonamasia, catachresis, metalepsis, allegory and irony; among the figures, protasis, apheresis, aspentesis, syncope, paragoge, apocope, metathesis, temesis, antithesis, sistole, ettasis, sineresis, dieresis, and sinalefa; among figures to express beauty, repetition, conversion, complexion and reduplication [. . .]

It may be objected – Oh, you want a player so learned that it will be difficult to find anyone up to it. He should indeed be perfect I reply, and the more informed he is in rhetoric, the better he will act. If he is less than perfect, then let him come as near to being so as he can, for then he will approach perfection. Yet naturalness too will be useful to him, for some people have fluent tongues and an innate eloquence, and that usually ensures success, natural ability making up for artistic limitations, just as in others art can redress the limitations of nature.

Further, it is known that rhetoric too is a gift of nature from which the precepts of art have been drawn. Nor can it be denied, finally, that the actor need not be wholly rhetorical, nor natural, nor artificial. This is the case as far as improvised dialogue goes when it is needed for different speeches and encounters involving fathers, women and servants. Indeed the lover should take pleasure in improvising some small conceit and in sustaining an impromptu speech that is equivalent to the premeditated speech he delivers, for if an actor first delivers a premeditiated sentence in a grand and exquisite style and then, in the course of his speech, falls into a style, not I grant of the middle sort, but one that is low and humble, then it is like witnessing the fall of Icarus. Again, if an actor begins by speaking like a hero, but in the course of his speech shows himself to be a vulgarian, he will expose the gap between what he has memorized from others and what he is capable of adding himself.

(Perrucci, *Dell'arte rappresentativa*, 1699, Regola I, pp. 193–7)

The roles of the Old Men (Parti dei vecchi)

Pantalone First, about Pantalone, whoever performs this part should be accomplished in the Venetian language, in all its dialects, proverbs and words, presenting the role of an ailing old man who nonetheless tries to appear youthful. The actor should memorize various things to say at appropriate moments, like advice to his son, counsel to kings and princes, curses, compliments to the woman he loves, and such other matters as he chooses, in order to raise laughter at opportune moments by his respectability and seriousness. He should depict a person of maturity, but one who is all the more ridiculous because while he ought to be a person of authority, setting an example and serving as a lesson to others, he is possessed by love, and behaves so like a child that one may say *puer centum annorum,* and his avarice, so typical of old men, is overcome by a greater vice, namely, love, something wholly unsuitable to an elderly person.

(Perrucci, *Dell'arte rappresentativa*, 1699, Regola VI, pp. 246–7)

Dottore The role of the Dottore need not be as serious as that of Pantalone, serving as it does for the second father's role. Thanks to the liveliness of the plot line and the superfluity of language there is some freedom to distance it from the serious, although not so far as to reduce it to the level of the second Zanni, for that would be unpardonably wrong. The language of this role must be perfect Bolognese, although in Naples, Palermo and other cities far from Bologna it need not be rigorously correct, for then many would not understand a word. It should therefore be slightly modified so that it is fairly close to Tuscan, but as spoken by the nobility of that illustrious city, not that of the lower classes, whose language when first heard is so barely comprehensible that when I had the good fortune to be there my companion felt he was among so many barbarians, for he could not understand them at all.

[. . .] Many years ago a way of performing the Dottore role was introduced that involved the distortion of words, by saying for example 'terrible urinal', for 'tribunal'. But it was recognized that the Dottore was thus made too stupid and doltish, and the practice was abandoned. Such jokes were left to the foolish servant for whom they are more appropriate, leaving Dottore Graziano to employ genuine knowledge and erudition, but accompanied by extremely long discourses.

(Perrucci, *Dell'arte rappresentativa*, 1699, Regola VI, pp. 252–4)

The roles of the Captains (Parti dei capitani)

The roles of the swash-buckling *capitani* were very popular among the ancients, like the *Miles Gloriosus* of Plautus, and Trasone in Terence's *Eunuchus*, and many perform them today in various languages, some in Tuscan and some in Neapolitan, like Tasso, Ottavia d'Issa, Stellato, Sgambati and other authors, foreigners doing them mainly in order to mock boastful Neapolitans. They have been played too in Spanish, Romanesque, Calabrian and Sicilian, being known as 'the giant killers'. The Capitano role is one rich in words and gestures, boastful about beauty, elegance and wealth, but in reality a monster, an idiot, a coward, a nincompoop, someone who should be chained up, a man who wants to spend his life passing himself off as someone he is not, as quite a few do as they journey through this world.

PLATE 27 *Portrait of the actor Marc Antonio Romagnesi as a Dottore. Permission of the Bibliothèque Nationale, Paris*

The boastful speeches are usually prepared in advance to suit the place and time, and a volume of these has been put together by Francesco Andreini, husband of the renowned Isabella, to whom we defer for the sake of brevity.

When performed in the Neapolitan language, it is necessary only to change the phrasing from Tuscan to Neapolitan.

Performance of it in Spanish however must be done with discretion, for that nation, ever haughty, cannot tolerate ridicule the way the others can. Neapolitans are mocked as fools and chatterboxes, the Bolognese as tongue-waggers, the Venetians as idiots, the French as drunkards, the Sicilians as garrulous and quarrelsome –

but far from taking offence, they enjoy it. The Spaniard, however, although he may laugh when he listens to boasting, is reluctant to accept cowardice in a military figure, albeit only in pretence . . .

[. . .] All these swashbuckling captains mentioned above may function as second or third lovers, yet in the main they are scorned, rejected, deceived and despised by women, servants and maids, for despite their vigorous side they are in truth lazy, they will pretend to be generous but are in fact mean, they will claim nobility and wealth, but are plebeians, scoundrels and poverty-stricken.

(Perrucci, *Dell'arte rappresentativa*, 1699, Regola VII, pp. 273–9.)

The ridiculous roles of first and second Zanni (Parti ridicole di primo e secondo zanni)

[. . .] There are two servants called first and second *Zanni*. The first should be amusing, quick, lively, witty, and able to devise intrigues, confusions and stratagems, which might deceive the world. He must be mordant, but not to excess, and in such a way that his witticisms, called in Latin *dicteria*, are piquant, not oafish. The *Zanni* are primarily go-betweens, and according to Festo and Pollux the ancients portrayed them as bald, possibly to indicate that they had hot brains.

[. . .] The role of the second servant, which the ancients also assigned to the parasite [. . .] should be foolish, dumb and witless — so much so that he cannot tell his left hand from his right. Now let us consider each of them separately, starting with the first *Zanni*.

The first servant or *Zanni* can be performed in any language, although it is usually done in Milanese, Bergamask, Neapolitan, Sicilian, or in other manners which imply ingenuity – Neapolitans and Bergamasks both being particularly noted for the astuteness and absurdity of their rough speech, and for the craftiness of their dealings. His function is to devise the intrigue and to confuse issues. Lombards perform the part in a mask, Neapolitans without the mask, and the Spaniards, in their scripted plays, do not use the role at all.

[. . .] The clownish and ridiculous roles continue to be performed in masks, these being dark in colour and gross caricatures: a large or squashed nose, small and weary eyes, wrinkled forehead and broad head. Additionally, false beards can be used together with ridiculous faces, or to represent old men or magicians, or to transform the appearance of those who perform more than one part, and they can be matched with wigs similar to the beards.

Masks are not used for Furies or Demons when they have long parts, in order not to impede the breathing, and because they prevent clear speech; their faces instead are usually painted in red and other colours and they wear very thick wigs.

But to return to the ridiculous roles. It is essential for the first *Zanni* in improvised drama thoroughly to memorize the whole scenario in, as they say, all its final detail, for he must advance the plot and stratagems smoothly, be quick and lively in his responses, and avoid deviating so far from the *soggetto* that no quick return can be made to it. At appropriate moments he should introduce sharp and witty phrases, without making them just absurdities, and he should not step out of role by incorporating the second Zanni's ridiculous buffoonery, an error often made by Neapolitan *Covielli* who, because they over-step the line between wit and stupidity, produce an unacceptable concoction – for *Zanni* should be either always witty or always stupid, and when first *Zanni* are stupid they transgress their role, the proper business of which is to draw out the intrigue by ingenuity and guile.

(Perrucci, *Dell'arte rappresentativa*, 1699, Regola VII, pp. 283–6)

[. . .] The second *Zanni* [like the first] is performed in many languages: in Lombardy and the greater part of Italy the language of the valleys of the Bergamo and Valtellina is used [. . .] The people born in these valleys are very simple and humorous, and whoever has had dealings with them cannot deny they are delightful in their foolery, as I myself have found when twice in their company and their delightful foolery eased the boredom of a journey. Indeed it seems that nature has given them life that they may make people laugh . . .

(Perrucci, *Dell'arte rappresentativa*, 1699, Regola VIII, p. 292)

Pulcinella

[. . .] In Naples we have the character of Pulcinella, a character invented, not as the Abbot Pacchielli supposed by the lawyer Andrew Ciuccio, who then decided to introduce it to the stage, but rather by an actor called Silvio Fiorillo, who played under the name of Capitano Matamoros. It is however true that some time later Andrea Calcese, called Ciuccio, a tailor not a lawyer, through study and natural talent refined the role – as is well know to all those who still remember him, for he died in the plague of 1656.

(Perrucci, *Dell'arte rappresentativa*, 1699, Regola, VIII, p. 293)

The appearance of the Zanni and Pulcinella

Because comedy consists in words and deeds [. . .] and because one speaks too with the actions of the entire body, the ridiculous can be created by actions, with or without words [. . .] And as we have said enough about words, let us consider improvised actions.

Ridiculous antics consist in exaggerations or deformities of nature – in distorted faces, caricatured noses, pointed foreheads, baldness, long ears, and shapeless legs. Such defects can be simulated both by masks and the skill of performers, and to the extent that in real life these defects would be pitiable and elicit compassion, so they seem ridiculous when imitated.

Thus the *Zanni* should be extremely ridiculous, with tiny eyes, black face, bushy eyebrows and absurd in all his poses. Pulcinella should be equally ridiculous, in his whole appearance a very ungraceful figure, with a long, hooked nose, and, in all his gestures, squalid, dumb and stupid. Both are ridiculous as far as dress is concerned: the Zanni's costume being multicoloured; Pulcinella wearing a sack in the manner of a peasant. Both are ridiculous in other aspects too.

[A *Zanni* or Pulcinella] should be ridiculous in his movements: in the way he puts on a hat, walks, runs, affects gravity or haste in his deportment. He should be ridiculous in the tone of his voice, which ought to be excessively shrill, or out of tune, or raucous. He should be ridiculous in the dignified roles in which a blockhead incompetently pretends to be a prince, a captain, and so on. He should be artistically ridiculous when he imitates a poet, musician, painter, sculptor, hairdresser or similar artist. He should be ridiculous in his behaviour when performing an incongruously low and base action, as when he sits unbecomingly on a throne, or falls over when making a bow, and such like. He should be ridiculous in other actions as was Margite, who would fight with his own shadow, or Psilli when he fought against the wind, or Don Quixote against windmills. He should be ridiculous in his costuming, as when a fool dresses up as a prince or king and stupidly mistakes sleeves for trousers and boots for gloves, and puts on clothes inappropriate to the character. He should be ridiculous with his accoutrements, using a sword as if it were a horse, a hat as a fan, and a scabbard as a sword. To conclude, the ridiculous in action is born from exploiting exaggerations and excesses in the matters mentioned above, for there are times when a ridiculous and amusing action is wholly welcome and can give more pleasure than any metaphor of language and wit, and a natural action can express as much as can be said by any motto or saying, and is far more welcome in the more diverting characters.

(Perrucci, *Dell'arte rappresentativa*, 1699, Regol XII, pp. 340–2)

CARLO GOLDONI ON THE ROLES AND MASKS

Comedy, which in all ages has been the favourite entertainment of polished nations, shared the fate of the arts and sciences, and was buried under the ruins of the empire during the decay of letters.

The germ of comedy, however, was never altogether extinguished in the fertile bosom of Italy. Those who first

PLATE 28 *The actor Fracanzani as Polichinelle, engraved by F. Bonnart. Late seventeenth century. Permission of the Biblioteca Burcardo, Rome*

endeavoured to bring about its revival, not finding, in an ignorant age, writers of sufficient skill, had the boldness to draw out plans, to distribute them into acts and scenes, and to utter, *extempore*, the subjects, thoughts and witticisms which they had concerted among themselves.

Those who could read (and neither the great not the rich were of the number) finding that in the comedies of Plautus and Terence there were always duped fathers, debauched sons, enamoured girls, knavish servants, and mercenary maids; and running over the different districts of Italy, they took the fathers from Venice and Bologna, the servants from Bergamo, and the lovers and waiting-maids from the dominions of Rome and Tuscany.

Written proofs are not to be expected of what took place in a time when writing was not in use; but I prove my assertion in this way; Pantaloon has always been a Venetian, the Doctor a Bolognese, and Brighella and Harlequin, Bergamasks; and from these places, therefore, the comic personages called the four masks of the Italian comedy, were taken by the players.

What I say on this subject is not altogether the creature of my imagination: I possess a manuscript of the fifteenth century [sic], in very good preservation, and bound in parchment, containing a hundred and twenty subjects, or sketches of Italian pieces, called comedies of art, and of which the basis of the comic humour are always Pantaloon, a Venetian merchant; the Doctor, a Bolognese juris-consult, and Brighella and Harlequin, Bergamese valets, the first clever and sprightly, and the other a mere dolt. Their antiquity and their long existence indicate their origin.

With respect to their employment, Pantaloon and the Doctor, called by the Italians the two old men, represent the part of fathers, and the other parts in which cloaks are worn.

The first is a merchant, because Venice in its ancient times, was the richest and most extensively commercial country of Italy. He has always preserved the ancient Venetian costume; the black dress and the woollen bonnet are still worn in Venice; and the red under-waist and breeches, cut out like drawers, with red stockings and slippers, are a most exact representation of the equipment of the first inhabitants of the Adriatic marshes. The beard, which was considered as an ornament in those remote ages, has been caricatured, and rendered ridiculous in subsequent periods.

The second old man, called the Doctor, was taken from among the lawyers, for the sake of opposing a learned man to a merchant; and Bologna was selected, because in that city there existed a university which, notwithstanding the ignorance of the times, still preserved the offices and emoluments of the professors.

In the dress of the Doctor, we observe the ancient costume of the university and bar of Bologna, which is nearly the same at this day; and the idea of the singular mask which covers his face and nose, was taken from a wine stain which disfigured the countenance of a juris-consult of those times. This is a tradition still existing among the amateurs of the comedy of art.

Brighella and Harlequin, called in Italy the two Zani, were taken from Bergamo; because, the former being a very sharp fellow, and the other a stupid clown, these two extremes are only to be found among the lower orders of that part of the country.

Brighella represents an intriguing, deceitful, and knavish valet. His dress is a species of livery; his swarthy mask is a caricature of the colour of the inhabitants of those high mountains, tanned by the heat of the sun.

Some comedians, in this character, have taken the name of *Fenoc-*

ATE 29 *Brighella and Trivellino* *)omenico Locatelli). Mid seventeenth* *ntury engraving. Permission of the* *'blioteca Burcardo, Rome*

chio, Fiqueto and *Scapin*; but they have always represented the same valet and the same Bergamask.

The harlequins have also assumed other names; they have been sometimes *Tracagnins, Truffaldins, Gradelins*, and *Mezetins*; but they have always been stupid Bergamasks. Their dress is an exact representation of that of a poor devil who has picked up pieces of stuffs of different colours to patch his dress; his hat corresponds with his mendicity, and the hare's tail with which it is ornamented is still common in the dress of the peasantry of Bergamo.

I have thus, I trust, sufficiently demonstrated the origin and employment of the four masks of the Italian comedy [. . .]

(Goldoni, *Memoirs*, trans. Black, 1814, Vol. II, pp. 55–6)

6

The Scenarii *and Materials*

The Extant *Scenarii*

CRUCIAL TO the improvised composition of plays were *scenarii* (scenarios) – which may briefly be defined as notational guides to elements in the dramaturgy and plot-lines of the pieces the players performed. About 800 *scenarii* (also called *soggetti* or *canovacci*) have survived, most in manuscript collections formed in the seventeenth and eighteenth centuries. An early important collection, and the only one published during the great period of the *commedia dell'arte*, was Flaminio Scala's *Il teatro delle Favole rappresentative* (Venice, 1611). Many of the rest were probably gathered in random fashion, eventually finding their way into libraries.[1] These extant *scenarii* provide a major source of information about *commedia dell'arte* performance, but they are fraught with interpretative difficulties. Most can be dated only approximately, their provenance is diverse and often uncertain, and they exist in various states from the skeletal to the more elaborate. By no means all were scripted by or for professionals, and, when they were, then literary modifications and distortions may overlay stage usage. Some provide very general, some much more specific technical indications of what actors might do at particular moments in the action; most however leave the actors very free to develop the individual parts, the contributions of which, and the inter-relationships between which, comprised the performed *favola*. They are neither simple plot summaries nor prompt copies of actual performance, and in reading them we have to guard against any tendency to take them as complete: they are not, as it were, 'miniatures' of the stage performance, nor the 'briefs' of, or for, stage directors. A *scenario* is at best a pointer to ways in which performers might through improvisation compose plays. But the *scenario* is not itself a particular play; the play composed from a given *scenario* could be radically different in the hands of different groups of players and, according to immediate needs and emphases, in different performances by the same group of players.[2]

Scenarii appear to have circulated in manuscript, among players and possibly between companies, hence in part the difficulty of defining the provenance of pieces in many of the collections. That they did so circulate contrasts them as repertory pieces with the play stocks of the English Elizabethan and Jacobean acting companies. The English players were keen to prevent their texts from falling into the hands of rival troupes, and plays were invariably published only for specific reasons: to counter the pirated printing of a popular piece (as with the 1603 Bad and 1604 Good Quartos of *Hamlet*); when a play had exhausted its immediate playhouse utility; or when a company had fallen on hard times and sought to raise money by publishing its play texts. But *scenarii* were not for the most part particularly original even as plot synopses, and the Italian players seem to have been rather less concerned than the English to deny them to other players. On occasions, however, the Italians acted firmly to protect their performance texts, as did the troupe in Paris in the 1670s when it asked Louis XIV to ban the publication of material it had in repertory. In this instance however the players may have had particular reasons for keeping the material out of print.[3] The essential value of a *scenario* lay in what a company was able to do with it – and that depended on the quality of the players in the troupe , on the individual players' mimic and verbal repertoires, their ability to work with and off each other, and on the knowledge and skill of the *capocomico* to harmonize the stage action. *Scenarii*, then, are at best guides for actors, and when read today may conceal much more than they reveal.

However, notwithstanding such *caveats*, the extant collections, and Scala's in particular, are central to our understanding of *commedia dell'arte* improvised performance. Not least important is their indication of the range of genres encompassed. Comedy, tragicomedy, tragedy, pastoral, and historical and mythological spectacle, all fell within the scope of the actors' *all'improvviso*, although information about the ways in which they performed the non-comic kinds is sparse. Of these kinds the pastoral form perhaps most readily lent itself to incorporation in the players' repertories, for the juxtaposition of the *commedia dell'arte* 'masks' and the conventionalized figures of Arcadia provided theatrically effective comic incongruities, not least in terms of the love entanglements such encounters generated. The players' readiness to embrace various dramatic genres in the improvised manner was no doubt

PLATE 30 *Watercolour illustration to the pastoral* scenario Il mago. *Corsini MS. Permission of the Accademia dei Lincei, Rome*

facilitated by the well-established use of improvised or semi-improvised *intermezzi* between the acts of scripted 'serious' drama, and by the fact that many of the players themselves performed in both scripted and improvised plays and were directly familiar with the range of scripted genres. Behind the more serious *scenarii* (that is, the heroic, tragic and tragi-comic pieces) lies, too, the influence of the Spanish drama of *sangue e spada*, as well as in the *seicento* the more local models of the *melodramma libretti*. When translated from scripted to improvised performance the masked figures emerge in roles defined by social status; the *vecchi* are advisers and counsellors, the *zanni* are servants or attendants. The *innamorati* were readily absorbed into 'serious' drama as princes and princesses. How effective the 'serious' improvised drama was, and for how long it remained popular, is now impossible to calculate, although we may note that while it made up one-fifth of the pieces in Scala's collection, fewer such pieces are found in later Italian collections, and Andrea Perrucci, writing at the end of the seventeenth century, has little to say about improvised drama other than that in the comic mode. In any event, it was comic materials which were the stock in trade of the improvising players and comic *scenarii* make up the bulk of those extant in collections.

Some *scenarii* provide useful information about properties and stage appurtenances and decorations – as can be seen by a glance at the prefatory lists to *L'ateista fulminato (The Atheist Damned*, see below, p. 164), or at the body of the scenario text itself of *Il vecchio geloso (The Jealous Old Man)*. In the main such items were few, practicable and easily transportable. Those called for in the Scala collection consist for the most part of utilities like lights and lanterns, ladders, bottles, glasses, letters, fruit cake and other foodstuffs, purses, chests, benches, chairs, ropes, tools, trunks and travelling bags, swords, daggers and pistols and, occasionally, inn and trade signs, pictures, miniatures and playing cards. Special items of dress or disguise are similarly simple and stock, like slave garb and iron chains, hunters' clothing, nightshirts, false beards, wigs and cloaks for ghosts. Scarcely any of the early comic *scenarii* require elaborate scenic units and scene changes of the kind stipulated in the stage directions to *L'ateista fulminato*: 'the facade of a palace that can be transformed into a temple; a temple with a monument in the middle; a wood on the other side.' Such spectacle was more appropriate to the serious *scenarii* of tragic or tragi-comic emphasis, and Scala's pieces in this vein seem to call for decidedly more sophisticated stage setting than is required by most of the other pieces in his collection. In the later seventeenth century and in the eighteenth century, however, comedy came increasingly to exploit scenery and machinery, as Luigi Riccoboni's early eighteenth-century *scenarii* indicate.[4] For the earlier comic *scenarii* comparatively simple settings suffice, the invariable *locus* of the action being a street or piazza backed by two or three houses or an inn, while basic props and accoutrements were functional rather than decorative and helped to establish a mood or locale at the same time as they served incidents in the plot. Nonetheless, if a splendid occasion called for it, the scenically simplest *scenarii* could be lavishly upholstered.

Scenarii may have been pinned up backstage to serve as action mnemonics for the players. But whether many of the extant *scenarii* served that function in the form in which they have come down is highly problematic. They certainly show a pattern of exits and entrances, of appearances at windows and aloft, and in some instances point specific 'business' and scene changes. But the utility of many as prompt texts seems rather limited. Like the evidence they provide about props and stage practicables, what they indicate of the players' actions and movements is fairly simple and basic.[5] This, however, is deceptive. It has often been remarked that many of the same kinds of situation recur in the *scenarii*; indeed a certain repetitiousness was virtually a condition of improvised performance, which depended for its composition on the actors and acresses being physically and verbally attuned to the roles they played, and able to ring innumerable changes on familiar situations. It does not follow, however, that the plots of the plays were thus naive and repetitive. In fact there is more range and diversity to the *scenarii* plots than is often allowed, and they are as diverse as the sources from which they were drawn. While many of the plot-lines were taken from the learned drama, much was early borrowed too from the *novelle*, from the oral tradition, from foreign drama known in text or performance and from popular quasi-dramatic entertainment. Individual units of action often turned on the same basic situations, but the plot-lines which tied them together were various. While it is true that performances were not *scenarii*-led, and it was the theatricality of the individual units more than theme and plot which engaged an audience, the plots cannot be dismissed as mere pretexts for performance. At the very least, the plot gave an overall patterning that to spectators was pleasurable in itself. Perhaps nowhere is the variety of the *scenarii* better seen than in the collection of pieces Flaminio Scala published in 1611.

The Flaminio Scala Collection

Scala's collection of fifty *scenarii, Il teatro delle Favole rappresentative*, is of considerable importance in so far as it was prepared during the heyday of the improvised comedy by a professional practitioner who was an actor, director for a time of the Confidenti troupe, and a dramatist who wrote fully-scripted plays as well as *scenarii*. How many of the pieces in his collection were devised for the Confidenti is not known. Some may have been prepared for other troupes: for a time Scala was possibly a member of the Gelosi, and the scenario in his collection called *La pazzia d'Isabella (The Madness of Isabella)* may have been an adapted version of the piece in which Isabella Andreini was so much admired (see above, p. 74). However, tempting as it is to take the Scala *scenarii* as pieces which faithfully reflect stage usage and practices, and thus to extrapolate from them information about performance conditions and techniques, to do so is rather hazardous, for the collection's reliability in this respect is problematic. Scala prepared his collection for publication, conscious that he was organizing a literary product intended primarily for readers.[6] The actor Francesco Andreini wrote in the preface to his friend's work that the book was intended to be read, although 'ladies and gentlemen' might, he speculated, like to consider staging the pieces in private performances. Amateur performance *all'improvviso* was common enough, and Scala may have made the texts available partly with such use in mind. But the collection seems to have been organized to be read, on a *giornate* basis, in the manner of Boccaccio's *novelle*. In preparing it for readers it is likely that Scala would have tried to clarify content and amplify detail, and probable too that he would have paid particular attention to matters of literary style and reference. The player who went into print was seeking to establish, or cement, a literary reputation. How much then Scala modified his stage materials for publication purposes remains open to conjecture, and must leave some doubt as to the degree and kind of evidence we can extract from the collection about actual stage practice.

The plot lines of *scenarii* run in many directions, and their tone and subject matter can be strikingly diverse, as Scala's collection amply illustrates, ranging as it does from, say, the mildly scurrilous domestic imbroglios of *Il finto negromante (The Fake Magician),* where the comedy turns on tricking the *vecchi* into allowing their pregnant daughters to marry the men of their choice, through the cruel farce of *Il cavadente (The Dentist),* in which Pantalone is deceived and humiliated, to the bitter, near tragi-comic action of betrayals and revenges that is *La pazzia d'Isabella (The Madness of Isabella).* Some plot-lines are simple, others intricate in the extreme. In *Li tragici successi (The Tragic Events),* for example, for all the use of devices like Isabella pretending to be dead and disguising herself as a man in order to follow her lover, Oratio, the latter's despair at hearing of her supposed death, and his mistaken assumption that he has killed Gratiano's son, Capitano Spavento, the story-line is nonetheless thin and the action rather padded out by repetitive stage business. *Isabella, astrologa (Isabella, Astrologer)* on the other hand, is a densely plotted account of tribulations in Naples among children lost years before into Turkish slavery, wives apparently abandoned, supposed deaths, wild misunderstandings, disguisings, imprisonments and threatened executions. Again, how totally different is the mood of this scenario, rooted as it is in the urban exotic and the picaresque, from that of *Il vecchio geloso (The Jealous Old Man)*, set at a villa near Padua and redolent of lounging summer days in the country, with dancing, music, hunting, feasting, and amorous entanglements all amicably resolved in the fulfilment of youth and the mild chastisement of age.

It is often said that the plot-lines of the *scenarii*, wherever the action is set, are wearisomely focused on intrigues generated by the *zanni* at the expense of their masters, and on the romantic entanglements of *innamorati* temporarily foiled in their matrimonial plans by the opposition of parents. There is some truth to this generalization. In the Scala collection servants very obviously scheme against masters in pieces like *Il cavadente (The Dentist), Li duo finti zingani (The Two Fake Gypsies)*, and *Il vecchio geloso (The Jealous Old Man)*. Similarly, young lovers are patently frustrated by the obstinacy of the *vecchi* in *Li tragici successi (The Tragic Events), La creduta morta (She Who Was Thought Dead)* and *Li duo fidi notari (The Two Faithful Notaries)*. But just as frequently the scheming of the *zanni* can be directed elsewhere – against particular *innamorati* for example – or masters and servants can unite in plots against the young, or in tricks against enemies of the family. The *zanni* too can pursue their schemes for what they see as strictly their own interests, exploiting everyone else in the process, as in *Li tre fidi amici (The Three Loyal Friends)*, or seeking revenge on outsiders, as Pedrolino does on Il Capitano in *La caccia (The Hunt)*. Lovers' discord too can be quite independent of parental interference: the turbulent emotions of Oratio in *La pazzia d'Isabella (The Madness of Isabella)* have nothing to do with parental restraint, but turn rather on his love for two women; Flavio in *Isabella astrologa (Isabella, Astrologer)* has had his mistress stolen from him not by his father, but by the Turk who had taken him into slavery. Again, the love affairs of the young *innamorati* are not always central; matrimonial discord for example underpins much of the action in *Il ritratto (The Picture)*. In fact the character relationships, love pursuits, comic misunderstandings and deceptions are as various in the *scenarii* as they are in the popular *novelle* collections. It is only when the *scenarii* are encountered on the page that the recurrence of stock roles tends to give a superficial impression of excessive plot repetitiousness. Nor do some of the generalizations of the early commentators seem wholly borne out by the evidence of the *scenarii*. Cecchini, for example, speaks of the first *zanni* as being the spring of the comic intrigue. But this is by no means always the case; indeed many of the intrigues are generated not so much by the *zanni* as by the lovers – yet another indication of the important functions the *innamorati* served in the comic actions of *commedia dell'arte* improvised performance.

Scala's collection was probably edited, organized and refined to serve the reader and amateur performer. He prefaces each *scenario* with an 'Argument' that explicates the essentials of the plot and gives crucial information about the earlier fortunes of the characters, information of a kind the players would almost certainly have explicated themselves in rehearsal and then conveyed in performance. He sets out a list of the *dramatis personae*, pointing domestic relationships and particular, distinctive features ('Capitano alone'; 'Burattino, an inn-keeper', 'A dirty damp shirt for the Capitano'; 'Ridiculous hunter's dress for Arlecchino') – some of these could usefully have served as stage-management mnemonics, but others the players would early in preparation have settled for themselves. Occasionally he supplies snippets of dialogue, as when in *Isabella, astrologa* Pedrolino cries 'Where the hell is the astrologer?', and Isabella enters straight away with 'Here I am.' Again, Scala provides brief examples of speeches, like that of the grief-stricken Oratio in this same *scenario* who laments, 'Am I alive? Am I breathing? Am I Oratio? Then I will kill him!', or instances of the mad ravings of Isabella in *La pazzia d'Isabella*: 'I recall the year I cannot recall when a harpsichord sat next to a Spanish *pavane* dancing a *gagliarda* of Santin of Parma, followed by the lasagne, macaroni and polenta all in brown, but incompatible because the stolen cat was the friend of the beautiful Algerian girl, although it pleased the Caliph of Egypt to decide to put both in the stocks the next day.'[7] Such details seem to be provided for the reader, not for players performing the roles – if ever verbal improvisation had unfettered licence it would surely have been in Isabella's mad discourses. However, as the only early printed collection of *scenarii*, Scala's *Il teatro delle Favole rappresentative* was highly influential and may have conditioned the form of later *scenarii*.

Not least of the problems with the *scenarii* when we encounter them on the page is that they rarely seem very entertaining; the apparently naive nonsense of the situations, comic or serious, can be offputting. Again, their skeletal, mnemonic nature militates against identification in them of character 'individuality' and 'psychology', and can strengthen a tendency among readers to take them as plot synopses embodying the antics of stage figures who were no more than recurring 'types'. In his preface to *Il teatro delle Favole rappresentative* Andreini said that Scala wished, with the publication of his work, to leave 'to the beauty of the imagination (which delights in the quality of its own language) the business of creating the speeches.'[8] For twentieth-century readers that is a tall order, and a great deal of imaginative work has to be done to get beyond the text to some awareness of the performance possibilities latent in these actors' briefs. Yet many of the *scenarii* make for fascinating reading if we allow imagination free play.

PLATE 31 *Late sixteenth century drawing by Ambrose Francken,* Scene from the Commedia dell'arte. *Permission of the Amsterdams Historisch Museum, Museum Willet-Holthuysen*

The Materials

The nature and amount of the contribution made by premeditated materials to an improvised play is peculiarly hard to calculate for we lack any early detailed accounts of how the players worked, and how such plays were actually put together. The art of improvisation would seem however to have been based on wide and systematic study of literary works, and on careful selection from a host of potentially utilizable materials appropriate to the individual player's role specialization. Barbieri, writing in 1634, towards the end of a lifetime spent in the professional theatre, tells how 'the players study and stock their memories with a great load of things, like wise-sayings, conceits, love discourses, imprecations and outbursts of desperation or despair, in order to have them ready when needed, and their studies are in tune with the lineaments of the figures they perform.'[9] Cecchini confirms that the players enriched their minds with literary materials of high quality.

The nature of the material they drew on is ironically, but not altogether inaccurately, described in one of the prologues written by Domenico Bruni, an actor who had been in the Gelosi and Confidenti troupes. The prologue is cast in the form of a complaint by the players' servant woman, who is kept running to get one book after another as the players study to prepare their roles:

> Oh Lord! just listen to it. In the morning the Signora calls me: 'Hey, Ricciolina, bring me the material I need to study for the lover's role of Fiammetta.' Pantalone insists I get the letters of Calmo. The Capitano wants the *Bravure* of Capitan Spavento. Zanni asks for the witty pieces of Bertoldo, the Fugilozio and the Hours of Recreation. Graziano need the Sentenze dell'Erborente and the Novissima Poliantea, while Franceschina wants La Celestina to learn vulgarity. The *innamorato* asks for the works of Plato, and almost at the same moment one demands this, and another that, so curse them! Why even on stage they order me to do the Prologue![10]

Other reading could include Petrarchan sonnets, soliloquies and heroic speeches from plays, wise sayings and apophthegms, fine Platonic arguments on love, life, beauty and virtue, and pungent macaronic verses on senile lasciviousness or female frailty.

By reading such work the players familiarized themselves with literary materials and absorbed their diction, imagery, styles and tones. By so enriching their minds they sought, as Cecchini tells us, to attune the dialogue they were later to improvise to a level appropriate to the stage situations in which they would find themselves. By memorizing particularly choice passages, lines or turns of phrase (either directly from the printed texts, or more probably from *zibaldoni*, or commonplace books), they built up a stock of materials which they could insert into their dialogue as occasion permitted. Such passages were in effect the very bricks of improvised composition, and included *concetti, metafore, rodomontate* and *colloqui*. Similar gatherings were doubtless made of potentially useful physical and verbal 'business', (*lazzi* and *burle*), and matter relevant to song, dance and theatrical effects. While much was drawn, especially for the serious roles, from works of the high culture like those remarked above, the players borrowed too from the popular tradition, particularly for the comic roles. They seem to have had a marked preference for the rhetorically colourful and complex, and there was a tendency to traffic a lot in mythological reference.

The variety of material was such that it does not easily lend itself to classification, but we can conveniently identify four broad groups, while granting that the groups themselves frequently overlapped:[11]

1 *tirate*, or lengthy speeches of complaint, reprimand, praise, description or analysis, sometimes directly delivered to other characters in a stage situation – like a *vecchio* advising his son, or a *servetta* addressing an amorous suitor – or given as soliloquies,

reflective, argumentative or pugnacious, to reveal, or more frequently expatiate on, a situation in which a character finds himself or herself – like a lover abused or rejected, a *vecchio* baffled or frustrated;

2 *dialoghi amorosi*, emotionally extravagant and rhetorically sophisticated exchanges between lovers caught in specific situations of reproach, confession or apology, verbally and imagistically apposite to the mood of the moment but inflated nearly to the point of the comic – lovers' roles were 'serious' roles from the players' point of view, but they functioned within comic or potentially comic situations;

3 *bravure*, highly rhetorical rhodomontades characteristic of stage *capitani* which were structurally parts of dialogue exchanges between the Capitano and his servant, but which tended to be high-flown monologues prompted by a question or comment of the Zanni;

4 *lazzi* and *burle*, absurd verbal and physical comic antics and extended passages of comic stage 'business', particularly characteristic of *zanni* performance, but not confined only to them. These interweaved imaginatively extravagant verbal and physical play, either within running comic situations or developed as set-pieces quasi-independent of the plot-line. Where appropriate, and particularly in the performance of *zanni, lazzi* could also be interpolated to build out soliloquies with unspoken, pantomimic statement.

It seems likely that it was players early in the heyday of the companies who laid down the bases on which many later performers worked. While players may have guarded their *zibaldoni* more jealously than the troupes apparently did their *scenarii*, nonetheless the push to achieve cultural recognition and status in the early decades of the seventeenth century led, as we have remarked, to actors publishing materials, and these provided matter which later players could borrow from, or model their own preparations on. These included most notably Francesco Andreini's collection of his rhodomontades, *Le Bravure del Capitano Spavento, divise in molti ragionamenti* (1607), but among them too Lodovico Bianchi's early published collection *Le Cento e quindici conclusioni in ottava rima del Dottor Graziano* (1587), Isabella Andreini's pastoral *Mirtilla*, (1588) and the later *Rime* and *Lettere della Signora I.A. aggiuntovi di nuovo i ragionamenti piacevoli dell'istessa* (1607), and Domenico Bruni's *Prologhi* (1621) and *Fatiche comiche* (1623), as well as Scala's *Il teatro delle Favole rappresentative* (1611), some of the *scenarii* in which include examples of stage discourse. These publications not only supplemented materials which circulated among the players, but in various ways provided later performers with examples of literary discourse carrying the *imprimatur*, as it were, of the most distinguished actors and actresses of the age. What many of them indicate too, of course, is that many of the leading players were competent writers themselves. While most players, as we have seen, drew the materials with which they composed from a wide range of apt, approved or fashionable literary models some, like the player poets and poetesses, quite certainly contributed their own inventions.[12]

Documents

From such a large number of extant scenarii *it is difficult to select pieces which can reasonably be called representative; it can be claimed, however, that the three* scenarii *given below are among the most interesting which have survived. They are followed by a selection of* lazzi *and literary materials.*

AN EARLY SCENARIO, *LA SCHIAVA (THE SLAVE GIRL)*

One of the earliest extant scenarii, *dating from the sixteenth century, is the two-act* La schiava, *first published by Emilio Re in 1910 from a manuscript in the Biblioteca Estense in Modena. In its plot line, intrigues and character relationships it shows the strong influence of classical comedy, particularly perhaps that of Plautus, yet contains too many of the distinctive features of the Italian improvised comedy, notably the* lazzi *of Zane and the characteristic comic 'business' and garrulity of Gratiano. The latter, it should be noted, is not of Bologna, like many stage* Gratiani, *but is a gentleman from the region of Ferrara.*

The scene is Ancona
Pantalone
Capitano Tremante
Dottore Gratiano
Zane, as a Turk, servant to Pantalone
Hortensia, as a female slave, daughter to Pantalone
Marsilia, a courtesan
Franceschina, her servant
Leandro, a young lover
Burattino, servant to Gratiano

PLATE 32 *Watercolour illustration to the* scenario Li tre matti. *Corsini MS. Permission of the Accademia dei Lincei, Rome*

ACT I

1 *Pantalone – Capitano*
As they enter from the street Pantalone is arguing with Capitano Tremante and rejoicing in the fact that he has such an honest man for a friend. The Capitano boasts that as Pantalone stands in the protection of his shadow he is safe from all danger, and

proceeds to hold forth about wars fought, numbers killed, countries visited, and friendships with princes. Pantalone is astonished at his valour. The Capitano enquires about the business that has brought Pantalone to Ancona. Pantalone explains that his daughter was abucted five years before by pirates and was sold in Schiavonia. He sent his servant Zane to ransom her, but when he failed to return had himself set off from Venice on the journey to Schiavonia. Fate has brought him to Ancona, where he is awaiting good weather in order to continue his journey. The Capitano consoles him and before leaving offers his services. Pantalone remains, declaring his intention to knock at the door of Gratiano, a ship's master, as he wants to know when Gratiano will be setting sail for Schiavonia.

2 *Gratiano – Pantalone*

First at the window, then in the street, Gratiano behaves in a ridiculous way. Pantalone asks him when he intends to set sail. Gratiano replies that the sea is rough and he waits for a favourable wind, and he elaborates in an absurd way on the names of many different winds. Pantalone asks him how he came to take up this business in Ancona. Gratiano replies that he was once a doctor in Francolino, but ran into trouble and fled his country. During the flight he lost a young son. He later settled in Ancona where he had set up in business. Talking together they exit to the harbour to look for signs of favourable weather.

3 *Zane – Hortensia*

Zane in the street dressed as a Turk and Hortensia dressed as a slave. Zane announces that because chance has brought them to Ancona, and they have no money, and he cannot take her on to her father, Pantalone, he has therefore decided to raise some money by selling her. Hortensia begs him not to abandon her, but to get her to Venice as best he can. Zane explains that it is very dangerous for him to lead a beautiful woman around with him and so he intends to sell her. At which,

4 *Buratino – Zane – Hortensia*

Buratino from within the house announces that he acts as treasurer to his master Gratiano, and buys and sells goods and women of all kinds. He says he tours the world, and mentions all sorts of places and regions. Seeing Zane, he greets him, believing him to be a Turk. Zane responds as if he were. The two engage in a comic exchange. Finally Zane draws up a contract with Buratino and sells Hortensia to him for one hundred gold saraffi. Zane exits, and Hortensia remains bewailing her plight. Buratino consoles her, and Hortensia begs him to protect her honour. At which

5 *Franceschina – Buratino – Hortensia*

Franceschina enters from the square with a basket of lettuce and runs into Buratino who is her lover, but he pretends not to see her. She greets him and fondles him. He tells her he has found another lover, and points to Hortensia. Taken in, Franceschina curses him and flies into a fury. Buratino confesses that he was only joking, and they are reconciled. Then Buratino tells Franceschina to call Signora Marsilia as he wants to talk to her. Franceschina does so.

6 *Marsilia – Franceschina – Hortensia*

The courtesan Marsilia fondles Buratino, complaining that her master no longer visits her. Buratino assures her that business has prevented him. He hands the slave over to her care saying that all she need do is keep her in the house while he goes to the harbour in search of his master. He explains that the slave was bought in his master's name. Marsilia orders Franceschina to take the slave into the house. Hortensia begs her to accompany them and the three women enter the house, while Buratino exits for the harbour.

7 *Leandro, alone*

Entering from the Street, Leandro says that in Schiavonia he had fallen in love with Hortensia, the slave of a very rich merchant. She had been sold to an Italian servant who had gone about dressed as a Turk. Now he is pursuing her in order to ransom her or rescue her by force from this same servant. Knowing him to be in Ancona, he is now looking for him.

8 *Zane – Leandro*

Entering from the street Zane says that thanks to the one hundred gold saraffi he received for the sale of Hortensia, he intends to retire to his own country and never return to Venice again. But Leandro, having seen and recognized him, greets him warmly and enquires about the slave. Zane explains he sold her to a local merchant who is taking her to the harbour. The distraught Leandro asks the way to the harbour, and with *lazzi* Zane directs him. Leandro exits, and Zane remains jabbering away.

9 *Pantalone – Zane*

Entering from the street, Pantalone announces that he has been to the harbour and doubts he will be able to leave for some time as the weather is unfavourable. Seeing Zane, and thinking him a Turk, he greets him. Fearful he will be recognized, and astonished that his master, Pantalone, is here in Ancona, Zane is downcast, but manages to reply as if he were a Turk. But Pantalone recognizes him, and warmly embraces him, asking after his daughter Hortensia. Seeing he has been recognized, Zane resorts to absurd lies in order to explain to Pantalone that

Hortensia is dead. Pantalone is grief-stricken. Zane consoles him. Both exit into the house.

ACT II

1 *Zane, alone*

Zane enters from the house still dressed as a Turk. He says he has left Pantalone in bed grief-stricken by the loss of Hortensia. He declares he will look for a horse or a ship in order to make his getaway. At which

2 *Buratino – Zane*

Buratino enters from the street saying he has been at the harbour. As he has not found his master there, he thinks he will remain no longer in service, but will take the slave away himself and sell her in some other country. Seeing Zane dressed as a Turk he greets him. Zane returns the greeting. They agree to go off together as travelling companions, and plan to become rich merchants by purchasing women and setting themselves up as pimps. At which,

3 *Capitano – Zane – Buratino*

Capitano Tremante enters, kicks Zane, slaps Buratino, and acts belligerently. Buratino retreats. Zane addresses the Capitano in the Turkish manner, and the Capitano replies in kind. Buratino begins to talk in an odd language, but understanding that he knows no Turkish the Capitano terrifies him and bears down on him. Buratino is petrified. The Capitano insists the pair accompany him to the war. They don't want to go. The Capitano threatens them. Finally Zane draws his scimitar from its sheath, and Buratino seizes hold of his weapon and they both attack the Capitano, who runs off shrieking, leaving behind him his cloak and hat. Buratino takes up the cloak and hat and enters the courtesan's house, and Zane, after strutting about the stage, exits by the street.

4 *Gratiano*

Gratiano entering from the street says that now he has finished his business for the day he intends to pass the evening having a good time with Signora Marsilia, a courtesan who is in love with him. He praises himself for being an accomplished gallant, a very excellent poet, and a doctor of the most rare skill. At which,

5 *Buratino – Hortensia – Gratiano*

Buratino and Hortensia outside the house of the courtesan. He consoles her, telling her not to worry as he will take her away to beautiful countries. Hortensia begs him to take her to her father in Venice, promising he will be rewarded four times over for what it will cost him. Buratino agrees to do so, but Gratiano, having seen Buratino, questions him about her. On seeing his master Buratino claims he bought her for one hundred saraffi, but that she will sell for two hundred as she is young and beautiful. Gratiano rejoices, and after making her walk about and bow to him, orders Buratino to take her into the house. So Buratino and Hortensia go into the house, and Gratiano remains on stage.

6 Marsilia – Franceschina – Gratiano
Marsilia and Franceschina entering from the house say that they have seen the Dottore and wish to greet him. Seeing Marsilia, Gratiano makes lascivious and ridiculous gestures, and then greets her in the way stage *Gratiani* do. With the wiles of a courtesan, Marsilia extracts ten scudi from him in order to buy earrings. Franceschina too, with fine words, gets a scudo out of him to buy a bonnet and a pair of clogs, then all three go into the house to dine and sleep together.

7 Buratino – Hortensia
Buratino and Hortensia entering from the house say they wish to leave for Venice before Gratiano returns home. At which Leandro arrives.

8 Leandro – Buratino – Hortensia
Leandro, entering from the street, is desperate because he has found neither the merchant nor Hortensia. But when he sees Buratino and Hortensia he is delighted, and Hortensia too, on seeing her Leandro, greets him, and he greets her, and with great rejoicing they embrace. Buratino is surprised and asks why they behave in such a way. Leandro says that she is his beloved and that he wants her. Buratino declares that he wants from him what he has paid out. Having agreed on this Leandro and Hortensia exit to their lodging and Buratino remains with the money.

9 Zane – Buratino
Zane says he could find neither horses nor a ship to get away on and that he is desperate, fearful that Pantalone will discover the deception. Buratino sees him, and he sees Buratino, and they agree to leave together. In order not to be recognized Buratino begs Zane to sell him some Turkish clothes. Zane charges him ten gold saraffi and in addition to cash Buratino gives him his cloak and his beret on account, and then on stage he dresses himself as a Turk.

10 Capitano – Zane – Buratino
Capitano Tremante, with a hat on his head but without a cloak, jumps on Buratino, grabs him by the neck and demands that he return his hat and cloak. Buratino screams; Zane attempts to defend him using his pouch as a weapon; they make a great deal of noise. At which

11 *Gratiano – Franceschina – Zane – Buratino – Pantalone – Capitano*
Both Gratiano, wearing a night cap and shirt, and carrying a piss pot, and Franceschina with a handloom, are brought out by the noise. At which the noise brings Pantalone too from his house, clutching his clothes and waving a pistol, and Zane and Buratino run away. The Capitano boastingly declares that he has beaten off more than a hundred men, mortally wounding many of them, but has lost his coat and beret. Franceschina says the cloak and beret have been taken into the house by her mistress, and they will be returned to him. Gratiano removes his nightcap and shirt and asks Franceschina to give him his clothes, then exits with Pantalone to find out if anyone has actually died or been wounded. Franceschina takes Capitano into the house where she says her mistress is waiting for him.

ACT III

1 *Leandro – Hortensia*
Leandro and Hortensia thank Heaven they have found each other and plan to marry, then return to Schiavonia. At which

2 *Gratiano – Leandro – Hortensia*
Gratiano enters from the street saying he has not heard of anyone who has died or been wounded, and seeing the young man with the slave girl asks him where he got her from as she belongs to him. Leandro insists she is his, and that he has paid for her. Gratiano aggressively replies that if that is the case then he wants his slave back, and they begin to insult each other. At which

3 *Pantalone – Gratiano – Leandro – Hortensia*
Pantalone enters from the street saying he has not heard of anyone who has died or been wounded, and seeing the two fighting he withdraws. But then he sees and recognizes Hortensia, and she recognizes her father, and they fall into each other's arms. Pantalone tells Gratiano that she is his daughter and Gratiano demands his money back. Pantalone acknowledges he has a duty to pay him. Hortensia tells how Zane sold her to Gratiano's servant. Pantalone calls Zane a felon, and swears he will punish him. Leandro tells how he later bought her from Buratino for one hundred and fifty gold saraffi, intending to marry her. Pantalone says he wishes to give her to a gentleman of status comparable to his own, not to someone he knows nothing about. Leandro reveals he is a gentleman from Francolino, and the son of a Dottore called Gratiano, but that as a result of certain disputes had been taken away into Schiavonia. Gratiano questions him and recognizes that he is his son. Pantalone is happy to give him his daughter in marriage, and so they embrace. At which

4 *Buratino – Gratiano – Pantalone – Leandro – Hortensia*
Buratino enters from the street dressed as a Turk. He announces

he will no longer leave his master, but Gratiano, seeing and recognizing him, asks him what sort of clothes he is wearing. After speaking in Turkish in a deliberately comic way, Buratino says he bought them from a merchant, who also sold him a slave girl, whom he had then sold to a young man, and he gives Gratiano one hundred and fifty saraffi. At which

5 *Zane – Pantalone – Gratiano – Leandro – Hortensia – Buratino*
Zane enters and as he goes towards Buratino talking, he bumps into Pantalone. Pantalone pulls out his gun and makes as if to kill him, but Zane begs to be spared. Hortensia too begs her father to forgive him. Pantalone finally does so, and Zane returns the one hundred saraffi Leandro had given him for Hortensia. Gratiano asks them all to enter his house, and tells Buratino to call the courtesan out. Buratino knocks at the door.

6 *Marisilia – Franceschina – Capitano – and all*
Marsilia, Franceschina and Capitano come out, and Gratiano invites Marsilia to the wedding saying that he has found his son Leandro, and has given him the slave girl, Pantalone's daughter, for his wife. Marsilia and the Capitano are delighted, at which Buratino dances with Franceschina in delight.

(From Re, 1910 pp. 333–8)

A SCALA SCENARIO, *IL VECCHIO GELOSO (THE JEALOUS OLD MAN)*

One of the finest of Scala's scenarii, Il vecchio geloso *is notable not for its plot-line, which has few of the intricacies characteristic of so many other pieces, but rather for its country setting and the detail of its individual scenes. Interesting too is the earthy directness of some of the comic 'business' and the dialogue called for.*

The Argument

There lived in Venice an old merchant named Pantalone de' Bisognosi, who had for a wife a beautiful young woman called Isabella, who was most ardently loved by a very handsome young man, rich and respectable, by name Oratio Cortese, also from Venice. Much to the young man's misfortune the old merchant was jealous of his wife, and in order to remove her from the eyes of her admirers, and to be quite certain of her, he decided to take her to a villa he owned near Venice. The lady was followed there by her lover, and with her agreement he enjoyed with her a lovers' assignation, which she found all the more pleasant as it was conducted right under the watchful eye of her husband. It came to pass that talking one day with the same merchant, Oratio told him, as if in jest, everything he had done with his wife, at which story the old man, conscious of his importance and of his foolish mistake (in living in constant jealousy) graciously handed over the woman to be the young man's wife.

Characters in the comedy
Pantalone, an old merchant
Isabella, his wife
Pedrolino, a servant
Gratiano, a family friend
Capitano Spavento, a hunter
Huntsmen
Oratio and Flavio, friends
Burattino, a kitchen gardener
Pasquella, his wife
Olivetta, his daughter
Cavicchio, a peasant
Flaminia, a widow, sister to Isabella

Props for the comedy
Huntsmen's clothes, weapons, horns, dogs and the like
A chest
Silver vessels
Flasks of wine
Drinking glasses
Food on silver plates
Vestments for the entertainers
A lute or theorbo
A plate with figs or other fruit

Scene: A villa near Padua

ACT I

Oratio, Flavio

Oratio tells his friend Flavio that he has come to that country house for love of Isabella, the wife of Pantalone, that he is loved by her in return, and that his servant Pedrolino knows of their love. He says that he has never possessed Isabella, but that she has promised to satisfy him, and his being at the villa will provide opportunity. Flavio says that he has no need to worry as he has a good go-between. At which,

Pedrolino

with a straw hat and a stick, tells Oratio that Pantalone is approaching together with his wife. Flavio immediately goes to meet him. Pedrolino asks Oratio whether Tofano, who has a villa only two miles from Pantalone's house, is a friend of his and whether Pantalone is aware of it. Oratio confirms this. Pedrolino says he wishes to make use of Tofano's house at the appropriate time. At which, he sees Pantalone arrive. Oratio remains. At which,

Pantalone, Isabella, Flaminia, Flavio, Gratiano [enter]

Pantalone leads his wife, Isabella, in by the hand. Flavio leads the widow, Flaminia. Oratio greets Pantalone and all his companions, delighting in the fact that he has come to favour the villa with his presence. As a long bench has been made ready for them, they all sit down, begging Dottor Gratiano to tell them a story. For a while Gratiano allows them to beseech him, but finally tells them that story by Boccaccio called [*title not given in Scala*]. They all praise it, save for Pantalone, who objects that it was inappropriate with ladies present. At which,

Pedrolino

panting, tells Oratio and Flavio that some Bergamask gentlemen have arrived and are asking for them. They immediately depart in search of them, and the rest remain. At which, they hear singing from within.

Cavicchio

a peasant, [enters] first singing *alla norcina*, then singing about the suffering endured by an old husband who is jealous of his wife. They all laugh, then ask Cavicchio to tell them a story. Cavicchio tells the story of the painter who used to portray the devil as a beautiful person etc. They all laugh at the fine story. Cavicchio invites them to go to a place he rents where they may enjoy themselves. They accept his invitation. Gratiano takes Flaminia by the hand, making lascivious gestures, and leads the way. Pantalone remains with Isabella, urging her to take care of her honour, at which she is angry. Pantalone placates her, embraces her, and together with her follows the others out.

Burattino, Olivetta

Burattino, a kitchen gardener, [enters] with his daughter Olivetta, whom he reproaches because she can neither hoe nor plant although she is now old enough to be married, and he gives her some lessons in how to handle the hoe. At which,

Pedrolino

greets Burattino and his daughter, telling them that he would like them to earn ten scudi. Pedrolino orders them to take a plate of the finest figs or peaches to Oratio, and to tell him that Tofano Braghettini has sent them to him from his place, begging him to go there because he wishes to speak to him about a very important matter. He gives them two scudi on account, and asks Burattino to send out his wife, Pasquella. Burattino enters with Olivetta, and Pedrolino remains.

Pasquella

comes out. On behalf of Oratio, Pedrolino makes suggestions to her. Pasquella says Oratio is a very courteous gentleman, and that for him she will do anything. Pedrolino tells her that Oratio loves Pantalone's wife and that in order to possess her needs to hide in one of the rooms in her house, and when a time comes that Isabella wants to urinate in her house she should take her to that same room, and make sure that no one but Isabella goes into the house. Pasquella is agreeable. Pedrolino gives her two scudi and Pasquella goes in. Pedrolino says that things are well in hand. At which,

Gratiano

saying that the gentlemen have left, reminds Pedrolino not to forget his love for Flaminia. Pedrolino promises to help him. At which

Oratio, Flaminia, Flavio, Isabella, Pantalone [enter]

Oratio holding Flaminia by the hand, and Flavio leading Isabella, and Pantalone following them, encounter Gratiano and

Pedrolino. They ask if the meal is being prepared. They are assured it is, and that they will be well served. At which,

Burattino

the kitchen gardener, enters with a most beautiful plate full of figs or peaches, and presents it to Oratio on behalf of Tofano Braghettino, begging him to be so kind as to go to his house after dinner. Oratio accepts the present, gives him a tip, and says that he will go without fail. Burattino exits. Pantalone calls for water to be brought in for them to wash their hands. At which,

Pedrolino

with a silver bowl

Gratiano

with a silver jug and a hand towel. They all wash, then go inside to eat in a merry mood, and so ends the first act.

ACT II

Three Strolling Musicians

enter. They carry instruments and are poorly dressed. They make their living by going from villa to villa performing and singing. They play on their instruments. At which,

Pasquella, Olivetta

come out. The musicians beg for something to eat, offering to sing and play in return. Pasquella sends in for bread and wine. At which,

Pedrolino

comes from the house and tells Pasquella that the time for the business with Oratio is drawing near, and the musicians provide the opportunity. Olivetta is despatched to invite some young ladies from the villa to come and join in the dancing. Olivetta exits. Pedrolino orders the musicians to play and promises them that they will be well paid. The musicians perform. At which,

Olivetta, Girls [enter]

Olivetta arrives with her companions and the girls from the villa. Pasquella goes into the house to get benches and chairs, then returns with her husband.

Burattino, Pasquella

come out with benches and chairs. They arrange seating for everyone while the musicians are performing. At which,

Pantalone, with Isabella, Flavio, Oratio, Gratiano

comes out of the house with his companions and sits down with the others. All begin to dance – first one, then another, as is customary among such women. In the middle of the dance Oratio takes his leave of the company, declaring that he must visit Tofano. He exits. Burattino goes into the house to look for his own musical instrument. They dismiss the musicians, who leave after Flavio has paid them. Burattino suggests that he take them all for a walk and that he will play to them as they go, and

PLATE 33 *Watercolour illustration to the* scenario Le mogli superbe. *Corsini MS. Permission of the Accademia dei Lincei, Rome*

agreeing to this they all exit save for Pasquella, who remains in charge of the house. At which,

Oratio

arrives and greets Pasquella. After rehearsing everything Pedrolino had told him earlier she leads him into the house: there she will take him into the room already prepared, in which he will enjoy Isabella. They go in.

Gratiano with Pedrolino

enters. He has been drinking heartily in the houses of peasants. Gratiano reminds Pedrolino of the love he bears for Flaminia. Pedrolino replies that he will arrange for him to have her for the whole day. At which they hear the sound of huntsmen and their horns and

Capitano Spavento with Huntsmen

enters, in hunting clothes, with dogs and horns, and paying a visit to the villa out of the love he bears for Flaminia, the sister of Isabella. He asks Gratiano after Pantalone, Flavio and Oratio. Oratio replies that they are nearby the villa, and he exits to summon them. Pedrolino warns the Captain that Gratiano is his rival for Flaminia's love. The Captain brushes this aside. At which

Flavio, with Pantalone, Gratiano, Isabella, Flaminia, Burattino

enters with his companions. They greet the Captain delighted at his arrival. Immediately Flavio suggests they sit down. They first take refreshments, then begin to dance again, then all sit down once more. At which,

Pasquella, Olivetta

join the others. At which,

Pedrolino, Gratiano, Servants

enter with dishes loaded with food, flasks of wine, fruit, glasses and saucers. They serve lunch, and all eat and drink. Later they begin to dance the *piantone*, and during the dancing Isabella intimates to her husband that she must go in and urinate. Immediately Pasquella, with Pantalone's permission, leads her into the house. Ever jealous, Pantalone promptly plants himself in front of the door. Meanwhile all dance again, and as they are doing so

Flaminia

is taken short and needs to go into Pasquella's house, but Pedrolino, to prevent her disturbing Oratio, forces her to dance. In similar fashion each one is taken short and tries to enter Pasquella's house, but Pantalone stops them, saying 'Please don't disturb my wife, she's relieving herself.' Finally,

Isabella

comes out of the house dripping with perspiration. Pantalone dries her with his handkerchief, insisting that when she has needs to satisfy she must not resist but give in to them. They all stop dancing and wander off to enjoy themselves. Pantalone follows them out, mopping his wife's face, while she feigns coyness and caresses her husband. All exit, and so ends the Second Act.

ACT III

Flavio with Pedrolino

Flavio longs to see Oratio again to find out how the business went. At which,

Oratio

comes from Pasquella's house and tells them about the brief pleasure he had with Isabella. Pedrolino wishes to play a trick on Gratiano, who is in love with Flaminia; the Captain is deeply in love with Flaminia, and it is for her sake that he has come on the pretence of going hunting. At which,

Capitano, Pantalone, Isabella, Flaminia

arrive, see Oratio, and congratulate him on his rapid return. They all embrace each other. Isabella begs Oratio to get his *tiorba* and sing some songs *a la Romana* to entertain the company. Being in a happy mood, Oratio sends Pedrolino in to fetch the instrument. Turning to the Captain, Oratio asks him if he would marry. The Captain, looking at Flaminia, says that he would. Oratio says that the Captain should make him responsible for making the arrangements. The Captain agrees and as Oratio is about to discuss this with Pantalone,

Burattino

arrives, and taking Oratio aside asks him to be so good as to pay for the bed he broke while he was closeted with Isabella. Oratio agrees to pay, and sends him away, then asks Pantalone to give Flaminia's hand to the Captain. Pantalone is happy to do so provided Flaminia agrees. Flaminia indicates her assent and touches his hand. At which,

Pedrolino

enters with the guitar and hands it to Oratio, and all sit down. At which,

Gratiano

enters. Pedrolino promptly tells him to go into the house to Flaminia's room, close the windows, throw himself on her bed, and wait for her to join him. Gratiano goes in. Oratio begins to sing, and so sweetly that Pantalone falls deeply asleep. At which Oratio, still singing, leads Isabella away. Capitano, Flaminia and Flavio follow them. Pedrolino remains. At which,

Pasquella

comes out and Pedrolino tells her that Isabella waits for her in the house, in her sister Flaminia's room, in order to give her a tip. She should go in quietly, however, as she is lying down on the bed. Delighted, Pasquella leaves. Pedrolino remains. At which,

Pantalone

wakes up, sees Pedrolino, and asks where Isabella has gone to. Pedrolino [says] he too was asleep, and so has no idea. Pantalone is surprised at this. At which,

Burattino

[enters] and asks Pantalone if he has seen his wife, Pasquella, and Pantalone asks in return if he knows where his wife has gone to. At which,

Oratio with Capitano, Flavio, Isabella, Flaminia

Oratio enters singing, followed by all his companions. On seeing Pantalone they tease him for falling asleep, saying, 'Oh what a suspicious husband: he can't guard her closely enough when he's awake; just see how he guards her when he's asleep!' Pantalone flies into a rage, at which

Pasquella with Gratiano

Pasquella enters running away from Gratiano, who is trying to embrace her. Burattino comes between them. Pasquella says Gratiano has taken her honour by force. Gratiano apologizes, claiming he has been betrayed and is for the moment speechless, but intends in due course to get his revenge. Burattino asks Pantalone if he is now a cuckold seeing as Gratiano has had his wife. Pantalone confirms this and hearing it Burattino replies, 'Signor Pantalone, your excellency should know I am not alone, for there are other cuckolds not so far from here.' He says too he would like him to hear about what happened to an acquaintance of his. He recounts how a jealous old man stayed at a country villa with his wife, whom he watched over very closely. A young man was in love with her, but had no idea how to win her. With the aid of his servant he arranged to be called away by a friend who lived nearby. After taking his leave he hid in the house of a woman friend, and stayed there, while awaiting an opportunity to carry out the arrangement he had made with the woman. At the same time the girls of the villa wanted to dance, and after a beautiful group of men and women had been assembled, the dance began to the strains of a fine instrument. Shortly after the start of the dance the jealous old man's wife pretended to her husband she had to go to the lavatory. On hearing this the lady who had loaned the lover her house led the wife into it with the husband's permission, and lodged her in the arms of her lover. Meanwhile the good old man, racked with jealousy of his wife, set himself before the door and told all who tried to enter not to disturb her because she was on the job. Her amorous work over, the wily wife came out of the house covered in sweat from her labours, and was told by her trusting husband that whenever she had similar needs she should not resist them but satisfy them, and the old man caressed her as he dried the sweat on her face. On hearing the conclusion of the tale turned against him, the old

PLATE 34 *Watercolour illustration to the* scenario Li sei contenti *showing a comic* finale. Corsini MS. Permission of the Accademia dei Lincei, Rome

man immediately cried out he had been betrayed and destroyed by his wife. Oratio then tells him that his wife, not he, was the one destroyed, for in the cause of making love to her he had discovered she was a virgin, and therefore Pantalone, by not making love to her, was destroying her by his impotence. Finding himself thus exposed, Pantalone confesses the truth and agrees that Isabella should become Oratio's wife. Weddings were therefore arranged for Oratio and Isabella, the Captain and Flaminia, and Pedrolino and Olivetta. Burattino's dishonour is forgotten, and it is agreed to celebrate the nuptials in Pantalone's house. Thus ends the comedy of *The Jealous Old Man.*

(Scala, *Il teatro delle Favole rappresentative*, 1611, giornata VI, pp. 20–3.)

A SEVENTEENTH-CENTURY SCENARIO, *L'ATEISTA FULMINATO* (*THE ATHEIST DAMNED*)

This interesting early seventeenth-century scenario *is one of many dramatic versions of the Don Juan theme, and may have been known to Molière when he wrote his version of the story. The basic role composition of a* commedia dell'arte *company could have accommodated without overmuch difficulty the large cast of this piece, allowing for doubling and the use of supernumeraries: the kinds of accommodation made can be seen in the appearance of Il Magnifico as counsellor to the king. For all that it has a serious plot, and is an example of the* opere regie, *there are ample opportunities for the comic servants, Bertolino and Buffetto, to engage in intrigue and* lazzi. *The props and scenic effects are noticeably more elaborate than those in the other* scenarii *translated here. The emphasis on spectacle in this* scenario *was not uncommon by the early to middle decades of the seventeenth century, particularly in the more serious pieces. This* scenario *is manifestly a product of the baroque theatre. The deletions of some short passages in the Ms. were made at a later date, probably because they were found morally offensive.*

The King of Sardinia, without an heir
The Queen, his wife, who does not appear
Count Aurelio, a prince of the line, banished
Duke Mario, also of the line
Bertolino, servant to Count Aurelio
Buffetto, servant to Duke Mario
Learco, father to Duke Mario } both statues
Teandra, mother to Duke Mario } both statues
Leonora, sister to Duke Mario
Cassandro
Angela, his daughter
Romito, an old man

Count Aurelio's bandits
Duke Mario's soldiers
Highwaymen
Olivetta, of the Court
Several peasants
Counsellors to the King
[Magnifico]

Props

Trumpets and drums. Armour for the white statue. Trousers, socks and all necessary clothing, including gloves. Two white masks, one for a male and another for a female, with flaxen hair. A friar's gown and a white sword. Weapons and collars for the bandits. Two garments for hermits. A female wig made of flax; straw matting; beards and ringlets. Two panniers for carrying food for the table. Halbards for the guards. Two peasant gowns.

The facade of the palace that can be transformed into a temple; a temple with a monument in the middle; a wood on the other side.

Things to eat; plates; a table cloth; napkins; knives with glasses; a white dress for Leonora in Heaven; for dressing Pluto, a trident, a royal crown, a dressing gown, a large and unkempt black beard; different garments and clothing for spirits; pitch; things with which to impale Zanni.

ACT I

A city: Cagliari in Sardinia

The King, Counsellors and the Court

The King bewails his misfortune in having a sick wife and no further hope of having children by her to secure the succession of the kingdom. The Counsellors console him. At which,

Duke Mario

exaggerates the insult he has received from Count Aurelio, who abducted his sister Leonora from the house of the Vestals, and who, having returned to the country, offends the realm and his royal house in a thousand ways. The King gives him full authority over all the soldiery of the land and charges him to apprehend Count Aurelio, whom he intends to punish. Duke Mario accepts the charge and the authority. At which,

Bertolino

enters, a bandit, disguised as a peasant, together with

Peasants

bearing various petitions against Count Aurelio for damages they have suffered to their goods and honour. The King assures them that justice will be done, then all exit to the Court.

A wood

Aurelio, Leonora, Bandits

In a short love scene Aurelio and Leonora declare their mutual passion and swear never to forsake each other. Then Aurelio hears from all the rest the reason why each has become a bandit. At which,

Bandits

lead in the bound

Cassandro

who was taking

Angela

his daughter to the City of Cagliari to be married. Aurelio frees Cassandro, but retains Angela, and Cassandro departs in tears, having to find a ransom of ten thousand scudi if he hopes to recover his daughter. Angela throws herself on Aurelio's mercy, and he reassures here. Pricked by jealousy Leonora intercedes for her, but Aurelio insists he will not set her free. At which,

Bertolino

dressed as a peasant, says that he took the petition to the King, and found other peasants there making complaints. He tells of the King's order to Duke Mario, Aurelio's enemy. Aurelio scoffs at this, and then, so that all may take their rest, he sends them to their caves, instructing that Angela be well guarded. The others exit, taking Angela with them. Aurelio remains with Bertolino and Leonora. He sees

The Temple

which opens, revealing the statues of Mario's father and mother. Aurelio behaves in a savagely aggressive way towards them as if exacting revenge. Leonora pleads with him, he loses his temper with her and she, unwilling to witness more, exits in a downcast spirit. The others remain, and there is a dramatic scene between them. Bertolino betrays his fear. Finally the statues speak, saying 'Do not disturb the peace of the dead.' Aurelio, parading his contempt before Bertolino, retorts, 'And what if I do disturb it?'

The Statues

reply, 'He who lives by the sword dies by the sword.' He responds that he is now leaving, so if they want an encounter with him they will have to follow him.

The Statues

reply that they will, and the Temple closes. The others exit into the wood.

The city

Mario, Buffetto

Mario has given orders that as soon as all is ready he will go himself to fight against Aurelio, and will perhaps also kill

Leonora, even though she is his sister, because she agreed to run away with his great enemy and to his dishonour.

Buffetto

wants no violence against Leonora, but says he wants to make mincemeat of Bertolino. At which,

Magnifico

tells Mario that a royal order summons him to Court to receive new and secret orders from His Majesty. Exeunt Magnifico and Mario; Buffetto remains; at which,

Olivetta

enters and there is a love scene between them with *lazzi*. Buffetto invites her to accompany him and his master against the bandits; she accepts and all go to Court to arm themselves.

The woods

Aurelio, Angela

Aurelio praises her for her beauty, she reveals that she is in love with him, and they promise to make love, and in order to prevent Leonora from finding out they agree to simulate hatred, so that their love can be the better concealed. At which

Leonora

who has witnessed the scene, sees them embrace, makes *lazzi* of fury that she wants to shoot him. Finally Aurelio calls out to

Bertolino

and hands over Angela to him, so that he can take her to the caves. Bertolino departs with Angela. Aurelio remains, at which

Leonora

tells Aurelio that she heard everything. He denies it; she reproaches him; finally she is so petulant that Aurelio, driven to fury, kicks her. She falls to the ground, he scornfully disarms her and departs saying: 'Go wherever you wish, and do your worst to me'; and he leaves. She stays and laments; at which,

Hermit

an old man comes out of his cave to breathe fresh air; sees the young woman distraught; she tells him everything, and he tells her who he is, and says he will keep her hidden and that Heaven will protect her, and with a pious exhortation leads her into the cell, and so concludes the act.

ACT II

The wood

Aurelio, Bertolino

Aurelio orders Bertolino to go to the Court disguised as a peasant and try to discover when Duke Mario will set out against him with his army and the number of men he will have with him, for he wishes to prepare an ambush. Bertolino tried to

PLATE 35 *Late sixteenth century drawing by Lodewyk Toeput* Allegory of January, *showing travelling players in a village. Permission of the Yale University Art Gallery*

persuade him to repent, and reminds him of the statues' words. Aurelio laughs at this and finally says he too wants to go in person in disguise, and remembering the Hermit says he wants his habit. They knock at the cell.

Romito

fearful lest they learn about the hidden woman, and that they intend harm, falls to his knees and begs forgiveness. There follows a scene of misunderstandings, and they talk at cross purposes. Finally they tell him they want his habit, remove it and depart. He remains complaining, but praises Jupiter for them, then exits.

The city

Buffetto and Olivetta

enter dressed in a ridiculous way and carrying weapons, ready to move against Aurelio with their master.

The Magnifico, Duke Mario, People

The Magnifico encourages Duke Mario to be diligent and watchful, and alert to danger. The Duke tells him not to worry, as before the day's end he will have left to avenge himself against the Count, and at the same time will root out many other monsters, securing the Kingdom and making the roads safe for travellers. They all go into the Court. Buffetto encourages them and then exits.

The wood

Leonora
enters dressed in a sackcloth [phrase deleted in Ms.]. She laments the sins she has committed against Heaven, then falls into a swoon. At which,

The Hermit
enters carrying a straw mat, and catches sight of her. She regains consciousness and he takes her back into the cell.

Bertolino
enters on his way to Court, dressed as a peasant and carrying concealed weapons. He exits.

Aurelio
enters dressed as a hermit. Not wanting to be recognized he has avoided changing clothes in front of the others before going to the Court. At which,

Duke Mario, Olivetta, Soldiers and Buffetto
enter. Duke Mario says they have searched the wood under the King's order that gives them supreme authority to command the entire Kingdom against Aurelio and the bandits. Aurelio, dressed as a Hermit, hears this. He steps forward, and pretends to encourage Duke Mario, disparaging himself and offering to put Aurelio into the Duke's hands by a trick. Mario believes him and says he will do whatever the Hermit advises. All leave.

The city

The King, with the Magnifico
The King gives vent to his sorrow: Aurelio is a Prince of the Blood, like Duke Mario, and one of them will lawfully succeed him as the Kingdom has no other heir; Leonora, Mario's sister, is missing, and so many complications have arisen, for Aurelio has escaped into the countryside after seizing her from the Vestals. On the one hand he is happy that Aurelio has removed himself from the Court, for being King he could do no other than condemn him, but on the other hand he regrets that Aurelio is rampaging through the Kingdom. The Magnifico replies that this is a grave matter, and he cannot think what advice to give, for it concerns two of the foremost members of the Court and the Kingdom. The King regrets that he gave Mario so much authority to use against his enemy Aurelio, as he will not act in a just way. At which,

Bertolino
enters dressed as a peasant, with a list of complaints against the

Count Aurelio. He exaggerates the great destruction Aurelio is doing in the Kingdom. The King tells the Magnifico to heed the peasant and to ensure that justice is done, then he exits. The Magnifico listens, then says that Duke Mario has already gone into the country with an army to destroy Count Aurelio, then shows some hesitation as he recognizes Bertolino. They make various *lazzi*, and finally the Magnifico goes into the Court, and Bertolino returns to the wood in order to warn the Count.

The wood

Aurelio [with soldiers]

enters dressed as a hermit, and asks his soldiers where the rest of the troops are. They reply that all are in their assigned places in the caves and woods. He orders them to go and warn the others to be ready for his signal, and then explains the plan he had devised to separate the Duke's forces by means of a skilful stratagem, and now the Duke is left with little support. At which,

Bertolino

enters and after engaging in *lazzi* they recognize each other. At which,

Duke Mario and Buffetto

enter and Aurelio acts out a scene of disarming Duke Mario. Bertolino does the same with Buffetto. Then they reveal themselves and call out.

The Soldiers of Aurelio

all come out with weapons. Aurelio has Mario bound to the door of the Temple ready for execution and, thus bound, sends him with two soldiers to be impaled. Just as this is about to be done,

The Temple

opens revealing two kneeling statues which speak:

'Moderate your fury Count
Before the setting of the sun.'

They all flee. Mario unties himself and flees too. Aurelio wants to chase after him but cannot. He calls to his soldiers. The statues speak:

'Repent for you are not the sole lord
Whosoever lives badly, dies badly.'

The Temple closes. Aurelio exits. End of the Act.

ACT III

Aurelio, Bertolino

Aurelio complains that his army is frightened of stone statues. Bertolino reminds him that men die, and that there is a Heaven and a Hell. But Aurelio scorns this, and says he regrets the Duke escaped from him. At which,

A Soldier

enters leading

Olivetta

bound. He tells how Duke Mario's army has fled, and says that a number of soldiers have been killed or wounded. He claims that Olivetta is one of the Duke's soldiers. Olivetta explains that they should not assume she is a man and treat her accordingly. She reveals that she is a woman, and is Olivetta from the Court. Aurelio says he does not wish to treat a woman cruelly, but orders that she be taken to the grotto where his soldiers can enjoy themselves with her, after which she can be set free. Olivetta says that if the punishment is no worse than that, she will laugh at it, and will enjoy having a few soldiers herself. Bertolino performs *lazzi*, at which

A Soldier

announces that the Buffetto business has been carried out. Olivetta asks what this is. Aurelio orders it to be shown.

Buffetto impaled

The curtain opens to reveal Buffetto impaled. It then closes again. Olivetta and the soldiers depart. The Count and Bertolino remain, at which,

The Soldiers

sit at the table and eat a hearty meal of the things they most like, and toast confusion to their enemies. Signora Angela drinks merrily, with the utmost pleasure and delight. At which,

The Hermit

comes out from his cell and begs for alms. [phrase deleted in Ms.] Aurelio ridicules him laughingly, then asks him if he enjoys the good things in life, and orders a soldier to search his cell. The soldier exits. At which, enter

A Soldier and Leonora

dressed as a penitent. Aurelio asks the Hermit if this is an example of his good charity and one of the good things in life he enjoys. The Hermit replies that she is a soul from Heaven exhausted by her great penances. Leonora falls lifeless and dies. Aurelio rises from the table and threatens the Hermit. The others clear the table. Aurelio orders that Leonora be carried to the Temple. The Hermit and the others bear her away. Bertolino remains.

Aurelio

returns. The Temple opens and the Statues can be seen with swords in hand, and Leonora's body at their feet. Bertolino performs *lazzi*. Aurelio asks Bertolino to enquire what the sword-carrying Statues want, and whether they wish to fight with him. Bertolino performs *lazzi*, then asks them.

The Statues

indicate that they do. Bertolino shows fear. Aurelio asks, 'When?' A Statue replies, 'Today, Count, before sunset.' Aurelio accepts this, and all depart. *The Temple closes.*

The city

The King and the Magnifico
discuss the question of Mario and the bandits, at which
The Hermit and Cassandro
who have accompanied each other on the road, tell the Magnifico of Leonora's death and how she lies in the Temple. Cassandro tells of his daughter Angela, kidnapped by the bandits. At which,
Olivetta
who has escaped from the bandits, tells of the defeat suffered by Mario's army and about the impalement of Buffetto, and says she fears for Duke Mario. At which,
Mario
enters without hat, weapons and [phrase lost in Ms.] in the act of escaping, fearful and nearly beside himself in the belief that the Count and the bandits are in close pursuit. Finally he says that he will explain everything when he gets to the Court, and all exit.
[*The wood*]

Aurelio and Bertolino
wish to go to the Temple to fight as arranged. At which,
The Temple opens
The Statues
standing, with swords in hand, tell the Count to approach. The Count says that he wants their hand on it that they will fight like gentlemen in personal combat. One of the Statues offers its hand, holding the Count firmly, and then says:

'Repent Count before the sun sets.'

Aurelio replies that he has done nothing of which to repent. After the Statue has repeated its warning three times, it raises its voice:

'Beware, the sun is setting.'

Aurelio replies, 'And even after the sun has set, shall I not still be the Count?'

A Statue speaks:

'He is yours, Heaven!'

The Count still seeks to fight. The Statues prevent him. At which
The Heavens open
thunder and earthquake are heard, the lights dim, and a bolt of lightning falls from Heaven at the feet of Aurelio who is immediately engulfed, and the Temple closes. Bertolino flees with Angela.

The city

The King, Duke Mario, the Magnifico
at which,

The Hermit and the Priest of the Temple
tell what has befallen the Count. At which,
Cassandro
tells the King about his daughter who was kidnapped by the Count. At which,
Bertolino and Angela
tell what they saw befall Count Aurelio. Cassandro recognizes his daughter, and all exit.

Hell

Aurelio
lamenting in Hell, and in

Heaven

The Statues with Leonora
in a white gown. At which,
Pluto, Devils
At which,
A Chorus of Angels in Heaven
and
A Chorus of Devils in Hell
sing of the glory of Heaven and the pains of Hell, of rewards for the just, and punishment for the wicked.

(From F. de S. Brouwer, *Rendiconti dell'Accademia dei Lincei*, 1901, and Biblioteca Casanatense Ms 4186, Ciro Monarca, folios 19–24)

LAZZI AND LITERARY MATERIALS

A definition of lazzi, *and an example of a* lazzo *are given by Luigi Riccoboni in his* Histoire du Théâtre Italien *(1728).*

We call *lazzi* what Arlequin or the other masked players do in the course of a scene when they interrupt it with shows of fear, or crack jokes remote from the play's subject matter, for all that they constantly resort to them. Thus what Italian actors call *lazzi* are those interpolations conjured up by the actor's inspiration.

(Riccoboni, *Histoire du Théâtre Italien,* 1728, p. 65)

Riccoboni gives an example apparently drawn from the repertory of the Théâtre Italien; he points out that the scenario *was a very old one, and the 'business' too was doubtless traditional and handed down through generations of players.*

I will give an example of this art which will serve as a guide to players ignorant of it, and as instruction to spectators wishing to understand it: I will take one of the oldest plays in our theatre.

PLATE 36 *An early seventeenth century engraving by Stefano della Bella of the actor Carlo Cantù (Buffetto). Permission of the Biblioteca Burcardo, Rome*

In the Arlequin piece *Devaliseur de maisons* Arlequin and Scapin are servants to Flaminia, a poor girl separated from her parents and reduced to extreme misery. Arlequin complains to his companion about his difficult situation and the meagre rations he has been confined to for so long. Scapin commiserates with him and says that he will sort it all out, telling him to create a hubbub in front of the house. *Flaminia*, drawn by Arlequin's cries, demands to know the cause, and Scapin explains why they have quarrelled, while all the time Arlequin cries and declares he will leave her. *Flaminia* begs him not to go, calling on Scapin for help. He comes up with a reasonable proposal designed to relieve her from the misery afflicting her. While Scapin is explaining his plan to *Flaminia*, Arlequin interrupts the scene with various *Lazzi*: sometimes he pretends to have cherries in his hat and mimes eating them and throwing the stones in Scapin's face, at other times, after supposedly catching a fly, he comically pulls off its wings and eats it, and so on. Such are the theatrical games called *Lazzi*. These *Lazzi* constantly interrupt Scapin's conversation, but at the same time give him the chance to respond vigorously. These *Lazzi* are inessential to the scene in the sense that if Arlequin did not perform them the action would carry on unaffected; nonetheless I insist that however inessential they are, they do not detract from the purpose of the scene, because even as these antics break up the action, so too they bind it together, and indeed are the very essence of the scene.

These inessentials, which are added to what they break up and bind together, were rightly called by our predecessors *Lazzi*, with two *z's*, because the word *Lazzi* in the Lombard language in the fine Tuscan language means *Lacci*, and this in French means *Liens*. This word was used in order to make it clear that although the action was broken up by these *Lazzi*, they must also bind it together, and in a way so skilful that the spectator is unaware of the interruption.

(Riccoboni, pp. 67–9)

Some examples of lazzi

Examples of lazzi *occur in many of the* scenarii, *although for the most part they are more noted* en passant *than described in any detail. One of the richest collections is that made by Padre Adriani di Lucca in the early eighteenth century, although the examples gathered date from much earlier, being the kinds of material which circulated widely and were handed down from player to player over many generations. There is a useful English account and collection of* lazzi *in M. Gordon,* Lazzi: the comic routines of the Commedia dell'Arte, *New York, 1983.*

The lazzo *of fresh urine* The *lazzo* of fresh urine is when Pulcinella says that all urine is warm. The maidservant quibbles on the word *fresca* [meaning both 'cool' and 'fresh'] and says it is fresh only when it is made there and then, and she shows him.

The lazzo *of laughing and crying* The *lazzo* of laughing and crying is when one deceives the other, as when an old man cries at the departure of his son, and laughs because he is free to enjoy his son's beloved without fear of the son's jealousy. The same can be applied to the son.

The lazzo *of politeness* The *lazzo* of politeness is when Pulcinella asks his wife whether any man has paid compliments to her, and she answers that she returns a man's greeting politely, and then follows this up by opening the door, asking him in, and inviting him to sit down. Pulcinella says that thanks to this sort of politeness he is made a cuckold. The same can be said of any other character.

The lazzo *of fruit and kisses* The *lazzo* of fruit and kisses is when Coviello imitates the voice of a woman Pulcinella loves. Pulcinella asks for the fruits of love and Coviello, who is behind him, beats him instead. Pulcinella says these are not the fruits of love, kisses are, and Coviello, from behind, beats him again.

Lazzi *of confusions* *Lazzi* of confusions occur when Coviello teaches Pulcinella to speak in a loving way, and then concealed behind him, whispers a lot of nonsense that Pulcinella repeats. Coviello, from behind, makes as if to strangle Pulcinella, who does the same to the woman.

Lazzi *of sewing and tying* The *lazzo* of sewing is when Coviello is talking with Pulcinella, and Pulcinella begins to move away. Coviello calls him back and tells him to keep sewn up close to him. Pulcinella takes a needle and thread in order to sew himself to Coviello. Coviello asks what he is doing; he replies that he is sewing himself close to him. Coviello says, 'Attach yourself to me!' Pulcinella produces a rope in order to tie himself to Coviello. Coviello asks him what he is doing, and tells him to take care of his every word. While Coviello is speaking Pulcinella seizes the words from his mouth and puts them into his cap. Then Coviello asks him if he has taken care of his words. Pulcinella opens up his cap and finds nothing there.

The lazzo *of Pulcinella's goodness* The *lazzo* of Pulcinella's goodness is when, on hearing from the Capitano or others that they intend to kill him, and not being recognized, Pulcinella praises himself saying, 'Pulcinella is a lively chap, simple and good.'

The lazzo *of the fly* The *lazzo* of the fly is when Pulcinella, having been left in charge of his master's house, and being asked by his master whether anyone is in the house, replies 'Not a fly!' The master then finds people there and reproaches Pulcinella, who replies, 'You found men here, not flies.'

The lazzo *of the pulse, the urine and the prescription* The *lazzo* of the pulse and urine is when Pulcinella touches the patient's foot and says 'It is a headache!' He then has urine brought to him, drinks it and spits it out. So that he can write out a prescription he makes Coviello go down on all fours with his backside to the audience. He then asks Coviello to stretch his hand back, makes him hold an ink-pot and then, after dipping his nib in the ink, writes on Coviello's backside, 'Galen, I thank you, *ego medicus*.'

The lazzo *of the shoe* The *lazzo* of the shoe is when Pulcinella is taken to prison. He says he wants to tie his shoe-lace, and bending down grabs the two officers by the ankles, pulls them over, and runs away.

The lazzo *of 'o'* The *lazzo* of 'o' is when Coviello asks Pulcinella the name of his beloved. Pulcinella says it begins with an 'o', and invites him to guess it. Coviello tried 'Orsola, Olympia, Oriana', then Pulcinella says she is called Rosetta. Coviello complains that that begins with an 'R' and not with an 'O'. Pulcinella replies 'I like to start with an 'O', any objections?'

The lazzo *of the pigeons* The *lazzo* of the pigeons is when Pulcinella tells his master that he went to the pigeon coop, opened it up and told the pigeons to fly to their master. If they have not done so, that's their fault not his.

The lazzo *of the pig* The *lazzo* of the pig. Pulcinella says that in order not to pay toll duty he hid the pig inside the carriage, and when he reached the toll gate the customs officers asked him who he was carrying in the carriage. He replied, 'that pig of my master', and so they let him pass. But when they heard the pig grunt 'Ru, ru', the officers confiscated the pig, so it was all the pig's fault because he had not kept quiet.

The lazzo *of the beggar* The *lazzo* of the beggar is when one begs from another, first with the right hand, then with the left, and repeats it many times, or pretends to be Spanish, then German, then French.

The lazzo *of the school of humanity* Pulcinella says that his wife or sister runs a school of humanity from his house; what he means, is that she is a prostitute.

The lazzo *of a dialogue with a third person* The *lazzo* of a dialogue with a third person is when the *Innamorati* are angry with each other, and call on Pulcinella to act as go-between. The *Innamorato* says to him, 'go tell her she is unjust.' Pulcinella goes to the woman and says, 'According to him you've got no bust.' She replies, 'Oh tell him there was never such a wickedly cold brute,' at which Pulcinella returns to the man and says, 'She thinks without your wig you are as bald as a coot.' The *Innamorato* says to Pulcinella, 'tell her she is cruel and barbarous to her slave.' Pulcinella returns to the woman and says, 'He thinks you should go to your barber and get a shave.' Then the woman cries to Pulcinella, 'How disloyal he is, and how cruelly he mocks!' Pulcinella goes across to the man and tells him, 'She says you've got boils and maybe the pox.' The man replies, 'She can be cruel and contrary, yet she has no peer!', and Pulcinella returns to the woman and says, 'You've been keeping it hairy for more than a year.'

(From the Placido Adriani collection, Biblioteca Comunale, Perugia, A. 20, f.141–352)

SOME EXAMPLES OF VERBAL MATERIALS

The improvised commedia dell'arte*, as we have said, was not just a visual, but very much an aural theatre. Verbal virtuosity was much admired in the period of the improvised drama's heyday, and players were as much celebrated for their skill at using language, within the parameters of their role specializations and the needs of the particular* scenario *part they were playing, as for their acrobatic and musical skills. Below is a brief selection of materials, from Perrucci, but probably characteristic of performed reprimands, tirades, 'flytings', lovers' exchanges and* bravure.[13] *Inevitably much of the verbal quality of these is lost in translation, and they can do no more than suggest something of the delight in wit, word games and verbal and vocal dexterity that characterised* commedia dell'arte *performance, and constituted much of its audience appeal, at least in Italy.*

Il Magnifico reprimands his son

What do you hope to achieve, my son, by leading such a licentious life? Can't you see that my house is going to the dogs? You've abandoned your studies and waste your time in the company of these drifters, whoring with these hot-heads all day long, and hanging round the *Ridotto*. Don't you realize that even the treasures of Croesus, Crassus and Midas would be used up, let alone the few bits and pieces we have in our house?

Because of you my coffers have become coffins; you have gutted my caskets; you have turned the table silver into quick-silver and it's gone up in smoke; like magic the tapestries have vanished; my pictures have disappeared into thin air; I am reduced to sleeping on wooden boards, and through all the rooms one can twirl a sword in both hands. Don't you realize these bulls, in order to get money from your purse, are like so many leeches which will attach themselves to you as long as they can suck the blood from your veins, these whores are like cesspits, after you have done what you have to do they stink. Gambling is like the wolf: the more it devours the more it wants to eat. Vices are companions which will make you reach like Hercules no further than the pillars of Marco and Todaro.

Come to your senses my son, and remember that the road you have taken will lead to the Orphan's Canal, for should I die, then left without possessions and virtue you will be an awful beast, baited by everyone, mocked by children, avoided by friends, abhorred by relatives, abandoned by the very same people who now court you. So turn away, my son, from bad companions who, more than those with the plague, contaminate you with their disease; and from women who, worse than basilisks, poison you with their eyes; and from gambling which, worse than fire, destroys houses. Get back to your studies, return to your home like a man, and thus you will become the support of my old age, the protector of the family, and the pillar of the House of Bisognosi.

(From Perrucci, *Dell'arte rappresentativa*, 1699, Regola VI, pp. 249–50)

A Servetta's address

Jove was not so pleasing and graceful when he changed his shape
For love of a cow, and translated himself into an ox;
Nor did Bacchus show himself so beautiful
When he transformed himself into a billy-goat;
Nor did Neptune neigh so well for his nymph when,
Hungry with love, he transformed himself into a horse;
Nor did the god of weapons run so beautifully
With foam at his mouth,
As when, to send Adonis to the Orco,
He changed himself into a pig;
Nor was Lucius Apuleius more beautiful to the pretty Lucida
When, as a token of love,
He became a donkey,
As you are handsome,
You thief of my affections,
You by whom my entire soul is moved,
You are Lucius, Mars, Neptune, Bacchus and Jove,
Amiable, beautiful, gentle, agreeable and precious,
Ox, goat, horse, pig and donkey.

(From Perrucci, *Dell'arte rappresentativa*, 1699, Regola IX, pp. 303–4)

A Servetta on old men

Old men are like trees when they produce no more fruit they're cut out for the fire.

Whoever in old age tries to fire on the fortress of love is like the ancient cannon of leather, having shot off the first and second balls, shrinks and withers, or bursts.

Old men are like plants, having wilted from age there's no chance they'll straighten up again.

Such old men, weighed down by the gross burden of marriage, are just like camels, unable to raise themselves from the ground.

Deer and old men are alike, for in old age both have a head so heavy with horns they can no longer lift it.

The love of an old man is like quicksilver, it can be congealed and fixed, but it can't resist hammer blows.

What happens with lions happens with old men – when in the grip of an amorous fever they can't get their tails up.

(From Perrucci, *Dell'arte rappresentativa*, 1699, Regola IX, p. 305)

Dialogue: the woman begs, the man is indifferent

Woman: Don't flee, my idol!
Man: What do you expect, you Fury?
Woman: I want to set you afire.
Man: With what?
Woman: With Cupid's flame.
Man: You can dowse that in Lethe.
Woman: Not so, for that's in the other world.
Man: I too am beyond your fire.
Woman: My flames aspire to reach you.
Man: Drive them away and they'll abate.
Woman: The opposite; when driven away the greater they become.
Man: Without fuel they'll fade.
Woman: Your looks supply that.
Man: My coldness will kill them.
Woman: Mine is a spiritual fire.
Man: Therefore it cannot torment you.
Woman: It burns me, but is not consumed.
Man: It must be an ideal fire.
Woman: Why then does it torment me?
Man: Who not flee from it?
Woman: Because I have the soul of a moth.
Man: Then assume the heart of a lion.
Woman: I am too blind to face it.
Man: Open your eyes and look on it.
Woman: It is too beautiful for me to look on.
Man: It will be cruel if you touch it.
Woman: And yet it delights me.
Man: Torment delights you?
Woman: Yes, it is dear to me.
Man: And is that a fire from Heaven?
Woman: No, it's from Hell.
Man: And you wish me to love you?
Woman: Yes.
Man: When the fire is from Hell?
Woman: You can make it Heavenly.
Man: Fire always gives pain.
Woman: Not the fire that beatifies.
Man: Is it not a fire from the abyss?
Woman: When not reciprocated.

Man: I don't believe it.
Woman: Try it, and you will find it's so.
Man: Fire given by woman is always infernal.
Woman: No, for it's not just mine; infernal fire is on your lips, in my breast, in your eyes, and in my heart.

(From Perrucci, *Dell'arte rappresentativa*, 1699, Regola IV, pp. 230–1)

A laconic dialogue improvised on a detail – about the fall of a handkerchief; man begs, woman rejects

Man: Oh, how lucky I am!
Woman: Oh, how unhappy I am!
Man: Here is the one I adore.
Woman: Here is the one I loathe.
Man: I shall approach and address her.
Woman: I shall flee to avoid meeting him. *(A handkerchief falls from her hand)*
Man: Stop, my dearest.
Woman: What do you want?
Man: That you listen to me.
Woman: I have no time, farewell.
Man: At least see . . .
Woman: What?
Man: That love had pity on me.
Woman: How?
Man: By making you drop your handkerchief.
Woman: Give it to me.
Man: I cannot.
Woman: What do you want it for?
Man: To dress my wounds.
Woman: What use, if there's no liniment?
Man: I shall hope for that from your pity
Woman: I'm no doctor for your ills.
Man: Yet you promised me peace.
Woman: I? . . . peace? You deceive yourself.
Man: The whiteness of this handkerchief suggests it.
Woman: But don't you see, that fell by accident.
Man: I know how to pick it up.
Woman: Will you trust yourself to a piece of cloth?
Man: As a sail to my fortune.
Woman: A wind can tear that.
Man: It will serve as a flag.
Woman: But to call you to war.
Man: How, if it's white?
Woman: It's the flag of enlistment that will take you away.
Man: Not unless I'm allied to you.
Woman: The alliance is too frail.
Man: But pure.

Woman: A sign you'll be left alone.
Man: It will serve as a sash for my Cupid.
Woman: It will serve as a veil for your shame.
Man: You are cruel!
Woman: You are obstinate!
Man: Lighter than this fragment of cloth.
Woman: Harder than iron.
Man: Destiny gave me this handkerchief.
Woman: Chance gave it to you.
Man: To dry my tears.
Woman: To cool your ardour.
Man: It will serve as a canvas . . .
Woman: It will serve as a paper.
Man: To paint your cruelty on.
Woman: To write your importunity on.
Man: I shall keep it.
Woman: You can burn it.
Man: For by its whiteness . . .
Woman: For among its arches.
Man: In my heart.
Woman: In your breast . . .
Man: Fidelity will live eternally . . .
Woman: Your love will perish.

(From Perrucci, *Dell'arte rappresentativa*, 1699, Regola IV, pp. 228–30)

Two soliloquies of a Lover

Thoughts, where are you tending? Heart, where are you flying? Soul, where are you fleeing? Yes, my thoughts, knowing you can no longer stay hidden, you wish to reveal the innermost secrets to my beloved; yes, my heart, unable to bear any longer the wound given by the piercing arrow of a glance, you beg for a cure; yes, my soul, desperately enduring a solitude you have never known before, you wish at least that she who has enchained you knows of the chains that she may take pity on you.

But stop, oh thoughts! hold firm, oh heart! stay, oh my soul! What will you do, oh thoughts, if she disdains you? How will you respond, heart, if by rejecting you she doubles the pain of the wound? Where will you turn, unhappy soul, if she laughs at your chains?

Return to me, thoughts, heart and soul. And yet, no! Fly to that beauty of which you are enamour'd. Disclose the secrets, show the wounds, display the chains – perhaps you will find pity, balm and courtesy. Thus love tells me:

> That in amorous calm in that beautiful breast,
> Thoughts, heart and soul will find joyful rest.

My heart, are you made of flesh? My breast, can you feel? My thoughts, can you speak? My soul, can you reason? If you are made of flesh, my heart, then why not extinguish a fire that seems to burn in vain? If you can feel, my breast, then why not tear out those arrows, which give you incurable wounds, soothed by no balm save that of disdain? If you can speak, my thoughts, then why not abhor she who abhores you? And if you can reason, my soul, why not use your freedom to flee this tyranny? Alas, my heart is made of flesh that it may burn – a willing sacrifice to a cruel idol; my breast feels only to adore its wounds; my thoughts debate only the impossibility of escaping an adorable chain; and my soul has lost its freedom, captivated by too beautiful an object.

If, then, you cannot escape the pain afflicting you, the fire consuming you, the arrow piercing you, the chains holding you captive and the tyranny ruling you,

By so much ardour in silence be oppressed
Oh soul, oh thoughts, oh heart, oh breast!

(From Perrucci, *Dell'arte rappresentativa*, Regola II, pp. 202–4)

A bravura of Capitano Spavento: on changing roles with Death

Capitano Spavento and Trappola

Capitano: Being tired and fed up with so much killing and the shedding of human blood, one morning Death came to have lunch with me. After eating a most delicate broth, made of the finest ingredients, and after drinking human blood in place of wine, Death begged me to take over her job for a month.

Trappola: If Death, that indefatigable Goddess, gets tired, then even more does a poor peasant who tills the ground from morning to night, and if she needs to rest from the heavy labours endured in her work, and has to hand over her weapons to someone else, so poor peasants need respite from their work sometimes, and should have their masters toil and hoe in their place.

Capitano: I could not but agree to so just a demand and reasonable favour asked of me by Death, one of my dearest friends. But as such a task could not be carried out without assuming the appearance and features of Death, what did I do? I took hold of Death and skinned her with my own hands, and then I put on her skin.

Trappola: What a superb transformation! What a superb metamorphosis! What a superb masquerade!

Capitano: After I had skinned Death and donned her skin, I took her lethal sickle in my hand, and she, after putting on my clothes, hung my sword about her waist. Then she set off through many lands and was mistaken by everyone for Capitano Spavento, consumed and wasted away by an attack of the French disease.

Trappola: Oh, poor Death! What if she had encountered your enemies? She would probably have got a blast of gunshot, and been blown to miserable bits!

Capitano: Meanwhile, I myself entered onto the great stage of the world, and after taking a look around, gave such a great swipe with my sickle, and in such fury, that I slaughtered a third of the men in the world. If Death had not rushed to stay my arm, with a second blow I would have wiped out all human kind.

Trappola: Bloody shit, master! If Death had not stayed your arm, you'd have swept away the world in a flash, without even covering it with water and dust either!

Capitano: Then Death, aware of the huge destruction I would have caused with her sickle in my hand, took it back from me, along with her skin and weapons, and I too took back my sword and my clothes, and in a friendly way we took leave of each other.

(Andreini, *Le Bravure del Capitano Spavento*, 1607, Dialogue Twenty Two.)

7

Improvisation and Performance

The Evolution of Improvisation

EARLY REFERENCES to professional players are rather cursory (see above p. 52), but indicate that by the 1560s improvised playing was well established, and was defined more by that particular technique than by the fact that some of the lead players wore masks. Flaminio Scala was early credited with bringing the form of the improvised *commedia dell'arte* to perfection by refining subject-matter and accommodating entertainer skills to the needs of a coherent dramatic action (see the account of Scala below, p. 225). But it is doubtful that any single player was responsible for bringing about those changes which signal the emergence of technically accomplished professional troupes regularly acting sophisticated repertories of plays. The contributions of the Andreini, and possibly of Cecchini, seem to have been equally important. Scala acquired something of his later reputation on the strength of the *scenario* collection he published, and the same repute attached to Francesco Andreini's published 'literary' versions of his stage materials, which again were later widely influential. Significant too was the work of other writer-practitioners like Silvio Fiorillo and Domenico Bruni. These writings signal a conscious attempt by players in the first decade or so of the *seicento* to assert the cultural respectability of the profession.

But however changes were initiated, and whoever were the prime movers, improvised performance as a *modus operandi* for the professional companies almost certainly pre-dated them. Improvisation may initially have been prompted by the professional need to wed within companies the entertainer virtuosity of mimes, singers, acrobats, dancers and other solo performers, and to harmonize their materials and strategies in a manner appropriate to the performance not of short sketches, but of full-length plays. Fully-fledged improvised performance of plays may early have developed out of comic encounters between Il Magnifico and Zanni, as Appollonio has suggested.[1] But this is not the only possibility, persuasive as it may seem to be. Few of the early *scenarii* suggest such beginnings from a nuclear situation, nor do they foreground encounters between Il Magnifico and Zanni in such a way as to suggest any gradual development from the simple to the complex.[2] On the contrary it may be that the trestle-stage master and servant sketches, archetypal comic situations in themselves, were not nuclear, but were simply absorbed, along with other kinds of popular entertainment, into an emerging, more structured, pattern of full-length improvised plays, which were modelled on, and to some extent were at times a vulgarization of, the Renaissance academic scripted drama, which itself had taken over, and made more familiar, materials from the classical tradition. Performance of a play *all'improvviso* was a process of collaborative 'making', the success of which was rooted in virtuoso skills and the players' familiarity with each other in the performance situation. That process of collaborative 'making' may have governed the devising of plays *ab initio*: even as they created the masks and roles, according to their particular personalities and performer skills, so too the actors devised the dramatic narratives in which the masks and roles achieved stage life. More than anything else it was perhaps the introduction of actresses some time in the 1560s that helped both to occasion, and to give impetus to, the formal organization and elaboration of performed materials into sustained and coherent dramatic narratives.

The Techniques

Although improvisation was early recognized abroad to be a distinctive characteristic of performance *all'Italiana*, exactly in what it consisted remains elusive, from the accounts of early commentators, whether Troiano's description of the amateur performance at the Bavarian court in 1568, or those of P. M. Cecchini and Andrea Perrucci in the seventeenth century, lack the kinds of precision we could wish. Exactly how much was prepared or 'composed' beforehand? In what ways were performances put together? Did the players prepare in small groups – Zanni and Il Magnifico, the pairs of *innamorati*, Zanni and Capitano – then bring prepared sections together? If so, when were sections brought together, at preparation or performance stage? How did improvisation actually function in performance? Few of these questions can be answered with great confidence. Cecchini tends primarily to emphasize timing and co-ordination. Perrucci's account is more wide-ranging, but in those sections of his *Dell'arte rappresentativa premeditata ed all'improvvisso* (1699) which treat of improvisation it is obvious that he addresses *dilettanti*, and was writing what was in effect a manual for novices; professional practice may have been different in some respects.[3]

Perhaps the one thing we can say with confidence about improvisation is that it was not entirely spontaneous; it was not devised wholly impromptu and off-the-cuff while the players were actually on a stage in performance. Spontaneity was of course a feature of improvised playing, and Perrucci, Riccoboni, Gozzi and others all remark on this as a strength that distinguished it from premeditated acting: but what they seem to suggest is that improvised acting gave the *impression* in performance of being more spontaneous than premeditated acting. The actors did not, then, simply spawn new plot-lines, dialogue and *lazzi* as they went along. Successful improvised performance, when done not as an amateur *jeu d'esprit* like that of Troiano and his colleagues, but as a professional activity for a paying audience, was the outcome of long deliberation by, and close collaboration between, members of a troupe accustomed to playing together, and familiar with each other's stage *personae*. Disciplined performance did not exclude the introduction of unpremeditated verbal arabesques and the elaboration of 'business' on the spur of the moment; it was indeed spontaneous to the extent that it permitted a certain free play in performance for the expression of the performer's character, temperament, particular specialist skills, and personal performance ways with assimilated materials. But it was rooted in careful preparation.

Cecchini and Perrucci discuss both premeditated and improvised drama and, like the *settecento* commentators, Riccoboni, Goldoni and Gozzi, make a clear distinction between the two. The distinction seems to be not just between two different kinds of acting, but rather between two very different techniques of 'composing' plays. Improvisation entailed not simply the performers' freedom to explore stage space, and to exploit their physical performance means, although as Scala indicates in the prologue to *Il finto marito* (see below, p. 197) movement and gesture lie at the root of drama. But improvisation was conspicuously concerned too with the verbal; indeed both Andreini and Scala in their different ways tend to suggest that improvising players were as much masters of words as of physical means. The iconographic tradition has tended to foreground in our awareness of the *commedia dell'arte* the physical antics of the masked players, and more particularly of the *zanni*. But improvisation equally displayed a delight, enjoyed by performer and spectator alike, in verbal virtuosity. Quite striking in fact is the number of late seventeenth- and early eighteenth-century reports of *commedia dell'arte* performances which refer to *hearing* rather than *seeing* improvised plays. Equally striking is the number of eighteenth-century complaints about the extent to which stage dialogue had become facile, monotonous and repetitious – so much so that many of Carlo Gozzi's contemporaries thought that performances by then were basically premeditated, the same stock sentiments, attitudes and jokes being regurgitated from play to play.[4]

The strength of improvised playing lay in the ability of the players to exploit the uniqueness of each particular performance. The absence of a fixed authorial text left performance 'open' to group composition: to an accumulation of suggestions from stage-managers and players within the predetermined narrative line. But those suggestions drew on traditional materials and 'business', and in the hands of inept, 'coasting' or hidebound performers could easily become repetitious. A tendency on the part of too many players to settle too frequently for the stock dialogue of familiar stage situations may in part account for the ossification of improvised playing remarked by the eighteenth-century commentators.

According to Cecchini and Barbieri, premeditated material was prepared for insertion by the players at appropriate moments in the acting out of a scene. We can take this to reflect amateur as well as professional practice, for Perrucci advised much the same thing. The skill of the performer resided in his or her ability to exploit interpolated material both as an appealing set-piece and as an integral part of the stage dialogue. Cecchini and Perrucci were at one, too, in stressing the need for fluid congruity between the improvised and premeditated elements of what was delivered, and both emphasized the importance of maintaining verbal and imagistic decorum in discourse between improvised speech and the borrowed material interpolated. What they looked for, then, in the intermeshing of improvised and premeditated elements, was such a fine harmony and decorum in thought and expression between the player's own words and what had been appropriated as to give auditors the impression of a seamless web of discourse seemingly wholly of the speaker's invention. The player's verbal inspiration lay precisely in this ability to cover the tracks of borrowing by making what was appropriated apparently his or her own. The ability to do so derived from a combination of quick-wittedness, innate talent for verbal expression, sensitivity to the levels of language most appropriate to particular types of discourse, and familiarity with the performance styles and the vocal and verbal characteristics of fellow performers, more particularly those with whom the player was most frequently joined in the network of scenic units which characterized the structure of the improvised plays.[5]

Performances may have been prepared on the basis of these scenic units, players composing and rehearsing together individual sequences, which were then knitted together to make up the whole. For just as the individual player's dialogue was 'composed' by intermeshing the improvised and the premeditated, and as particular sequences were devised by interweaving the contributions of individual players into a coherent scenic unit, so the *fabula* that was the entire performed play was collectively 'composed' by a process of accumulating and interconnecting the scenic units within a carefully orchestrated whole.[6] Like a molecular chain, the units of the action formed a lattice, the delight of which for spectators lay in the quasi-autonomous theatricality of the units and their overall patterning. Hence the emphasis placed by Cecchini and Perrucci (although more particularly by the latter) on the proper bonding of units, and the dangers of straying, in the course of 'composing' a unit, so far from the through-line of the plot that both players and spectators lost the thread of continuity (see below, pp. 200–4). Improvisation was, then, a technique for 'composing' plays. The composers could be amateur or professional. From the latter however greater ensemble expertise would have been expected. Effective ensemble work by professionals was a consequence of regular and full-time practice, and a necessity if a company was to compete successfully in the theatre market.

Performance

In an important respect of course, what the above indicates is that *commedia dell'arte* players did not so much dispense with the writer, as take advantage of the absence of copyright controls to pillage and make their own appropriate literary work from a wide variety of genres. Material was taken according to the needs of each player, and used according to the requirements of individual *scenarii* as these were developed for performance by particular troupes. There is a sense too in which this practice can be seen as a variation on the working methods of actors who memorized and delivered parts in scripted plays. The Italian *dilettanti*, as is quite clear from Leone de' Sommi's account above (see p. 41), like the English Elizabethan actors, did not work with full scripts of a play they were preparing, but only with their parts, or 'sides', written out separately and topped with cue lines. In effect, what the improvising players did was to prepare their own 'sides' by plundering printed and inherited materials for what they needed. Sometimes this was done directly from texts, sometimes by recourse to the *zibaldoni*, in which utilizable passages had been gathered, but more frequently among the more skilled and experienced players by drawing on a stock of memorized material, either of their own composition or which over the years they had become so familiar with, and had so accommodated, by modification and elaboration, to their individual temperaments and kinds of performance expertise, that they had made it altogether their own.

As will be clear from what has been said above, the effective composition of plays by improvisation depended not just on individual performer skills, but on ensemble playing. Hence the great importance of the balance of players within a company, and the prominence in so many of the pieces they performed of units of action involving either just a single player, or groups of two or three players. Solo turns and opportunities for soliloquy and single actor address abound, as do set pieces for two or three players in many of which a single figure may dominate the verbal discourse – the monologues of a Dottore or the *bravure* of a Capitano are obvious instances. This was, we have emphasized, a decidedly verbal and rhetorical theatre. Soliloquies in particular frequently punctuate the units of action, and are invariably cast in the form of direct comment to the audience, underscoring the extent to which so much improvised performance capitalized on close player–spectator contact. Many tend to be set-pieces expressive of basic responses: the diatribe of the slighted woman; the speech of perplexity, bewilderment or disgust; the plaintive lament of the lover spurned or ignored by his or her beloved; the familiar chat of the comic servant who marvels at the cunning and shrewishness of women, or despairingly curses and denounces his master. Speeches could cover a wide range, from those merely overheard by the audience, to those delivered directly to it in the most colloquial and informal way. What was done on stage complemented what was said through appropriately patterned movement, gesture and 'business', including *lazzi*, which were verbal as well as physical.

The apparent organization of plays on the basis of units of action, which seems to be reflected in the way many of the *scenarii* were structured to bring small groups of players together on stage in short scenes, was not just a preparational convenience. It was probably a necessity if plays were to be 'composed' in the improvisatory manner and for purposes of rapid and flexible production to meet market needs. The conjunction of characters was, too, visually and verbally theatrical in so far as it pointed the strong contrasts between them in appearance, language and gestures: between Pantalone and Zanni; Capitano, Zanni and an *innamorata*; Dottore, the *servetta*, a young lover, and so on.[7] The advantage for performers of working in such clusters of contrasting figures was that they gave each player a great deal of 'space' to operate in within the ensemble unit. The sharp contrasts and the rapid turnover of scenic units required the establishment of 'character' by graphic strokes rather than through the accumulation of psychological detail.

PLATE 37 *Watercolour illustration to the* scenario L'arme mutate *showing stage business. Corsini MS. Permission of the Accademia dei Lincei, Rome*

Scenarii were probably prepared for performance under the direction of a stage-manager, called a *corago* or *concertatore*. This was common academy and court practice, as we know from the activities of Leone de' Sommi and Angelo Ingegneri (see above, pp. 40ff.), and seems to have been taken over by the professional companies quite early on. In all probability a stage-manager was needed to help street and *piazza* entertainers make the transition to acting proper, and to ensure the effective blending of their skills to those of performers drawn to the profession from the courts.[8] In the professional companies this function was sometimes but not necessarily undertaken by a lead player or troupe leader (*capocomico*): Scala may well have performed the task in the companies he was attached to. Unfortunately concrete evidence about the activities of *coraghi* is wanting for the early period, and while it may well be that lead players and *capocomici* acted as *coraghi*, most of our knowledge about what they did comes from Perrucci. Like his remarks on improvisation, what Perrucci has to say about the *corago* is manifestly advice to amateurs, but he had first-hand contact with professionals, and was concerned to encourage *dilettanti* to adopt a disciplined approach to play-making by taking the best of professional practice as a model. Perrucci's account may, then, spell out, even if rather ingenuously, what was common professional practice.

The duties of a *corago* seem to have included reading a new scenario to the assembled players, distributing parts which were less than obviously assignable, pointing aspects of character and kinds of dialogue appropriate to particular scenes, indicating key emphases in the plot lines, arranging the location of the action and the use of space, streets and houses, identifying exits and entrances, settling on relevant props and stage accoutrements, and suggesting possible ways of 'blocking' a scene and orchestrating stage 'business' and *lazzi*. His or her function seems to have been decidedly more than just that of an explicator and adviser. The *corago* was perhaps the closest an improvising company came to having a resident troupe dramatist, for it was the business of the *corago* to give structure and coherence to a play that was 'composed' by the players through the accumulation and intermeshing of various units of action, all of which had to be co-ordinated with dramaturgical precision and theatrical flair.

The standard structure of a performance in a *stanza* or hall may well have been that indicated by Garzoni in his satirical account of strollers (see above, p. 69). The programme probably began with some kind of musical introduction (how elaborate it was no doubt depended on the performance place, the audience, and the abilities of the players); this was followed by a formal prologue, containing the customary compliments to the audience and basic information about the locale and action of the *fabula*; then came the play itself, with interludes (again of variable nature and elaboration depending on troupe, occasion and venue); finally, if the troupe was playing in the *stanza* for some time, the announcement of the next day's offering. No matter what the dramatic genre – comedy, tragicomedy, or quasi-operatic pieces – performances were quite certainly lively and colourful. Music and dance were invariable and prominent features; costuming was marked by contrasting primary colours; variety was given to the stage world by the appearance of minor figures like servants, soldiers, innkeepers, tradesmen, messengers, old women, slaves and courtesans. Use of animals, birds and natural decoration was not unknown. Diversity too was given by exotic settings, whether established simply through the dialogue, or visually by scenic means like pastoral, rustic, military or Oriental costumes and effects.

The variety of the extant *scenarii* we have already stressed. In nearly all, however, there is the core base of two *vecchi*, two *zanni*, two sets of lovers and a *servetta*, the patterning in role composition complementing the patterning of the plots. That schematic balancing of roles is obvious enough in the standard comic pieces set in Renaissance Italy. But it allowed, too, for great flexibility in accommodating performer skills to the needs of many very different *scenarii*, as can be seen by a glance at the role disposition in *Il vecchio geloso* (*The Jealous Old Man*) and *L'ateista fulminato* (*The Atheist Damned*) (above pp. 158 and 164), or in one of the more picaresque of the comic pieces found in Scala, like *Isabella astrologa* (*Isabella Astrologer*). Costume changes on and off stage were frequent, and recourse to disguise is a feature of many *scenarii*. Disguise served many purposes: lovers took to it to abscond or pursue each other; *zanni* adopted it to advance their schemes; Captains found it a useful device by which to evade enemies or deceive women, as too did the *vecchi*; quite frequently principal characters assumed the guise of ghosts or spirits. Madness at times was a form of disguise. Flavio in *Il finto negromante* (*The Fake Magician*) pretends to be mad in order to deceive the *vecchi*. Conventions permitted a change of character by change of clothing, and disguise needed very little justification: donning a dress over, or in place of another, or switching a hat and cape, made a character unrecognizable even to members of his or her own family. An extension of this convention was the assumption that some characters were able to see through disguise immediately, while others remained blind to the deception. Disguise functioned like invisibility, enabling characters to hear things about or relevant to themselves. It often operated, too, as comic relief, punctuating the emotionally inflated tensions of lovers' scenes or the more disturbing implications of the plot imbroglios. Cross-dressing in the *scenarii* is so frequent as to suggest that the improvised drama exploited the complexities and social implications of gender difference as much as did the scripted drama, but in the absence of textual dialogue it is difficult to explore this dimension in detail, and it is hard, too, not to conclude that such switches were frequently no more than expedients of plot, without marked referential significance. The half-masks used by some of the players were of course not a form of disguise, but they served, too, along with the stylized verbal and physical delivery, and the non-naturalistic, generalized and impressionistic decor, to distance, and thus to underscore, the theatrical dimension of the stage world.[9]

The Quality of the Improvised Drama

The reputation of the English Elizabethan and Jacobean theatre survives in part in the extant play texts; about Elizabethan acting and staging we know very little and ultimately must speculate about its quality, on how the texts were translated to the stages and delivered on them, and as to the kinds of emphases given in performance to the interpretation of popular stage characters like, for example, Tamburlaine and Shylock. As we have no such texts, and no early detailed analytical descriptions of the Italian players' impromptu performances it is even more difficult to define the spirit and quality of the improvised drama. It is clear from the mingling of masked and unmasked figures that it was distinctly stylized; yet it was rooted in, and in many respects reflected, the life and concerns of its time. This was particularly the case with the comedy, but was almost equally so, too, with the other improvised kinds like the tragedies, pastorals, *opere reali* and *opere eroiche*.[10] Improvised pieces of all genres were distinctly of the baroque, as much in their histrionic, emotional exaggerations as in the grotesquerie of their physical 'business'. Characteristically baroque too are the extravagantly convoluted plot-lines of comic and 'serious' forms alike, and much of the literary material employed by some of the players in the comic pieces was as inflated and artificial as anything in the scripted tragedy of the time, or in the work of Mannerist poets like Giambattista Marino (1569–1625).

In this there is nothing surprising: players levied heavily on contemporary scripted drama and other literary forms, both Italian and foreign, and followed, or led, verbal and stylistic fashions. The serious improvised plays seem to have had only a brief and intermittent vogue, and primarily perhaps in the elite venues where their subject-matter most appealed, and their staging demands could best be met. By the mid seventeenth-century they seem to have been eclipsed by the comic and tragi-comic modes, in both of which a delicate balance was maintained between the natural and the artificial. The advent of Neapolitan players at the end of the *cinquecento* may have strengthened the musical and imaginatively fantastic dimensions of performance, redressing the earlier more moralistic emphases of the northern Italian companies.[11] The individualism of the age delighted in *virtuosi* performances, and these new dimensions may have encouraged increased performer exhibitionism, which by mid-century was aggravated by the players' need to compete with the appeal of opera singers.

Yet for all that the improvised drama was patterned and stylized, and drew attention to its own theatricality, it was, too, engaged with the life of its time. We have remarked above the strong influence on *commedia dell'arte* players and their performance materials of 'popular' traditions, both literary and oral, and of literary forms deeply rooted in the 'popular' like the *novelle*. Engagement with immediate life in comedy is manifest in the extent to which the *scenarii* traffic in domestic and small community incidents, trade in human peccadilloes and are coloured by the inclusion of familiar details of the everyday. A not uncharacteristic feature of popular entertainment, the bawdy and scatological elements, seems to have been prominent in improvised performance, as too of course was that standby of popular story, knock-about comic 'business'. As examples we may instance those in Scala's *Il finto negromante* (*The Fake Magician*): the Dottore jokes about making women pregnant; Pedrolino force-feeds Arlecchino with medicine, pretending it is wine; Arlecchino is sent to collect cheese for breakfast, and in a long *burla*, or extended sequence of *lazzi*, after eating most of it and making himself ill, vomits over the remainder; Gratiano, the Captain, Pedrolino and Franceschina get drunk together, engage in drunken antics before an astonished Pantalone, collapse in a stupor, and are carried into the house one by one by a complaining Arlecchino.

Scholars have disagreed as to the extent to which the improvised comedy was satirical. Some have argued that its stage figures were rooted in sharp socio-political observation, that it was alert to, and cutting in its treatment of, class and sectional interests and the political realities of its time. Others have seen it as pre-eminently a comedy of style and skill and in no way particularly satiric in intention.[12] There is perhaps no way adequately to resolve these disagreements, for in this regard too the extant descriptive and evaluative accounts are insubstantial. Opportunities for satirical play can certainly be found in the improvised comedy. The *Capitani* provided occasion to mock Spanish military rule. The pedantic garrulousness of stage *Dottori* by implication could embrace ridicule of Humanism and humanistic earnestness and pretension. What more generally was exposed and subverted in these, and in other figures too, like the *Pantaloni* and the *innamorati*, was power, whether expressed in domestic, intellectual or military terms. The power of the patriarch, the scholar or the soldier, acknowledged, admired and feared in real life, was paraded for amusement on the stage: much in this comedy turned familiar authority structures and relationships upside down. In amatory relationships, too, lovers enjoyed in their stage world freedom in pairings, deceptions, elopements, revenges and abductions, rarely available in everyday life, and their activities by implication satirized familiar and traditional conventions and restraints. We cannot, however, readily assume that this comedy directly and deliberately sought to challenge the *status quo*, whether domestic or political. The comic subversion of order invariably later endorsed order by reinstating it at the end of the stage game.

Again, how purposeful and persuasive the challenge from the stage was at any particular time is peculiarly hard to calculate, given the freedom improvised playing allowed. To ask whether the comedy of the *commedia dell'arte* was or was not satirical is to assume that its comedy was a single and readily refinable entity: we might as reasonably ask whether Elizabethan comedy or music-hall comic routines were or were not satirical. The likeliest answer for the Italian improvised comedy is perhaps yes and no: that much depended on the time, the place, the immediate issues and opportunities, the choice of the comedians, the particular play they happened to be performing, the slant they chose at any moment to give their material, the audiences and their disposition at any moment to see satire, whether intended or not. Perhaps the most we can say is that in the more physical comic scenes, although the bias may have been towards extravagance and hilarity, buffoonery was not dominant, that dialogue in improvised comic plays was very prominent and characters were highly stylized but recognizably of their society, and that therefore the possibilities for satiric comment, whether mild or pungent, general or specific, were latent in the comedy and may or may not have been brought out if the occasion permitted. In the later French and Italian scripted comedy which to some extent drew inspiration from *commedia dell'arte* example sometimes satiric emphasis is developed, sometimes not. Molière, supremely, fashioned a comedy of satiric purpose; the bias of Goldoni was towards a comedy of character and social observation on the one hand, and the imbroglios of pure farce on the other.

What this dependence on the conditions of performance returns us to is recognition of the diversity of Italian professional drama, and the extent to which so much *commedia dell'arte* playing was commercially oriented, and was deliberately geared, by many different kinds of company to entertain at different social levels, from the *piazze* to the courts. The plurilingual nature of much of the stage dialogue reflects the influence of the 'popular' tradition, but was, too, calculated both to exploit available talent and to appeal to a wide range of audiences, albeit with a distinct bias to the sophisticated at the higher reaches of the profession. Conspicuous too was the fact that performance operated on many physical and verbal planes, rough 'business' and the earthy and scatological in dialogue coexisting with elegant posture and refined delivery, and exchanges rich in intellectual wit and learned reference. This mingling of 'high' and 'low' styles in performance was not unlike that found on the English Elizabethan and Jacobean stages. Like the Elizabethan and Jacobean theatre, the theatre of the Italian players had a dual orientation, to the broader populace and to the more exclusive courts. Both theatres were rich and diverse, drew their materials from a range of sources, and pitched their play composition and interpretation to the tastes and interests of various social and cultural sectors. Both were commercial in orientation and sought paying audiences where best they could find them, capitalizing on an increasing public taste for theatrical entertainment. Many of the companies and practitioners, both English and Italian, aspired to status and social advancement, and were no strangers to the 'high' culture; indeed it permeated their work and they identified themselves with it in innumerable ways, and often looked to courts and patricians for patronage, approval and support.

Far more than the Elizabethan theatre, however, the *commedia dell'arte* has invariably been described as a species of 'popular' theatre. The former obviously drew much from the 'popular' tradition, and for a time at least attracted 'groundlings' to the pits of its playhouses. Some indeed would argue that the Elizabethan theatre, in the late sixteenth century at least, was very much a 'popular' theatre; but on this there is no firm agreement, for others hold that its audiences were decidedly 'privileged playgoers'.[13] The case with the *commedia dell'arte* is assumed to have been much more clear-cut. Its many and deep tap roots in the entertainment traditions of the mass of the people have been frequently stressed. If it appealed to plebeian and aristocrat alike, as too perhaps did the early Elizabethan theatre, its credentials as the entertainment of the people have been thought the more secure in that being itinerant it went in search of its audiences, was able to accommodate easily, by virtue of its improvising techniques, to the tastes and predilections of its various audiences, sought those audiences directly through street performances, and for long maintained close links with the styles and techniques of the trestle-stage entertainment world from which it had partly sprung.

But the *commedia dell'arte* was not distinctively 'popular' in the way the mythology would have it. In a number of respects the theatre of the Italian professionals was not unlike that of the Elizabethans and Jacobeans. There were of course many differences between the two, a number of which have been touched on above, most notably the radical difference in their modes of play production. The *commedia dell'arte* like the Elizabethan theatre, is perhaps best seen as something new. Rather than characterize it and its products as a species of 'popular' theatre, we should perhaps accept it for what it was, a distinct and definable new theatrical formation: 'public' professional theatre – that is, an organized, commercially sophisticated business operation, engaged in by full-time professional players bound together in legally constituted companies for the purpose of marketing plays for a living – the *commedia mercenaria*, not wholly dissimilar in its variety, status, economy and concerns to the English theatre as it had become established, particularly in London, by the 1580s and 1590s.

Documents

The following documents include some of the most lengthy and valuable which have come down, and while they bear particularly on the art of improvisation, they say much on other matters concerning acting and performance.

THE PROLOGUE TO SCALA'S *IL FINTO MARITO*, 1619

One of the most important documents for our understanding of the professional actors who performed all'improvviso *is the following Prologue to Flaminio Scala's play,* Il finto marito (The Fake Husband). *This fully-scripted play was based on a scenario,* Il marito (The Husband), *which Scala had included in his collection* Il teatro delle Favole rappresentative *(1611), and in which he himself had probably performed. In it Scala takes up the issue of the status of the performer, and more particularly the performer who 'composes' a play by the techniques of improvisation. Scala argues for the primacy of the actor in the theatre as the one who, by virtue of his practical experience, has established those rules which should govern the composition of plays. Dramatists, in Scala's opinion, learnt how to fashion plays by following the rules established by actors.*

PLATE 38 *Watercolour illustration to a* scenario *with an Eastern setting,* Elisa Alii Bassa, *Corsini MS. Permission of the Accademia dei Lincei, Rome*

The Player: Hey, sir, where are you going? You can't go that way.
The Stranger: Oh, what way then?
The Player: This way, damn it.
The Stranger: Wait a minute. Isn't this the setting, the scene, and the place where the comedy will be acted?
The Player: And that's the place for the audience, not here. This isn't a passageway either.
The Stranger: Very well, we'll go some other way. But what sort of buffoonery's going to be performed?
The Player: Oh, this man's a real bore! It's *The Fake Husband* by Flaminio Scala.
The Stranger: Who's it by?
The Player: By Scala, of course, who in his day wrote a thousand scenarios. Why do you turn your nose up? Are you surprised?

The Stranger: Yes, I *am* surprised, because it's one thing to devise a scenario for improvised performance, but quite another to produce a pleasing comedy that is fully scripted, and to find good, lengthy dialogue with beautiful and well-turned periods, instead of things like 'give him the bed-warmer', 'the *lazzi*', 'at which', 'remains', 'exits' – the sorts of thing we get from improvising comedians. Also, to tell the truth, I don't want to be jostled about as you usually are when you are down there with the crowd. Anyway we'll have to trust in God, because as I've said, it'll be a buffoonery.

The Player: Now just a minute! Scala's invention has always been inspired, and that counts for everything in comedy.

The Stranger: But some of his things haven't impressed me at all.

The Player: It must take a lot to impress a chap like you – the way you go on you seem to know it all, or think you do . . . maybe that's because you fancy the idea of writing for the stage yourself. But you're on your own when you damn someone who's always been universally praised in print. What you can't deny is that wherever Scala took his scenarios they always gave pleasure and won high praise.

The Stranger: Very true, but why? Because he strove to get them realized in performance, and good acting companies can improve scenarios by the quality of their performance. Nonetheless a composition just sketched out, and not embellished by the art of fine writing, remains cold and hollow.

The Player: In that case, the one to be acted now should go well, because the actors have chosen the characters.

The Stranger: Very well, but as the dialogue has been memorized, it will amount to nothing unless it's really well turned, and cast in fine language.

The Player: That's true if what you want is to praise someone in a beautiful and dignified speech, or narrate a sequence of events. But in comedy, as long as the imitation is good and true to nature, and as long as the diction is neither scurrilous nor crude, that ought to be enough. In fact a familiar and none too elevated style of diction is particularly appropriate, for comedy deals with mundane actions, not those of men in high position, thus anything extravagant would be out of place.

The Stranger: Very well said, but in order to imitate a range of parts and allow each to speak appropriately you have to be well informed. You can't just make any variations you wish on the Bergamask, Venetian or Bolognese dialects; your imitation must be accurate in propriety of diction, otherwise you will distort the dialect. And to be accurate you have to be good. So I'll say again, I don't expect much from this buffoonery, because each should stick to his own art.

The Player: I think the real art of making plays well belongs to those who perform them well, because if experience is what teaches, then those it can best teach to write them down well are those who best have the ability to shape and perform the actable scenario – provided they were not born in the backwoods, or where they say 'I' for 'me'. But tell me please, in what does such an art consist?

The Stranger: In observing the rules and imitating as much as possible.

The Player: Who can know the rules of the art better than the players themselves? Every day they put them into practice by exercising the art, and thus they learn by doing. Who is better in the art of imitation than they? They not only imitate emotions and plausible actions, but by introducing a number of dialects are obliged to give accomplished imitations not just in their own dialect, but in other dialects too. Of course there would be nothing remarkable about that if a Venetian had no problem speaking in Florentine, nor a Florentine in Bergamask!

The Stranger: But the rules have to be drawn from those fine writers who have dealt with the art of poetics, because there is little value in imitating a dialect if there's no sense of joy or sorrow, or fear, or bravado in the tone and language of what's said. Such things are taught by orators and philosophers, not by players.

The Player: Indeed, all rules are desirable, but the essence of any art or science lies in putting things into practice.

The Stranger: Agreed, but rules must precede practice; or rather, forms can be derived only from rules.

The Player: Experience produces art. A rule is made by the frequent repetition of actions, and if rules derive from experience, then the valid rule is that which comes from such actions. Thus the player may give rules to the playwrights, not they to him.

The Stranger: Since when did you take to syllogizing?

The Player: This is natural logic, and based on nothing but reason.

The Stranger: Then I'll use logic to refute you. An artist cannot perfect his art without material, instruments, and an end in view.

The Player: I grant you that.

The Stranger: Now the material of the art we are discussing is oration, or better, locution. The instruments are concepts and inventions, the end is to imitate and delight, and the result that should follow is utility.

The Player: Very good.

The Stranger: Right then, in order to achieve the end of useful imitation and delight, in addition to inventions it is necessary to find appropriate concepts with which to express and signify what one seeks to imitate, together with well-organized oration or locution, that is representative and expressive, and can convey to people what one seeks to imitate, in order to achieve the ends of delight and utility.

The Player: Who doubts that?

The Stranger: It is therefore proven that valid rules, derived from those who best know how to give them, establish good concepts which appropriately express and signify what one wishes to imitate. Such rules provide the inventions too, because in distinguishing between a rule to be followed and one to be avoided, we are able to tell the good from the bad. Oration in performance, and words which are appropriately expressive, judiciously linked, and worthy of being delivered for imitative purposes, cannot be learned or used without recourse to rules and precepts, and one cannot even begin to know those without reliance on such texts as provide a proper function.

The Player: Your scholastic reasoning is ingenious, but I think its sophistry will be defeated by my simplicity.

The Stranger: Fire away!

The Player: Your argument would be sound if writers had given us valid precepts concerning oratory, locution and dramatic speech, in addition to concepts and inventions relevant to dramatic poetry. But remember, for you must have read it, just I've heard it said, that your Aristotle gave rules only for tragedy. He never got down to the detail of comic style, and nor can one find anything substantial in Horace. As far as comedy goes, the only rules and precepts are those of good practice and good dramatists, and it's from these that the forms habitually used today have been derived, it being the case that rules are always taken from usage and not usage from rules. That's the reason why many great men of letters, including some of the finest, have written plays in an elegant style, full of fine concepts, graceful speeches, and noble inventions; but what they lack is experience of the stage, and so when these same plays are performed they prove lifeless – they lack that imitation proper to comedy, are remarkably dull and insipid, and at times are not just unpersuasive, but preposterous. So they disgust audiences, and fail to achieve the end of pleasure, let alone of utility. Because audiences don't listen to them, they're not only useless, they're forgotten. Thus good concepts should be identified from effects not rules, for as those who know about such things say: people with no feelings must be made to feel, and you have to take a stick to them to make them laugh.

For this reason, then, oration, or even locution, and words alone, have little to do with imitation, because even the smallest gesture at the right moment, and made with feeling, can achieve a greater effect than all the philosophy of Aristotle or the rhetoric of Demosthenes and Cicero. That feelings are aroused more by gestures than words is obvious, for intelligent men, and even brute beasts, will always better attend and obey those who use a stick than those who rely on words – for as the Bergamask says, 'There's a great gulf between asking and doing.' And this is the case with everything that bears on the senses. Just remember this, it was the power of stones not words that drove the man out of the fig tree – for with regard to actions, they are more imitative than narrations, and plays properly and in essence consist in actions, and only incidentally in narrations. Thus in the comic genre whoever wants to imitate actions will achieve more with actions than with words. This is to be seen in lovers, who are more moved and influenced by the beloved's tear, or glance, or kiss or suchlike, to go no further, than by the persuasions of any great moral philosopher who, with well-composed writing, immaculate concepts, excellent locution, exquistite words and the subtlest arguments, exhorts to virtue and urges the rejection of sensuality. The senses are more easily moved by the senses than by anything in the abstract, just as like is drawn to like.

The Stranger: Truly you argue well, and I am beginning to be persuaded. I could say something in reply, but for the moment I'm satisfied with what you've said [. . .]

(Scala, *Il finto marito*, 1619, pp. 6–15)

IMPROVISATION

Unfortunately, the two most detailed seventeenth-century commentators on the commedia dell'arte*, Cecchini and Perrucci, are neither as explicit nor as analytical as we could wish in their discussions of improvised performance. Cecchini's rather querulous tone breaks through in his comments,* *which in this brief passage are concerned primarily with the technique of effectively intermeshing the improvised dialogue of actors, whether on stage together, or when one joined another. This interestingly points, however, to what was one of the trickiest features of delivering dialogue impromptu: the timing of speech and entrances, when cue-lines could not be relied on.*

Cecchini on improvisation

Improvised performances need to be undertaken by someone who has thoroughly considered beforehand those elements mentioned earlier [language, voice, gesture], and above all the actor must be careful not to speak when his partner is holding forth, so as to avoid that confusion so tedious to those who are listening, and so disagreeable to the one speaking; and before responding he should allow the one speaking to reach the end of his sentence, although it is necessary too to remember that long sentences are awkward and unpleasant, therefore the new speech must be of a length that can be received easily by those listening.

Further, it is important for the actor to remember that when he is speaking on the stage alone he must cease as soon as he is joined by another speaking character; and he must be more concerned to observe this point, than to do violence to the idea he is prevented from expressing. It is prudent however not to enter until the other actor is about to conclude his speech: that conclusion can be signalled by the speaker, having reached the end of his line of thought, making some easily understood gesture. But it is better to agree the moment of entrance, than to disturb the flow.

(Cecchini, *Frutti*, 1628, pp. 17–18.)

Perrucci on improvisation

Perrucci is rather more forthcoming and informative than Cecchini, but his remarks are primarily addressed to dilettanti, *and it is their practice he seems primarily to have in mind. But much of his incidental comment is interesting, more particularly the suggestions that improvised playing was widespread, at all social and cultural levels, that vulgarities characterized the performance of street entertainers and mountebanks, and that improvised playing at its best should be considered superior to acting off scripted texts – a view quite widely held by seventeenth- and eighteenth-century commentators.*

The acting of comedies *all'improvviso* was an invention of our centuries and was unknown to the ancients; indeed I cannot find that any of them so much as used the word. Furthermore, it seems that only in fair Italy has this so far been achieved, for a famous Spanish player called Adriano, who came with his fellows to perform comedies in Naples, could not understand how a comedy could be prepared and mounted in less than an hour, merely by assembling the different characters. The undertaking is indeed most extraordinary, although very difficult and dangerous, and is not one to be attempted by other than the capable and expert; they need to be familiar with the rules of language, with figures of speech, tropes, and all the arts of rhetoric, for they must do *all'improvviso* what the poet does by premeditation. Thus although scripted performance may be more highly valued, and is prized and esteemed, that is because the poet is careful in composing it, and all is controlled by one person alone – considering all the assistance, effort and toil that goes into so many preparations and rehearsals, the end-product should perforce be successful; and if it is not, then those who give birth after such a prodigious labour, not to a perfect specimen but to a mangled embryo full of oddities and distortions, wholly deserve criticism. This is not the case with improvised plays, in which the vanity of so many tends to produce irregularity, for some are necessarily less perfect and less skilful than others, and it is impossible to avoid mistakes when one speaks *quidquid in buccam venit*. However, when an improvised comedy is performed by good actors it can succeed as well as a scripted piece, and as has been finely and elegantly said: *Meditatum et impromptu habere quod quisque modis dicatur, magnum ad perspicuitatis habet adiumentum.* Therefore I laugh at those, accustomed to perform only in scripted pieces, who conclude that actors impromptu are no good, for those who can act perfectly in the more difficult *all'improvviso* style will have no problem acting in the easier, scripted way. In fact the improvising player will always have the edge, for if his memory lets him down, or some mistake occurs, he is able to remedy the situation without the audience being aware of it, while the actor who performs like a parrot will be thrown by every mistake.

Unfortunately these days everyone fancies he can dabble in improvised playing, and the very dregs of the populace attempt it, imagining it to be easy, not realizing the peril that lies in their ignorance and presumption. Thus the most vulgar ruffians and mountebanks get it into their heads that they can draw crowds and entertain them with words, and like so many bumptious Hercules in golden chains they try to perform improvised plays in public squares, mangling the *soggetti*, speaking off the point, gesturing like lunatics and, what's worse, indulging in a thousand scurrilities and obscenities, in order to extract a sordid income from the purses of the spectators by selling their fake potions of boiled oils, poisonous antidotes, and remedies which produce illnesses where before there were none. They are like those utterly ignorant painters who, aspiring to copy the works of the most distinguished and celebrated artists, make crude daubs rather than fine strokes, but with the difference that good artists draw from Apellis and Titians, while these blotchers take from Agatarchi or Zannini da Capugnano. But let us turn from these vile creatures, infamous and deserving of total contempt, and say that whenever a group of *virtuosi* come together *all'improvviso*, it is always possible to perform something distinguished by imitating the finest players in this kind (and they have never been in short supply), and it is possible to do for pleasure what the professionals do for money. There are many academies practising this virtuoso skill – in Naples, Bologna and many Italian cities – and some years ago even in Palermo there was the Academy of the Squinternati, which had for its sign an unbound book and a motto, *Non qui Internati*, and whose rules obliged whoever attended the academy to perform *all'improvviso* if called upon to do so. Is this a fine example of Sicilian ingenuity?

As improvisations need to be carried off with decorum, in practice it is necessary to observe all those rules formulated for acting in scripted plays, for both kinds of acting are the same in the theatre in that they involve costume, voice, pronunciation, memory, gestures and actions. All that is needed is some preparation to effect greater smoothness and harmony, to ensure as far as possible that all is consonant with a well-organized performance. If all does not then turn out as expected, this will be the more readily excusable, for scripted performances too are not always successful, as can be seen in the case of Terence, his *Hecyra* being given only once or twice and then set aside, while his *Eunuchus* was done many times and with great applause. Why then should the failure of an improvised performance occasion any surprise when, far more than a scripted play, for it to be successful is a matter of luck? An improvised performance has to satisfy the opinion of many. According to Laerzius *populari multitudini multorum capitum belluae servire servitutem*, and the performer even more than the orator is *servus populi* [. . .] and that it is indeed difficult even for the most learned I have discovered many times, [finding] that poets, scholars and literary men, when they have acted impromptu, have been so confused and upset that they have been incapable of saying a word, notwithstanding that they were highly competent with language or pen, on the rostrum, or on paper, or from balconies. Now in order to make this fine and unusual entertainment all the easier by the application of rules, they should recognize that they ought not to essay an undertaking without preparation, but should arm themselves with certain general compositions adaptable to any play. These might include, for the *innamorati* and the women, conceits, soliloquies and dialogues, and for the *vecchi*, advice, disquisitions, greetings, word-play and certain gracious expressions.

(Perrucci, Dell'arte rappresentativa, 1699, Proemio, pp. 187–92)

Gherardi's late seventeenth-century remarks on improvisation

The reason [Italian plays cannot be published] is because the Italians are not actors who learn off texts; in performing a play it is sufficient if they have read its subject shortly before they go out on to the stage. Also the greatest beauty of their pieces is inseparable from the action, for the success of their plays depends entirely on the actors, who make them agreeable or not according to the degree of their ability and intelligence, or to the situation in which they find themselves performing.

And it is this requirement to sustain performance without preparation, that makes it very hard to find a substitute for a good Italian actor when he is not available. Anyone can learn a text and then deliver it; but it is something else to be a good actor in the Comédie Italienne. Whoever refers to 'A good actor of the Comédie Italienne' is identifying a player with a personality of his own, one who depends more on the strength of his imagination than on his memory, and who composes what he performs even as he delivers it; one who knows how to adjust to the player he acts with; one who can, that is, so perfectly marry his own words and actions to the words and actions of his colleague, that he can blend with the action of his companion and react as required, making all believe that his acting was premeditated.

(From Gherardi, *Le Théâtre Italien de Gherardi*, 1700, Avertissement)

Riccoboni on improvisation

Improvisation allows for variation in acting, so that even if the same scenario is seen more than once it is possible to see a different version of it each time. The player who acts *all'improvviso* performs in a more vivacious and natural way than the player who has learned a part. Feeling comes more readily, and thus one can better say what one has composed oneself, than what is drawn from others by the help of memory. But these advantages of the *commedia all'improvviso* are won at the cost of many drawbacks: improvisation demands skilful players, and players who have more or less comparable talent, for the disadvantage of improvisation lies in the fact that the acting of even the best player depends wholly upon the player with whom he exchanges lines; for if he finds himself with a player unable to calculate precisely the moment of his response, and who interjects at the wrong time, his dialogue withers and the vivacity of his thought is stifled. Appearance, memory, voice, identification do not suffice for an actor who wishes to perform impromptu, unless he enjoys a live and fertile imagination and a facility in expression, or if he lacks delicacies of language, and has not acquired all necessary understanding of the nature of his role.

(Riccoboni, *Histoire du Théâtre Italien*, 1728, pp. 61–2)

THE NATURE OF THE COMEDY

The following passage from Barbieri attempts to define the nature of improvised comic performance and to distinguish it from the buffoonery of trestle stage players.

In both comedy and buffoonery laughter is laughter, but in comedy it is provoked by a misunderstanding or a witty remark, while in buffoonery it is produced more by excessive nimbleness: the one has as its goal instruction to virtuous conduct, the other is concerned more to ridicule human beings. The comic actor uses laughter to season his trenchant speeches, but the foolish buffoon makes it the *raison d'être* of all he does. A potter paints the pots he makes, but is not thereby called a painter – for his skill lies not in painting, but in making pots. An actor can provoke laughter, but that does not make him a jester, for the essence of comic performance is not to provoke laughter but to entertain with brilliant inventiveness, and with historical and poetic pieces. Again, who is so foolish as not to recognize the difference between being and seeming? The buffoon is himself actually a buffoon; but the actor who plays a comic role only pretends to be a buffoon, and for that reason wears a mask, or a false beard, or make-up that he may appear to be another [. . .]

(Barbieri, *La Supplica*, 1634, chapter IX)

PERRUCCI ON THE FUNCTIONS OF THE *CORAGO*

Perrucci's late seicento *account of the duties of the* corago *probably reflects professional stage practice; it can usefully be read in conjunction with the passage from Leone de' Sommi's* Dialoghi *on Renaissance academic staging (above, p. 40).*

The *corago*, the leader or the *maestro*, the one most capable of instructing others, should rehearse the *soggetto* before it is performed so that the actors are familiar with the content of the play, know where to conclude their speeches, and can explore in rehearsal some new witticism or new *lazzo*. The person in charge of the rehearsal does not restrict himself just to reading the scenario, but explains the names and qualities of the characters, the argument of the play, the location of the action, the stage houses, the distribution of the *lazzi* and all the necessary details, taking care of the props required for the play, like letters, purses, daggers and such like, as listed at the end of the scenario.

He will say, for example: 'The play we are to perform is *La Trappolaria*.

The characters are Tartaglia, father of Fedelindo and master of Coviello; Policinella, a slave-merchant, and Turchetta, his slave;

Isabella, a courtesan, and her servants, Pespice, a parasite, and Pimpinella; Capitano, a master, and Pasquariello, his servant; Tartaglia's wife, Donna Laura, who arrives from elsewhere with her servant; a pedlar; people who play the parts of guards and those pretending to be guards; and these parts will be played by X and Y and Z. [. . .]'

He will then consider the stage houses, establishing the first on the right as Tartaglia's house, the second on the left as Pulcinella's, and the second on the right as Isabella's. He will then recount the plot. [Perrucci then gives the argument of the *soggetto La trappolaria.*]

The actors must above all ensure that they make no mistake about the location of the action: where any character comes from and for what purpose he comes. They must remember proper names, for it would be a gross error and an unforgivable impropriety if one spoke of being in Rome and another in Naples, or if one had arrived from Spain then announced that he had come from Germany, or for a father to forget his son's name, or a lover the name of his mistress.

[. . .] Actors need to be equally alert to the way the stage houses are assigned, so that each one knows his own house; for unfortunately it would be laughable and invite ridicule if someone were to knock at or enter another house instead of his own – indeed he would be thought stupid or drunk. These are the worst possible mistakes which can be made on the stage [. . .] Some lapses of memory or slips of the tongue can be forgiven, for this is a game in which the greatest men make mistakes, and the tongue is not infallible, but to make mistakes about stage houses and characters' names, or to leave the stage empty, is the way only fools would behave.

Next, the stage-manager should explicate and interpret the *lazzi* and the plot, saying: 'Here we need such and such a *lazzo*, here this metaphor, there that hyperbole or irony,' and do this for all the *lazzi* and witticisms, satisfying any objections the players may raise, and doing his best to avoid any improprieties [. . .]

The actors must be careful not to bump into each other when they make their entrances. This is easier to avoid in improvised than in scripted drama, because as they speak in the course of improvising it is easy to see which part of the stage is accupied by the player about to exit, and so avoid entering that same way, choosing rather a way where part of the stage is empty – although an infallible rule is to exit up-stage and enter down-stage as long as necessity does not require something different.

It is easier in improvised than in scripted drama to avoid an empty and silent stage, for each player can improvise on the subject of the previous scene and speak as long as necessary until the arrival of the actor whose turn it is to appear.

Once the actors have heard what is expected of them about

entering on to the stage, performing and terminating the scene, along with their companions they will be able to repeat the scenes and agree among themselves any new *lazzo* and 'business' they may fancy. They should be at pains not to wander so far from the *soggetto* that they cannot return to it, and be careful that the audience does not lose track of the plot or have difficulty in keeping up with it because the *lazzi* are too drawn out and inappropriate. Therefore it is advisable that everything added should be pertinent to the subject of the play – not stray too far away from it, and always be capable of being brought back to it – for it is a fact that some actors stray so far that they forget the scenario, and the whole thing becomes a chaos of confusions.

All the players should make a circle and receive instruction as a group. They should not be overly confident because they know the play by heart or have acted in it before, for as far as the plot is concerned it is possible that different *coragi* might stage it differently, altering both names and places. Nor should anyone expect to receive personal instruction, nor should he urge the *corago* to give it [. . .]

Once the players have heard this explication of the *soggetto* they should consider adding it to something they have prepared beforehand or have devised specifically for that comedy, or what seems suitable for it, such as some particular fact, some tale, something either directly connected with the play, or of universal significance – things which are memorized can be applicable to any comedy or play, like for example the opening lines mentioned above, expressions of despair, conceits, dialogues, reproaches, greetings, parallelisms, and anything else we have mentioned, whether serious or ridiculous. They should know how to insert these in such a way that they seem not borrowed, but an essential part of the play, and they must not, as some do when they have something fine to say, whether it be ridiculous or serious, be indifferent to where they interpolate it, and whether it fits logically, thus producing a result like a white patch on black, and marring the poor *soggetto* with something ill placed, a practice of which I have been a very rigid opponent.

(Perrucci, *Dell'arte rappresentativa*, 1699, Regola XIV, pp. 364–70)

PERRUCCI ON NIGHT SCENES AND PLACE

In scenes which are supposed to take place at night Neapolitans are superior to Lombards and those of other nations, and indeed in the comedy of words and incidents foreigners say, 'Neapolitan *lazzi* (meaning what is witty in words and incidents) and Lombard *scenari*', and in night scenes one sees this in the Neapolitan way of walking cautiously, encountering each other, grimacing, mounting

PLATE 39 (overleaf) *Eighteenth century players in Venice performi[n] open air on a large platform stage. Permission of the Museo Correr, Venice*

steps and other mute acts, so that nothing more ridiculous and verisimilar can be imagined, as is evident when the most the Lombard *Zanni* can do to provoke laughter is to use gunshots, which delight boys and ignoramuses, but irritate the more sagacious who recognize that *Zanni* resort to gun shots when they are short on comic material.

(Perrucci, *Dell'arte rappresentativa*, 1699, Regola XII, p. 342)

When a scene is followed by one taking place at night, those who are in the first scene should try and prepare for this, saying: 'Night is already coming on,' or, like Virgil, '*cadunt altis de montibus umbrae*' (and the same goes for when dawn breaks and day approaches), so that the audience will realize that the characters who come on next, make their entrance at night. In the margin of the *soggetto* one should write, 'Night, Dawn, Day'. Again, when a scene change is needed one should write in the margin 'City, Wood, Room' and suchlike in order to alert the performer and prepare the machinist who will make the scene change. The stage-manager too should point out such matters by saying, 'These scenes take place during the day, and these at night.'

(Perrucci, *Dell'arte rappresentativa*, 1699, Regola XIV, p. 371)

8

Some Leading Players

Provenance and Status

THE EMERGENCE of the acting companies in the middle decades of the sixteenth century led to radical readjustments and realignments in theatrical culture. Aspirant comedians, whether drawn from the court sphere or the world of popular street entertainment, were obliged to accommodate their skills to the needs of the more organized, structured and sustained entertainments the companies purveyed.[1] Thus buffoons had to adapt, for if they did not they found their kinds of entertainment less regularly in demand, and declined from the court to the street. Former jugglers, acrobats, musicians, singers, dancers and mimes of the *piazza* attracted to the new companies had necessarily to adjust their performer expertise to the requirements of dramatic situations and plot-lines. Even those admitted to the professional troupes from the court fringes, like singers, writers, poetesses and courtesans, however eager they may have been to find more regular and financially secure outlets for their talents, were no less constrained by company structures, performing schedules and performance demands, to learn new styles, techniques and habits.

We have said that if anything marked off the professionals it was that they earned their living by acting. By virtue of that fact they were a definable social group with a particular, if variable, social status, conditional on the kind of position they managed to secure in the courts and market-place. Some companies and individual players accumulated capital to tide them over difficult periods; they could look to receiving some support from wealthy patrons and admirers; a few may have been economically independent. As the brief accounts above of some of the leading companies have indicated, a small number of players and troupe leaders were courted by domestic and foreign royalty, and by the nobility and the *letterati*. By the end of the century players in at least the major companies had achieved the status of respected and sought-after artisans: on a level, as Barbieri tells us, with 'painters, sculptors and others of similar ilk'.[2] Inevitably, however, it was the successful, the exceptional, and the surprising which the records tended to report. The esteem in which Isabella Andreini was held is well attested; Tristano Martinelli was admired and favoured by Maria de' Medici; Pier Maria Cecchini was ennobled for his services to a foreign ruler; Flaminio Scala was a friend of the Roman academician Locatelli – instances of the respect enjoyed by leading players are readily found in the records. So too is evidence of the extent to which the major troupes were favoured by the great families like the Medici, the Gonzaga and the Farnese.

What characterized the work, and to some extent even the social tone, of many of the troupes was a certain mingling of the plebeian and the would-be aristocratic. Many who entered the later *cinquecento* acting companies sought not just a regular living and the opportunity to exercise trade or artistic skills, but possibilities for social and financial advancement. Such players and companies were able in large measure to satisfy their aspirations not least because theatrical conditions were peculiarly propitious. The new acting companies were able to capitalize on possibilities initially opened up by the early sixteenth-century court patronage of amateur and academic drama.[3] That patronage had licensed experiment and innovation, expanding the verbal, scenic and interpretative resources of the theatre, and locating comic drama in particular firmly in the realities of recognizable life. Building on the new-won theatrical freedoms of the immediate past, and wedding the dramaturgy and literary materials of the 'high' culture to the more physical and pantomimic skills of popular *piazza* theatricals, the professional actors and actresses, drawn from a variety of social and cultural backgrounds and fusing and exploiting a wide range of performer expertise, were able to elevate themselves above the hitherto largely undifferentiated mass of medieval and Renaissance professional theatrical entertainers. Indeed, by the turn of the century or even earlier the activites of the leading players and troupes seem characterized by a deliberate bid for upward social and cultural mobility, evident not only in the publication by players of their performance materials (Andreini, Martinelli etc.) and scripted plays (Fiorillo, Scala etc), but in the vigour with which they sought to distance themselves from the ruck of itinerant entertainers and to define themselves as a distinct theatrical formation. The extent of their success in so doing seems evident in the willingness of moralistic critics to distinguish between their work and that of entertainers and troupes of more humble standing.

Among the acting companies proper a hierarchy seems to have developed. Indeed the more successful the major troupes were in establishing themselves socially and culturally – whether they were companies under direct noble patronage, and therefore almost by definition of some status, or whether they were autonomous or familial troupes – the more a hierarchy was affirmed. Members of, say, the Gelosi or the Confidenti appear in many respects to be as far removed socially and financially from players in indigent strolling troupes as they were from performers on the trestle stages of mountebanks. Yet the bounds between all three of these broad groups in a number of respects remained imprecise and ever shifting. The status of companies rose and fell, there were frequent breaks and realignments and, of course, major companies were formed or recruited from the ranks of the less prosperous. Again, more than one outstanding player began on mountebank stages (as did, it seems, Barbieri); Silvio Fiorillo apparently began his career in the theatre as a member of travelling troupes working in the Naples region, before moving on to more distinguished companies. That kind of upward mobility is in no way surprising. As we have seen above, some mountebank entertainers were admired at all social levels, strolling players often performed in a variety of performance places, including the more socially exclusive. Whole companies were well capable of reorchestrating their street entertainment skills to meet new opportunities: interesting mid eighteenth-century instances of the rapid transition troupes could make from *piazza* to playhouse are found in Carlo Goldoni's engaging account in his *Memoirs* of the mountebank Compagnia dell'Anonimo and the rope-dancing family headed by Girolamo Medebach.[4]

Economic Conditions

At the level of the strollers, the actor's life was not an enviable one. Most lived in poverty and on the margins of society, widely considered to be rogues, vagabonds and thieves. But even members of major companies lived a somewhat precarious existence. Noble patronage offered a degree of protection and financial security, and service with a noble patron, or the regular provision of entertainment to a patrician and his circle, gave social status to a troupe, and brought benefits in money and kind – hence the extent to which the leading troupes organized their activities and itineraries according to the court calendars. But the *largesse* of the courts not only brought obligation and subordination, it was often erratic and limited, and few players were for long securely established. Companies not

PLATE 40 (overleaf) *The actor Giovanni Gabrielli. Permission of the Biblioteca Burcardo, Rome*

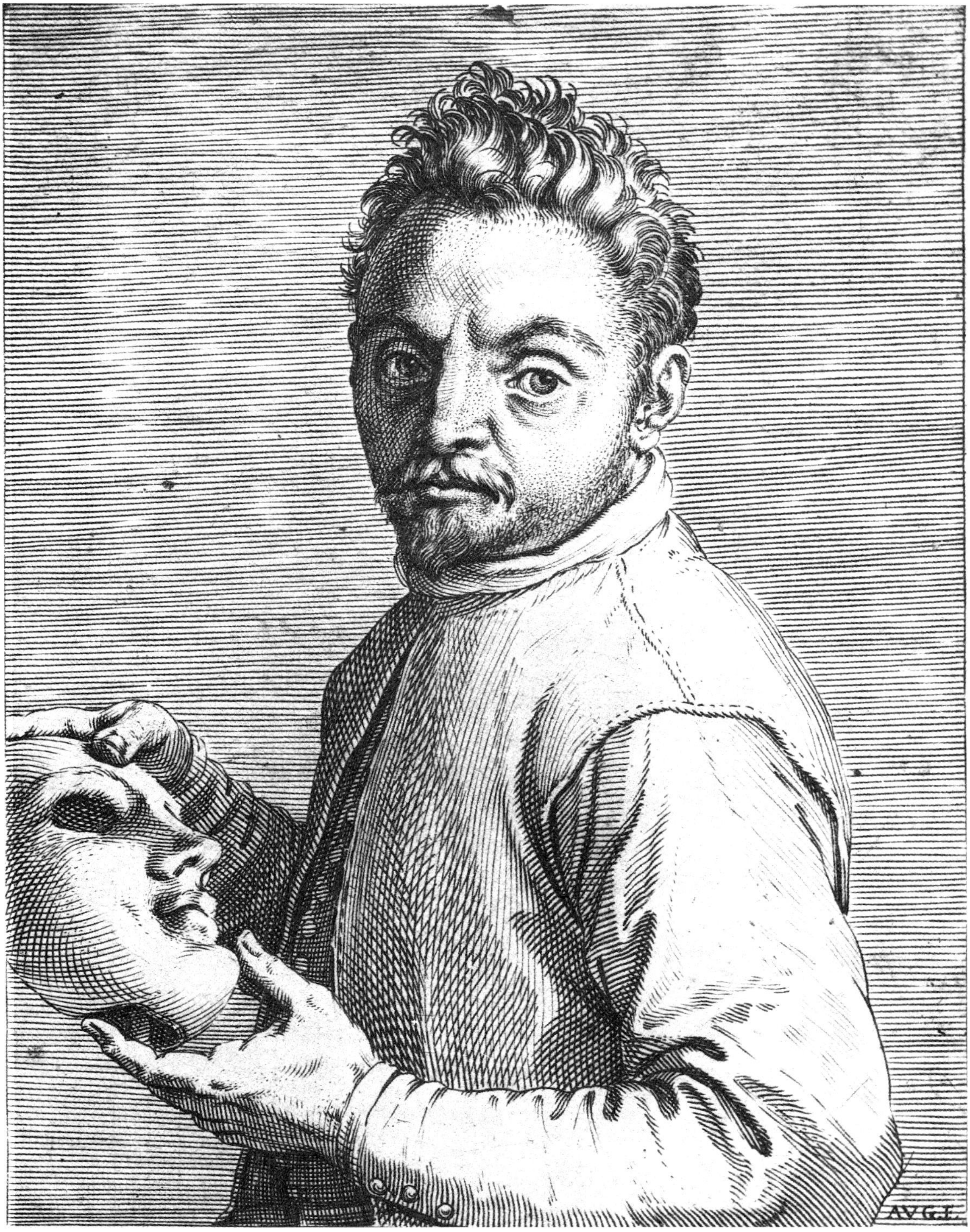
AVG.F.

under regular ducal patronage depended for much of their economic well-being on the takings they could command from court visits and the general public. Even a celebrated company like the Gelosi, at the height of its success, could suffer potentially damaging setbacks by events beyond its control, like plague, famine and local wars (see above, p. 95).

Although no longer co-operatives in the manner of the early troupes of the 1540s and 1550s, in many respects companies were self-contained economic communities. With a complement of about ten or twelve principal performers and support players, together with families, servants and elderly dependants (Francesco Gabrielli's domestic unit numbered fourteen – see above, p. 126), they lived, travelled and worked together, the quality of their livelihood fluctuating according to the degree of noble patronage or the box-office returns they could command. Unfortunately, their livelihoods seem all too often to have been threatened by problems of their own making. The balance of players within a troupe was a delicate one and often difficult to sustain (see above, chapter 5). If the many extant letters, reports and petitions of the players, and of court officials and advisers, are anything to judge by, company instability was all too common. A great deal of this material documents splits, mergers, quarrels and departures, most of which arose from internal disputes over personal relationships or disagreements over relative professional status.[5]

Inevitably, for many less established players their communal, nomadic and often economically precarious existence separated them from other members of society and made them objects of suspicion. That suspicion, from the perspective of civic and church leaders, is understandable, even if often unwarranted and frequently expressed in exaggerated terms. For the administrator and the moralist alike, players were elusive transients, not readily able to be incorporated within the pattern of a community's affairs — their life-styles, activities, and indeed their very appearance when on the move, seemingly alien and potentially disruptive. There was little the players could do to counter such suspicion, for it was generated by the very nature of their trade. For many, and certainly for those at the lower reaches of the profession, the actor's life must have been a hard one, travelling from place to place in a small caravan of carts, pack-horses and foot-sloggers, sleeping in inns or hostels, or in covered waggons or under the sky, and living much of the time cheek by jowl with others in a tight-knit, socially marginal group.[6] In the eyes of moralists, actresses in particular were stigmatized as much by their communal, wayfaring life-style, as by the fact that they paraded themselves before the public gaze in lascivious comedies. Actresses, not excluding even the celebrated, were regarded by some as little better than common whores (see in particular below, chapter 9). Although the conditions of their living were not always consonant with maintaining that life of virtue called for by their clerical and moralistic critics, many were doubtless unjustifiably defamed. But unfortunately, too, moral obloquy, social ostracism and the inclination of critics to dub all actresses loose livers, tended perhaps to foster what the moralists condemned.

For players in the major companies, existence was not in the main hand-to-mouth, as doubtless it was for many in the lesser troupes. Yet for the most part even the members of prestigious companies lived on fairly narrow margins – dependent on patronage, box office and a propitious social climate. In this respect the economy of many of the best Italian players and companies was not perhaps significantly different from that of the leading Elizabethan and Jacobean acting troupes, both their 'sharers' and 'hired men'. The latter were likewise heavily dependent on takings at the door; for them, too, royal and noble patronage offered the social benefits of status and protection, but produced usually no more than a financial supplement to income primarily derived from public playing; they similarly could suffer ruinous economic setbacks by civil disturbance or natural disasters, the severe consequences for the London acting companies of the long closure of the theatres by plague between 1592–3 being but one case in point. Unlike the English companies, however, in time of need the Italian troupes, being itinerant rather than playhouse-based, and working more improvised than scripted drama, probably had few assets they could sell off. The English troupes could realize something on wardrobe holdings and play scripts – the latter, in particular, being the property of the company not of the dramatist, were often a useful fallback.[7] Indeed it is conceivable that the spate of publications from the hands of Italian players in the early decades of the seventeenth century had an economic as well as cultural motive. Recent Italian scholarship has emphasized the extent to which the tendency of the players to go into print with their own scripted dramas, performance materials and other writings, was a conscious bid to win acceptance of their art by demonstration of their cultural credentials. At the same time, however, the occasion, conditions and timing of the individual publications call for scrutiny. Some were self-advertisement of potential if indirect economic utility, like the publication usually ascribed to Tristano Martinelli, *Compositions de rhetorique* (1601), others appeared when the writers were either close to, or had already entered into, retirement, like those of Andreini and Scala, and yet others, like the writings of Cecchini and Barbieri, were products of the later years of players whose lives had been spent in a profession beginning now to feel the effects of the economic retrenchment remarked above.

Training and Skills

Many players lived out their lives in their own craft community, intermarrying, travelling in family units and introducing their children to the profession at an early age – hence the Italian phrase traditionally used of so many actors and actresses, *figli d'arte*, perhaps best expressed in English as 'born to the profession'. Acting, it must be emphasized, was a trade, and one learnt by many of the young not least by their domestic immersion in the profession from childhood, by being in the train of touring companies, learning skills from relatives and friends, and often inheriting traditions of playing, items of stage 'business', and even roles, from parents or grandparents. Other players, however, were quite certainly drawn from without the profession. It would be altogether wrong to conclude too that most performers, by virtue of their itinerant existence, were of little or no education. It is clear, in fact, that both men and women of education and bourgeois background took up acting in the later decades of the sixteenth century. Many performers were highly cultivated, some had studied at the universities, and a few were of the cultural and intellectual *milieux*. Most of the extant portrait paintings of celebrated players depict them as figures of authority and dignity, poses which are not wholly to be explained by the conventions of the genre.[8] Some children of players attended university, probably with the encouragement of patrician patrons. A number of educated semi-professionals, as we have seen, probably took to the craft full-time. Acting provided, too, an outlet for artistic skills not readily marketable elsewhere, and offered careers to some restless and renegade talents. But once committed to it there was not usually any easy going back. Hence, in part, the tendency for players to remain within the world of the profession. Some players had very long careers indeed: Giovan Andrea Zanotti was still playing the Lover role until he was seventy; Giovanni Pellesini acted Pedrolino until he was eighty seven; Fiorilli was not only appearing as Scaramouche in his eighties but remained so agile that he was able, it was said, to touch his forehead with his foot.[9]

The versatility of the players we have already stressed; it complemented the wide range of their repertories. At the root of their performance were the twin early entertainer skills of acrobatics and rhetoric, and the juxtaposition of contrasting figures in the units of action of a *scenario* (see above, chapter 7) invariably exploited these skills. They point, too, the founts of the players' inspiration: comic 'business' and literary discourse. Given the kinds of material they performed, and the manner of their improvisation, it is clear that a fundamental requirement of most actors and actresses, particularly perhaps those playing Lovers' roles, was a retentive memory and rapid recall, together with good diction and the ability to deliver witty repartee or verbally sophisticated speeches with panache. In improvised performance, pacing and timing was of the essence, as too was an instinctive talent for playing off fellow performers and the audience. The sheer number of opportunities signalled in the *scenarii* for soliloquy and aside indicates how close was the rapport between player and spectator. In that rapport the player was exposed, physically and verbally, and the effective performer needed an innate sense of the way pictorial and theatrical effects could be achieved through posture, movement and gesture, and how inflection and shifts of vocal register could help carry the most verbally and imagistically complex rhetorical flights. Fundamental as requirements, too, for the successful actor or actress were an appearance appropriate to the role specialization, an awareness of how to turn physical, vocal and temperamental indiosyncracies to performance ends, and the ability to sing, dance and play musical instruments. Obviously few players possessed all these skills; but no player could hope to be successful if deficient in most of them.

At the highest reaches of the profession more, too, was often called for than performance expertise: a good business sense, and a taste for the niceties of compliment and persuasion; a knowledge of fashions in dress, deportment, literature and the fine arts; the bearing and manners of one accustomed to move in the sphere of the social and cultural elite. By the turn of the *cinquecento* some players may have succeeded in winning the same degree of artistic and social recognition as was accorded a few of the great artificers of the age like Buontalenti, Bernini and Torelli. Barbieri and others suggest this may have been so. But the status achieved by even the most distinguished players must not be exaggerated. Nor were other artists always ready to accept the pretensions of the players. In 1645 the great scenic designer Giacomo Torelli prepared the *pièce de machines*, *La finta pazza*, for the entertainment of the French court at the Petit Bourbon. The Italian players brought to Paris to act and sing in the production found him aloof and unwilling to consider them fellow artists; his cooperation had to be imposed by the instruction of the French Queen.[10] Even in the artistic community the standing of actors and actresses was decidely qualified.

Documents

The following documents are necessarily highly selective, and here it is possible to include only a few pieces on some of the most distinguished players of the heyday of the commedia dell'arte. *Of none of the actors and actresses, however, have detailed records survived, and our knowledge of the lives, careers and performance abilities of the players is as sketchy as it is for the companies.*

A PLAYER LAMENTS BEING IN THE PROFESSION

The following complaint, although part of a dramatic prologue, Prologo da Ragazzo, *and so in that respect not first-hand evidence directly from the mouth of a player, nonetheless expresses sentiments which probably would have been echoed by many an actor and actress, for the profession could be disputatious, hard on itinerants, and material rewards, save for the most distinguished, were as few then as now, while subsistence living was decidedly more precarious.*

I shall leave, for as you are in agreement you oblige me to do so, but if I had not been wise from the beginning to this extraordinary farce, nothing would have kept me here. Curse this profession and whoever invented it! When I threw in my lot with these people I thought I would have a happy life: but I find that in truth it's the life of a gypsy, never settled in any place. Here today, there tomorrow; sometimes by land, sometimes by sea; and what's worse, forever living in inns where the charges are high and the service poor. I wish my father had consigned me to another trade, one where I think I could have done better with less trouble. As my companion Farfanicchio used to say, if you've got a profession you've got a position in the world. But patience! I'm stuck with it, and in this trade if you are in it long enough to wear out a pair of boots, then you are in it for good. As that applies to me, I want to be sure I am always in the best and most honourable companies, for as well as learning from them, I shall not fear, as many do, the charge of being ignorant or infamous.

(Bruni, *Le Fatiche Comiche*, 1623, pp. 6–7)

Another of Bruni's prologues, this one in the mouth of a servetta, speaks eloquently of the tribulations of a travelling life.

But let us mention too all the fun to be got from travelling through a world of rain, frost and snow, of miserable inns, vile innkeepers, dreadful horses, ramshackle carriages, impertinent boatmen, importunate coachmen, spies at city gates and customs houses, and similar such delights which are always part of the players' happy life. But enough, dear people, you'll gather I'm none too happy with them.

(Bruni, here cited from MS AG XIV 24, Biblio. Bradiense, Milan, pp. 25–25v)

The Jesuit critic of theatre, G. D. Ottonelli, remarks on the players' tendency to stress the difficulties they encountered in exercising their profession, and notes their complaint about travelling.

[. . .] all too often the consequences of travelling are double-edged, for in addition to the peril of journeying itself, money made in one town can be spent on travelling to another where, if their plays are unsuccessful, the players incur the danger of running into debt in order to survive.

But Ottonelli counters this with a report:

In the year 1640 I was told by the leader of a company of players that some performers possessed their own houses and similar tokens of wealth, and that every leading and prominent player had four or six thousand *scudi* of his own in costumes and other properties.
(Ottonelli, *Della Christiana Moderatione del Theatro*, IV, 1652, p. 128)

SOME LATE SIXTEENTH-CENTURY PLAYERS

Zan Ganassa (Alberto Naseli)

We have already touched briefly above (p. 60) on the few facts available about the career of this player, who was one of the earliest recorded troupe leaders to take a company abroad. Of his work in Italy next to nothing is known, although in the mid-1560s he is found performing in Ferrara. His presence in Paris in 1571 is often taken to mark the beginning of that long tradition of Italian acting company visits to the French capital that ran through to the formation of a permanent company there in 1661.

He used to act the comic part of the second *zanni* and was very restrained, avoiding any obscenity. He was prolific only in absurd and tasteful witticisms, and so modest that every virtuous spectator could be much delighted by him and truly hold him in affection.

Ganassa was in Spain in the service of Philip II around 1570, at the head of his well-disciplined comic company, and although in the beginning neither he nor his companions were much understood by that nation, nonetheless he tried with gestures and the occasional word to please and provoke laughter until, having become more proficient in the language, he managed to mix some Spanish words with his own Bergamask dialect so that he could always be understood to the infinite satisfaction of the court and the King. This troupe leader was very highly regarded then for his modest and lively style of playing as well as for his great enterprise in the management of his fine company. He became rich in Spain and was highly esteemed and generously treated by that nation's king. The Spaniards learnt from him to produce their own plays, which hitherto were neither customary among them nor done by them. Niccolò Barbieri mentions this player in his *Supplica ricorretta* in chapter 25, and Father Giovanni Domenico Ottonelli in his *Christiana moderazione del teatro* praises him highly, saying that he tried to give instruction and pleasure with his delightful witticisms and by performances devoid of obscenity.

(Bartoli, *Notizie istoriche*, 1782, vol. I, pp. 248–9)

Further information about Ganassa is supplied by Ottonelli, writing in the mid seventeenth century from hearsay.

[. . .] in the year 1644 in Florence I heard from a Florentine, a highly intelligent man and very knowledgeable on Spain, that about the year 1610, finding himself in Seville, he heard from certain of his friends, elderly men and eye-witnesses, that the Italian actor Ganazza, who was very diverting in his witticisms, went there with a company of Italian players and began to act in our [improvising] style. Although he and all his other colleagues were not fully and perfectly understood, nonetheless by virtue of the little that was understood he succeeded in making audiences laugh a great deal and earned much money in those cities, while the Spaniards learned from his example to make comedies in their own way, which they had not done previously. All this I take to be true, and believe that just as Ganazza sought to provide utility and pleasure with his delightful witticisms and by performances free of all obscenity, so the Spaniards learned from him to make refined rather than obscene plays.

(Ottonelli, *Della Christiana Moderatione del Theatro*, 1655, II, p. 37)

Giovanni Gabrielli

An early player as elusive as Ganassa is Giovanni Gabrielli. As the following account indicates, he was a popular, street and piazza entertainer, and brought up his children to the profession. Most brilliant of these was Francesco (1588–1636), the Scapino referred to below, who worked in many of the leading companies of his time and was particularly noted for his musical talent and expertise on a variety of instruments.[11] *The little information we possess about the Gabrielli family underscores the close connections which existed throughout the great period of the companies between actors proper and itinerant street and banquet performers. Giovanni's solo performances of plays have something in common with the antics of the Venetian buffoon Cimador described by Aretino and cited above (p. 24).*

A celebrated and exceptional comedian was the father of Scappino

[. . .] he used to give solo performances of an entire play, acting the various characters it required. He would step on to a trestle stage in a square and narrate the most delightful and persuasive stories to the crowd that gathered and stayed to hear him. Then he would get his servant to bring on a large suitcase, saying he kept two vessels in it – a large one and a smaller one. As he continued with a varied and entrancing speech, he would draw from the suitcase first one of his older sons, saying 'Here is the first vessel,' and then, extracting another and younger son he would add, 'Here is the second vessel.' Then he would graciously continue 'This first child needs two portions of food, and this second, only one. Therefore, ladies and gentlemen, pay me a penny each and come and hear my comedy.' The curious crowd would follow him and then, all on his own, he would act out the entire play. Now masked he would pretend to be one character, now without mask he would portray another, and in his pieces he never introduced any woman in the flesh, and never dressed as a woman, but wanted to have on the stage only the voice of a woman. It was in such a way that Sivello entertained the people, pleasing them with witty jokes and with the various characters he represented by changing costumes, transforming his face and altering his voice to the occasion and as he thought appropriate to those scenes he had judged it appropriate to perform. All would depart content, praising him highly, and were pleased to return frequently to hear him.

(Bartoli, *Notizie istoriche*, 1782, vol. I, pp. 246–7)

Vittoria Piissimi

*With the exception of a few like Isabella Andreini and Vincenza Armani (of whom Adriano Valerini left a glowing encomium – see Rasi, (*I Comici, vol. I*), little unfortunately is known about the careers of the leading actresses of the golden age of the* commedia dell'arte. *Their importance, however, cannot be doubted: not only were they great audience draws, but several were troupe leaders in their own right. Much of the information we have about them comes from the panegyrics of admirers, and bears witness to the range and variety of their skills, as does the piece below on Vittoria. The dates of her birth and death are unknown, but she flourished in the later years of the cinquecento and was a member of a number of leading troupes, including the Uniti and the Gelosi. It was she who vied with Isabella Andreini at the court in Florence with her performance of* Zingana *(see above p. 74). A leader for a time of the Confidenti, like many of the great players of her time she moved particularly in the sphere of the court at Mantua.*

But above all worthy of the highest honours is the divine Vittoria who metamorphoses herself on the stage: a beautiful sorceress of love, she entices the hearts of a thousand lovers with her words; a sweet siren, she enchants with smooth incantations the souls of her devout spectators. Without doubt she deserves to be ranked as an embodiment of the arts, for her gestures are proportionate, her movements harmonious and co-ordinated, her actions disciplined and pleasing, her language sweet and affable, her sighs measured and stealing, her laughter suave and delicious, her deportment noble and generous, and her whole person has the perfect decorum that belongs to and befits a perfect actress.

(Garzoni, *La piazza universale*, 1595 ed., 738–9)

Tristano Martinelli

Perhaps the outstanding Arlecchino of his age, some think Tristano Martinelli (1556–c.1630) may have been the Italian actor who created that mask. Few players were as much sought after by royalty and nobility as he, and for much of his career he had close ties with the Gonzaga and with the French court. The brother of Drusiano Martinelli, one of the first Italian players to appear in England in the 1570s, Tristano appears to have had a curiously droll and eccentric wit, evident in the letters he wrote to Maria de' Medici[12] *and the curious publication he may have brought out in France in 1601,* Compositions de Rhetorique *(Lyons), many of the pages of which were blank sheets. The following letter is a useful corrective to the arguments of those who have taken the familiar tone of his letters to Maria de' Medici as evidence of the independence some players could exercise in their relations with powerful patrons. It interestingly shows, too, how ready players were to change troupes, the tense relations which could exist within companies, and how even the most outstanding actors, perhaps by virtue of their gifts, found it difficult to work harmoniously with their fellows.*

This letter [dated 11 December, 1595] is intended to bid Your Lordship farewell, and to beg that you condescend to favour me on the matter about which I write, and with regard to which I shall be much obliged to you. What I wish Your Lordship to do for me is to tell His Serene Highness that if he wishes my service in the line of comedy this Carnival, he need but command me, for I shall be very willing to come and serve him on the slightest sign. If I left the Company of Pedrolino, I had a thousand reasons for doing so: they wish to be masters but not companions; and as I am not accustomed to serving, it seemed to me they were treating me ill. For that reason, as well as for others, I left. Nor was I the first, for thanks to the insolent ways in which they treat their companions three or four others departed before I did. Therefore I beg and implore Your Lordship that for the love of God you fail not to report this to His Supreme Highness, for I would not have him think I have no wish to serve him, when with all my heart I am his servant and quite without self-interest. If he wishes me to serve him, Your Lordship should advise me here in Cremona through the Company of the actress Signa. Diana, addressing letters to the actor M. Giambattista Lazarone who will forward them to me. I beg you to inform me, one way or another, so that I may know what action to take. No more. May Our Lord preserve you in His highest grace. From Cremona.

Tristano Martinelli, called Arlecchino, actor.

(From Jarro, *Epistolari*, 1895, p. 8)

Isabella Andreini

The Andreini were one of the great Italian theatrical families of the late sixteenth and early seventeenth centuries. How the Paduan Isabella Canali (1562–1604) acquired her skills as an actress is not known, but she may first have entered the profession on her marriage in 1578, at the age of sixteen, to Francesco Andreini (1548–1624). She quite rapidly became one of the most celebrated actresses of the age, and was perhaps even more admired by the cognoscenti *and* literati *as a poetess of distinction. Her poetic writings are so informed by the literary mannerisms of the age that they now make for heavy reading, but they may well reflect something of the elaborate, highly figurative language that contemporaries so admired in her stage discourse. In so far as we can judge, she appears to have been an intelligent, subtle, mercurial performer, possessed of powerful and very flexible vocal skills: one of her* tours de force, La pazzia d'Isabella, *runs the gamut of emotions from gentle declarations of love, through bewilderment and despair, to rampant, hair-tearing abandon and lunatic gabble in a hotchpotch of languages – the sort of virtuoso showcase performance beloved of stage* dive *(see above, p. 74). Although Isabella is known to have performed occasionally in other companies, she and her husband are indelibly associated with the Gelosi Company (see above pp. 61–4), which on her death at Lyons he disbanded. Francesco was probably already a player at the time of their marriage, a profession he took to after serving as a soldier and spending some eight years as a Turkish slave. After acting Lover's parts early in his stage career he switched to that of the Capitano, a role he immortalized by publishing a collection of sixty-five dialogues between the Capitano and his servant, Trappola,* Le Bravure del Capitano Spavento *(1607), and to which he later added more. A player of vigour, assurance and wide culture, he and his wife were among the handful of great players who in the final decades of the century gave dignity and status to the work of the professional performer. Francesco Bartoli's panegyric below, if not accurate in all its details, wholly reflects the reputation Isabella enjoyed in her own time and among later generations.*

Isabella Andreini, a celebrated player, was born in Padua in 1562 to parents of modest means who nonetheless did not fail to give her an excellent education, making her learn to read and write, of which study the girl became so enamoured that she desired to make greater progress in the field of letters. At the age of sixteen, in 1578, she became the wife of Francesco Andreini and, in the company directed by Flaminio Scala then touring Italy under the name of the *Comici Gelosi*, performed in theatres in the roles of the lead actress and maintained with great skill her strenuous task. After being nine years an actress she wrote a pastoral in verse that she called *La Mirtilla* and had it printed in Verona by Girolamo Discepolo in 1588, dedicating it to the most illustrious and excellent lady Donna Lavinia della Rovere, Marchesa del Vasto, dated 24 February. It was clear from this her first work that she would produce greater progeny of her talent, as she did in her very elegant *Rime* in no way inferior to those of the most famous poets of that century; and they were published by her in Milan in 1601 by the Bordoni and Lorcarni press in quarto. Isabella was praised by the most famous pens of that golden century: Jacopo Castelvetro, Gabriello Chiabrera, Torquato and Ercole Tasso, Ridolfo Campeggi and others honoured her with their verses, bestowing great praise on her; to all of which praise she modestly responded with sonnets so distinguished that at times, according to certain knowledgeable people, the response was superior to what had prompted it in the nobility of feeling and grace of style that could clearly be heard between the sweetness and the robustness of the lines. Finding herself in Rome, this virtuous actress not only had her portrait painted but was crowned with laurel on a decorated bust between Tasso and Petrarch: following a banquet offered to her by the very eminent cardinal Cinthio Aldobrandini, great patron of the virtues, where the guests were six very knowledgeable cardinals, the above-mentioned Tasso, Cavalier de' Pazzi, Antonio Ongaro and other most illustrious poets, in magnificent competition with them in writing and improvising sonnets Andreini wittily came out best, after only the great Torquato himself. But because in her the strong desire was, so to say, innate to leave after death an immortal reputation, not satisfied with having published her poetic work, under the patronage of the very eminent Aldobrandini she began to compose her *Lettere*, stealing (as she herself says) from Time and the demands of her exhausting acting career, a few hours she could devote to the production of those letters which are adorned by the most beautiful flowers of rhetoric, a vigorous philosophy and witty sayings, and which gave endless pleasure. They were so universally well received that six printed editions appeared between 1607 and 1647 [. . .] She then moved to France in the service of that Majesty, together with her beloved consort from whom she was never separated thanks to the love that jointly bound them. When the fame of this celebrated woman was firmly established in Paris, intending to return to Italy to see her children, she paid a visit to Lyons with her troupe and there received very gracious letters from Great Henry then reigning, who showed her marks of high esteem and regal munificence. The Academy of the Intenti in Pavia thought it a great honour to register her among its members under the name of Accesa, an honour especially devised for this rare woman and not readily bestowed on others. But in the meantime the Lord was pleased to crown her merit in Heaven, for she fell ill with a miscarriage and succumbed to the force of the illness [. . .] As her lasting memorial her husband, Francesco Andreini, had an epitaph sculpted for her in bronze. According to Pietro Mattei in his *History of France* many writers in the past century and today speak of this virtuous woman, and the celebrated Lawyer in his modern *Dictionary* mentions her, claiming that she knew the French and Spanish languages and was accomplished in dance and music [. . .]

(Bartoli, *Notizie istoriche*, 1782, vol. I, pp. 31–4)

Garzoni refers several times to Isabella Andreini in his Piazza universale, *always in a highly complimentary way, as in the following passage.*

The gracious Isabella, a decoration of the stage, an ornament of the theatres, a superb spectacle no less of virtue than of beauty, has herself so distinguished her profession that, while the world lasts, while the years remain, while the prevailing orders and times survive, every voice, every tongue, every cry, will echo the celebrated name of Isabella.

(Garzoni, *La Piazza universale*, 1595 ed., p. 738)

Isabella's husband, Francesco Andreini, was no less profuse in praise of his wife in Le bravure *(1607), putting into the mouth of his stage Capitano the following:*

If Signora Isabella, beautiful in name, beautiful in body, and most beautiful in spirit, had not decided to reward my fidelity and love, I had decided and resolved, conquered by this bitter passion and the torments of love, to take myself off to the wars, like a lover who no longer hopes.

(Scala, *Le Bravure*, 1607. Ragionamenti 4, p. 24)

Flaminio Scala

One of the most important figures in the history of the great companies, Scala (1547–c1620), stage name Flavio, was an actor and writer, and possibly for a time director of the Confidenti. He was much admired in his own age for his contribution to the artistic organization and refinement of the professional drama, although there are few references to his particular skills as a player. Perhaps his major achievements lay in direction and stage management, and in devising, and giving coherence and intellectual substance to, improvised performance. Something of his abilities in these respects is suggested by the collection of scenarii *he published,* Il teatro delle Favole rappresentatativa *(1611). Notwithstanding the difficulties involved in reading these for evidence of actual stage practice (see chapter 6), assuming that many were by him they make amply clear his brilliant dramaturgical gifts, theatrical flair and eye for detail. The Prologue he wrote to his own literary play,* Il finto marito *(1619), shows his attempt to advance a reasoned and coherent aesthetic for actor-devised drama. Scala's tendency, in defining the essence of playing, is to give more importance to movement and gesture than to language.*[13] *The following brief documents are witness to his skills and the esteem in which he was held.*

Flamino Scala was born of noble parents, and after completing his initial studies dedicated himself in his youth to the business of acting comedies. He became an illustrious actor, in part for the beautiful conceits he delivered on the stage while playing the role of the lover, under the name of Flavio, but in part too because he was the first to organize the *commedie dell'arte all'improvviso* in a systematic way, and to formulate all the exact rules for it, having devised a large number of them himself.

(Bartoli, *Notizie istoriche*, 1782, vol. II, pp. 155–6)

Flaminio Scala, called *Flavio*, a distinguished player and troupe leader, acted only in those comedies which had always been supreme, namely improvised pieces with our Arlequin, while in the academies [. . .] regular comedies were performed which had been prevalent in Italy for about a century. In 1611 this same *Flaminio Scala* published his theatre, which consisted of no more than simple scenarios without dialogue: they are not so short as those we employ, and which we fix to the walls of the theatre in the wings, but nonetheless they are not so lengthy that one can get an impression of the dialogue from them, for they set out only what the actor does on the stage and the action in which he appears [. . .]

Flaminio Scala was the first to compose and publish scenarios of plays. Their structure is slight and, I must confess, awkward, and even more than that they are for the most part decidedly offensive. But he possessed skilful invention, and so was praised by the best poets of his time: their verses preface his book and they held him in the very highest regard for having produced the finest drama seen up to that time [. . .]

The finest comedies printed in the early sixteenth century had opened *Flaminio Scala*'s eyes: by his manner of improvising and his mimic skill he gave a better form to his theatre that others might improve the quality of performance, but they quite failed in this way to make theatrical actions harmonious, and to assume reason and good sense [. . .] It is appropriate to note here *en passant* that it was in *Flaminio Scala*'s time that women were first employed on the stage – that is, about the year 1560. Although Flaminio Scala had not yet by then become an actor, he could certainly have witnessed that event.

(Riccoboni, *Histoire du Théâtre Italien*, 1728, pp. 39–42)

Pier Maria Cecchini

A Ferrarese actor whose stage name was Frittellino, Cecchini (1563–1645) played the primo zanni, *and in the course of his career worked with most of the great performers of his day. Awkward and irascible, he seems to have quarrelled with nearly all of them, but undoubtedly was one of the most successful and influential figures of the golden age of the companies: his ennoblement by the Emperor Matthias is a measure of the respect he won abroad. Early under the patronage of the Gonzaga family, he was leader of several companies, the Accesi in particular. He wrote several plays, probably devised* scenarii, *and in his critical and theoretical work was the first to attempt a systematic codification of the improvised theatre. Although his* Brevi discorsi intorno alla comedia e comedianti e spettatori *(1616) is general and rather derivative, it is particularly valuable in coming from the hand of a professional practitioner. It is less important, however, than his* Frutti delle moderne comedie et avvisi a chi le recita *(1628); written from a rather conservative position, at least to the extent that Cecchini was scathing of many newfangled innovations and austere in his analysis of roles and playing, it was, too, intentionally or not, a defence of the professional theatre, not least in the emphasis it put on the responsibility of theatre to entertain and morally edify. Cecchini's links with the Gonzaga are well indicated in the following letter written to the Duke in 1622.*

It was God's pleasure after many years to send me a son, who has been dear to me as a son, but all the more dear in that on my return from Ferrara I found him to be under the patronage of Your Serene Highness of whom I hope one day to be a permanent subject, just as I have been a servant of long standing – for my service began in the year 1583, at which time as a tender youth I first performed some comedies for his most Serene, the Duke Guglielmo, Your Highness' glorious ancestor. That event became a regular occurrence, and in the course of thirty-eight years I have always, with few breaks, served your most Serene House. I served your Highness when you were still in your mother's womb, and I hope to serve your progeny while still in the womb of your Serene Consort [. . .] and I trust this will soon be the case. Meanwhile I advise you of the arrival of Cinthio and others, and we shall open in one of the theatres here on Tuesday, 5 April. At which my wife and I devoutly send our respects and pray that God may bless you.

From Venice, 30 March, 1622.

Most humble and devout servant, Pier Maria Cecchini.

(From Rasi, *I Comici*, 1897, II, p. 626)

The high opinion in which he was held is evident from the following account, revealing for the emphasis it places on the conjunction in the great professional players of careful study and natural talent.[14] *It points, too, the extent to which the profession of player attracted aspirants from the world of late Humanist learning, many no doubt drawn to it as outlets at the courts and universities for their talents began to dry up in the changed social and economically tighter conditions of the later sixteenth and seventeenth centuries.*

What can one say of Pietro Maria Cecchini who, when he acted before her very holy Majesty Emperor Mathias, was accorded the great privilege of being admitted to the nobility? His Majesty proclaimed him and his descendants noble for three generations. This was done because he and other modern players are not of that number who defile the art through their ignorance and do not deserve to be counted among the worthy for whom study and assiduous application is a necessity. Furthermore, a player must be helped in a special way by nature or all effort will be in vain, as has been the case with many in my day who, despite their proficiency in knowledge, were obliged by need to abandon the academic life and aspired to become players. But after their first appearance on the stage, realizing that knowledge unsupported by the gift of nature was inadequate, they withdrew from the theatre, acknowledging the art to be too difficult.

(Bruni, *Le Fatiche Comiche*, 1623, p. 8)

SOME SEVENTEENTH-CENTURY PLAYERS

Giovan Battista Andreini

PLATE 41 *The actor Giovan Battista Andreini. Frontispiece to Andreini's* L'Adamo, *Milan, 1613. Permission of The British Library, 84 e12*

The eldest son of Francesco and Isabella Andreini, Giovan Battista (c.1579–1654), stage name Lelio, was perhaps the major troupe leader of the first half of the seventeenth century. University educated, he acted first in the Gelosi with his parents, thus beginning a long association with the Dukes of Mantua, then with his own company, the Fedeli. He twice married within the profession, his first wife, Virginia Ramponi (Florinda), a brilliant actress, singer and dancer, being until her death perhaps the mainstay of his troupe. Not himself a great actor, he was a fascinating and talented homme de théâtre *and a prolific dramatist. Notwithstanding the attempts of the modern Italian director, Luca Ronconi, to revive some of his plays, his literary-dramatic talents were modest, and none has survived in the regular modern repertory. But he had a sharp eye for theatrical effect, a willingness to experiment with unusual dramaturgy, and was a master of theatrical* mise-en-scène. *One of his best plays,* Due comedie in comedia *(1623), is* inter alia *a mine of information about amateur and professional performance; one of the most curious is* La centaura *(1622), each act of which is cast in a different dramatic genre; his religious piece,* Adamo *(1610), may have been known to Milton.*

Gio. Battista Andreini wrote eighteen plays [. . .] but all are marked by a spiritual decadence, and some are distinctly obscene. Nonetheless, Giovanni Battista Andreini was a man of wit and letters, and I am sure if he had lived fifty years earlier he would have followed the same road as authors did then, and we would have had some fine comedies from him. But he was both an author and a player, and so could write only in the way authors of his own time wrote, and as accorded with his own interests.

(Riccoboni, *Histoire du Théâtre Italien*, 1728, p. 71)

Tiberio Fiorilli

One of the most celebrated commedia dell'arte *performers of the* seicento, *what little we know of Tiberio Fiorilli (c.1605–1694), stage name Scaramouche, comes in part from Angelo Costantini's picaresque life of the actor.* La Vie de Scaramouche, *published in Paris in 1695. Some scholars have dismissed Costantini's account as a mere fabrication, but he was a fellow-actor with Fiorilli and produced his biography only a year after the great actor's death, when many were around who could have exposed it as no more than a fiction. Extravagant, selective and anecdotal, and factually often wrong, it cannot simply be dismissed out of hand as wholly untrustworthy.*

Possibly born in Naples, Fiorilli seems to have played in companies the length and breadth of the peninsula, from Naples to Mantua, and in troupes in and about Palermo in Sicily, where he married the actress Marinetta. He may have been the son of the actor Silvio Fiorillo, but this detail, although remarked by Costantini, is much disputed. He was early taken up by Cardinal Mazarin and was possibly at the French court by as early as 1639. From 1644 he acted with his wife, and with Domenico Locatelli (Trivellino) and Marc Antonio Romagnesi (Orazio), at the Petit Bourbon, probably returning to Italy only in early 1648. References to his activites in his homeland are few, but throughout the 1650s he seems to have divided his time between Paris and the major Italian cities, and was evidently in Italy in the autumn of 1659, when a false account of his death was put out in Paris. By 1661 he was back in Paris with a brilliant new company that included the Arlecchino, Domenico Biancolelli, and played at the Palais Royal on alternate days with Molière's company. His influence on Molière is well attested.

The mask of Scaramouche, or Scaramuccia, *he appears to have assumed early in his career, and it was in this that he won fame in Paris and elsewhere. It was a highly original combination of elements of the* Zanni *and the* Capitano, *with a certain Spanish emphasis in dress and manner that bespoke its Neapolitan origin. Fiorilli dispensed with the half-mask, white-powdering his face for striking visual effect against his black costuming, and substituted a guitar for the Captain's sword. He was above all a physical performer, a mime and an acrobat, who is said to have retained his agility through to his death at the age of nearly ninety. Of his mimic skill*

Evaristo Gherardi wrote: 'he moved more hearts by such simple and natural means than can the finest speakers of the most persuasive rhetorical arts.' Although Gherardi indicates Fiorilli's ability to play with and off other players, many contemporary reports so single him out as a performer that Mario Apollonio is surely right in seeing him as one of those mid and late seventeenth-century commedia dell'arte *actors who brought about a shift of focus in performance from the ensemble to the individual entertainer. John Evelyn, for example, who saw Fiorilli in Italy in the 1640s, and again when he played in London in the 1670s, noticeably speaks of the performer rather than the troupe (see below, chapter 10).*

Fiorilli seems to have delighted Charles II and the English court as much as he did the court of Louis XIV: he visited London at least twice at Charles's request. He appears to have returned to Italy less and less in the final decades of his life, his fortunes evidently being secure in Paris, where in his private life he enjoyed a comfortable living in the court circle and bore two illegitimate children – one with a twenty-three-year-old girl whom royal opinion obliged him to marry after the death of his wife Marinetta. It is known that he played before the ex-Queen Christina of Sweden at her house in Rome in 1669.

Fiorilli was an original, but facets of his style and approach were doubtless absorbed by younger players who worked with him, like Giuseppe Tortoriti, and figures like Scaramouche were conscripted into the literary drama.

Scaramouche having bought some Cloaths, suitable to his small Ability, went from *Ancona* into a City of Romania, call'd *Fano*, where he found a scatter'd Company of Players. Tho' he had never been upon the Stage, yet he presented himself to them, and said boldly that he was an able Player, as if he had fore-seen what he was to be one Day.

PLATE 42 *The actor Tiberio Fiorilli. Permission of the Biblioteca Burcardo, Rome*

The Players receiv'd him with Joy, and having ask'd him what part he intended to act, he answer'd the Comical one, under the Name of *Scaramouche*, and that he would dress himself after such and such a Manner. They found his Name as Comical as his Habit, and 'twas not without very good Reason, that such a Person was look'd upon by them as a very extraordinary Man, since he had prov'd in his Kind an Original, that as yet has had no Copy, and that perhaps never will have any.

They ask'd him too in what Play he would act, he chose the *Libertine*, which he esteem'd above all others, because there's eating in it.

That Play was then put up, to be represented with a new Actor. Curiosity brought thither an extraordinary crowd of People, and *Scaramouche*, who acted his whole part of the Play with very good Success, did likewise acquit himself at the Feast so well, that he was almost ready to burst in the midst of Applause.

The Publick was so charm'd with his first Appearance, that a second was eagerly desir'd; *Scaramouche* very willingly consented to it, and whereas the first time he fill'd his Belly only with hard Eggs, he had in this a Turkey-Cock, too young Patridges, and a Pidgeon-pie.

He restor'd his Company to their former credit, and he who had never before been upon the Stage, was look'd upon by his Partners as the greatest Man in the World, for they found in his Person, all the Mirth and Humour of *Plautus*, and even sometimes the Majesty and Gravity of *Terence*.

It is true that *Scaramouche* had not apply'd himself much to learning but to make Amends, He had so easy and so natural a Way with him, that one would have thought he knew perfectly those things, which he never had learn'd in the least.

These Players went to spend the Carnaval at *Mantua*, where the Young Prince had seen *Scaramouche* two or three Times upon the Stage, was very well pleas'd with him, and gave him soon after considerable Proofs of his Liberality, and you may be sure *Scaramouche*, who was naturally given to Covetousness, knew how to make his Best of so good an Opportunity.

(Costantini, *La Vie de Scaramouche*, 1695, English trans. 1696, pp. 10–13)

Some Players happening to be in *Naples*, he desir'd to be receiv'd into their Company, which they willingly agreed to: and he acted the Part of *Scaramouche*, so divertingly, that the Duke of Satrian hearing how the new Actor was universally commended, sent for those Comedians to have them act in his House, for the Entertainment of his own Family.

The Day was appointed, and according to the usual Custom in the like Feasts, a great part of the Nobility met in the Duke's Palace: *Scaramouche* behav'd himself to a Miracle, and forc'd from all the spectators such Praises as would have feasted the Mind, and therefore satisfy'd the Appetite of any other: but *Scaramouche* when at Table (where he was plac'd by the Duke's Special Command) was so hotly engag'd among the Dishes, that it was easily perceiv'd the Diet he fed upon most was not Glory.

(Costantini, English trans., pp. 35–6)

The following from L'Avocat pour et contre *in Gherardi gives an indication of the kind of pantomimic business of which Fiorilli was a master.*

Scene VII

The scene represents Harlequin's room

Scaramouche, Pasquariel

Scaramouche, after repairing everything in the room, takes his guitar, sits on a chair, and strums on it while he waits for his master to appear. Pasquariel creeps quietly behind him and beats time with the music on his shoulders. This terrifies Scaramouche. In a word, it is now that the incomparable Scaramouche, the ornament of the stage and a model for the most illustrious players of his time – who had schooled them in that most difficult art, so necessary to people of their quality, of rousing passions and reflecting them in the face – it is now, I say, that he holds the audience in helpless laughter for a quarter of an hour together with a scene of terror in which he utters not a single word. It must be acknowledged too that this excellent actor possessed this marvellous talent to the highest degree of perfection, so that he could touch all hearts merely by simplicity and naturalness, far more effectively than is usually managed by the most skilful orators with the charms of the most persuasive rhetoric. A great Prince who saw him act in Rome once said, 'Scaramouche never speaks, but expresses the most beautiful things in the world.' And to mark the esteem in which he held him, when the comedy was done sent for him and made him a present of the coach and six horses which had collected him. He was ever the delight of all the Princes who knew him, and our invincible Monarch never tired of showing him favour. I am even of the opinion that were he not dead, the Italian company would still be active.

(From Gherardi, *Le Théâtre Italien de Gherardi*, 1701, I, pp. 308–9)

PLATE 43 *Frontispiece to C. Cotolendi,* Arliquiniana *(Paris, 1694). Permission of the Biblioteca Burcardo, Rome*

Domenico Biancolelli

A brilliant, imaginative and highly innovative Arlecchino, *under the name by which he was known in Paris, Dominique, Biancolelli (c.1636–1688) was a pivotal figure in the process by which Italian materials were gradually accommodated to French taste. Trained by Carlo Cantù (Buffetto), he quickly acquired a high reputation and was called to Paris in 1661, where he remained until his death. His daughters followed him into the theatre, Caterina in particular being a notable and novel Colombine (see p. 260). He was with Fiorilli and other players in the troupe which performed in London in 1673 for Charles II. His playing was noteworthy for meticulous, very stylized pantomimic detail. Many of the* scenarii *in the Gherardi collection are versions of pieces in which he performed. The following brief passage describes one of his* lazzi, *and clearly indicates that the quality of such 'gags' turned most of the time not just on a sequence of imaginative comic antics, but on the technical skill and the comic instinct of the performer.*

I arrive on the stage. I find Trivelin there on the ground, and thinking him dead I try to pull him to his feet, dropping my wooden sword, which he seizes and uses on my buttocks. I turn without a word, and he gives me a kick in the back and I fall over, get up, pick him up, carry him, and prop him against the right cantonade. I turn away to the theatre footlights, during which time he gets up and sets himself against the left cantonade. This *lazzo* is repeated two or three times.

(From Nicoll, 1931, p. 221, n. 2, citing Gueullette, *Traduction du Scenario*)

Luigi Riccoboni

One of the great early eighteenth-century actor-managers, Riccoboni (1676–1753) was born to the profession and acted first with his parents but, as the letter below indicates, he was initially reluctant to pursue an acting career. A player of intellectual and scholarly inclinations and firm religious convictions, it is perhaps scarcely surprising that he was in the vanguard of those who sought to reform the improvised commedia dell'arte, *to re-establish on the stage the scripted drama of the past, and to encourage new scripted drama in his own day. This he attempted particularly in the work of the company he established in 1706 with his actress wife, and in which he played a Lover role under the stage name of Lelio. Its repertory over the next few years included Corneille, Racine and Molière, as well as Italian Renaissance classic plays like Trissino's* Sofonisba, *and the company achieved considerable success with a contemporary tragedy, Maffei's* Merope *(1713). But in the longer run Riccoboni's attempts at reform were only marginally successful. Given his strong literary inclinations, it is ironic that it was Riccoboni who led the attempt of the Regent's troupe in 1716 to re-establish the improvising Italian comedians on the Paris stage. In the 1720s he performed in London, and was a keen admirer of the English theatre. A deviser himself of* scenarii,[15] *he retired in 1729 and in his later years turned increasingly to writing, producing the first history of the Italian theatre in 1728, several studies of the art of acting, and* Reflexions historiques et critiques sur les différens théâtres de l'Europe *(1738). His writings have done much to inform modern understanding of the* commedia dell'arte.

Serene Highness, Luigi Riccoboni, humble servant and subject of Your Highness, begs to inform you that he has exercised the comic art for four years, doing so as the son of Antonio, who for many years served His Highness' house as Pantalone. In that time he came clearly to recognize that it was impossible for him to save his soul while he exercised the comic art, and on the basis of this conviction he decided last year to leave the art and retire to a monastery. The truth of that can be seen in the negotiations on the matter he has had with the Father Superior de Zocolenti di Cento. But as those who exercise the art are soulless and altogether iniquitous, they arranged for him to be summoned to perform before the Serene Duke of Mantua, and that he could not deny. But he told the said Father Superior of his engagement, showed him the letters exchanged in connection with it, and made plain his inclination and wish to become a religious. Thus, with a thousand worries gnawing his soul, he agreed to continue as an actor. His companions however tried to marry him off to the actress Argentina, but that he managed to avoid. Thus at the end of the year, before being re-engaged, Sig. Co. Cesare Rangoni, in charge of Your Highness' players, was advised that Riccoboni should not be re-engaged as he no longer wished to continue in the art, preferring to earn his bread by God's grace and in a more honourable way. As he has since heard that Leandro, the *primo amoroso,* with the approval of the said Count has selected him to be *secondo amoroso*, albeit against his own wishes, he appeals to the innate goodness of Your Serene Highness to absolve him from practising an art that is alien to him. He is confident he will obtain this, knowing that Your Highness is a true Christian and would permit him neither to offend God by exercising the art nor run the danger of marrying the aforementioned Argentina, who is in the same Company, for were he to do so then he could no longer give up the art and would end in Hell. With profound thanks etc.

(From Courville, 1943, vol. I, p. 35, note 4)

9

Opposition and Defence

Clerical and Moral Hostility

IF THE emergence of the professional acting companies was a product of the changed social, political and cultural climate of the early to middle decades of the sixteenth century, so too was the active hostility to mercenary theatre that persisted through to, and indeed well beyond, the triumph of neo-classical moral reform in the final years of the next century. Anti-theatrical church polemic was of course nothing new but it was accentuated by the post-Trentine reassessment of the role of the church in society, and of the contribution which specific social, intellectual and cultural activities might make to the realization of the Christian way of life.[1] It was led by a formidable opponent, Carlo Borromeo, Archbishop of Milan from 1565 to 1584. Borromeo established the lineaments of a sophisticated theoretical position which later churchmen were to amplify and rework. In essentials this sought to undermine the very bases of theatre by attacking its social functions as both perverse and irrelevant. Theatre was seen by its very nature to subvert the Christian social order in that it substituted an artificial for a real world, denied temporal space and time, and trafficked in dreams and imaginings. Far from leading man to a profounder understanding of, and a wish to commune with and eventually enter into, eternal life, theatre was a place that revelled in fabrications and seduced man from a confrontation with the actual. Further, theatre encouraged identification with the fictional world it presented; by implication it thus denied the value of the contemplative life by stimulating the desire to participate vicariously in its own fictional life. Church and theatre assemblies were seen to be polar opposites: the former, celebrants of the Christian spirit in the world of men; the latter, pursuants of vacuous and profane diversions.

Lay moralists joined clerics in condemning the innumerable temptations which made the theatrical place, with its parade of females, sometimes in scanty attire, its emphasis on luxurious dress and living, and its trading in tales of love and adultery, an evil fascination for the weak, misguided and unwary. The effect made by theatre was seen as comparable to that of painting and sculpture, but much the greater in that theatre presented live and moving pictures, was a public activity, and its subject-matter less easily stipulated or controlled. Most educated and successful players, however, could assume that clerical and moral hostility would be amply offset by the support they received in the late sixteenth-century and throughout much of the seventeenth century from lay patrons of prestige and influence. In this respect they were not unlike Elizabethan and Jacobean actors, who in the main could be confident of royal and aristocratic support in their disputes with Puritan and City opponents.[2] Yet in an important respect the Italian actors and companies were in a very different position. Comparatively centralized rule in England helped to protect the English companies, but it also made government control over the troupes, and censorship of what they performed, all the easier. In England between the 1580s and 1604 royal control of theatre markedly increased, and that control was never effectively challenged until the Civil War. In Italy the divisions of the peninsula, the absence of a single cultural and administrative centre, and the itinerancy on which the economy of many troupes depended, all tended to encourage a fragmentation and gradual diminution of aristocratic control as the market trading possibilities for the companies increased. Surveillance and regulation were the less easy to enforce, and the position of the companies, both major and lesser, if in one sense more free, was in another more precarious, in that it was more open to arbitrary decision and prey to the covert machinations of its enemies from place to place.

But dismissal of theatre and players was by no means blanket in polemical writing, for churchmen hostile to theatre had perforce to reconcile their opposition to certain inescapable facts: the church itself had long been implicated in theatrical activity through its association with the religious drama, and some priests, cardinals and popes past and present maintained a keen interest in theatre. Cardinals like Bibbiena had written plays in their youth and had them performed; the Medici popes were among those who had contributed, however unwittingly, to the emergence of professional companies; actors, if not actresses, were invited to perform in papal palaces.[3] The strategy of many critics was to damn the majority of players by adversely comparing their talents, purposes and morals, to those of a socially approved and culturally respectable few. What comes through much of the polemic is hostility not to court theatre, but to theatre of the kind that spectators paid for in the *piazze* or at the *stanze* box offices. Public theatre was seen as pernicious and dangerous in a way that court theatre was not. The latter served the interests of established order and was under its direct control. Popular public theatre was another matter: the more theatre as trade flourished the more it served, in the eyes of its critics, not social and civic needs, defined in terms of the Christian community, but the mercantilist, acquisitive spirit. Hence an emphasis in the writings of moralists on the willingness of players to indulge in any taste, however perverse or reprobate, for monetary gain.

The Players' Licence

In the eyes of its moral critics part of theatre's fascination for many male members of its audiences lay in the opportunities it provided for indulgence in the lascivious, particularly as manifest in actresses, provocative situations, suggestive gestures, vulgar stage 'business', imagined fantasy worlds, and scanty or exotic costumes. Actresses in particular came in for a great deal of stick, being classed in the main as whores and kept women, and not only by clerics and moralists. Indeed, the strength of the opposition case lay very much in its ability to capitalize on part-truths and popular prejudice. For it is difficult to deny that many acting companies, like mountebank troupes, deliberately exploited sexual suggestion, *double entendres* and the physical charms of actresses, and some players could be downright crude and prurient. Much depended in this respect not simply on the professional and social status of the players, but on their knowledge or calculation of particular audience tastes. There is certainly no reason to suppose that the titillating and scatological appealed only to rough popular audiences at street shows: the description above (p. 24) of Cimador's banquet entertainment antics is but one of many instances which could be given of the taste for the earthy at all social levels.[4] The *scenarii* indicate that there were ample opportunities, when occasion offered, to turn stage 'business' to the bawdy and explicit: cross-dressing, night scenes, abductions and attempted rapes, as well as dressing and undressing on stage, provided the requisite cues. Instances supplied as illustrations in the writings of clerics must obviously be taken with caution, but there is no reason to suppose that Ottonelli fabricated the following incident:

the actors introduced a licentious attempt on the part of an ardent lover to assault a woman he desired. The woman, getting down from a window, escaped in an almost naked condition. She tried to cover herself with a large sheet, but, in point of fact, she remained upon the stage a shameful, naked figure.[5]

Such scenes were probably not that uncommon, for situations as well as dialogue could be uninhibited, and when performance conditions allowed there was probably much play with sexual innuendo, provocative flirtation between the sexes, and easy discussion of sexual matters and natural functions. In *Il finto negromante* (*The Fake Magician*), for example, Flaminia is pregnant by Oratio, and Isabella by his friend Flavio; Pantalone notices Flaminia's belly is beginning to swell and broods over the problem with Pedrolino, who blames it on her recent stay in the country and recommends he find her a husband; in a night scene the two young women appear at their respective windows and discuss their pregnancies with the two young men. In Scala's *La gelosa Isabella* (*The Jealous Isabella*) Pantalone and Gratiano dine at an inn and arrange to spend the night with courtesans; Gratiano's daughter, Flaminia, and the *servetta*, Franceschina, engage in lewd by-play, and Isabella quarrels with her lover because of his interest in whores. The illustrative materials often point the players liberality: one of the elegant sixteenth-century frescoes at Trausnitz Castle in Bavaria, depicting scenes from an improvised comedy, shows a naked woman at a window (plate 44); many other paintings and engravings of *commedia dell'arte* figures have them engaged in sexually explicit 'business' probably not wholly remote from stage practice (for instance, plate 50). These various illustrations may depict the stage activities of both amateur and professional players, and stand firmly in the traditions of both 'popular' and elite art, literature and performance.

Of course in the popular mind, as in that of clerics and moralists, the confusion of a professional actress's stage and private life was all too easily made, and hostile polemic traded in extreme instances. Probably few actresses were as free-living as their critics maintained. Similarly, few companies of players were as libertine in their domestic arrangements as that described by the hostile Petrus Hurtado de Mendoza (see below, p. 251). But an itinerant life-style in a somewhat close and closed profession, and often on the margin of society, doubtless provided examples enough of conduct contrary to Christian spiritual and domestic propriety to fuel the indignation of the theatre's opponents, and by the morally righteous many of the poorer strollers were classified with other social outcasts, like prostitutes, thieves, witches and gypsies, as objects of contempt and obloquy.

PLATE 44 (overleaf) *Fresco in Castle Trausnitz, Bavaria, showing a scene from an improvised play. Late sixteenth century. Permission of the Bayerische Vewaltung der Staatlichen Schlösser Gärten und Seen, Schloss Nymphenburg, Munich*

A Moderate Critic: Ottonelli

Perhaps nowhere is this emphasis in argument more pronounced than in the prolific writings of one of the theatre's most illuminating and provocative critics, the Jesuit, Giulio Domenico Ottonelli, whose five-volume *Della Christiana Moderatione del Theatro* is a monumental disquisition rich in its descriptions of theatrical activity, particularly at the street and *piazza* level.[6] As Ottonelli's title suggests, his stance is essentially that of a moderate critic, a mediator who sought to identify and castigate the scandals and excesses of the mercenary trade, and by banishing them to recuperate a responsible, morally respectable theatre for positive Christian civic purposes. In important respects his writing anticipates, at least by implication, many of the formal and stylistic reforms later to be carried through by the Arcadian movement and the activities of the Venetian dramatist, Carlo Goldoni, in the early and mid eighteenth century (see below, chapter 11). Ottonelli took as the cue for his discussion of theatre the actor Niccolò Barbieri's defence of his profession, *La Supplica*, and in his critical analysis of this is neither unjust to the actor's arguments, nor unwilling to acknowledge the many valid points Barbieri makes. Ottonelli, like other moralists, directed much of his criticism against the practitioners of popular street entertainment. His objections turn on the spiritual and social evils attendant on forms of playing in which commercial motives have displaced any concern for artistic or instructional purpose: fianancial gain is the players' driving force and the *raison d'être* of their performances; wholly concerned as they are with the monetary end-product, players, he argues, all too readily resort to the prurient and trivial, exploit vulgar language, suggestive movement and gesture, and obscene stage 'business', and traffic in unedifying and potentially subversive comic *fabulae*. Such players, prepared to trade in anything for commercial gain, are judged by Ottonelli to be incapable of self-regulation, indeed he argues that they have a vested interest in actively evading any kind of control. In this they are aided by their technique of improvisation for which nothing save the *soggetto* is set down. Anything can be interpolated in performance, and their activities cannot easily be censored when there is no text to censor and when what is done can change radically from one performance to another.[7] Like other critics of the popular stages, Ottonelli is supportive of the major troupes, whose forms, values and organizational structures were closest to the tastes of the high culture, and like most moralists he is more inclined to endorse past tradition than current practice. Ottonelli must be seen perhaps, not so much as a critic of 'popular' theatre, but as a precursor of those reformers who eventually, by the late *seicento*, succeeded in large measure in bridling what they saw to be an unruly trade, and in reining in its materials and energies to conform more closely to the views and interests of the social and religious *status quo*.

What lies behind Ottonelli's disquiet, and that of other critics of theatre far less moderate than he, is then, above all, suspicion of the considerable freedom many actors often enjoyed in their public improvised performances, and concern at the inability of civic authorities to control and direct theatrical work to the ends of approved social and religious ideology. Players of distinction often had perceivable affiliations with the established order and had, too, professional reputations to protect. Many, too, had fixed bases out of which they operated, whether a theatrical centre like Mantua, or home territory in which they were known, respected and could, if necessary, be brought to account. Cecchini, for example, always gravitated back to his birthplace, Ferrara; Fiorilli for long had a house in Florence. The major troupes, too, were more readily definable entities for legal purposes, could if necessary be traced across frontiers, and considerations of long-term interest served to bind them to regulations and contracts.[8] Players and companies low in the hierarchy were another matter. It was perhaps the itinerancy of the lesser troupes that particularly fuelled the suspicion of clerics and administrators: troupes of no fixed abode or means, and owing no evident allegiance to a particular patron or community. These enjoyed a degree of freedom that in the eyes of authority was at best socially uncontributive, at worst potentially or actually subversive.

In Defence of the Profession

Trained neither as philosophers nor as theologians, the defenders of theatre tended to eschew discussion of theatre in terms of religious ideology, and tried to ground their case on past and present theatre practice. They argued that theatre gave innocuous pleasure and delight, and yet was at the same time purposeful and instructional. Where their opponents cited biblical and classical authority to challenge the worth and functions of theatre, they advanced similar authority in support of theatre's utility. Instances were adduced of prelates and princes who had not merely favoured, but had themselves actually performed in plays and had encouraged others to do so. Thus the theatre's defenders sought to demonstrate that at the very least theatre was a harmless diversion: but more, it could claim too to be an instrument of personal, social and moral instruction. Acting, so the arguments ran, could scarcely be a reprehensible activity when it was keenly and voluntarily engaged in by the social and cultural elite for the delight and edification of their peers. Recognition of theatre's worth by the worthy perforce gave it an unassailable seal of approval to which only bigotry could be blind.

PLATE 45 *The actor Niccolò Barbieri. Frontispiece to Barbieri's* La Supplica *(1634). Permission of The British Library, 11795 aa16*

Ottonelli's debating opponent in *Della Christiana Moderatione*, Niccolò Barbieri, wrote the most substantial early defence, based on a lifetime's experience in the theatre as actor, stage director and writer. A player with a marked religious cast of mind, in his *La Supplica* (1634), Barbieri refuted the charges of beggary, theft and promiscuity so often levelled against players, arguing that all could not be condemned for the vices of some, and that most in the profession were honourable and cultivated, concerned seriously with the practice of their craft, and dedicated only to obtaining respect and status in the world.[9] His defence of the morality of players in their personal lives was complemented by a defence of the art of acting as a worthy profession and of play performance as an activity both diversional and instructional. Comedy, particularly vulnerable in that it traded in the local and familiar, and displayed a bias to mockery and ridicule, he defended on the traditional grounds that it served a social function by exposing folly and excess. According to Barbieri, as we have seen above, what distinguished comedy from mere buffoonery was that the laughter it provoked was rooted in observation and imitation of the actual; if not all comedy all the time was correctional, it strove always to be honest and true. Actors, like painters and sculptors, he argued, practised a craft the specialist skills and merit of which had long been acknowledged; like such fellow artisans they sought merely to earn their livelihoods by practising that which they could do best.[10]

The value of Barbieri's account lies in its solidity and sincerity, and in the fact that it was a measured and structured defence. But Barbieri was not alone in speaking out in support of the profession. Pier Maria Cecchini's writings as much as Barbieri's speak eloquently for the social and moral purpose of theatre, and defence of it is overt or implicit in a number of *scenarii*, in some of which actors appear playing actors, as is the case in *Il ritratto* (The Picture) from the Scala collection. There the actress, Vittoria, while neither sentimentalized nor idealized, but a much admired woman of the world, is clearly far from promiscuous, and provides the astute Arlecchino with a chance to advise the Captain that men can hold quite wrong ideas about actresses:

> *Cap. Spavento [Arlecchino]*
> The Captain tells Arlecchino his servant, how, having been going more and more frequently to the theatre, he has fallen in love with the actress Signora Vittoria, and has no wish to leave Parma for Naples before he has enjoyed her. Arlecchino tells him he is wasting his time, for such women are not as easy to get as men suppose.[11]

In the prologues and dedications written for the players' published work, too, we find various kinds of defence. In a sense, the very publication of players' work, as we have said, was a bid for acceptance and respectability. But further, letters and verses of either compliment or dedication bespoke the status of the stage and its cultural and educational worth. From the artistic and technical point of view, one of the most important pieces was the prologue Flaminio Scala wrote to his *Il finto marito* (see, p. 197). While concerned more particularly to explore the relative merits of improvised and premeditated acting, in the seriousness of its discourse and in its high moral tone it speaks seriously of, and for, the profession. Again, many players and troupes exercised a considerable degree of self-censorship, sometimes consciously, sometimes no doubt quite unconsciously in so far as they perforce absorbed the mood and tone of their times. By the late sixteenth century the spirit of the Counter-Reformation had become strongly felt. It is noticeable, for example, that the freedom Machiavelli enjoyed about 1520 to ridicule priests, as in his portrait of Fra Timoteo in *La mandragola*, was not one much exercised by the improvising comedians, and figures like the lecherous, venal monk and the amorous novice nun, so prominent in the *novelle*, are conspicously absent from the *scenarii*.

Documents

The official documents authorizing players to give public performances often defined with some care the kinds of moral and sartorial propriety they were expected to observe. City administrators were particularly alert to the hostility theatre could excite among some clergy, and to the dangers implicit in allowing players to treat of potentially contentious religious subject matter.

AN AUTHORITY FROM THE STATE GOVERNOR OF MILAN, 13 MAY, 1596 FOR THE UNITI COMPANY TO PERFORM PLAYS

It being proper, dignified and appropriate to help and favour those who, by their virtuous study, bring especial benefits and afford satisfaction to the the public in general, and since, from our own knowledge, the Uniti Players, by acting and interpreting in a laudable manner do not only profit many in particular, but give great contentment to the entire city in general, we therefore wish to affirm here the virtue and valour of the same, and grant them, as we do, permission freely and without hindrance to perform their worthy plays as much in public as in private, not only in this city, but in all the other cities, lands and places of this present State of Milan. They cannot, however, act on Christmas Day, nor during the days of Easter, nor on Fridays and those other festive days proclaimed by Holy Church, nor perform while Mass, Vespers and Compline are celebrated . . . nor may they assume religious vestments, nor anything similar, nor may they include divine matter, nor use improper and obscene words, and in all else they must observe, in the exercise of their profession and in the performance of plays, such instructions as they are given by the Honourable Dr Orazio Archinto and the Excellent Dr Marcello Rincio, to whom they are required to show and deliver their plays before they are performed, these persons having formerly been designated, and now by us being so delegated, for this purpose, such being done in order to avoid any possibility of scandal. Thus with this authority we instruct all officials, and all other of our subjects, that they offer no let or hindrance to the fulfilment of this authority, nor occasion any dispute, but show them all due favour and appropriate assistance, and no one wishing to be in our good graces should fail to observe what is set down above. 13 May 1596.

(From Castiglione, *Sentimenti di S. Carlo Borromeo*, 1759, pp. 165–6)

The Governor followed this authority with a letter of instruction to the two officials whose business it was to oversee and approve the subjects and content of stage plays. The passage from his letter below spells out in rather more detail the restraints imposed on the use of anything bearing upon the Church and religious belief.

These players, each and every one of them in their plays, must in no way be permitted to use vestments pertaining to the priesthood nor any other religious, nor use church garments of any kind, nor anything similar to them.

They must not speak in any way of Holy Writ, nor of subject matter contained therein – that is, of anything pertaining to religion and the ecclesiastical state – nor use the particular language of the Holy Sacraments of the Church, nor employ words or topics of ambiguous interpretation concerning matters bearing on the Holy Catholic faith, nor treat of things which might breed superstition in the minds of simple auditors, nor invoke magic spells nor any like evil. [. . .] they must not perform any play the *soggetto* of which has not first been seen and approved by at least one of you two delegates.

(From Castiglione, *Sentimenti di S. Carlo Borromeo*, 1759, pp. 167–8)

OTTONELLI ON CHARLATANS AND PLAYERS

The Jesuit Ottonelli was one of the seventeenth-century commentators on actors and acting who made little or no distinction between charlatans, street entertainers and itinerant players. His comments are the more interesting in that his hostility to players was qualified: he approves and writes admiringly of the comedianti, *like Vittoria Piissimi and Francesco and Isabella Andreini, who acted in the more socially exclusive centres, and were therefore culturally because socially respectable, but is scathingly critical of* ciarlatani, *the performers of the streets and market places. His hostility is manifestly directed at the popular entertainers, and for that reason may well be coloured somewhat by the prejudice of the post-Trentine reformer, but it would have carried little polemical weight if it had not been grounded in some fact.*

I cannot deny that charlatans and players collect money quickly, for they are diligently helped by actresses to gather it in a variety of ways, on the trestle and on the stage, and also in private *conversazioni* in their homes. To treat first of charlatans, the woman who treads the trestle helps to earn money in many ways.

1 Because some who would not [otherwise] buy the charlatan's nostrum [literally, secret], do so thanks to the woman. And to what end? In order to throw a handkerchief at her with money in it – throwing it with the intention of hitting her face or breasts, and then to receive it back later from her hands with a thousand crude and improper thoughts, indifferent to the quality of the secret [itself], whether it be good or bad . . .

2 The woman earns money on the trestle because sometimes she acts as a saleswoman, offering certain fine commodities, whether perfume, or soap, or lozenges or such similar things, which are pretty and appealing; and there is no danger of her not getting rid of them quickly and successfully, for many vain and lascivious men rush to play the part of customer.

3 The woman earns money on the trestle too because she pleases by singing and playing an instrument; moreover she often entertains the crowd with various physical and captivating games, after which a cup is circulated among the spectators to solicit a tip for the lady; nor are many slow to give it. Further, as Beltrame noted, because beautiful actresses are often praised, flattered, and occasionally courted by people of rank, and are virtually raped with presents, great monetary gain undoubtedly accrues to many of them

(Ottonelli *Della Christiana Moderatione del Theatro*, 1648, Bk. I, pp. 121–2)

But although Ottonelli argues that charlatans and popular street players alike merit condemnation, he nonetheless distinguishes between performers of the trestle and those of the stage:

But let us leave the trestle and move to the stage, and turn from charlatans to players, to whom women [likewise] give a great deal of help in earning money; for attendance at mercenary drama is the greater when the actresses are the prettier and fairer, and when it is not just a case of listening but also of looking – and looking with pleasure. Off-stage, actors make a lot of money out of actresses in other ways. First, from the presents of food and clothes which are often given to actresses. Second, from the private gaming that accompanies *conversazioni* with actresses. Third, from the large sums of money paid out to enjoy filthy and improper lewdnesses of the flesh with actresses, of whom many show themselves madly enamoured . . .

(Ottonelli, 1648, I, p. 122)

Ottonelli had no doubt about the mercenary purpose and appeal of theatre, but his strictures were the more effective in that he was in no wise blind to the benefits theatre could offer – albeit that some of the benefits he perceives seem now somewhat curious.

Mercenary drama is popular for economic reasons: that is, at little cost you can buy a great deal of pleasure. Indeed as Beltrame [Niccolò Barbieri] says in his forty-third chapter, people attend plays mainly for economic reasons, for all other entertainment is

PLATE 46 *Late sixteenth century drawing by Joos de Momper* February, *showing players in a piazza. Permission of the Rijksmuseum, Amsterdam*

more expensive than drama: during the winter, for little outlay you can save three hours of light and fuel; during the summer there is less wear and tear on shoes and clothes, for they are protected from the dust; and you save money on alcohol, which might also do you harm. Additionally, dramatic entertainment allows you to study without weakening your eyesight by reading books, for it can amount to a two-hour lesson in which you hear speeches, conceits, *sententiae* and witticisms, to the consolation of the soul and the senses.

(Ottonelli, II, 1649, p. 66)

In the opinion of Ottonelli, and others like him, the actors' pursuit of monetary reward tainted the lower reaches of the profession, and offered irresistible temptation to the avaricious and weak-willed. He thinks many spectators all the more at risk in that they attend plays which treat of love relationships, and has scant sympathy for those who argued that such plays extolled the virtues of wedlock.

Now let us touch briefly on the earnings of certain miserable and depraved actors that a wise man has called double earning – although it is doubly improper, shameless and contemptible. It is this.

Occasionally one finds in a company of players one, two or more women who are clever, beautiful and charming, and who therefore fascinate the eyes and hearts of lascivious admirers. These admirers attempt to assault and conquer their rock of virtue with a battery of gold, but encounter double resistance: that of the actress herself, who resists like an honest woman, and that of the actor who resists as a husband . . . What follows? The assault is redoubled with twice as many gifts, one to the wife, another to the husband, and soon this double and infamous payment opens the way to victory and the multiplication of the ugliest adulteries . . .

(Ottonelli, 1648, I, p. 128)

So I do not think I am a bad judge when I conclude that a public performance in which men and women talk about love, pretending to promote the desirable end of matrimony, should not be permitted, especially in the presence of many who are weak in virtue; for these public and lascivious expressions of loving affection and amorous concern are unlawful because they are scandalous.

But further, the principal aim of actors and actresses is not to champion matrimony, but to look out for their own interest. They all acknowledge this, and address all they do to the business of making profit, professing the comic art in order to live grandly on the comfortable return they get from their work. If they entertain in a modest way, they do so in order to bait the hook, thus enticing and catching a few fish and raising the small sums necessary for their upkeep. In sum, the ultimate aim of actors is gain, as it is the aim of any other artist. I think no practitioner of the comic art could object to my suggestion, for I would convince him by citing the authority of his own Beltrame [Barbieri], who wrote very aptly thus: whoever errs along with common opinion does not deserve particular censure; and whoever is led by experience will not stray from the path. The common aim motivating all human activity is the expectation of gain, and it is the lure of gain that draws a man to achievement. Advancing oneself in reputation is a way to ensure greater profit, therefore this common aim is shared by actors too, and so like others they direct their aims towards gain. He says furthermore that they undertake their mercenary comedies for no other purpose than to obtain board and lodging.

(Ottonelli, 1648, I, pp. 209–10)

THE RANGE OF HOSTILITY TO THEATRE

The following documents illustrate the different kinds of hostility theatre attracted, and something of the devious strategies its opponents adopted in their attempts to limit or curtail the players' activities. The moralists whose views are cited below were decidedly less tolerant that the basically affable Ottonelli.[12]

A letter from the Bishop of Cremona, 26 March, 1572

I am advised that certain players have come to this city and are preparing themselves with great care to give their usual obscene and improper entertainment to the people and, because such creatures are no less insolent than they are presumptuous, I doubt whether they will have patience enough to let the first day of Holy Easter pass before they begin performing.

(From Castiglione, *Sentimenti di S. Carlo Borromeo*, 1759, p. 62)

A father complains to Cardinal Borromeo, Milan, 3 May 1572

Is it not possible for Your Illustrious Lordship, who has banished and expunged from the city of Milan all evil and loose conduct, rather as a farmer eradicates thorns and weeds from an orchard, to eliminate too the terrible virus of those abominable and pernicious comedies given here each year to so much scandal, and which set a bad example to all who hear them? I myself can assert this with confidence, for my only son, on whom all my hopes were pinned, has been seduced and corrupted by these profane men and shameless women who defile the young, so that very often married men stint on their wives in order to give to those shameless women, and children steal from their fathers and, what is worse, these infamous mummers portray on their stage such vulgarities and lewdnesses,

women dressing as men, and boys as women, that I nigh blush as I write this and my notepaper near trembles seeing as it must come into the hands of Your Illustrious Lordship, whom I humbly beg no longer to close his eyes to this plague, but to drive it so far away that one cannot whiff the smell of it, for summer is now coming, when these depraved people are accustomed to come to Milan.
(From Castiglione, *Sentimenti di S. Carlo Borromeo*, 1759, pp. 63–4)

A churchman's scheme for getting rid of players, 24 September, 1581

The proposal I once made as to how public players can be cleverly prevented from ever performing comedies in Milan, even though given permission to do so by the *Governatore*, was that on news on their arrival (something easy to learn of because they put out notices and beat the drum) they should be summoned and kindly advised that before they act any play your Illustrious Lordship, as befits his position, should see their pieces to ensure they contain nothing improper and contrary to the faith. They will almost certainly hand them over, and that once done, assure them that the pieces are being examined, but take as long as possible doing so. Thus they will be unable to bear the expense they normally carry of having to feed many mouths, for they will have no money coming in and will encounter great trouble getting their comedies approved. So they will be forced to depart. This has happened elsewhere here in the Papal States, even though the players had been given permission to act by persons it was impossible to oppose.
(From Castiglione, *Sentimenti di S. Carlo Borromeo*, 1759, p. 117)

Venice bans professional players but eventually reinstates them

This prohibition was for long observed, much to the acclaim of our Republic, but for several years now it has been decided that this Council will license the acting of comedies on two-thirds of the ballot, and to these comedies, men and women, young and old, turn up. Therefore, as a result of the skill that evil people have to subvert the ingenuousness of the young, innumerable follies ensue against the honour of God, the wellbeing of souls, and to the shame of public government, since in this city not only is ordinary hospitality given to the actors but more than one place has been erected in which they act their most shameful plays [. . .] There will be an edict to the effect that a licence for acting such plays or eclogues, meaning however those performed by mercenary people, can only be granted by a decision of the Most Serene Prince, by the six Counsellors, and by the three *Capi*, and taken with five-sixths of the ballot of this Council assembled to the full number of seventeen.

(From Sforza, FM Fiorentini, p. 798, cited Povoledo, 'I Comici professionisti', 1983.)

23 May [1607], the Eve of the Ascension. A company of players began to act plays publicly in the town for six or eight soldi per person (it is already thirty years since the Jesuits got these comedies banned). They acted first in S. Alvise in Ca' Lipamano, then in Rio Marin in S. Basegio in Corte [in rooms] hired by the actors. Then, as the taste for this entertainment grew in the city, the theatre in S. Cassano was built by the Tron family, the theatre in S. Moise by the Zustiniano family, and the theatre in S. Salvador by the Vendramin family. Things so developed that sometimes there were at one and the same time three companies acting, all of which drew large audiences, and they are accustomed to act from S. Martin to Lent, and from Sensa to the middle of July.

(From G. Cozzi, 'Appunti sul teatro e i teatri a Venezia', *Bollettino dell' Istituto di Storia della Società e dello Stato Veneziano*, 1959, vol. I, p. 189)

Players persuade Cardinal Borromeo to let them perform c.1583

That the blessed Priest did not write against capable players, and was not unappreciative of the *Arte Coraica* I conclude from the following. The Company of the Signor Andriano Valerini, a gentleman actor from Verona who was a Doctor and an excellent poet both in Latin and the vernacular, found itself in that same city. The very excellent Signior *Governatore* of Milan invited the company to entertain in his city. The actors accepted the invitation, but having arrived in Milan and staged their first play, that selfsame *Governatore* rescinded their licence and they were supplied with money to return to Verona. The actors were astonished at this, and appealed to the *Governatore*, asking for an explanation, as they had no idea what wrong they had done to warrant such an insult. He replied that certain people had advised him that acting of plays was a mortal sin, and had shown him what their Archbishop had written on the subject. The actors attempted to justify themselves, but the *Governatore* replied, go to the Cardinal and resolve it with him, for as far as I am concerned I shall be happy to hear the company some time, for I like it, but I have no wish to commit mortal sin. And so the actors went to the good Shepherd and were instantly admitted. There they found two of the very same people who had denounced them in audience, advising their superior of what they had said to the Signor *Governatore*. The good Prelate listened to the actors' case. Their two opponents were not slow to produce texts against comedies, and were loathe to allow the players to counter their arguments, almost assuming that the authority of their habits sanctioned their opinions. But the kindly Superior insisted that the players be allowed to speak, saying all were entitled to have their views heard. However, as the matter became drawn out, discussion was adjourned until the following day. Thus the next day, at the agreed time, the actors appeared armed with a defence drawn from learned authorities. Their enemies did likewise. The two parties, one on one side and one on the other, debated for a while, and finally the blessed Cardinal decreed that comedies could be acted in his diocese, citing what Thomas Aquinas had to say about them. He instructed the players to show the *scenarii* of their plays to his office each day, and in that manner many were approved by that Saint and by his Very Reverend Representative. But after a while the preoccupations of the Cardinal's office were such that the order was relaxed, the actors promising their other *soggetti* would be no less respectable than those which had already been inspected. Not so long ago Braga (as the Pantalone of the company was called) and Pedrolino still had some of those approved play *soggetti* or *scenarii*, while those signed by San Carlo are preserved. Indeed in the company of which I am a member now there is a person who possesses two, and keeps them at his home so as not to lose them. The decree is in the Archbishopric of Milan and should anyone be curious enough to wish to look it up, it was issued about three years before the Glorious Saint's death, and can easily be found.

(Barbieri, *La Supplica*, 1634, chapter XXXVI)

Hurtado de Mendoza on actresses

The women are always, or nearly always shameless. Players enjoy a free life together, and the women are not segregated in separate rooms. Thus the men can often see them when they dress, undress or comb themselves, and at times when they are in bed, or when they are half naked. And they are forever exchanging indecencies.

The husbands are cowards and the women do not respect them, nor do lovers fear them.

Often the women are prostitutes, and rapacious. Often players find themselves performing together, and in order for a woman to effect a quick change and take on a new role a man helps her to undress and then dress again. What more can one say? A young actor, for example, will help an actress put on her shoes, and will tie the laces on her leg, and will not just do this on a stage, but also near a bed; those who are familiar with troupes of players are witness to this, and by them I have been told it.

On stage, players portray the love exchanges of characters in plays, and such exchanges between men and women act like burning darts. Players likewise embrace, squeeze hands, kiss, fondle each other, and make secret assignations on stage. Why should they not perform for real in the bedroom what they feign on the stage?

Thus I conclude that these many and frequent opportunities bring some into grave danger of adultery and other crimes, and it is thus impossible for such people to avoid immorality [. . .]

(P. H. de Mendoza, *Scolasticae et morales disputationes*, 1631, in F. Taviani, *La Commedia dell'Arte*, 1969, p. 87)

An anecdote by Hurtado de Mendoza on the immorality of players

On one occasion a friend of mine, a priest, found himself at an inn, and a company of players happened to arrive at the same place. When the priest attempted to admonish one of them, and to persuade him to give up the life, he heard from him of the many sins they all, both married and single, were committing. The astonished priest asked him how it could be that the married men were not satisfied with their own wives, and in reply was told 'Good father, the bridle is changed every second night.' He was alluding to a common mistake made by those who travel with packs of mules, who often put the bridle of one mare on another by accident. Thus the witty actor implied that in their community his companions frequently made use of each other's wives.

(Mendoza, op. cit. in Taviani, *La Commedia dell'Arte*, 1969, p. 88)

Ottonelli on the stage conduct of a player

Further proof (of the iniquity of some players) I have read in a letter written to me on 12 July by a reliable person from a major city. He writes that an actor in his Company named X, dressed in the manner of a certain religious order, portrays the actions of a father confessor. These conclude, there on the stage in public, with him entering a woman's house by a window, cajoling her, and sinning with her, having first pretended to obtain her confession and repentance. This is a very scandalous act. I myself heard the play as I had gone to it in the belief it was a moral piece. I can attest that when it was over I met many who thought these players deserved to be brought before the Inquisition.

(Ottonelli, *Della Christiana Moderatione del Theatro*, V, 1652, pp. 49–50)

Censorship and scenarii

The *Italian* theatre depends upon ancient and modern Sketches which are impossible to be criticized; for the most exact and the chastest Outlines may produce a very scandalous Comedy, especially if the masqued Actors are not People of Virtue. The Liberty of speaking whatever comes uppermost may sometimes seduce the most cautious Players; Criticism would therefore be useless; for that Reason perhaps at *Rome* these Pieces pass no Examination: they therefore go another way to work. They have taken Care to put a kind of Interdict upon Women's going to the Playhouse, as being most liable to be corrupted . . .

(Riccoboni, *An Historical Account* 1741, pp. 214–15)

NICCOLÒ BARBIERI DEFENDS THE PROFESSION

Barbieri wrote what was perhaps the most sustained defence of the theatre in his La Supplica, *a work all the more effective as it came from a long-time actor of great moral integrity.*

Here Barbieri's defence of players becomes a defence of the art of comedy, and reminds us of his vigorous arguments for comedy being superior to mere buffoonery, *above p. 205.*

Many princes and great nobles have acted, and continue to act, before their relatives and associates when it so pleases them, and sometimes they take great trouble over performing the stage characters. Although they do this for their own pleasure, nonetheless they would not commit disgraceful acts in the presence of so many distinguished people for either pleasure or jest. Thus drama is not something scandalous. Many princes, kings and emperors have performed publicly in their theatres, and in our time I have seen the most illustrious Dukes of Mantua – Francesco, Ferdinando and Vincenzo – act with some of our players; and the most illustrious Prince of Urbino, and many others I shall not mention, have often done likewise. Now if an illustrious person can act without detracting from his nobility, why should ordinary decent men lose their reputation when they act for a living, particularly when they perform at times with more care than do their masters? Indeed, I believe that if an illustrious person, albeit for pleasure and without reward, frequently undertook a disgraceful activity in the presence of many, then somehow he would tarnish the splendour of his reputation. So if he does not jeopardize his nobility by acting, then nor can the acting profession be considered base. Many academies perform plays, and as well as incurring the expense of the scenery, they take great pains over their acting, and one cannot believe that they would devote study and expense to a disgraceful activity. Thus drama is an honourable business, and as mercenary players often act the same plays as are done in the academies, they too are respectable. Who influenced the thinking of those who in certain periods despised drama? It was certainly those practitioners who diverged from the right method and devised plays full of improprieties, and in the name of drama produced sordid, unregulated buffooneries. The blame therefore must be placed not on all, but on those who do things improperly.

(Barbieri, *La Supplica,* 1634, chapter VII)

If [players] converse with the common people they are judged to be plebeian, and if they consort with the nobility they are regarded as clowns. Indeed some think comedy is a species of buffoonery, and perhaps for this reason when they see something extravagant, use stock phrases like, this is certainly a fine comedy! or, don't act the comedian here!, or, you are always ready to act the comedian! or, what a comedy!, or I've other things to think about than your play-acting, rather as if every vulgar word or ridiculous gesture were the equivalent of a comedy. Many think players study nothing but foolery; this opinion I shall neither challenge nor defend, for I am

PLATE 47 *Late sixteenth century painting by Leandro Bassano of a* Carnival Scene. *Permission of the Staatliche Schlösser und Gärten, Potsdam-Sanssouci*

convinced that Alcides had less trouble severing the Hydra's new-born heads than in battling with the perfidy of the malicious. But this I will say to those who do not disparage my arguments: to call a sentry a spy because he challenges anyone passing his post, or to call a metal-worker a rubbish sweeper because he gathers gold and silver fillings, is downright stupidity. Similarly, to describe players or other performers as buffoons because occasionally they make people laugh, is to traffic in arguments of either clever sophistry or plain idiocy. The player aims to entertain by way of his skill, but pleasure is not always found in laughter, and there are times when a wondrous thing is more delightful than any action that provokes laughter, and to an informed mind a well-organized tale constitutes the height of pleasure. Players study and stock their memories with a wide variety of things like maxims, conceits, love-speeches, reprimands, and outbursts of desperation and madness, in order to have them ready when needed, and their studies accord with the nature of the characters they perform. As most of them perform serious rather than comic parts, more of them direct their study to serious rather than to jocular things. The greater part of their study is directed more to making audiences weep than to making them laugh, for while laughter springs more from a word or an extravagant gesture than from what is performed in a very studied way, it is a difficult art indeed to make people weep at something they know to be false. It is possible for a man to die in torment without a tear being shed for him, but an ugly grimace, a flamboyant pratfall, the gesture of a monkey, or the playfulness of a puppy or a cat, or some similar animal, is enough to provoke laughter. There is a difference between pleasure and laughter: one often laughs in anger or derision, but someone can give pleaure without mouthing, and will prefer to raise an eyebrow than smirk. [. . .]

(Barbieri, chapter VIII)

10

Diffusion in Europe

Touring Abroad

As we have said above, extant records undoubtedly chart only a small part of the Italian acting companies' activities abroad. We know, for example, that troupes were touring in the German states by the 1570s, and others were active in the French provinces, especially in the south, where Molière perhaps first encountered them, but little record of their work has come down. Inevitably it was court visits which found most frequent mention in the records, and French sources are particularly rich.[1] Royal or noble invitations were often the occasion of foreign touring and these usually attracted mention, but of the regular bread-and-butter activity of the many different troupes which travelled we know little. It is likely that the greater part of the work abroad of all the companies, great or small, consisted in improvised plays. Probably even the major troupes, when *en route* to or from Paris, Dresden or Vienna at royal behest, performed too in some of the towns they passed through: the economy of the companies would have made it more than likely that they did.

Long-distance travel was certainly not easy for an acting company in the sixteenth and seventeenth centuries. The players were naturally not strangers to sea travel. Sometimes, as with the Confidenti troupe Drusiano Martinelli took to Madrid in 1587, the journey was made directly by ship, in that case from Genoa. But in general companies travelled overland, by the principal highways and river and canal routes. Such travel was time-consuming, could be expensive and, as the letters and diaries of contemporary travellers show, might sometimes be dangerous even for those moving in large parties: disease, theft and banditry were not uncommon.[2] Local social and political disturbance and the suspicion or hostility of officialdom could occasion delay or worse. It will be recalled how in 1577 the Gelosi players were taken prisoner in France by religious and political dissidents and had to be ransomed by Henry III. Other vagaries of lengthy travel, from natural disasters to personal accident and illness could never be discounted. In some respects the companies were inured to these difficulties, for theirs was an itinerant profession, and a taste for the nomadic was rapidly acquired by, where it was not already innate to, the professional player. But traversing familiar routes in the peninsula was one thing, travelling long distances into less familiar foreign parts was something else. Early pioneers of the 'grand tour' did so of course; but they were usually the economically privileged, and rarely took their families and chattels with them, as the players often did. It is perhaps to merchants and traders that the acting companies are more analogous, for in one way or another dependence, obligation and economic considerations motivated the travels of both.

Actors travelled for three main reasons. First, when foreign royalty invited a troupe, or when an Italian patron for his own personal and political reasons wished to dispatch to a foreign court either a troupe under his own direct patronage, or one he had expressly formed for service abroad in order to please a foreign power. Second, when the players felt that the anticipated rewards of a foreign tour were such as to make the long journey seem worthwhile. Third, when economic fortunes at home were bleak enough to prompt companies to look further afield for their livelihoods. The Gelosi Company's visit to France in 1571 seems to have been occasioned by the first; Zan Ganassa's activities in Paris in the summer of that same year were possibly an example of the second; some of the Fedeli Company's travels of the late 1620s may have been an instance of the third. When company visits were under royal auspices, troupes could normally expect to have their travel expenses paid and to receive other rewards and subventions in addition to what they made by their public performances. But whatever the economic advantages to the troupes, the longer-term implications of foreign touring were to be enormous. The versatility that enabled many companies to perform both scripted and improvised pieces, and to improvise drama of a distinctly verbal and rhetorical kind, necessarily gave way to an increased emphasis on non-verbal performance before audiences mostly ignorant of the Italian language. Abroad the Italian players were to become increasingly identified with improvisation alone, and improvisation of a distinctly physical rather than verbal kind.

Spain

Spain was from early on an attraction for some troupes. Even before the formation of the professional companies, entertainment by Italian acrobats and dancers, and performance of the Italian learned drama, were familiar in Spanish court and aristocratic circles. Zan Ganassa as we have already noted was active in Spain from 1574 onwards, and it seems that other Italian companies touring in southern France also visited Spain – the troupe of a certain Massimiliano Milanino undertook such a visit in 1581. The activities of Ganassa and these other troupes of the 1570s and early 1580s apparently spawned small itinerant Italo-Spanish companies, but of their activities little is known.[3] There was probably much more *commedia dell'arte* activity in Spain than appears in the extant records, for political and cultural links between Spain and parts of both northern and southern Italy were close, and the travel routes into Spain comparatively easy. For all that Zan Ganassa was a vigorous and imaginative performer and entrepreneur, it is unlikely that his work alone could have exercised the influence on Spanish theatre that Italian example seems to have had: the Spanish scripted *commedia* of dramatists like Lope de Vega shows marks of Italian inspiration; Italian habits seem to have helped to shape the Spanish players' approaches to company organization, use of performance places and technical means. Few Spanish dramatists however seem to have drawn so directly and extensively on the work of the Italian comedians that their influence can be considered incontrovertible; nor did the Spanish professional players themselves pursue, other than in the activities of the Italo-Spanish troupes remarked above, techniques of improvised composition. In this respect the activity of the Italian comedians in Spain is like that of their work elsewhere: their presence was at times quite strongly felt, but the influence of their performance modes and materials is difficult to isolate from that of native entertainment kinds, and thus peculiarly difficult to identify and characterize with confidence.[4]

France

Exactly when the first Italian companies went into France is unclear, but it would seem highly probably that the visits of the Gelosi Company and the Ganassa troupe to Paris in 1571 had been preceded by those of other players. Particularly striking is how quickly after the formation of the professional companies they took to foreign touring. Paris in particular was to draw their talents for some two centuries, although other French towns like Lyons, Bordeaux and Orléans attracted them with equal regularity. What of course made Paris appealing to the companies, in addition to the welcome they could expect from the court, was that for size of population, and so of a potential public theatre audience, no city in Italy could rival it. Italian political and dynastic links with the French throne were undoubtedly crucial, too, in fostering the migration of Italian players to France, above all the patronage bestowed in the early years by Caterina and Maria de' Medici. The Parisian court circles of the two Medici queens were centres of Italian cultural influence in France; French Renaissance culture drew extensively on Italian example in drama as well as in the other arts; the Italian language, while not widely spoken outside the Medici *entourages*, was decidedly a less alien tongue to French courtiers than was, say, English; and the French social and educated elite, at least through to the middle of the seventeenth century, looked to Italian tastes, fashions and practices for inspiration. Nor in the late sixteenth and early seventeenth centuries could French theatre at the time boast professional performance expertise equivalent to, and as abundant as, that of the Italians.

In the late *cinquecento*, and in the early decades of the *seicento*, the companies as a rule made short visits, at least to Paris, of about four to six months. From early on the companies seem to have acted not only in and for the court, but in public theatres to paying spectators, a privilege which, when first granted by the French king, was to the evident disquiet of the vested theatrical interests of the Confréries de la Passion, and through them of the French Parliament. Most of the major companies were in Paris at least once, and allowing for the sketchiness of extant records, their visits to the French capital and elsewhere may have been more frequent than now appears. Visits to the French court bolstered the prestige of the major companies and players, augmenting the status they already enjoyed in Italy and supplementing the income of both players and companies. It was a common European court practice to bestow presents, like purses of money, gold medals, gold chains and suchlike, on departing players, and in this French *largesse* was especially generous.[5]

French theatrical, literary and social influences were doubtless felt by those early visiting Italian companies; but they appear to have been easily assimilated, and do not seem significantly to have modified or contaminated the Italians' traditional performance materials, decorative emphases and acting styles. In the second half of the seventeenth century, however, the case was different. Exactly when Italian players became more regularly based in Paris is uncertain, but from the early 1640s a troupe may have been there on at least a semi-permanent basis. In the 1640s Italian players already in Paris were augmented by performers brought in on the express instruction of Cardinal Mazarin to perform at the Petit Bourbon in the first spectacular *pièce de machine, La finta pazza*. The companies were usually assembled as visiting troupes, probably under *capocomici* who were more spokesmen and business managers than acknowledged leaders. Evidence of the Italian players' activities in the 1650s is thin, but it would seem that they consolidated their position in that decade sufficiently to warrant their instalment in the prestigious Palais Royal in 1661, which theatre they occupied jointly with the company of Molière. These Paris-based Italian players of course returned quite regularly to Italy, and new talent was as regularly imported from the peninsula. Nonetheless by the 1670s, and possibly earlier, the effects of more permanent residence in France became increasingly marked in their playing. There was an ever greater drift towards accommodation of traditional materials, stage 'business', mask emphases and styles of costuming to French social and cultural preferences. French writers prepared *scenarii* or even scripted scenes for the actors to perform.[6] Virtuoso rather than ensemble playing became ever more a feature of performance, and comic and sentimental elements more pronounced. By the 1640s, too, spectacle, music and dance were prominent in the Italian shows, as was an increase in purely pantomimic 'business'; they were to become ever more pronounced in their work, serving to replace the verbal and rhetorical emphases in improvisation characteristic of their performances in Italy, but which were largely irrelevant to playing abroad. Other changes also came about, nowhere perhaps better illustrated than in the début in 1683 of Caterina and Francesca Biancolelli, daughters of the great Arlecchino, Domenico. Biancolelli had joined the Paris company in 1661: his daughters were not merely bred to the Comédie Italienne, but were essentially Franco-Italian in their education and stage leanings. Caterina (1665–1716) in particular introduced strikingly new, and manifestly French, emphases in the stage role of Colombina, which her grandmother had played before her. In her performance this *servetta* role was refined and sentimentalized, and was given, too, a dramaturgical importance that brought it close to the *prima amorosa*: plot devices, including last act discoveries, revelations and confessions, engineered the *servetta*'s elevation into high society, noble family and matrimony.

Whether these changes signal the beginning of a decline in the quality of the Italian drama is a moot point. We have emphasized that the Italian players were above all professionals, and the changes they introduced were clearly calculated in relation to foreign audience tastes and preferences. But the shift away from traditional methods was to have consequences for the Italian players which the early travelling companies could not have contemplated. Accommodation of language, costuming and performance emphases to French tastes must have seemed sound business practice. New role emphases in tune with French predilections, like Pierrot and Columbine, offered exciting possibilities for new players to define

PLATE 48 *The actress Caterina Biancolelli, daughter of Domenico, in the role of Colombine, in which she trïumphed in the late seventeenth century at the Comédie Italienne in Paris. Permission of the Bibliothèque Nationale, Paris*

fresh lines of interpretation. The French king's decision in 1662 to subvent the Italian company with an annual grant as the Comédiens Italiens du Roy, their move to the Hôtel de Bourgogne, and then the formation of the Comédie Italienne in 1680, must all have seemed to the players not just signs of favour, but an endorsement of the Parisian patina they gave to their work. But the patina came later to include a modish satirical thrust that eventually brought about their downfall. In 1697 the Italian players were evicted from their theatre and banished, not to return until 1716, after the death of Louis XIV. The expulsion of the Italian players has traditionally been ascribed to their performance of a play that ridiculed the King's mistress, Mme de Maintenon, but that may merely have been the pretext exploited by officialdom, increasingly suspicious of, and finally incensed by, the satirical emphases in their productions.

Much more important than accommodation to French cultural preferences, however, were the radical adjustments the players made in their working methods. Notwithstanding that a number of Italian players learnt French and were capable of performing in that language, the focus of improvised composition and performance moved away from the verbal to the physical, and the range of their repertories, scripted and improvised, became drastically more confined. What had been a routine method of composing plays came to be seen as the norm, and a norm distinctly different from that characteristic of performance in Italy. The Italian players, as Riccoboni's comments indicate (above, pp. 122–3), came to be thought of as capable only of improvised performance of a distinctly physical and decorative kind. The Europe-wide cultural authority of France helped to endorse that view not only in countries elsewhere, but among many of the players themselves. It was a view the more strengthened by an image of the *commedia dell'arte* fostered by nostalgic recollection and the work of French painters and illustrators during the period of the Italians banishment from Paris.[7]

England

Where the activities of the Italian professional companies and the influence they exercised in France are well documented, in England both are much less tangible. Some educated Englishmen were certainly familiar with the Italians' distinctive modes of playing from encounters they had with them abroad, in France, the Low Countries or Germany, as well as in Italy itself. English visitors to Italian cities could no more have missed them or their mountebank affiliates than did Coryate in Venice, and English players who toured abroad, as many did in the late sixteenth and seventeenth centuries, may have met up with Italian players, although no documentary proof exists of such direct contact. By as early as the 1570s Italian performers were active in England itself. A troupe probably did a pastoral play at Windsor and Reading in 1573, in 1576 a group worked with the musician Alfonso Ferrabosco on an entertainment for Queen Elizabeth, while a leading Italian actor,

Drusiano Martinelli, was in England with his wife Angelica between 1577 and 1578.[8] Apart from the visit of one Flaminio Curtesse in 1602, however, these visiting Italian players of the 1570s may well have been the last between then and the closing of the theatres in 1642, for no concrete evidence of their presence later has come down.

Their apparent absence is, to say the least of it, curious, for the sheer number of references in the Elizabethan and Jacobean drama to comic *lazzi* and figures like Pantalone and Zanni suggests that the performance characteristics and techniques of the Italian improvising players were familiar enough to English playgoers for such references to be immediately meaningful. Some possible indebtednesses have been detected by scholars in the work of major Elizabethan dramatists, particularly in the plays of John Marston and Ben Jonson. Certainly rooted in the assumption that English audiences were familiar with the Italian technique of improvisation is the scene in John Day's *The Travailes of the Three English Brothers* (1607) (see below, pp. 275–7). What the scene points up is the English comic actor Will Kemp's versatility, and his instinctive ability to play the comedian when required, without dependence on a dramatist's text: he too could improvise. It does not necessarily of course indicate that extempore performance was his or any other player's habitual mode of performing on the English stage. Hamlet's celebrated reprimand to the clown not to exceed the licence allowed by the text obviously indicates that some comic players were inclined to do just that, but again does not in itself mean that such licence was common practice.[9] Evidence of the freedom enjoyed by English comic players in the period is perhaps best found in English low comedy, works popular but of more marginal literary merit, like Marston's *Jack Drum's Entertainment* or Barrey's *Ram Alley*, but even in these little influence of the Italian comedians can be incontrovertibly detected.

Some extravagant claims have been made for Shakespeare's knowledge and use of *commedia dell'arte* materials and techniques. One scholar has gone so far as to claim that the insistent introduction of comic elements into Shakespeare's plays of serious concern, particularly when taken in conjunction with textual awkwardnesses and corruptions, indicates that the interpolation of improvised comic business was considerable.[10] Others have argued that the influence of the improvised drama can be felt, too, in the early comedies, like *The Comedy of Errors, The Taming of the Shrew* and *The Merry Wives of Windsor*, while some characters, like Berowne in *Love's Labour's Lost*, Jacques in *As You Like It* and Parolles in *All's Well*, echo, even if at some distance, figures familiar on the Italian comic stage. But the close inter-relationship between some of the materials of the Italian drama *a soggetto* on the one hand, and those of the Italian *cinquecento* scripted drama and the classical comedy on the other, makes identification of influences and borrowings virtually impossible. Quite simply, these various faint similarities and correspondences can be accounted for without reference to the work of the Italian actors. Here and there in other plays by Shakespeare (like the *Merchant of Venice* and *Othello*) some details are indeed striking, but in no respect are they conclusive as evidence that Shakespeare and his fellow dramatists knew and used the example of the Italian improvising players. Perhaps the firmest links which can be established with Shakespeare's work are certain tenuous correspondences between *The Tempest*, for which no sure plot source has been identified, and certain pastoral *scenarii* which treat of scheming *magi*, aided by satyrs or demons, who exercise control over young lovers and shipwrecked enemies, and steer the plot to final revelations, reconciliations and the promise of a new order. Unfortunately no single extant *scenario* contains sufficient correspondence to count as a certain source.[11]

PLATE 49 *Design by Inigo Jones for the* Envious Lover, *a figure in the court masque* Love's Triumph through Callipolis *(1631) by Ben Jonson and Inigo Jones. Unlike most of Jones's drawings of* Commedia dell'arte *figures, this may not have been taken from Callot. Devonshire Collection, Chatsworth. Reproduced by permission of the Chatsworth Settlement Trustees (photograph: Courtauld Institute of Art)*

Only marginally more rewarding as evidence of Italian actors' influence in England are a few Caroline theatre activities. An Italian mountebank, Francesco Nicolini, performed for a time in London, though whether solo or with a small troupe is not known. His presence may account for an increased interest in the period of plays featuring charlatans and their like.[12] The only English play of the Renaissance indisputably based on a *commedia dell'arte scenario* was a Caroline piece, Sir Aston Cockain's *Trappolin, Creduto Principe*; it was scripted by Cockain on the strength of two performances he saw in Venice by the Affezionati in 1632.[13] One or two of the Caroline court masques, like *Love's Triumph through Callipolis*, make specific reference to *commedia dell'arte* figures, and Inigo Jones's extant designs show that he occasionally looked to such figures for inspiration. In the main, however, Jones took as models for his drawings the engravings of Jacques Callot and, notwithstanding his several possible visits to Italy, nothing in his work suggests that he had any developed interest in, or knowledge of, the work of the improvising comedians.[14]

It is hard not to conclude from such evidence as has come down that throughout the period of their heyday the Italian acting companies quite failed to penetrate the English market. It seems to have been too remote and difficult of access, entailing Channel crossings for players and effects, as well as permits and customs clearances; actresses, a staple in Italian company performances, would not have been welcome; and London was already dominated by highly efficient, organized and competitive native companies resistant to the incursions of foreigners. Possibly no less important was the fact that English writers, particularly dramatists, had, perhaps not undeliberately, fostered an image of the Italian improvising comedians and their kinds of performance which helped to identify them in the public mind as mere *farceurs*. Throughout the period of the English Renaissance there was little or no acknowledgement in England that many Italian companies had quite transcended whatever roots that may have had in trestle-stage *piazza* entertainment, and were considerably more than the denizens of street corners and below-stairs that they were in the main depicted as being by English theatre practitioners. The direction Italian playing had taken in France, and the French view of where the nature and quality of Italian playing lay, almost wholly conditioned English educated response.[15]

Nor did the reopening of the theatres in 1660 bring any immediate change in this view. Although the English court in exile probably had ample opportunity to witness performances by Italian players in France, it was not until the 1670s that an Italian company visited London. In April 1673 a troupe arrived that included Tiberio Fiorilli, and may have had in its complement, too, the Arlecchino, Domenico Biancolelli, and the celebrated Dottore, MarcAntonio Romagnesi. On 29 May the diarist John Evelyn saw them perform at court, renewing an acquaintance with the Italian comedy he had first encountered on his travels through the peninsula in the 1640s. The company was evidently popular at court, for it remained throughout the summer, attracting the satirical attention of the playwright John Dryden. It returned to Paris in mid-September, bearing with it gold chains and medals given by Charles II to six of its members, including Scaramouche and the 'Harlekin'. So successful was the visit that the company was invited to return the following year. Whether it came or not is unknown, but a stage was built 'for Scaramouche' in St George's Hall at Windsor Castle. A year later, however, Fiorilli was certainly in England again, and unprecedentedly, although in all probability at the Italians' own insistence, the King gave permission for the troupe to perform regularly to a paying public at the Hall Theatre in Whitehall. Negotiations may have been entered into in the spring or summer of 1683 for yet another visit by Fiorilli, and Sir Christopher Wren was asked to prepare a theatre in Windsor Castle, but the visit seems not to have materialized.[16]

The only other Italian company known to have been in England in the last half of the seventeenth century was that of the Duke of Modena, resident in London between November 1678 and February 1679. Duke Francesco II had evidently arranged this visit for the pleasure of his sister, Maria d'Este, the second wife of King Charles's brother James, Duke of York. What came was a company of some size, including at least twelve players of the Duke's troupe, among them such distinguished performers as Antonio Riccoboni (Pantalone), Guiseppe Tortoriti (Pasquariello), Giovan Antonio Lolli (Dottor Brentino), and four members of the Costantini family.[17] Of particular interest is an extant list of the visitors, a number of them the wives and children of the twelve identifiable performers. Not all the families of the players travelled with them. The wife of Riccoboni for example was one who stayed behind in Italy, for she wrote at this time to the Duke of Modena requesting financial assistance for herself and her children while her husband was on the Duke's service in England. Yet the number on the list amounts to thirty-six. Even allowing that some of these were accompanying court functionaries, the number gives an indication of the size of the groups which travelled when the acting troupes took to the road on long-distance travel. The baggage this company imported was formidable enough in itself, including six portmanteaus, two great baskets and twenty-two trunks!

Unfortunately its stay in London was far from successful: in three months it gave only six plays 'to very little applause'. This was not a reflection on the quality of its performance, but an unfortunate outcome of the political climate of the time. The Titus Oates plot exacerbated anti-Catholic feeling to the embarrassment of the Duchess of York, and to the acute discomfort of the players — as is clear from a letter written by one of the actors, Lolli, to the Duke of Modena complaining of the miserable situation in which the players found themselves. They obtained the 'much desired permission' to leave England, and departed some time in February 1679. In a close profession like that of the Italian players, news of their misfortune in England would soon have spread. It is scarcely surprising that no further visit of an Italian company is recorded for the rest of the century.[18]

If post-Restoration visits were few, however, they left a very distinct impression. The quality of Fiorilli's playing could scarcely be gainsaid, although the more austere and jingoistic Restoration dramatists did their best. It possibly contributed to the consolidation of the genre of farce in the late seventeenth-century English theatre, and certainly encouraged some popular playwrights to take up Franco-Italian plays and materials, as did Edward Ravenscroft with *Scaramouch* (1677), Aphra Behn with *The Emperor of the Moon* (1687), and William Mountfort with *The Life and Death of Doctor Faustus* (1688). It prepared the way too for the eventual emergence in the early eighteenth century of the English pantomime.[19]

Elsewhere

Although we have more records of the activities of the Italian players in France than in other countries, that may be a matter of historical accident. There seems good reason to believe they may have been at least equally active in the German states: they were easy of access, there were many political ties between them and Italian rulers, and Italian players are early recorded touring in Bavaria and elsewhere. Vienna was close to the peninsula, and there are scattered records of the companies' activities there, although patronage inevitably fluctuated according to the interests of the particular ruler.[20] Innsbruck, Graz and Linz seem to have been equally popular with the troupes, and on occasions they were summoned to entertain dignitaries assembled for administrative and political conferences: for example, a company (probably the Confidenti) under the direction of P. M. Cecchini was called to Linz for that purpose in 1614. As so often in the records, it is not always clear whether an entire troupe or only some players made a particular visit, nor can actors readily be distinguished from dancers, acrobats and other kinds of entertainer. Such is the case with a certain 'Franciscina, Comedianten,' who was at the Viennese court in 1575, and with some of the later visits there of G. B. Andreini. Prague too attracted players and companies from an early date, while some troupes touring into France almost certainly went into the Low Countries.[21]

In the later seventeenth, and in the eighteenth century, actors and actresses travelled even further abroad, to Poland, Russia and Scandinavia, often at the request or instruction of a monarch. Antonio Sacchi, for example, was in Russia in 1742, and played with companies in Lisbon in 1753 and at Innsbruck in 1765 (see the account of Sacchi below, p. 301). Some players abroad found great favour, as we have seen Cecchini did when the Emperor bestowed a title of nobility on him at Linz in 1614. But some fared less well, particularly if they abused their position as guests. The brilliant Mezzettino, Angelo Costantini, won great success in the service of Augustus II of Saxony at Dresden, a city long welcoming of Italian players and companies, but became amorously involved with one of the Elector's favourites and was thrown into prison for twenty years; on his release he returned to the boards, but while 'resting' had not kept up his skills, and the old fire was no longer there.

The sparse and scattered records of players and companies abroad quite certainly do no more than hint at the amount and extent of the foreign touring undertaken by the Italian comedians. But their presence seems to have been ubiquitous in the theatrical culture of early modern Europe, or so we must conclude from the wealth of non-Italian iconographic material of the period recording their appearance and antics, and the extent to which people of many nationalities, and at all social levels, seem to have been familiar with their stage masks and performance techniques: sufficiently so at least for pictures of, and references to, the Italian improvising players to be instantly understood. In some of the foreign court circles where they played, of course, such knowledge as they had of French was a help, but above all it was their improvised, pantomimic playing that provided them with a kind of *lingua franca* which enabled them to cross language boundaries with some ease. That they exercised an influence, sometimes very considerable, on

PLATE 50 *A scene from the Recueil Fossard collection. The exact order of the illustrations in this collection is a matter of much debate, but some at least appear to show the action of a particular* scenario, *and may conceivably be a depiction or recollection of what was actually staged. Permission of the National Museum, Stockholm (photograph: Statens Konstmuseer)*

the drama and theatre of many nations can scarcely be questioned, although frequently, too, and particularly at the popular level, it is difficult to separate them and their contribution from the many theatrical forms more indigenous to particular national cultures; difficult, for example, to calculate what debts are owed to them by the Austrian and German popular stage comedy of Handswurst and Pickelharing, or by the early French *farceurs*, or by the Elizabethan comic performers of the Richard Tarleton generation.[22] Perhaps the best one can remark is that few European comedians of the late sixteenth and the seventeenth centuries can have been unaware of their distinctive styles of play composition and performance, whether or not they have seen them on their stages. But what for the most part were known and influential were the materials and performance methods which the Italian players devised for performance abroad to spectators ignorant of the Italian language: performance that capitalized on the physical rather than the verbal.

Documents

The documents below amount to a very cursory and random selection indeed, not least because many of the early notices of the Italian players abroad, save perhaps in France, amount to little more than short mentions.

EARLY ITALIAN COMPANIES IN FRANCE

The following pieces expand somewhat on aspects of the Italian players' activities abroad which have been briefly discussed above. Like most of the records which have survived, they refer primarily to the work of the Italian players in Paris.

French criticism of Italian players and their influence, 1577 and 1608

In this month [February, 1577] the troupe of Italian players called the Gelosi, which the King had expressly brought from Venice for his diversion, and for which he had paid a considerable ransom to the Huguenots Christmas last, began to give their plays in the hall of the Chateau at Blois, and the King has allowed them to do so for all who wish to see them.

[. . . In May] the Queen Mother gave a great banquet at Chenonceau which cost her (so it is said) 100,000 francs [. . .] at this splendid banquet the most beautiful and virtuous ladies of the court appeared half naked.

[. . .] On Sunday 19 May [1577] the Italian actors called the Gelosi began to perform their plays in the hall of the Hôtel de Bourbon in Paris, requiring four *sols* a head from each French spectator wanting to see them act, and such a throng assembled that the four best preachers in Paris would not draw so great a crowd to their preaching [. . .]

[. . .] On Wednesday 26 June the court assembly instructed the Italian Gelosi actors to cease performing their plays, for it was asserted in this assembly by some court counsellors, among them some of the youngest [. . .], that all these plays taught nothing but licentiousness and adultery, and served merely as a school of vice for both sexes in the city of Paris. In truth, even without such teachers, excesses in that city are already great enough, particularly among ladies and young women, who seem to have learned their manners from the soldiers of this age who, when they want to impress, flaunt their breast plates, all gilded and gleaming – in just the same way these females flaunt themselves in low-cut dresses, with their breasts and everything else in perpetual motion, yet all controlled by these ladies with great precision like the swing of a pendulum, or better, like the rhythm of a pair of blacksmith's bellows fanning the flames of a forge.

[. . .] On Saturday 27 July [1577] the Gelosi players from Italy presented the court assembly with letters patent they had from the King giving them permission to perform their plays, notwithstanding the court's decision, but their appeal was rejected and they were forbidden to raise the issue again on pain of 10,000 francs fine [. . .] but notwithstanding this decision at the beginning of the following

September they began to give their plays again at the Hôtel de Bourbon just as before, the corruption of the times being such that fools, buffoons, prostitutes and tarts enjoy all the credit and influence.

(Pierre de L'Estoile, *Memoires-Journaux*, ed. G. Brunet et al, 1865, vol. 1, pp. 179–202)

[A dispatch by the Mantuan agent at the French court to the Duke of Mantua, 19 May, 1608.] A French gentleman, of noble descent and a close relative of Monsieur le Grand Ecuyer, went to the theatre, and instead of the money requested of him by Battistino on the door, gave him a slap on the face, and ignored regulations by pushing him aside. The player pursued him, complaining at the fact that he had been beaten and once again requested payment, at which the Frenchman said, "I paid you in the coin you deserve." Then Battistino, full of rage and stepping forward, said, "As that's the case, here's your change," and straightaway gave him a blow on the nose, which poured with fresh blood. The Frenchman, along with many others, drew his sword, but the player was helped by other Italians who were on the spot, and managed to save himself. Two nights later the same gentleman, with a large band of well-armed companions who pretended to be the Royal Guard, went to the players' lodging house to kill the poor man. But they were recognised, the door to the stairway was shut, as too were the bedroom doors, and the poor player, thanks to a very honest landlord, managed to make his escape by a back way. Still, he had been well prepared to defend himself, having a pistol in one hand and a sword in the other. When the King returned and heard of the affair he ordered Monsieur le Grand to sort it out, which he managed to do. I am surprised that neither Frittellino nor any of his troupe mentioned this to me, for in the hope of serving Your Highness I would have tried to help them. Perhaps they did not require my intervention, for they appealed to Signor Don Giovanni, who has shown them much favour.

(Baschet, *Les Comédiens Italiens*, 1882, pp. 169–70)

An Italian travelling company in Avignon, 1598

During my stay in Avignon I have also seen performances of some very fine plays. These were mainly given by Italian troupes, and notably that of Zan Bragetta, which consisted of four actors and two actresses. In the tennis court theatre they took for several weeks they presented on stage some very jolly pieces which frequently ran late into the night – so much so that one was obliged to wind up in candlelight. I recall that on one occasion a player imitated to perfection the sounds of all kinds of birds and animals, doing so by means of a small whistle which he held in his mouth by his tongue and without ever using his hands. On another occasion a player cut off the head of an actress, behind a curtain, and put it on a bench on a plate. I swear one could see the mutilated neck of the decapitated actress, with her arms hanging down to the ground. Yet there was nothing of magic in this. They also gave three fine *pastorals*, in which the *Pantalone* and the *Zani* made one die with laughter to see and hear their dialogue, dances, gestures and tumbling. Their language consisted of a medley jargon of Italian and Languedoc. Every so often they played very pleasantly on the lute, harp and viola.

When they saw that the audience was beginning to fall off, for the cost of the hall was too much, they set up a trestle on the Place au Change. The show began after dinner with a very amusing comedy, which lasted for a good hour or two, and before a throng of spectators. Following this, *Zani*, the head of the troupe, having opened up a large chest which they had brought with them, was asked by his companion, dressed as a doctor, what the chest contained. *Zani* promptly replied in a high-sounding way that he had brought it from Turkey, where he had bought marvelous prescriptions and acquired many occult recipes [. . .] and forthwith pulled from the chest a small casket of pomade rubbed it on his hands and face, smelling it and making his companions, who were disguised and masked like him, savour it and lauding to them its astonishing properties. There were denunciations and comic resistance from the doctor, *Zani* being dismissed as a mountebank and vagabond, and his pomade made out to be just butter, and so on and so on.

(From *Felix et Thomas Platter à Montpellier*, 1842, pp. 392–3)

Tristano Martinelli meets Henri IV of France, 1599

Arlequin and his troupe arrived in Paris at that time, and when he went to greet the King, which he was disposed to do in his own good time, and His Majesty having risen from his chair, Arlequin mimicked him and, just as if he had been the King himself, said 'Ah, excellent! Arlequin, you have come here with your troupe to entertain me; that greatly pleases me; I promise I shall protect you and will give you such and such a pension etc., etc.' The King did not dare contradict a thing, but said to him, 'Right, you've been imitating me long enough; now allow me to do so.

(From *Les Historiettes de Tallement des Réaux*, ed. Monmerqué, n.d. pp. 89–90)

The French Queen attempts to attract Martinelli to France, 1606–7

Dear Brother,

When my sister the Duchess of Mantua left here I begged her to intercede with you on my behalf that you should send me a company of good players, for indeed I well know that the best in the whole of Italy are frequently in your state. However I am not sure if she remembered to do so. In any case, I wish to write to you and request this favour: that you use your authority quickly to provide for us the best possible company, and I particularly want Arlecchino to be a member, even though I well know he no longer wishes to continue in the profession except in your presence and by your command. But he and all his companions will be so rewarded and reimbursed for the expense of the journey, both here and back, and in addition we shall take so much care to please them and treat them well, that they will be wholly satisfied. This is something both the King and I very much desire. Therefore I beg you to arrange it. (Letter from Maria de'Medici to the Duke of Mantua, 10 November, 1606)

Arlecchino,
I have begged my brother, the Duke of Mantua, to send us a company made up of the best Italian actors – you yourself among them, so agree to the orders my brother will think fit to give you. Ensure that you are all in Lyons in the month of September, and I promise I shall arrange for you to find my treasurer there, or someone else in place of him, who will not be gout-ridden, but who will see you are amply compensated for your journey, and in such a way that you and your troupe will be satisfied. Do not fail me then, just as I will not fail you. (Letter from Maria de'Medici to Tristano Martinelli, *c.* August, 1607)

(Both letters from Baschet, *Les Comédiens Italiens*, 1882, p. 161)

The poet, Malherbe, sees an Italian company at Fontainbleau in 1613

On Saturday evening I shall be at the Italian Comedy at the express bidding of the Queen; without that I would not have gone to see it before we returned from Fontainbleau. Arlequin is certainly very different from what he once was, as too is Patrolin: the former is fifty six years old, and the latter eighty seven, neither of an age any longer appropriate to the stage, where one needs lively temperaments and firm minds, and those one rarely finds in such old bodies as their's. They are putting on the comedy they call *Due simili*, which is Plautus *Menechmi*. I dont know whether the source of the piece was poor or my taste corrupted, but I came away with no sense of satisfaction, other than in the honour done me by the Queen in requesting me to be there.

(From *Oeuvres de Malherbe*, ed. L. Lalanne, 1862, vol. 3, p. 337)

An English visitor to Paris in 1666 sees Scaramouche perform

Palais Cardinal is a fair place with handsome walks. Here Madame Henrietta, the Duchess of Orleans, lives. At one side of this house is a publick stage [the Palais Royal] where the Italian and French comedians act by turns. I saw here *Il maritaggion d'una Statua*, a merry play where the famous buffoon, Scaramuccio, acted. Three antick dances pleased the spectators. The *Quattre Scaramuccie* was another pleasant Italian comedy. We stood in the parterre, or pit, and paid 30 *sols* apiece for seeing the first, and but 15 *sols* for the last. (From Philip Skippon's account of his time in Paris in 1666, and published as an *Account of a Journey through Part of the Low Countries, Germany, Italy and France* in *A Collection of Voyages and Travels*, London, 1732, vol. 6, p. 731)

The expulsion of the Italian players from France in 1697

The French actors detested them [the Italian players] heartily. They took advantage of the great esteem then enjoyed by Mademoiselle Rasin to get rid of them [. . .] and it was through her that the late King (Louis XIV) learned how the Italians intended to perform a comedy in the manner of Le Noble entitled *La Fausse Prude*, and that it was a most vicious satire directed at Madame de Maintenon. This last point was wholly false. However, M. d'Argenson, then Lieutenant General of Police, was ordered to shut their theatre permanently, and to seal up the dressing rooms, which he did on the 14th May, 1697.

Here is the account we were given by Mezetin [Angelo Costantini], at Sieur Riccoboni's house, about their expulsion, for which he claimed he was in no way to blame. There had appeared (he told us) in Holland at that time a dreadful libel called *La Fausse Prude*. According to him it was the history of the late Madame de Maintenon and contained a ferocious satire on that lady. The King was outraged, and gave very firm orders for the book to be suppressed and prevented from being made public [. . .] The Italian actors of the day begged M. de Fatouville, a man of spirit who often worked for them, to re-work in French an Italian piece called *La finta Matrigna* (*La Fausse Belle-mere*) [. . .] and the actors were very imprudent, not to say insolent, to entitle it *La Fausse Prude*, and to present it. Their enemies vigorously attacked this imprudence. They roused the King's anger, who could have had the players punished even more severely for such a manifest lack of respect, but he was content to expel them, and to close their theatre for good. Yet I greatly fear the story Mezetin told us in 1729 is not altogether true, and that he invented it to exonerate himself for being the prime mover in their disgrace, which he had not anticipated. For if such a libel had existed, as he maintained it did, then for all the King's most rigorous orders (*pace* Mezetin), some copies would have reached France, and there would have been some report of it in Holland where, however, no one has seen a book called *La Fausse Prude* concerned with the adventures of Madame de Maintenon.

(From Thomas Simon Gueullette, *Notes at souvenirs sue le Théâtre-Italien au XVIII siecle*, 1938, reprinted 1976, pp. 23–4)

The Italian players are called back to Paris, 1716

Paris, 21 March, 1716 [to the Duke of Parma]
Monsieur Mon Cousin,
I have received with great pleasure the letter you wrote me, and which Count Pichetti (*sic*) delivered, saying you will select a troupe of Italian players and send them, and I ardently hope an occasion will present itself for me in turn to let you know of the high esteem and profound consideration in which I hold you.

Your very affectionate cousin, Philippe d'Orleans

Paris, 16 April, 1716 [from the Parese agent at the French court to Parma]
I have the honour to advise you that the troupe of players is anxiously awaited, and that you will do a singular favour to the Duke d'Orleans if you allow it to set off immediately, assuming it has not departed already.

Paghetti.

(From Courville, *Un artisan de la rénovation théâtrale*, 1943, vol. 1, pp. 4 and 17, note 1)

ENGLISH VIEWS OF THE ITALIAN PLAYERS

The following documents, most of them very short notices, indicate something of the English view of the Italian players, which in the main was not very sympathetic, and was rarely based on any considerable knowledge of the players' work. Included here too is the passage from The Travailes of the Three English Brothers *referred to above.*

English and Italian players compared

Our Players are not as the players beyond the sea, a sort of squirting baudie Comedians, that have Whores and common Curtizans to playe womens partes, and forbeare no immodest speech, or unchast action thay may procure laughter, but our Sceane is more stately furnisht than ever it was in the time of Roscius, our representations honorable and full of gallant resolution, not consisting like theirs of a Pantaloun, a Whore, and a Zanie, but of

Emperours, Kings and Princes, whose true tragedies they do vaunt.

(Thomas Nashe, *Pierce Penilesse*, 1592, p. 27)

Will Kemp, the English Arlecchino

Coming from Venice the last summer, and taking Bergamo in my ways homeward to England, it was my happe, sojourning there four or five days, to light in felowship with that famous Francatrip' Harlicken, who perceiving me to be an Englishman by my habit and speech asked me many particulars of the order and manner of our playes which he termed by the name of representations: amongst other talke he inquired of me if I knew any such Parabolano here as Signor Ciarlatano Kempio. Very well (quoth I) . . . He hearing me say so, began to embrace me anew, and offered me all the courtesie he colde for his sake, saying that altho' he knew him not, yet for the report he had heard of his plesance, he colde not but bee in love with his perfections being absent.

(From Thomas Nashe, 'An Almond for a Parrot', in *Works*, ed. R. B. McKerrow, 1904–10, vol. 3, p. 342)

John Day's The Travailes of the Three English Brothers (1607)

Enter Servant

Ser.: Sir, here's an *Englishman* desires access to you.

Sir Ant.: An *Englishman*? What's his name?

Ser.: He calls himself *Kemp*.

Enter Kemp

Sir Ant.: *Kemp!* Bid him come in. Welcome, honest *Will*.
And how doth all they fellows in England?

Kemp: Why, like good fellows, when they have no money live upon credit.

Sir Ant.: And what good new Plays have you?

Kemp: Many idle toys, but the old play that *Adam* and *Eve* acted in bare action under the fig tree draws most of the Gentlemen.

Sir Ant.: Jesting *Will*.

Kemp: In good earnest it doth, sir.

Sir Ant.: I partly credit thee, but what Play of note have you?

Kemp: Many of name, some of note, especially one; the name was called *Englands Joy*. Marry he was no Poet that wrote it; he drew more Connies in a purse-net than ever were taken at any draught about London.

Enter Servant

Ser.: Sir, here's an Italian *Harlaken* come to offer a play to your Lordship.

Sir Ant.: We willingly accept it. Hark *Kemp*,
Because I like thy jesture and thy mirth
Let me request thee play a part with them.

Kemp: I am somewhat hard of study, and like your honor; but if they will invent any extemporal merriment I'll put on the small sack of wit I ha' left, in venture with them.

Sir Ant.: They shall not deny't; Signior *Harlaken* he is content: I pray thee question him. *Whispers*

Kemp: Now Signior, how many are you in company?

Harl.: None but my wife and my self, sir.

Kemp: Your wife! Why, hark you, will your wife do tricks in public?

Harl.: My wife can play.

Kemp: The honest woman, I make no question; but how if we cast a whore's part or a courtesan?

Harl.: Oh my wife is excellent at that; she's practised it ever since I married her; 'tis her only practise.

Kemp: But, by your leave, and she were my wife, I had rather keep her out of practise a great deal.

Sir Ant.: Yet, since 'tis the custom of the country,
Prithee make one; conclude upon the project:
We neither look for Scholarship nor Art,
But harmless mirth, for that's thy usual part.

Exit

Kemp: You shall find me no turn-coat. But the project, come, and then to casting of the parts.

Harl.: Marry, sir, first we will have an old Pantaloun.

Kemp: Some jealous Coxcombe.

Harl.: Right and that part will I play.

Kemp: The jealous Coxcombe?

Harl.: I ha' play'd that part ever since.

Kemp: Your wife play'd the Curtizan.

Harl.: True, and a great while afore; then I must have a peasant to my man, and he must keep my wife.

Kemp: Your man, and a peasant, keep your wife? I have known a Gentleman keep a peasant's wife, but tis not usual for a peasant to keep his master's wife.

Harl.: Oh 'tis common in our country.

Kemp: And I'll maintain the custom of the country.

Offers to kiss his wife

Harl.: What do you mean, sir?

Kemp: Why, to rehearse my part on your wife's lips: we are fellows, and amongst friends and fellows, you know, all things are common.

Harl.: But she shall be no common thing, if I can keep her several. Then, sir, we must have an *Amorado* that must make me Cornuto.

Kemp: Of for love sake let me play that part.

Harl.: No, ye must play my man's part, and keep my wife.

Kemp: Right, and who so fit to make a man a Cuckold as he that keeps his wife.

Harl.: You shall not play that part.

Kemp: What say you to my boy?

Harl.: I, he may play it and you will.

Kemp: But he cannot make you jealous enough?

Harl.: Tush, I warrant you, I can be jealous for nothing.

Kemp: You should not be a true *Italian* else.

Harl.: Then we must have a Magnifico that must take up the matter betwixt me and my wife.

Kemp: Anything of yours, but I'll take up nothing of your wives.

Harl.: I wish not you should: but come, now am I your Master.
Kemp: Right, and I your servant.
Harl.: Lead the way then.
Kemp: No, I ha more manners than so: in our country 'tis the custom of the Master to go in before his wife and the man to follow the master.
Harl.: In.
Kemp: To his Mistress.
Harl.: Ye are in the right.
Kemp: Way to Cuck-hold's haven: Saint *Luke* be your speed.
Exeunt

(John Day, *The Travailes of the Three English Brothers*, 1607, pp. E4v-F1r)

Tiberio Fiorilli in London

[Treasurer Clifford to the Customs Commissioners, April 1673] That all such clothes, vestments, scenes, ornaments, necessaries and materials directly designed for the proper use of the Italian comedians lately arrived here should be admitted to entry as neither contraband nor prohibited and should be free of Customs.

(From CSP, Treasury Books)

[Letter to Lady Harvey, April 1673] There is arrived Scaramouchy, ye famous Italien comedian with his crew, to act again, & are to have ye King's Theatre in Whitehall for their use during their stay, and all people allowed to come there & see them, paying as they doe at other houses, so ye now a Papist may come to Court for halfe a crowne. This is not much lik'd by other players, for it will half break both our houses.

(From Richard Bulstrode, *The Bulstrode Papers*, London, 1879, I, p. 302)

[The Duke of Monmouth to Sir William Lockhart, April 1675] The King has commanded me to write to you to press the Italian players to hasten their journey, and for their better undertaking it Sir Stephen Fox will remit you by post 200 l. and a yacht shall be made ready at their time in any convenient port they desire to embark at. On their arrival here a place will be assigned them.

(From CSP, Domestic)

[Warrant 20 June 1675] [. . .] to deliver to Monsieur Brunetts, Custom free, and without opening, several vestments, habits, scenes and other necessaries belonging to the Italian comedians and lately brought from France in the 'Portsmouth' and 'Ann' yachts.

(From CSP, Treasury Books)

[Andrew Marvell in a letter of 25 July 1675] Scaramuccio acting dayly in the Hall at Whitehall, and all Sorts of People flocking thither, and paying their Mony as at a common Playhouse; nay even a twelve-penny Gallery is builded for the convenience of his Majesty's poorer Subjects.

(From *Works*, Oxford, 1927, II, p. 320)

[29 September 1675] I saw the Italian Scaramucchio act before the King at Whitehall, people giving money to come in, which was very scandalous, and never so before at Court-diversions. Having seen him act before in Italy many years past, I was not averse from seeing the most excellent of that kind of folly.

(Evelyn 1857, vol. 2, p. 102)

PRIESTS PERFORM *ALL'IMPROVVISO* IN POLAND

In the 1640s the interest of the Polish court in improvised drama all'italiana *was of great concern to the Papal Nuncio, Filomardi, and other seniors of the Church, occasioning reports on the involvement of priests in the theatricals commanded by Ladislav IV.*

I was told there were no priests in the comedy, and indeed I only recognised one. But someone who is more familiar with them reports that there were four: two seculars, one Augustinian, and one conventual. This time however they were wearing masks, and they were so concealed that one needed to be astute to recognize

PLATE 51 *Title page to an anti-Catholic pamphlet* The Divels Legend, *London, 1595, depicting Zanni and Pantalone. A rare English illustration (assuming it was not from a Continental version of the pamphlet) of* Commedia dell'arte *figures. Permission of the Bodleian Library, Oxford, 40.L.62(10)ART*

them. In view of the resolution taken last year and communicated by me to Your Eminence they were very reluctant, but finally His Majesty's authority prevailed, not least for the fact that there were none to replace them. They say the King's Father Confessor removed their scruples, notwithstanding what I myself had said on the matter to the said Father last year. On this occasion they wore the mask, which they did not use before. However, they recognise the impropriety of being before the altar in the morning, and in the evening on a stage acting the *zanni*. For this reason, and because they are ridiculed by the Poles themselves – both the Catholics and those heretics in the service of His Majesty who attend, notwithstanding that the entertainment is private – they are firm in their resolve to give up rather than continue. But they have no money. Indeed they are owed a great sum, but there is no way they can obtain it.

(From M. Brahmer, 'La commedia dell'arte in Polonia', *Ricerche slavistiche*, 1954, 3)

I I

Later Fortunes

The Condition of Theatre at the Turn of the Century

THE LATER seventeenth-century fortunes of the improvised *commedia dell'arte* are inextricably tied to the fortunes of the Italian players abroad, particularly in France. As has been said in the previous chapter, the actors adjusted to French tastes, habits and language and increasingly exploited scenic effects in order to attract French audiences and to compete with native French comedy, and eventually turned to use of texts prepared by French dramatists. Perhaps most important of all, however, in order to communicate effectively in France and other foreign countries, they radically changed their methods of composition. The formal, patterned rhetorical discourse and subtle use of dialect forms characteristic of their performances in Italy were perforce a liability in playing to audiences with no knowledge of Italian, and were rapidly jettisoned in favour of more physical, pantomimic playing, plots with clearly pointed 'through lines', reliance on a simpler, starked delineation of the stage figures, and the reduction of a plurality of 'masks' to a smaller number of immediately recognizable types. Inevitably there was greater emphasis on physical 'business' and the introduction of simple words, phrases and sentences in the language of the audiences to which they were playing in order to clarify stage action and relationships. Most of those changes are readily understandable. Being professionals the players were quick to accommodate their skills to audience expectations and requirements, and in Paris in particular the sheer quantity of French-oriented material encouraged them to look to French professional purveyors of it. Although the imaginative and theatrical quality of the repertory of the Paris-based Italian players was considerable, as is confirmed by a glance at the collections of pieces published by Evaristo Gherardi from 1694 onwards, *Le Théâtre Italien*. The impact of French culture and performance conditions gradually changed the style and materials of the Italian players through to 1697 when, as we have seen, they were banished from Paris. Touring elsewhere had a comparable, if less pronounced and pervasive, effect.

In Italy itself during the late seventeenth and the early eighteenth centuries the improvised drama began, it seems, to stultify and decline. The materials were becoming ossified, performer extravagances had crept in, public tastes had changed, and the form was progressively displaced by more winning novelties. As in France, elaborate stage decoration appealed to high baroque taste, and in performance, perhaps through the filtering back to Italy of the practices of the Italian players in France, there was a comparable tendency to over-inflate comic 'business' and build out the playing of the virtuoso 'mask' interpreters. Clearly all was not well with the Italian regular theatre; too many contemporary commentators bear witness to its decay, and not all can be dismissed as conservative champions of purely literary values.[1] Yet the factors, social, political, economic and aesthetic, which may be contributed to the gradual contamination and disintegration of the improvised comedy are bewilderingly complex. Modern scholars have posited a variety of reasons. They include the possible exhaustion through over-familiarity of the traditional plot materials; the falling away of aristocratic patronage; the emergence in the seventeenth and early eighteenth centuries of more appealing novelties, like *melodramma* and *opera buffa*; the threat provided by the growth of permanent theatre buildings to the viability of a theatre whose vitality lay very much in its itinerant nature; the increasing domination of the eighteenth-century theatre by predominantly middle-class audiences, whose tastes tended to foster the sentimental and decorative in theatre; the usurpation of certain *commedia dell'arte* materials and strategies by dramatists like Molière, Marivaux and Goldoni; and the gradual challenge to the stylized, non-naturalistic basis of improvised performance of a perceptible movement towards naturalism in the eighteenth-century theatre. Particularly important perhaps was the inability of improvised comedy to develop thematic content as effectively as scripted drama. Nor can we ignore the fact that times had simply changed, and along with them performers' inclinations and possibilities, and audiences' tastes and requirements. Each of the factors remarked may in some way have contributed to the decline; yet none is altogether persuasive as a determinant destructive agent. For example, any disposition to see the improvised comedy as a victim of the growth of naturalism needs to be countered by awareness of the popularity in the period of those eminently stylized and theatrical progency of the improvised comedy, albeit at several removes, the harlequinade and pantomime. Again, the establishment of companies in permanent theatre buildings need not necessarily have weakened improvised playing; it was perhaps the least of the factors which shaped the directions taken in Paris by the Comédie Italienne. Yet exactly what happened in and to the Italian professional companies in the eighteenth century perhaps needs more detailed examination than it has hitherto received. As has justly been remarked, the histories of the companies and changes at that time largely remain to be written.[2]

Varieties of Reform

Not least important too in determining the later fortunes of the professional companies was the longer-term impact of the Counter-Reformation, more particularly when its values converged with those of neo-classical aesthetics. We have already touched in chapter 9 on the increasing pressures felt by the theatrical profession from clerical and administrative authorities anxious to curb the freedom of itinerant improvising public players, and have remarked the suspicions accumulated against entertainers apparently concerned more with monetary aquisitiveness than with serving those moral and civic ends endorsed by the dominant culture. Neo-classical emphases on regularity, decorum, refinement and instructional purpose were felt as strongly in the theatre as in literature. By the end of the seventeenth century even that most patrician of stage forms, *opera seria*, under the influence of French-inspired neo-classical notions of the artistically proper, was made more austerely fit by Apostolo Zeno and others, who banished light material and low-life characters from high musical drama. By doing so they helped to spawn a new comic form, *opera buffa*, but that in its turn was conditioned by prevailing assumptions about structure and content. The comedy of the regular theatre could scarcely hope to escape the reformers' concern. Indeed, as we have seen, within the profession, troupe leaders like Pietro Cotta and Luigi Riccoboni sought to discipline improvised performance by banishing crudenesses and banalities and restoring a significant dramatic structure, and both were concerned to advance literary drama. Riccoboni indeed undertook an ambitious programme to restore to the stage the great literary drama of the past and to encourage new, classically regular, modern comedy and tragedy.

In the event Riccoboni had rather more success with tragedy than with comedy, although in neither genre can he be said to have had any lasting success. Nor were his attempts to restore the more traditional balances in improvised performance between the 'serious' and 'comic' *parti* any better rewarded when he led the Prince Regent's Company to Paris in 1716, after the twenty-year banishment of the Italian players was lifted on the death of Louis XIV. The troupe Riccoboni headed, put together by the Duke of Parma at the request of the Duke of Orléans, enjoyed only a short-lived success with improvised performances. Not least of its difficulties, as has been said, was that during the interim a myth of the *commedia dell'arte* had been fostered, and in the eighteenth century was to be sustained, by French artists like Watteau, Gillot, Picart and Lancret, who in their paintings of *commedia dell'arte* characters and scenes stressed the sentimental and picturesque, and helped to strengthen a conception of the improvised comedy which was neo-classical in its formal and decorative features.[3] The returning players could scarcely compete with that myth once the novelty of their reinstatement had worn off, and quickly turned to scripted or semi-scripted pieces prepared by dramatists, the most distinguished of whom was Pierre Marivaux. Of course, pantomimic work remained a feature of the company's playing in Paris, and what were now perceived as the four 'masks' of the *teatro dell'arte* decorated the stage, but the performance of the Italian comedians had become a far cry from what it had been a century before. Some of Riccoboni's extant *scenarii* from the second decade of the eighteenth century bear eloquent witness to the extent to which spectacle, for example, had become a feature of performance. His *Il giocatore*, prepared about 1715, includes an elaborate scene set in a ballroom, and has provision for a variety of formal dances including a minuet.[4]

Yet if by the turn of the century the improvised drama appeared to be in decay, the profession itself attracted many newcomers; indeed, its low standing among the erudite may have been occasioned by their hostility to the many of modest or negligible talent who sought to make a living on the stage. The large number of eighteenth-century troupes of whose existence we know cannot be explained wholly by the fact that by then there is greater likelihood of information surviving than is the case for earlier periods. Throughout Europe in the eighteenth century there was a marked increase in, and a greater commercialization of, nearly all fields of popular recreation and entertainment, including theatre. Understandably, many with few qualifications or opportunities to pursue other careers tried their luck as entertainers: deprivation and unemployment spawned performers. Many in the period, including those directly involved in theatre like Goldoni and Gozzi, bewailed the poor quality of acting talent, and one of the most interesting commentators of the period, the minor dramatist Gianvito Manfredi, in his *L'attore in scena* (1746), addresses the need in comedy to reform playing and renovate repertories. The mass of players seems to have been culturally limited, yet throughout the century there is found, too, a rich array of brilliant actors and actresses, like Antonio Visentini, Elena Balletti, Carlo Bertinazzi, Antonio Collalto, Teodora Ricci, Antonio Sacchi, Giuseppe Lapy, Cesare D'Arbes, Andrea Bertoldi, and Carlo and Camilla Veronese, as well as a number of adroit and inventive troupe leaders like Giuseppe Imer and Girolamo Medebach. The quality of that apex probably depended on the broad and modest base. Perhaps a sad reflection of the decline in support and patronage in Italy is the fact that many of the finest players were drawn abroad, to Paris, Warsaw, Vienna and elsewhere. The early and middle decades of the eighteenth century saw not just a proliferation of troupes, but the tendency of many to visit, and in some cases to settle in, towns across the length and breadth of Europe, northwards in Scandinavia and eastwards in Poland and Russia. As Allardyce Nicoll has justly remarked in *The World of Harlequin*, in some countries they provided a stimulus for the development of national dramas. In this they were following in the footsteps of their predecessors of the late sixteenth century in Spain and elsewhere.

Goldoni, Gozzi and the Venetian Theatre

Riccoboni's attempts within the profession to pioneer reform were carried further by the mid eighteenth-century dramatist, Carlo Goldoni (1707–1796). Partly inspired by Arcadian reformist ideals, but independently innovative, and with a keen instinct for what would take on the stage, Goldoni's reformation entailed the disciplining of masked and improvising players and the reassertion, by the eventual substitution of scripted comedies for *scenarii*, of the role of the comic dramatist in the Italian theatre. He progressively eliminated improvisation and masking in the service of a dramatist-orientated literary comedy. Goldoni was perhaps the first significant professional dramatist to work on a regular basis in the Italian theatre; to that extent at least it can be said that he had a vested interest in advancing the role of the playwright. During his long career, punctuated by periods as an advocate and a diplomat, for he long procrastinated before committing imself wholly to earning a living in the theatre by his pen, his output was remarkably varied and extensive, running to more than two-hundred-and-fifty pieces that included tragedies, tragi-comedies, *libretti* for serious and light opera, and scripted comedies in a wide range of comic kinds, as well as *scenarii* for improvising comedians.[5]

Most of Goldoni's work was done for theatre companies based much of the year in his birthplace, Venice. It was there that he worked with managers and impresarios like Imer, Medebach and the brothers Vendramin, although occasionally too he toured with companies on the mainland and worked in other cities like Rome. The theatrical activity of mid eighteenth-century Venice merits to rank as one of the most diverse and vigorous in the history of the European stage. Commercially oriented and audience-dominated, for a brief time its predominantly comic drama held equal rank with its opera *seria* and *buffa*. It was, too, an intensely competitive theatre, characterized by considerable infighting between performers, composers and literary men, evidenced in the squibs and pasquinades which seasoned cultural life, and the keen rivalry between theatres, both musical and dramatic. In such conflicts Goldoni was often deeply embroiled, and invariably gave as good as he got. His conflicts with popular dramatists like Chiari turned on competition for audiences; those with the reactionary patrician defender of traditional styles and values, Carlo Gozzi (1720–1806), on the nature and purposes of comedy, the purity of the language and the status of improvised drama.

Goldoni rejected what he felt to be the outworn materials and methods of the improvised comedy, condemning the tendency of 'mask' elements to dominate performance, and deploring the resulting reduction of comedy to the broadest farce and mere slapstick knockabout. Although Goldoni himself supplied *scenarii* for improvising actors throughout his career, by the 1740s he was scripting comedies, and by 1750 was vigorously attacking in some of his scripted pieces the crudities and excesses of the old form, as he did in *Pamela nubile*, his popular stage adaptation of Samuel Richardson's novel, and in his dramatized comic discourse on the ills of the stage, regular and musical, *Il teatro comico*. What he sought to bring about was a reform that would substitute for the looseness, repetitiveness and crudeness of the performer-oriented improvised comedy, a controlled and organized written comedy in which the playwright's plotting and dialogue would discipline and direct the exhibitionist tendencies of the players, and recreate in Italy a literary comedy, perhaps in emulation of the seventeenth-century French, but touched by Enlightenment ideals, with bourgeois domestic emphases, and coloured by distinctively local characteristics and appeal.

The evolution of Goldoni's reform was long and, at least in its earlier stages, less deliberate than he came later to claim in his play prefaces and *Memoirs*. Pivotal perhaps was the period between the no longer extant first version of his play *Momolo cortesan* (*Momolo the Courtier*), written in 1738 for the actor Golinetti, and crafted to include a mixture of scripted and improvised dialogue, and *La donna di Garbo* (*The Clever Woman*), a fully scripted piece written in 1742–3, and perhaps the first of his plays to carry the distinctively Goldonian comic tone. Goldoni's major early plays, like *Il servitore di due padroni* (*The Servant of Two Masters*), first written in 1645 in *scenario* form for the actor Antonio Sacchi, and *I due gemelli Veneziani* (*The Venetian Twins*, 1747), interestingly illuminate the dramatist's transformation of the scenario-type materials, improvised comic 'business', and the role lines of improvised drama, into a more formally organized, verbally refined and bourgeois character-oriented scripted comedy. He significantly advanced, too, the importance of the *servetta* role, both in regular comedy and in *opera buffa libretti*, in the composition of which he was a major innovator not least in accommodating traditional materials to deftly sketched characterization and familiar and domestic bourgeois situations.[6] Goldoni was essentially a performer's dramatist, in the sense that the strength of his best plays lies less in their dialogue than in their dramaturgy. Goldonian comedy serves to remind us of where the great strength of the improvised drama lay: it invariably gives far more to the perfomer and spectator than to the reader. Much of this dramaturgical skill Goldoni acquired working with improvising players, and for all his reformist intentions, even when the plot and character elements of his later comedy are directed more to social observations, as in *La Bettina*, and are furthest from the materials of the improvised *commedia dell'arte*, he rarely abandons altogether the model of fast and physical, even balletic, performance provided by the improvising comedians at their best.

In 1762 Goldoni left Venice to take up a position as house dramatist at the Comédie Italienne in Paris. It is invariably said that he was driven out by the success of his opponent Gozzi, but his move to Paris was probably as much inspired by the attractions of the salary and relative security he hoped to obtain there, and the possibility of gaining the patronage of the French monarch and those about the court. In the event, the best he got was a comfortable living, and in the longer term a pension for his services as Italian tutor. For these he cut the tap roots of his stage inspiration, and little of his later work in France stands comparison with his Venetian output.

Goldoni's rival, Carlo Gozzi, was a Venetian aristocrat of modest means. Highly conservative on literary and cultural matters, he took his reactionary bearings from the more patrician of the literary and artistic academies.[7] Hostile to Enlightenment ideas, and a champion of aristocratic decorum and linguistic purity, he deplored the Goldonian reform of improvised comedy, and the way in which Goldoni's comedy trafficked in the local, familiar and domestic. Against Goldoni's stylized yet often quasi-realistic depictions of Venetian society, family and street life, Gozzi set the curious and fantastically imaginative worlds of his *fiabe*, in an attempt to restore what were assumed to be the traditional 'masks' in plays like *L'amore delle tre melarance* (*The Love of Three Oranges*), first produced in 1761. Over the next five years he wrote nine more pieces in the same vein, the best known of which are *Il re cervo* (*The King Stag*), *Turandot, La donna serpente* (*The Snake Woman*), and *Il mostro turchino* (*The Blue Monster*). Fragile, fairy-tale pieces, these mingled the scripted and the improvised, and like some of the earlier improvised pastorals and heroic plays, translated the masked figures to a court world of kings, aristocrats and *maghi*. His plays enjoyed an immediate vogue, were later to be taken up as precursors of the romantic movement, and as *libretti* were set by many opera composers. But as plays in their own right they have little depth. Gozzi drew for them on popular story and romance, but was essentially parasitical on his sources. In a sense, certainly, he was a champion of theatrical theatre, but largely in the service of decoration, and the picturesqueness and grotesquerie of his plays are in many respects an extension of elements latent in some of the depictions of *commedia dell'arte* figures found in contemporary paintings and ceramics. Gozzi did not succeed in restoring the improvised drama. Replete with topical satire, his early plays were part of a deliberate assault on the popularity of Goldoni; but the competitive atmosphere of Venetian theatre encouraged rapid shifts in taste, and their success was short-lived. Ultimately Gozzi is important much more for the inspiration his work later gave to other kinds of theatre, particularly the musical, and for the extent to which his plays encouraged the development of a myth of what the *commedia dell'arte* had been.

Gozzi worked closely with a Venetian company the lead player in which was one of the finest comedians of the age, Antonio Sacchi. The brief overview of his career below indicates the extent to which he performed abroad, evidence in itself of how the improvised comedy spread to many countries, particularly in Eastern Europe: the Sacchi family of *figli d'arte* eventually settled in Russia, where it had gone to entertain the Empress Catherine. Antonio Sacchi's death in 1788, on ship from Genoa to Marseilles, is often taken to mark the demise of improvised playing, as too does the closure of the Comédie Italienne in 1782. In Italy some elements of improvised playing as it had become by the late seventeenth century lingered on, particularly in Naples and southern Italy, and in the work of mid nineteenth-century popular performers like Antonio Petito. The new kinds of comic theatre evolved elsewhere in Europe, like the harlequinade, pantomime and pierrot show, styled in some respects on the repute and iconography, and the Arlecchino and Pulcinella 'masks', of the *commedia dell'arte*, again as it was known in the eighteenth century, transmitted something of its spirit. But none of this was the theatre of Flaminio Scala and Virginia Armani, the Gabrielli and the Andreini. The *commedia degli Italiani* had become, in a sense, a victim of its own Europe-wide success. A myth or 'idea' of what the *commedia dell'arte* was had now largely displaced the historical reality in the European imagination. Nearly all the new forms exploited what the visual arts likewise emphasized, the potentially sentimental and decorative elements now foregrounded in the figures, costuming and situations of the *commedia all'improvviso*, and more particularly those of the 'four masks'. Much the same may be said of *commedia dell'arte* elements in the new *settecento* dramatic form, *opera buffa*, which levied heavily on the example of the improvising players.[8] In England a tendency to decorative treatment of figures based on the 'four masks' was indirectly reinforced by the restrictions of the Licensing Act of 1737, and the performances of English Harlequins between John Rich and David Garrick shifted emphases quite significantly. In the course of the century, similar formal tightening of performance regulations elsewhere in Europe including parts of Italy (like Venice in the early 1750s), helped to undermine the ability of players to work extempore. Increasingly players accommodated to the performance of scripted drama alone.

Documents

The eighteenth century is rich in documentary material, and here we can include only a brief selection of pieces in order to characterize some features, and draw attention to some of the more important players, of the period. The material gathered here is thus particularly disparate and wide-ranging.

A SUBMISSION BY THE REGENT'S COMPANY IN 1716

The company that returned to Paris in 1716 after the long banishment of the Italians, was anxious to secure itself on a firm footing. It anticipated that the lifting of the prohibition would encourage other Italian players to invade the Parisian market, and from the start sought a monopoly. It underscored its religious respectability, as well as its dependence on, and willingness to accommodate its playing materials to, court and church authorities. Intriguing is the reference to 'command of the French language' by possible Italian rivals; clearly there was a good supply of players with such expertise, not least because after 1697 many worked in the French provinces, as did the son of Domenico Biancolelli, Pietro Francesco, who returned to Paris with the Regent's troupe in 1716, and was skilled at performing in the French tongue. No less intriguing is the players' scapegoating of the Costantini family: Angelo Costantini had widely been thought the chief culprit in the activities which led to the expulsion of the Italian players from Paris in 1697.

PLATE 52 (overleaf) *An artist's impression of the return of the Italian players to Paris in 1716 after their long banishment; Luigi Riccoboni (Lelio) is shown introducing Arlecchino (Tommaso Visentini) to the French public, Musée Carnavalet, Paris (photograph: Giraudon)*

1. The entire company humbly begs that Your Serene Highness will grant it the same favour as was shown to its predecessor,

and that no other Italian company, no matter what the reason, will be permitted to perform in Paris, even if all the actors command the French language. The company begs too that none be allowed to use the costumes of the masked players of the Italian theatre, that is to say, Arlequin, Scaramouche, Pantalone, Dottore and Scapino, nor that of Pierrot which, although French, was derived from the Italian theatre.

2. Wishing only to serve Your Majesty in a peaceful and reputable way, the players request that no member of the Costantini family ever be enlisted into the company, for everyone knows that it was thanks to them that their predecessors in the Italian theatre fell into disfavour and disgrace.
3. They humbly beg that they be allowed to perform, as their predecessors were, dances and music in the interludes of their plays.
4. Should any actor be so unfortunate as to displease the court and the city, the company requests the authority to dismiss him with a gift and call for another to take his place.
5. The actors beg Your Serene Highness most humbly to request of the court that they be permitted, as in Italy, free use of the Holy Sacraments; especially as they will never perform a scurrilous play, and Riccoboni undertakes to submit play scenarios for the examination of the minister and also for the approval of the Church.

(M. T. Le Moyne des Essarts, *Les trois théâtres*, 1777, pp. 191–2)

AUDIENCES, COMPANIES AND PLAYERS

Throughout the century even major companies remained itinerant for considerable parts of the year: the troupes in Venice provide a particularly good example, being invariably playhouse based during the long Carnival season from Boxing Day through to Lent, and then touring the mainland at other times in the year.

A description of a Venetian theatre

A French visitor to Venice in the late seventeenth century has left perhaps the single, most detailed account of audiences in that city.

The Comedy is only at Venice in *Carnaval*-time; however, it sometimes begins in the end of *October* or beginning of *November*, in which Month one frequently finds here three several Gangs of *Comedians*, each infinitely worse than the other. The Theatres in which they Act, belong to the Noble *Venetians*, as likewise those of the *Opera's*, from whence they receive very considerable Profits; for they let their Boxes at such a certain Price for the whole *Carnaval*, or else so much a Day. The Profit of the Actors is only what they receive at the Door, which do's not exceed five Pence each Head. [. . .] The Young Nobility do not go so much to the Comedy to laugh at the Buffoonery of the Actors, as to play their own ridiculous Parts: They commonly bring Courtesans with them to their Boxes, where there is such a confusion and sometimes such surprizing Accidents, so contrary to the Rules of Decency, which are at least due in all Publik Places, that one must indeed see these Transactions before he can believe them. One of their most ordinary Diversions is not only to spit in the Pit, but likewise to pelt them with Snuffs and ends of Candles, and if they perceive any one decently clad, or with a Feather in his Hat, they are sure to ply him with the best of their endeavours, which they may do as being free from all notice or punishment; for the Nobles that are the Protectors of the Theater, having their Bravo's in disguise at the doors, who are well armed, and ready to obey Orders: Besides the *Comedy* and *Opera* are look'd upon as Privilege-places where the least Violence would be reckon'd a Crime of State.

The liberty which they in the Pit take, according to the Example of the Nobility, do's finally raise the Confusion to its utmost height. The *Gondoliers* chiefly do give their impertinent Applauses to some Actions of the Buffoons, that would be tolerated in no other Place; neither is it seldom that the whole House makes such terrible Exclamations against the Actors, who are not so happy as to please, that they are forced to retire to be succeeded by others; for the continual cry is, *fuora buffoni*. The Gentlemen find this so agreeable to 'em, that even they themselves are frequently this hissing Party; and if one inquires how it comes to pass, That they are so very prudent and wise at the Great *Ridotti* where they Game, and so extravagantly foolish at the *Comedy*; you are answered: That they sit at the former Place to take the hazards of Fortune, but that they come hither to divert themselves only; and as Masters, they are pleas'd to do it according to the method most agreeable to them.

Nothing can equal the noise which is made when a Play has given satisfaction to the Assembly, or to speak more properly to the *Gondoliers*; for when they come to name the Play to be acted the next Day, that Mob cries out *questa, questa*, play the same again, which must be of course obey'd. Whereby one usually brings away from these pitiful *Comedies*, the dissatisfaction only of having delay'd Supper until nine or ten at Night, yet they sometimes act such as are very serious. These compositions are in Verse, and these they call *Opera's*, with which they have indifferent good Success. At other times they represent such as would not be tolerated by the *Inquisition* anywhere out of the Territories of the State of *Venice*; as that of *Don Giles*, who in the Habit of a *Religious*, preaches against the Debauchery to which he abandons himself. Yet it is no way strange that these things pass unregarded, seeing the Nobles suffer themselves to be ridicul'd upon the Stage, in the Person of *Pantalon*, who is a real Copy of them, in Habits, Actions, and Words, which he really imitates with the greatest exactness.

(Limojon de Saint-Didier, *The City and Republick of Venice*, English translation, 1699, pp.65–7)

A company on the move

Some companies were regularly on the move, and Carlo Goldoni in his Memoires *provides a vivid account of a troupe travelling by boat that is probably not untypical, even if somewhat coloured by comic exaggeration.*

Twelve persons, actors as well as actresses, a prompter, a machinist, a store-keeper, eight domestics, four chambermaids, two nurses, children of every age, cats, dogs, monkeys, parrots, birds, pigeons, and a lamb – it was another Noah's ark!

The bark was very large, and divided into a number of apartments. Every female had her little corner with curtains. An excellent bed was fitted up for me beside the manager and all of us were comfortable.

The steward, who was at the same time cook and butler, rang a little bell which was our signal for breakfast. On this, we all assembled in a sort of saloon in the middle of the vessel above the chests, trunks and packages. An oval table was covered with coffee, tea, milk, roast meat, water and wine.

The Principal actress (*première amoureuse*) asked for soup. There was none. She was quite in a rage, and they had all the difficulty in the world to pacify her with a cup of chocolate. She was the ugliest and the most difficult to please of the whole.

After breakfast, play was proposed till dinner should be ready. I played *tresset* pretty well. It was the favourite game of my mother, from whom I learned it.

We were going to begin tresset and piquet, but a faro-table on deck drew everybody towards it. The bank was more a matter of amusement than interest, and the director would not have suffered it on any other terms. We played, laughed, joked, and gave ourselves up to all manner of tricks till the bell summoned us to dinner.

[. . .] The wind was unfavourable, and we remained three days at sea; always with the same amusements, the same pleasures, and the same appetite. We arrived on the fourth day at Chiozza.

(Goldoni, *Memoirs*, trans. Black, 1814, pp. 22–4)

Gozzi describes the Sacchi company

A rich mine of information about the Venetian theatre in the mid eighteenth century is Gozzi's Memorie inutili, *notwithstanding the author's frequently caustic comments on the selfishness and self-centredness of*

PLATE 53 *Players performing on an open air stage in the Arena at Verona in the mid eighteenth century. Engraving by P. A. Novelli to vol. XII of the Pasquali edition of Carlo Goldoni's plays. Permission of the Biblioteca Burcardo, Rome*

players. Although Gozzi writes primarily about the Sacchi company, much of what he says has bearing on the wider eighteenth-century theatrical scene.

It was composed for the most part of the close relatives, and bore the reputation of being better behaved and more honest than any others. Professionally, they sustained our old national comedy of improvisation with the greatest spirit. This type of drama, as I have said above, Goldoni and Chiari, under the mask of zeal for culture, but really with an eager eye to gain, had set themselves to ruin and abolish.

Antonio Sacchi, Agostino Fiorilli, Atanagio Zannoni and Cesare Derbes, all of them excellent players in their several lines, represented the four masks, Truffaldino, Tartaglia, Brighella, and Pantalone. Each of these men could boast of perfect practice in their art, readiness of wit, grace, fertility of ideas, variety of sallies, bye-play, drollery, naturalness, and some philosophy. The soubrette of the company, Andriana Sacchi-Zannoni, possessed the same qualities. Its other members, at the time when I took up their cause, were old men and women, persons of goods parts, but unattractive physique, lifeless sticks, and inexperienced children. Some time earlier, the troupe had been extremely well-to-do and popular in Italy. But the two playwrights in question, after having lived in partnership with them, had turned round and taken the bread out of their mouths. Sacchi, in these circumstances withdrew his company to the Court of Portugal, where they prospered, until a far more formidable enemy than a brace of poets assailed them. The terrible earthquake of Lisbon put a stop to all amusements in that capital; and our poor players, having lost their occupation, returned to Venice after an absence of some four years, and encamped in the theatre of San Samuele.

(Symonds, *The Useless Memoirs of Count Carlo Gozzi*, 1890, vol. 2, pp. 131–2)

Gozzi on actors and actresses

In what concerns the practice of their art, all that these people know is how to read and write; one better, and one worse. Indeed, I have been acquainted with both actors and actresses who have not even had that minimum of education, and yet they carried on their business without flinching. They got their lines read out to them by some friend or some associate, whenever a new part had to be impressed in outline on their memory. Keeping their ears open to the prompter, they entered boldly on the stage, and played a hero or a heroine without a touch of truth. The presentation of such characters by actors of the sort I have described abounds in blunders, stops and stays, and harkings back upon the leading motive, which would put to shame the player in his common walk of life.

Barefaced boldness is the prime quality, the chief stock-in-trade, the ground-element of education in these artists. Assiduous use of this one talent makes not a few of them both passable and even able actors.

These are the reasons why a civil war is always raging in our companies about the first parts in new pieces. The conflict does not start from an honest desire to acquire or to manifest theatrical ability. The players are actuated wholly by ambition by the hope of attracting favourable notice through the merit of their role, by the wish to keep themselves continually before the public, performing ill or well as their blind rashness prompts them.

Notwithstanding all these disadvantages, Italy would be able to make a good show in comparison with other nations if our theatres were better supported and remunerated. There are not wanting persons of fine presence, of talent, sensibility, and animation. What we do want are the refinements of education, solid protection, and emoluments sufficient to encourage the actor in his profession.

(Symonds, *The Useless Memoirs of Count Carlo Gozzi*, 1890, vol. 2, pp. 140–1)

INDIVIDUAL PLAYERS

Evaristo Gherardi

An influential player at the turn of the seicento, *Gherardi (1663–1700), who acted the Arlecchino role, was well educated and had a fluent pen. The six volumes of his* Le Théâtre Italien *is a major source of information about the work of the late seventeenth-century players. He disclaims vanity, but that need not be taken seriously.*

This comedy [*Le Divorce*] did not enjoy any great success in the hands of M. Domenico. It had been dropped from the repertory and the parts were burnt. I myself (who had never trod a stage before [. . .] chose it for my first attempt (1 October 1689) when, on the order of the King and Monsieur, I appeared before the public, and so prodigious was its success that it earned a great deal of money for the players.

If I were a man inclined to be vain of the theatrical talent nature had gifted him with for both masked and unmasked acting, and in both serious and comic lead roles – a talent which has brought me the applause of the most refined and intelligent – this would bolster my sense of self-importance. I might argue that I did more at the start and in the early years of my career than did the most illustrious actors of twenty years' experience when in their prime. But I protest that far from being swollen in vanity by my rare skill, I have always ascribed this more to a lucky star than any personal merit; and if anything of this kind has flattered my soul, it was the pleasure of hearing myself applauded in the wake of the inimitable M. Domenico, who had raised the gaucheness of the Harlequin role to such a high plane of excellence, that all who saw him perform always found something wanting in even the most famous arlecchini of the day.

(From *Le Théâtre Italien*, 1700, vol. II, pp. 153–4)

One of the most vivid accounts of the Italian players in Paris in the eighteenth century is provided by Goldoni in his Memoirs. *Below he writes of members of the Comédie Italienne he found on his arrival in 1762.*

Members of the Italian company in Paris in 1762

That I might have a better opportunity of knowing my Italian actors, I took apartments near the theatre; and in that house I had the good fortune to possess a charming neighbour, whose company has always been highly useful and agreeable to me.

This was Madame Riccoboni, who, having renounced the theatre, delighted Paris with her novels, which, for purity of style, delicacy of images, truth of passion, and the art of interesting and amusing her readers at the same time, raised her to a level with whatever was most valuable in French literature.

I applied to Madame Riccoboni to give me some preliminary account of my Italian actors. She knew them thoroughly, and favoured me with a description which I afterwards discovered to be prefectly correct, and worthy of her candour and discretion.

Mr Charles Bertinazzi, called Carlin, which is the diminutive of Charles in Italian, was in high estimation for his propriety of behaviour, celebrated as a Harlequin, and in the possession of a reputation which raised him to a level with Dominique and Thomassin in France, and Sacchi in Italy. Nature had endowed him with inimitable graces; his figure, his gesture, his movements, prepossessed every one in his favour. For his action and talents he was admired on the stage, and for his private character he was beloved in society.

Carlin was the public favourite: he had acquired the esteem of the frequenters of the pit to such a degree, that he spoke to them with an easy familiarity which no other actor durst presume to adopt. When the public were to be harangued, or when any excuse was to be made, Carlin was always employed, and his mode of communication was usually an agreeable dialogue between the actor and spectators.

Madamoiselle Camilla was an excellent waiting-maid, well suited to the Harlequin whom I have just mentioned. Full of wit and sentiment, she sustained comic parts with a charming vivacity, and played in touching situations with animation and intelligence. She was on the stage what she was in private, always gay, equal and interesting, possessing a cultivated mind, and the qualities of an excellent heart.

Mr Collalto was one of the best actors of Italy. He was the pantaloon for whom I exerted myself so much, and of whom I spoke so much in the second part of my Memoirs.

This man, who possessed the very soul of a comedian, had the art of conversing with his mask, but he shone still more without it. In Italy, he had acted in one of my pieces, called 'The Venetian Twins', the one of whom was stupid, and the other clever. He gave a new turn to this subject, and added a third twin of a headstrong and passionate character. He represented the three different characters in great perfection and with great applause, and I accorded to him, with the most sincere pleasure, all the merit of this new conception.

M. Ciavarelli played, under the name of Scapin, the characters of our Italian Brighellas. He was an excellent pantomime, and extremely accurate in his execution. M. Rubini filled occasionally the character of Doctor of the Italian comedy.

I have spoken of these five individuals before entering into any details respecting the male and female lovers, because they constituted the basis of the Italian comedy at Paris.

M. Zanuzzi was the principal lover. I had long known him: he made some noise in Italy, and was known there by the nick-name of Vitalbino, the diminutive of Vitalba, an Italian comedian of great celebrity, of whom I made honourable mention in the first part of my Memoirs.

He was seconded by M. Balletti, the son of an Italian father and a French mother; he possessed the two languages in equal perfection, and was acquainted with their respective genius. His talents had been injured, and his health affected, by accidents of a disagreeable nature; but in his acting we could still discover the school of Silvia, his mother, and Lelio and Flaminia, who had contributed to his education.

Madam Savi, the principal actress, and Madam Piccinelli, the second, were not very well adapted for comedy; but they were both young, and the one, from her desire of improvement, and the other, from the sweetness of her singing, might in time become useful. The former died a short time afterwards, and the second quitted the comic theatre to re-appear in the opera in Italy.

(Goldoni, *Memoirs*, trans. Black, 1814, vol. 2, pp. 143–6)

PLATE 54 *The actor Carlo Bertinazzi in* Le Prince de Salerno. *Permission of the Biblioteca Burcardo, Rome*

Carlo Bertinazzi

Known as Carlin, Bertinazzi (1710–1783), joined the Comédie Italienne in 1741, and was one of the last great Arlecchini *in the Paris-based company. An imaginative player, noted for his detailed and physically expressive mime, his death, with that of Sacchi in 1788, effectively marks the end of the great last phase of the improvised comedy.*

Carlin could play all instruments, and painted and engraved with talent. Gifted with an uncommonly quick intelligence he succeeded in everything better than anyone else. He once suggested he should serve his own servant for twenty-four hours in order to teach him a servant's proper duties, and to this purpose he dictated instructions which, if followed, would produce exemplary servants [. . .] If Carlin was the audience's favourite by virtue of his art, he was no less a favourite among those who knew him for his moral qualities: joviality, amiable good-heartedness and well-proven honesty were the qualities which principally made up his nature. He was an exemplary father, giving a fine education to his children. He was a faithful friend, keeping old and sincere acquaintances to the end of his life, and being sorely missed. Always fond of an organized life, he should have amassed a solid fortune, but his good-heartedness brought him misfortune from some whom he trusted absolutely. From then on this willingness to trust was less marked in him and his equanimity was shaken. At times, embittered in the depths of his soul, he would exclaim: *I am afraid I am the only truly honest person in the world!!!* He died in Paris on 6 September, 1783.

(From a report of Bertinazzi's death, published 17 October 1783, cited by Rasi, *I Comici*, vol. 1, 1897, pp. 369–70)

Antonio Collalto

Like Francesco Andreini before him, Collalto (1717–1778), who played in the Pantalone mask, transferred from the army to the stage, and after a period with travelling companies, came to celebrity when he replaced Cesare D'Arbes in Medebach's Venice-based company in 1750. His skills contributed substantially to Goldoni's success with the sixteen plays he wrote for the company the following season. His later fortunes too were partly in association with the Venetian dramatist, for he moved to the Comédie Italienne in Paris in 1759, where Goldoni was to join him five years later. An actor of originality and intelligence, he devised plays himself, and was much admired by Garrick, who saw him in Paris in 1773.

[Originally] from Vicenza. After following the profession of soldier in a Venetian company of dragoons, gifted with martial courage he had, too, a talent brilliant enough for him to appear on the stage, were he acted with infinite skill the mask of Pantalone. He played without mask in many Venetian dialect parts written for him in various comedies by the famous poet Carlo Goldoni. Girolamo Medebach's company gave Antonio Collalto both name and reputation, and he was summoned to Paris to join the Comédie Italienne, where he was much liked by the French and much appreciated by his colleagues, becoming indeed a redoubtable support to that troupe which was now in its decline. Among other things Collalto performed a comedy of his own devising called *The Three Venetian Twins*, the first character a military type, the second a fool, and the third astute. He did no more than change his wig, donning, according to the character he was representing, a black one and a grey one (both round), and a third in the French style with a bobble. Thanks to this very small but distinctive change, combined however with a total transformation of voice and deportment, many people found it impossible to believe that it was nonetheless he alone who depicted those three characters. He went into the provinces to perform his comedy, and there acted it all in French, and had it published in French too. [. . .] Collalto had great ability and was richly endowed by nature. A fine presence, a good voice, and an inimitable spirit contributed greatly to making him much idolized by his audiences. He earned a lot and spent a lot, because he liked to live in the grand style. He was over fifty when he fell ill in the month of June 1778, and when the help of doctors proved useless, he succumbed to the strength of the disease that in a few days carried him to the grave.

After the great comic actor's death the Comédie Italienne survived little more than a year. Our comedians were dismissed and the Comédie Italienne was entirely abolished. This would not have happened had Collalto lived and continued to support it with his talent that was so much admired. But destiny did not so allow, and with his passing it delivered the last blow to that society of which only he, together with Bertinazzi, was ever the ornament, the decoration and the true sustainer.

(Bartoli, *Notizie istoriche*, 1782, vol. 1, pp. 173–5)

Diana

Little of a hard factual nature is known about this actress of whom Bartoli writes so enthusiastically below. More than one actress played under the stage name Diana; one such was the Roman, Cecilia Rutti, known to have performed in Vienna and to have been a mistress of the Emperor, and she may possibly be the actress of whom Bartoli writes, notwithstanding that her death is recorded in 1711 – Bartoli's dates are not always reliable. Both this account below of Diana, and those above of Collalto, point the ability of players to perform in both improvised and scripted pieces.

A famous and distinguished actress who acquired great fame by her skill both in Italy and abroad. Her acting ability was so considerable that she truly enchanted spectators. In improvised pieces she was particularly vivacious, and together with Silvio, who was given the surname 'della Diana' from his association with her, she performed the most demanding scenes, superbly rich in sparkling phrases, forceful sayings, expressions of indignation, love and tenderness. She also sang pleasingly, and played several instruments with great skill. She was protected by persons of rank, among them crowned heads who made her an object of envy to other actresses by lavishing their immense wealth on her. These riches however were much depleted by her companion, Silvio, who cleverly got his hands on them, extracting them from her coffers by caresses and attentions more suited to a lover than a companion. Diana was considered a

PLATE 55 *Frontispiece to the British Library copy of James Miller,* Harlequin Horace, *1735. Although the piece is dedicated to John Rich, the caricature may not be integral to the edition. Permission of The British Library 11631 d27*

beauty, and was loved and respected, but her apparent physical charms were later found to be counterfeit. Suffice it to say that her teeth, praised as pearls, were not her own but were artificial and false. An accident exposed this deception which for long had been concealed from her admirers. After travelling throughout Europe, and conquering a thousand hearts, she died in Palermo about the year 1730.

(Bartoli, *Notizie istoriche*, 1782, vol. 1, pp. 194–5)

Antonio Sacchi

One of the most celebrated players of the eighteenth century, Sacchi (1708–1788) was born to the profession, and from the beginning worked with Venetian companies, travelling with them to Russia, Austria and Portugal. His work in Italy is above all associated with that of the dramatists Goldoni and Gozzi: the former wrote a number of scenarii *for him, including* Il servitore di due padroni, *and the latter both* fiabe *(fairy-tale-like pieces) and plays in imitation of Spanish romantic drama. The following amply testifies to his skills in improvised pieces.*

This actor, known on the Italian stage by the name of Truffaldin, added to the natural graces of his action, a thorough acquaintance with the art of comedy and the different European theatres.

Antonio Sacchi possessed a lively and brilliant imagination; he played in comedies of intrigue; but while other harlequins merely repeated themselves, Sacchi, who always adhered to the essence of the play, contrived to give an air of freshness to the piece, by his new sallies and unexpected repartees. It was Sacchi alone whom the people crowded to see.

His comic traits, and his jests, were neither taken from the language of the lower orders nor that of the comedians. He levied contributions on comic authors, on poets, orators, and philosophers; and in his impromptus we could recognize the thoughts of Seneca, Cicero, or Montaigne; but he possessed the art of appropriating the maxims of these great men to himself, and allying them to the simplicity of the blockhead; and the same proposition which was admired in a serious author, became highly ridiculous in the mouth of this excellent actor.

(Goldoni, Memoirs, trans. Black, 1814, vol. 1, pp. 280–1)

Conclusion

As we have seen, the players of the *commedia dell'arte* were quite unlike their contemporaries elsewhere in Europe in their method of 'composing' plays, and that method enabled many of them to foray profitably far beyond Italy comparatively untrammelled, at least for a time, by language barriers. But the accommodations they necessarily made in their repertories and performance emphases established for them abroad a reputation for being purveyors of a distinct and single kind of theatre, the 'idea' of which came largely to eclipse the reality of what they had once been and how they had once worked. That 'idea', seemingly endorsed by the rich iconography, with its stress on the 'masks', *al fresco* performance and the 'popular' ambience, was strengthened in the course of the nineteenth century. The sentimental and decorative features of the 'masks' were pronounced in musical adaptations of Gozzi's *fiabe* and in the pantomime of performers like Jean-Baptiste Deburau during the Romantic period, their picturesque charm was underscored in many of the comments in, as well as the illustrations to, Maurice Sand's influential *Masques et Bouffons* (1862), and was prominent too in some of the late nineteenth- and early twentieth-century pieces of Hugo von Hofmannsthal. The decorative was no less evident in much of the academic commentary of the time, which had a tendency as well to evaluate the work of the improvising players mainly in literary terms or from basically literary perspectives. The 'idea' of the *commedia dell'arte* flourished, as we have said elsewhere, and what in its heyday had been a vital and robust, a physical and pantomimic, but above all a verbal and rhetorical theatre, a theatre flexible and versatile in the skills of its performers and the range of dramatic kinds it performed, came all the more to be seen, when mediated through the rose-tinted filters of Romantic nostalgia and literary predilection, as a theatre essentially of 'masks' and comic routines.[1]

By the early years of this century that Romantic view was somewhat challenged by a number of innovative stage directors, although many of the assumptions in which it was rooted were not themselves abandoned.[2] Naturally the interest of practitioners lay not in 'reconstruction', nor in seeking merely to recover an historically accurate understanding of the *commedia dell'arte*; practitioners were concerned either to find confirmation in past theatre of their own theories, or with devising actor training materials and techniques. It was invariably for such immediate artistic purposes that they drew on, or drew conclusions from, what was known of the improvising players' method of preparation and presentation. Thus Edward Gordon Craig saw the theatre of the Italians as lending support to his own vision of a theatrical art liberated from its subservience to the word of the poet, and Vsevolod Meyerhold included study of *commedia dell'arte* techniques in the actor training programme of his experimental Studio Theatre to underscore the importance of physical performance. Nowhere in the early decades of this century was the *commedia dell'arte* taken up more fruitfully than in Russia. Several of the new generation of Russian directors, like Vakhtanghov, Tairov and Eisenstein, drew on its iconography for designs, and mounted plays inspired by it. The 'masks' in particular continued to exercise wide appeal in opera and ballet, as in Prokofiev's *The Love of Three Oranges*, and Stravinsky's *Pulcinella*, designed by Baskt and choreographed by Leonid Massine, and *Petrushka*, done by Diaghilev and Nijinsky. In the inter-war years theatre directors like Copeau and Reinhardt, Barrault and Jouvet, drew on the example of the *commedia dell'arte*, as too did a number of British and American directors and designers. Post-war theatre has been no less influenced, although in the main it has still been the decorative features of the 'masks' which have been drawn on, often to lend mood and colour to the stage orchestration of 'classic' plays, like Shakespeare's comedies of Italian setting. Perhaps the most celebrated post-war foregrounding of *commedia dell'arte* elements was that in Giorgio Strehler's several stagings of Goldoni's *Il servitore di due padroni*, the first of which he did at the Piccolo Teatro of Milan in 1955, and which utilized the work of the brilliant mask-maker, Sartori, whose historical and practical investigations into the qualities, characteristics and stage functions of the face mask continue to enrich our understanding. The influence of the *commedia dell'arte* in this century has spread, too, far beyond the theatre, and is to be found in the work of painters and sculptors, book illustrators and poster designers, and even in clothing fashions. Interest in it has also encouraged speculation about the extent to which many kinds of comedy in a variety of media may stand in its tradition, whether the silent film comedy of Chaplin, Keaton, Lloyd and the Keystone Cops, or more recent sound film or television situation comedy – even if in these its influence is acknowledged to be at several removes, and is intermeshed with echoes of, and borrowings from, many and diverse traditions of 'popular' comedy.[3]

One consequence of this practitioner interest has been to bring practical investigation and academic enquiry increasingly together. Perhaps the first significant instance of this was the seminal study of Constant Mic, *La Commedia dell'Arte*, published in Paris in 1927 (and based on a version brought out in Petrograd, 1914–17), for Mic had worked closely with Meyerhold and others in the theatre on productions, and in training and rehearsal sessions. Yet the romantic and sentimental view continued to prevail in some writing, and the *commedia dell'arte* was for long still viewed from essentially literary perspectives, even by theatre historians. Thus the early pioneering work of Pierre-Louis Duchartre, *The Italian Comedy* (first published in French in 1925), and a later expansion of that, *La Commedia dell'arte et ses enfants* (1955), tended to emphasize the childlike ingenuousness of the improvised comedy and its stage figures, and glossed over or bowdlerized the blunt, bawdy nature of some of the materials. By so doing it tended, however inadvertently, to point up a contrast between the apparent triviality of the improvised drama and the more serious concerns of scripted plays. Even Allardyce Nicoll, in his massively rich and perceptive *The World of Harlequin* (1963), in defining the 'types' of the *commedia all'improvviso* sought an analogy by likening them to the characters of nineteenth-century melodrama.[4] Such views are still to be found in many writings on the *commedia dell'arte*, and unfortunately a stress on the simplistic is no less evident at times in the work of some practitioners, particularly those who, attracted by the myth of pristine innocence, play up 'low' farce and facile buffoonery, and lean heavily on the stage interpretation of the 'masks' as infantile grotesques.

Many performance groups today either work directly under the inspiration of, or acknowledge indebtedness to, what they understand to have been the styles and techniques of the *commedia dell'arte*. Their reasons are various: some have looked to it as a once achieved actors' theatre, a theatrical art form *sui generis*, and free of the authority and literary emphases of the playwright; others have identified with it as a form of 'popular' theatre, rooted in the basics of comedy and of wide audience appeal; yet others have seen its traditional physical 'gags' and familiar, stylized 'masks' as offering opportunities to develop topical stage satire relevant to modern audiences; still others have been drawn to it more for the purely decorative qualities of the 'masks' and costuming. Companies in many parts of the world, from Britain, the United States and the Soviet Union, to Australia, India and Japan, now work in, or with, or are aware of the received tradition of the *commedia all'improvviso*, and nowhere more so is that the case than in Italy itself, whether specifically in productions like those of Carlo Boso, or through accommodation and assimilation, as in the work of the remarkably versatile comic performer, director and playwright, Dario Fo.[5] What twentieth-century uses of the *commedia dell'arte* have stressed, however, is in the main what increasingly in the mid and late seventeenth century, and in the eighteenth century, came to be foregrounded in the European imagination: the 'four masks', their distinctive costuming, the spontaneous and largely physical nature of improvised performance, the 'popular' and decorative dimensions, and the artistic coherence and distinctiveness of a theatrical form conceived of as a single artistic entity. The historical reality, as we have seen, was rather different. The *commedia dell'arte* was the product of economic, social and cultural change, and the need, opportunism and ambition of performers. It emerged from a confluence of talents from the world of street entertainment and the court fringes. It consisted of players banded together in acting companies in order to earn their livelihood by trading in plays. Those plays were various, as much verbal as physical, could be scripted, but were invariably improvised for reasons of economy and as a strategy for maximizing market opportunities. The role composition of the companies enabled them to accommodate their repertories flexibly to the needs and possibilities of the market. The *commedia dell'arte* was akin to the English Elizabethan, and to the later French and Spanish theatres, in that it was a mercenary theatre, yet had links with, and an orientation to, the 'high' culture of the courts and academies. It was a new theatrical formation, 'public' professional theatre.

Of course, few practitioners working today would claim that theirs is the authentic Italian improvised comedy of the late sixteenth and seventeenth centuries, nor indeed would many suppose that for modern performance it is even desirable to seek to reconstruct the historically authentic. Like the Renaissance professionals, modern practitioners accommodate what they understand and find usable of past styles, techniques and materials, to the interests and concerns of the audiences for and with whom they work. What their activities bear witness to of course is the enduring theatrical inspiration provided by the received 'idea' of the *commedia all'improvviso*, for the historical *commedia dell'arte* remains elusive. So various were its manifestations, so diffuse were its activities, and so receptive was it to many and diverse cultures, that in many respects it is irrecoverable.

Notes

INTRODUCTION

1 For English studies of the Italian Renaissance literary drama see particularly D. Radcliffe-Umstead, *The Birth of Modern Comedy in Renaissance Italy*, Chicago, 1969; M. Herrick, *Italian Comedy in the Renaissance*, Urbana, 1950; M. Herrick, *Italian Tragedy in the Renaissance*, Urbana, 1954; Louise George Clubb, *Italian Drama in Shakespeare's Time*, New Haven, 1989.

2 For select studies of the *commedia dell'arte* see the bibliography; recent works to which we are particularly indebted are C. Molinari, *La Commedia dell'Arte*, Milan, 1985; F. Taviani, *La Commedia dell'Arte e la società barocca: la fascinazione del teatro*, Rome, 1969; F. Taviani and M. Schino, *Il segreto della Commedia dell'Arte, la memoria delle compagnie italiane del XVI, XVII e XVIII secolo*, Florence, 1982; and R. Tessari, *La Commedia dell'Arte nel Seicento. 'Industria' e 'Arte giocosa' della civiltà barocca*, Florence, 1969; and *Commedia dell'Arte: La Maschera e L'Ombra*, Milan, 1981. The most comprehensive study in English of the Italian comedians and their influence on English Elizabethan drama is Kathleen M. Lea, *Italian Popular Comedy: A Study in the Commedia dell'Arte, 1550–1620, with Special Reference to the English Stage*, 2 vols, Oxford, 1934. Other major studies include, P-L. Duchartre, *The Italian Comedy*, London, 1929, (from the French, 1925), reprinted with the Receuil Fossard illustrations, New York, 1966; C. Mic[lashevski], *La Commedia dell'Arte, ou le théâtre des comédiens italiens des XVI, XVII et XVIII siècles*, Paris, 1927; M. Apollonio, *Storia della Commedia dell'Arte*, Rome, 1930, and two important studies by Allardyce Nicoll, *Masks, Mimes and Miracles: Studies in the Popular Theatre*, London, 1931, and *The World of Harlequin: A Critical Study of the Commedia dell'Arte*, Cambridge, 1963. Unfortunately Thomas Heck's excellent annotated bibliography arrived too late for us to use.

3 See Lea, *Italian Popular Comedy*.

4 See P. A. Wadsworth, *Molière and the Italian Theatrical Tradition*, York, S. C., 1977.

5 See H. Kindermann, *Theatergeschichte Europas*, 10 vols, Salzburg, 1957–74.

6 See M. Green and J. Swan, *The Triumph of Pierrot. The Commedia dell'Arte and the Modern Imagination*, New York, 1986.

7 The most useful collection of visual materials on the Elizabethan theatre is R. Foakes, *Illustrations of the English Stage 1580–1642*, London, 1985.

8 For a well illustrated account of Callot see G. Kahan, *Jacques Callot, Artist of the Theatre*, Athens, Georgia, 1976. The most valuable recent discussions of the illustrative materials are the articles of M. A. Katritsky, Bibliography C.

9 Another important collection of early illustrations is the Recueil Fossard, see figure 50; the collection is reproduced in Duchartre, *The Italian Comedy*, New York, 1966. Books particularly rich in visual materials, other than those listed above, are K. Kratochvil, *Ze sveta komedie dell'arte*, Prague, 1987, D. Esrig, *Commedia dell'Arte*, Nördlingen, 1985, and *Les Arts du Théâtre de Watteau à Fragonard*, an exhibition catalogue, Galerie des Beaux Arts, Bordeaux, 1980.

10 Luigi Riccoboni, *Histoire du Théâtre Italien depuis la decadence de la Comédie Latine*, Paris 1728, p. 89.

11 See Nicoll, *The World of Harlequin*.

CHAPTER 1 ANTECEDENTS

1 For a good discussion of possible classical roots and their transmission see Nicoll, *Masks, Mimes and Miracles*, p. 214ff. See also H. Reich, *Der Mimus*, Berlin, 1903, and Leach 4.

2 See M. Gigante, *Rintone e il teatro in Magna Grecia*, Naples, 1971.

3 See M. Bieber, *The History of the Roman Theater*, Princeton, 1961, p. 129ff.

4 Nicolò Rossi, *Discorsi . . . Intorno alla Comedia*, Vicenza, 1589.

5 Riccoboni, *Histoire*, p. 23ff., remarks links with Atellan farce, and examines the differences between actors and buffoons; Winifred Smith, *The Commedia dell'Arte*, New York, 1912, refers to the archeological discoveries. See also V. De Amicis, 1882.

6 Maurice Sand, *Masques et Bouffons*, Paris, 1862; Nicoll, *Masks, Mimes and Miracles* and *The World of Harlequin*. For the possible survival of mimes in Byzantium, see G. la Piena, 'The Byzantine Theatre', *Speculum*, April, 1936.

7 Such arguments are advanced by Mic, *La Commedia dell'Arte*.

8 For the relationship between Karagöz and the masks of the *commedia dell'arte* see M. And, *A History of Theatre and Popular Entertainment in Turkey*, Ankara, 1963, also arguments in Reich, Lea and Nicoll.

9 See N. Pirrotta and E. Povoledo, *Music and Theatre from Poliziano to Monteverdi*, Cambridge, 1982. The comic element is rarely found in Italian medieval theatre.

10 R. Redfield, *Peasant Society and Culture*, Chicago, 1956.

11 Vito Pandolfi, *La Commedia dell'Arte. Storia e testi*, 6 vols, Florence, 1957–61; P. Toschi, *Le origini del teatro italiano*, Milan, 1955.

12 For accounts of Carnival in Italian towns see *inter alia* A. Ademollo, *Il Carnevale di Roma*, Rome, 1883; G. Renier-Michiel, *Origini delle feste Veneziane*, 1817; for more general studies: F. Jesi, *La Festa*, Turin, 1977, and J. Caro Baroja, *El Carneval*, Madrid, 1965. See also P. Toschi, *Le origini del teatro italiano*.

13 Mario Apollonio, 'Il duetto di Magnifico e Zanni', 1971. See also Apollonio, *Storiadella Commedia dell'Arte*, p. 73ff. See also the Dialogue in Pandolfi, *La commedia dell'arte*, 1957, I, p. 174ff.

14 Toschi, *Le origini del teatro italiano*.

15 See Molinari, *La Commedia dell'Arte*, p. 16ff and Povoledo, 'Le bouffon'.

16 Pandolfi, *La Commedia dell'Arte*, vol. I.

CHAPTER 2 THE EMERGENCE OF PROFESSIONAL COMPANIES

1 Ferruccio Marotti has two very pertinent studies: *Lo spettacolo dall' Umanesimo al Manierismo*, Milan, 1974, which includes an anthology of writings, and *Lo spazio scenico*, Rome, 1974. For an account of the Renaissance revolution in ways of seeing, J. White, *The Birth of Pictorial Space*, London, 1957. See also Elena Povoledo, 'L'architettura del teatro in Italia dall'età greca al Palladio', in *Bollettino del Centro di Studi di Architettura Andrea Palladio*, Vicenza, 1974, and L. Zorzi, *Il teatro e la città*, Turin, 1977.

2 See Pandolfi, *La Commedia dell'Arte* vol. I, for examples.

3 For accounts of the Humanist theatre see: F. Ruffini, *Teatri prima del teatro*, Rome, 1983; F. Doglio, *Teatro in Europa*, Milan, 1982; A. Nicoll, *The Development of the Theatre*, London, 1966, and J. Jacquot (ed.) *Le lieu théâtrale à la Renaissance*, Paris, 1963.

4 See Leone de' Sommi, *Quattro dialoghi in materia di rappresentazioni sceniche*, ed. Ferruccio Marotti, Milan, 1968. Also in A. Nicoll, *The Development of the Theatre* London, 1927.

5 G. Padoan, *La commedia Rinascimentale veneta*, Vicenza, 1982.

6 *I Diarii di Marino Sanuto*, Venice, 1879–1903.

7 G. Calendoli, *Ruzante*, Venice, 1985; a good overview in English of Ruzante's work is F. Fido, 'An Introduction to Ruzante', in A. Dessen (ed.), *Renaissance Drama*, New Series, Illinois, 1973.

8 Calendoli, *Ruzante*, p. 9ff.

9 Vito Pandolfi, *Il teatro del Rinascimento e la Commedia dell'Arte*, Rome, 1969.

10 The Medici Popes in Rome were among those who encouraged the work of semi-professionals. For an account of theatre in Rome see F. Cruciani, *Teatro nel Rinascimento. Roma 1450–1550*, Rome, 1984; for the Venetian theatre in the early to mid sixteenth century see Padoan, *La commedia Rinascimentale veneta*.

11 L. Dolce, *Fabritia*, Venice, 1549, cited by Elena Povoledo, 'I Comici professionisti e la commedia dell'arte: caratteri, techniche, fortuna', in G. Arnaldi and M. P. Stocchi (eds), *Storia della Cultura Veneta*, Venice, 1983, p. 388.

12 Padoan, *La commedia Rinascimentale veneta*, p. 215. The first recorded appearance of the *commedia dell'arte* Accesi is in 1590.

13 B. Croce, 'Intorno alla Commedia dell'arte', in *Poesia popolare e poesia*

d'arte, Bari, 1957; Tessari, *La Commedia dell'Arte nel Seicento*, has a valuable discussion of the 'industrial' dimension of the players' output.

14 Taviani and Schino, *Il segreto della Commedia dell'Arte.*

15 Their professional status is indicated by the fact that they were taxed, while charlatans were not: see C. Molinari, *Pier Maria Cecchini.*

CHAPTER 3 THE MAJOR COMPANIES

1 See Apollonio, *Storia della Commedia dell'Arte*, and Povoledo, 'I Comici professionisti'.

2 The argument sometimes advanced that the only troupes active were those we know by name is in a sense irrefutable: there is no way of demonstrating that record of an unnamed company is not simply record of a company known by name from another source. There would seem to be sufficient evidence to suggest that companies existed of which we know little, not even their names. But a major difficulty is to distinguish in the comments of many Counter-Reformation critics between acting companies proper and groups of street entertainers and mountebank troupes. Nonetheless the court influence was crucial, and for discussion of the way the idea of a 'popular' theatre took root, see Taviani and Schino, *Il segreto della Commedia dell'Arte*, p. 395ff.

3 For an overview of Italian economic decline in the seventeenth century see Carlo M. Cipolla, 'The Decline of Italy: the case of a fully matured economy', *The Economic History Review*, 5, 1952; see also G. Aleati and C. Cipolla, Il trend economico nello Stato di Milano durante i secoli XVI e XVII: il caso di Pavia', *Bollettino della Società di Storia Patria*, 1950; of relevance too for the broader European scene are Henry Kamen, *The Iron Century: Social Change 1550–1660*, London, 1971, and *European Society*, London, 1984, T. Aston (ed.), *Europe in Crisis 1550–1660*, London, 1965, and P. Burke (ed.), *Economy and Society in Early Modern Europe*, London, 1972. For the effects of plague see C. M. Cipolla, *Fighting the Plague in Seventeenth Century Italy*, Wisconsin, 1981. The plague of 1630–1, according to Cipolla, reduced the population of Verona by 61 per cent, Parma by 50 per cent, and Milan by 46 per cent; that of 1656–7 was no less destructive, Naples for example losing 50 per cent of its population.

4 Riccoboni, *Histoire du Théâtre Italien.*

5 Francesco Bartoli, *Notizie istoriche de'comici italiani che fiorirono intorno all'anno MDC fino ai giorni presenti*, 2 vols, Padua, 1782.

6 The brief accounts of company activities below are drawn from a number of sources including D'Ancona, *Origini del teatro italiano*, 1891, Lea *Italian Popular Comedy*, Nicoll, *Masks, Mimes and Miracles* and *The World of Harlequin*, Pandolfi, *La Commedia dell'Arte*, Molinari, *La Commedia dell'Arte*, and N. D. Shergold, 'Ganassa and the Commedia dell'Arte in the Sixteenth Century Spain', *MLR*, I, i, (1956), but are primarily based on vol. 2 of I. Sanesi, *La Commedia*, Milan, 1935, and articles in the *Enciclopedia dello Spettacolo.*

7 Lea, *Italian Popular Comedy*, I, ch. 5, on Player Companies has an excellent amount of Ganassa and the later companies.

8 Nicoll, *Masks, Mimes and Miracles*, p. 304.

9 For a discussion see Charles Sterling, 'Early Paintings of the Commedia dell'Arte in France', *Bulletin of the Metropolitan Museum*, 1943.

10 Shergold, 'Ganassa and the Commedia dell'Arte'.

11 No lists of plays and performances can be drawn up comparable to A. Harbage, *Annals of the Early English Stage*, London, 1964, or Y. Kawachi, *Calendar of English Renaissance Drama 1558–1642*, New York, 1986; only in the eighteenth century for the Comédie Italienne is something of comparable detail possible.

12 The palace and gardens on this island in the Po were established as a court retreat for the Estensi family by Alfonso I.

13 Lea, *Italian Popular Comedy*, I, p. 261ff.

14 Sanesi, *La Commedia*, II, p. 7.

15 For the 1589 festivities see Pirrotta and Povoledo, *Music and Theatre*.

16 Sanesi, *La Commedia*, II, p. 12ff.

17 Luigi Rasi, III, p. 512ff.

18 The above particularly drawn from Sanesi, II, p. 19ff.

19 Ferrara had been one of the main centres for the production of Humanist drama in the late fifteenth and early sixteenth centuries. Its relations with the professional acting companies seem to have been rather more chequered, the Este family favouring patrician patronage, the players a more commercial *modus operandi*. The Gelosi seem to have been particularly in favour in Ferrara in the 1570s. The city's most notable late sixteenth-century activities were with pastoral plays and tournament theatre.

20 The above particularly drawn from Sanesi, II, p. 15ff.

21 Ibid. For Montaigne see *Journal du voyage de Michel de Montaigne en Italie en 1580–81*, Rome, 3 vols, 1774.

22 Rasi, *I Comici*, III, p. 304.

23 Robert Donington, *The Rise of Opera*, London, 1981.

24 Sanesi, *La Commedia*, II, p. 22ff.

25 Rasi, *I Comici*, passim.

26 Sanesi, *La Commedia* II, p. 27ff.

27 Riccoboni, *Histoire du Théâtre Italien*, pp. 75–9.

28 The situation is that the Duke of Mantua wishes to send three of the Confidenti, including Scala, with an acting company to France, but the other players object to the break-up of the company and seek the support of Don Giovanni de'Medici.

29 The players here show how distinguished was the Confidenti troupe: the Scapino was Francesco Gabrielli; the Beltramo was Niccolò Barbieri; the Pantalone was Marc Antonio Romagnesi. Note too the many family interconnections.

CHAPTER 4 PATRONAGE, PERFORMANCE PLACES AND REPERTORIES

1 D'Ancona, *Origini del teatro italiano*, II, p. 445.

2 Fynes Moryson, *Shakespeare's Europe*, I, 1903, p. 168. How socially heterogeneous such public theatre audiences were is hard to calculate, but by the turn of the century may have been somewhat comparable to the variable mix of patrician, bourgeois and some lower orders

found in the Paris theatres, see J. Lough, *Paris Theatre Audiences in the 17th and 18th Centuries*, Oxford, 1957.

3 Moryson, *Shakespeare's Europe*, II, 1903, p. 476. The travels undertaken by the Italian players may be compared to those of English touring companies on the Continent at the same time: see particularly Jerzy Limon, *Gentlemen of a Company: English Players in Central and Eastern Europe*, Cambridge, 1985. See also below, chapter 10. Travelling companies appealed to spectators of a wide social spectrum, as Garzoni's description indicates (see p. 69). Distinctions between public and private peformance places were perhaps most important in segregating audiences socially; some mingling of ranks at public shows was not unusual in societies where status and hierarchy were taken for granted, hence the availability of 'popular' culture at all social levels.

4 In 1598, for example, the political manoeuvrings of Cardinal Aldobrandini absorbed Ferrara into the Papal States, and the consequences of that subordination, compounded by other ills, included the eclipse of the great Ferrarese court culture and the decline of the city's population by some two-thirds in the course of the seventeenth century.

5 Rasi, *I Comici*, I.

6 For a general account of *feste* and their social and political significance, see Roy Strong, *Art and Power: Renaissance Festivals 1450–1650*, Woodbridge, Suffolk, 1984. It is worth remarking that one reason why court patronage was particularly important for the Italian professional players, is that there were comparatively more courts in the geographical area of the peninsula than was the case elsewhere.

7 As does, for example, P-L. Duchartre, *The Italian Comedy*.

8 T. Worsthorne, *Venetian Theatre in the 17th Century*, Oxford, 1954. The fortunes of the *commedia dell'arte* in Venice fluctuated considerably; for a period (between about 1584 and 1607) there was an interdiction on commercial performance, and for much of the seventeenth century, straight drama – scripted or improvised – was overshadowed by the popularity of *melodramma*.

9 N. Mangini, *I Teatri di Venezia*, Milan, 1974.

10 Coryate seems to distinguish between street performers and actors, as we have said in chapter 3, but it is further worth noting that this is his only reference to actors wearing masks; in his description of a visit to a theatre (see p. 100) it is masked members of the audience he remarks, rather than players. Possibly he, and his readers, took the masking of *zanni* for granted. We encounter here yet again, however, the difficulty of distinguishing clearly between street entertainers and acting troupes. That the Italian improvising comedians retained appeal at all social levels, in France as well as in Italy, seems clear from La Mesnardière's remark in his *Discours* (1639) cited by J. Lough, *Paris Theatre Audiences*, p. 70: 'the Zannis, the Pantalons, and other kinds of that species are the players appropriate to the capability of the people.'

11 John Evelyn, *Diary and Correspondence*.

12 For illustrations of street theatre and entertainment in Venice in the sixteenth, seventeenth and eighteenth centuries, see G. Perocco and A. Salvadori (eds), *Civiltà di Venezia*, Venice, 1976, particularly vols 2

and 3. The marked increase in the number of companies in the eighteenth century may in part account for the large number of illustrations in the century depicting *al fresco* performances.

13 See L. Zorzi, G. Innamorati and S. Ferrone, *Il teatro del cinquecento*, Florence, 1982, and Tessari, *La Commedia dell'Arte nel Seicento*. Italian players in Paris acted in public theatres from early on.

14 Padoan, *La commedia Rinascimentale veneta*, p. 23ff., for Venetian theatres and *stanze*. For references to amateur and professional performances in Florence see Roselli, Romby and Micali, *I teatri di Firenze*, p. 64ff. For the Baldracca see the important articles by Evangelista.

15 For a good account of Italian buildings see G. Ricci, *Teatri d'Italia*, Milan, 1978; for audiences and auditorium divisions at the Théâtre Italien in the 1690s see Lough, *Paris Theatre Audiences*, pp. 86–7. English Elizabethan companies similarly came early to recognize the box office advantage of the enclosed performance place: G. Wickham, *Early English Stages*, vol. 1, London, 1969.

16 Molinari, *La Commedia dell'Arte*, remarks that Mantua seems to have been not only a centre of patronage, but a kind of *entrepôt* for the theatrical profession in the late sixteenth and early seventeenth centuries; see too his comments on Modena in the later seventeenth century, pp. 179–82. Ottonelli emphasized too the importance of Bologna as a gathering place for the companies: *Della Christiana Moderatione del Theatro*, IV, 1652, p. 128.

17 *Tragedia del S. Cl. Cornelio Frangipane*, Venice, 1574, cited in Povoledo, 'I Comici professionisti'.

18 Rasi, *I Comici*, II.

19 See Apollonio, *Storia della Commedia dell'Arte* and 'Il duetto di Magnifico e Zanni'. *Il Pastor Fido* was widely performed, and was one of the most successful of the literary dramas of the late sixteenth century; several English translations were made of it, notably that by Sir Richard Fanshawe, 1647.

20 See P. Bjorstrom, *Giacomo Torelli and the Baroque Stage*, Stockholm, 1964.

21 For a good discussion of the Gabrielli see Taviani and Schino, *Il segreto della Commedia dell'Arte*.

22 A fine example of the visual magnificence with which amateur improvised performances could be invested is to be seen in the designs Bernardo Buontalenti prepared for the Viennese court in the early seventeenth century; a number of these are finely reproduced in Molinari, *La Commedia dell'Arte*.

23 The Vittoria referred to here and in other documents below was Vittoria Piissimi (see p. 221). For further details about the actors and actresses mentioned in these documents, see Rasi, *I Comici*.

24 The Buffetto mentioned here was Carlo Cantù (1609–*c.*76), who played a zanni role and was very popular in Italy and France: see plate 36. Rasi identifies Diana as Giulia Gabrielli, daughter of the famous Francesco (Scapino): Rasi, *I Comici*, II, p. 575. The players in the next letter giving unauthorized performances in Mantua may have been the Uniti.

25 Rinaldo Petignoni was an early leader of the Gelosi troupe.

26 The Vendramin were one of the most powerful of the Venetian impresarial families, and long remained so: see Mangini, *I Teatri di Venezia*.

CHAPTER 5 MASKS AND ROLES

1 Andrea Perrucci, *Dell'Arte rappresentativa ed all'improvviso*, Naples, 1699. The writings of Ferrone, Molinari, Tessari, and Taviani and Schino on this subject are particularly important.
2 Tessari, *La Commedia dell'Arte nel Seicento*.
3 See G. E. Bentley, *The Profession of Dramatist in Shakespeare's Time*, Princeton, 1976. A good account of working methods in the Elizabethan theatre is Bernard Beckerman, *Shakespeare at the Globe*, New York, 1962. Many of the Elizabethan plays were of course repeated.
4 G. E. Bentley, *The Profession of Player in Shakespeare's Time*, Princeton, 1984.
5 See Molinari, *La Commedia dell'Arte*, for a discussion of Guarini and the preparation of *Il pastor fido*, p. 41, and see also p. 141ff.; there is an account with documentation of the genesis of this piece in D'Ancona, *Origini del teatro italiano*, II, p. 420ff. Tasso wrote his *Aminta* in some two months and the preparation time for the first performance was much less, although well beyond what professionals could have devoted to a regular production. Centralization and censorship, too, in a sense worked for the Elizabethan theatre by giving it firm bounds within which to work; the Italians' position was much less clearly determined.
6 There is a valuable discussion of the role balances and patterning of the *scenarii* in L. Zorzi, 'Intorno alla Commedia dell'Arte', in *Forum Italicum*, 1980.
7 Molinari, *La Commedia dell'Arte*, p. 70ff.
8 The case for strong influence of the literary drama has often been made, including by Sanesi. Seventeenth-century *scenarii* are less obviously dependent on the learned drama than those of the late sixteenth century, perhaps underscoring the importance of court plays in providing partial models to the early professional players when they came to organize and structure their own plays.
9 Cf. discussion of these points by Molinari, *La Commedia dell'Arte*, p. 13ff., to whom we are particularly indebted here. Molinari justly remarks the inappositeness of Nicoll's linking of Hamlet and Arlecchino as dominant figures in the history of Western theatre since the Renaissance; it implies both are dramatic characters: Nicoll, *The World of Harlequin*, pp. 1–8.
10 Elizabethan theatricals, too, employed masks, even if their use was only occasional.
11 It is noticeable that scarcely any of the documents translated in this book refer explicitly to face masks; mention of them is conspicuously wanting, for example, in Scala's Prologue (see p. 197). For discussion of portraits of actors and masks, see Taviani and Schino, *Il segreto della Commedia dell'Arte*, pp. 11–14, and illustrations therein.
12 Riccoboni, *Histoire du Théâtre Italien*, p. 49: 'It is not only Arlecchino

who is a masked actor, there is a Pantalone, a Burattino, a Dottor Gratiano, a Cavicchio, peasant, a Pedrolino; under these names we find the four masked actors of our live theatre: one speaks Venetian, the other Bolognese, and the two Zanni Arlecchino and Scapino, Bergamask and Lombard.'

13 For a detailed and seminal discussion of the evolution of the four 'masks' in the seventeenth and eighteenth centuries, see Taviani and Schino, *Il segreto della Commedia dell'Arte*. See also Apollonio, *Storia della Commedia dell'Arte*, pp. 85ff. and 289ff.

14 Taviani and Schino, ibid., is particularly rich in new insights and suggestions to which we are indebted. For a good concise account see Marzia Pieri, *La nascita del teatro moderno*.

15 Emphasis on the 'popular' dimension is evident to a greater or lesser extent in, for example, P-L. Duchartre, *The Italian Comedy* and *La Commedia dell'Arte et ses enfants*, Paris, 1955, Mic, *La Commedia dell'Arte*, Lea, *Italian Popular Comedy*, and Nicoll, *Masks, Mimes and Miracles* and *The World of Harlequin*. So too is a tendency to see the 'masks' as parts rather like characters in a play: thus Nicoll, *The World of Harlequin*, describes Pantalone as a character 'interpreted by diverse actors', though one in which 'the actor's skill becomes of more significance than the part he plays' (p. 62), and remarks 'the whole collection of theatrical persons were transferred from one piece to another' (p. 22). The tendency in many writers to personalize the 'masks' suggests that a 'mask' was rather like a glove, always the same but worn by different actors.

16 According to Panigarola, in *Il Predicatore del Panigarola*, Venice, 1609: 'It is only a few years ago that the famous comedian Lucio, as close as can be to the modern Roscius, noticed when he was in Ferrara the fashionable dress and curious manners of an old barber called Messer Gratiano dalle Gotiche, from Francolino, and copied them for a very ridiculous stage role, taken in almost all its details, which was for a long time finely acted by Lodovico of Bologna, and since has been used to such a great extent that even off stage it has led to many good pieces both in prose and verse' pp. 36–7. It has been argued that the Lodovico of Bologna referred to here may have been Lodovico de' Bianchi, who in 1578 replaced in the Gelosi company the actor Luzio Burchiella, who was possibly the Lucio mentioned by Panigarola. Suggestive in this ascription of origins is the linking of the 'mask' to a particular actor. See Nicoll, *Masks, Mimes and Miracles*, p. 256.

17 For a detailed study see Delia Gambelli, 'Arlecchino dalla preistoria a Biancolelli', *Biblioteca Teatrale*, no. 5, 1972; see also F. Nicolini, *Vita di Arlecchino*, Milan, 1958. For the detail of Pantalone, Dottore and Arlecchino discussed above see Nicoll, *Masks, Mimes and Miracles*, p. 233ff.

18 See Molinari, *La Commedia dell'Arte*, pp. 17–18 for a concise account.

19 Compare for example early paintings, like plates 9 and 13, or the Buontalenti designs referred to above, chapter 4, note 22, with mid eighteenth-century coloured illustrations and ceramics.

20 For an account of the many players who performed the Arlecchino role see Nicolini, *Vita di Arlecchino*; Nicoll, *The World of Harlequin*, takes the figure of Harlequin as the focus for a general study of the

commedia dell'arte, and has much of great value on the performers. There were clearly great differences between Arlecchini, as a glance at the Recueil Fossard illustrations and those in Martinelli's *Compositions de Rhetorique* will indicate.

21 Plate 51 interestingly indicates how quickly the iconography of the 'masks' became familiar in England.

22 Nicoll, *The World of Harlequin*, p. 121ff.

23 For identification of other players mentioned in the letter see Rasi, *I Comici*, II, pp. 965–6.

24 Pulcinella was to become one of the most celebrated, influential and widely disseminated of the 'masks': in France it became Polichinelle, and in the English puppet theatre, Punch. Of Neapolitan origin, the name was possibly derived from *pulicinello* (little chick, but with an implication too of little rascal), denoting its rustic links, as too did the traditional loose-fitting white garb and the black half-mask. The role was probably first developed by Silvio Fiorillo. The painter Tiepolo was but one in the eighteenth century who delighted in depicting the figure. See A. G. Bragaglia, *Pulcinella*

CHAPTER 6 THE *SCENARII* AND MATERIALS

1 For a full list see the bibliography. For a good concise account, see Apollonio, *Storia della Commedia dell'Arte*, p. 219ff. and, in English, Lea, vol. I, ch. 3.

2 No doubt extant *scenarii* omit as many changes made by later players as they include.

3 How widely *scenarii* circulated between companies is uncertain. Ironically it was primarily through published material that the work of the Italians, or Franco-Italians, became known in England, and plundered by writers of English Restoration stage farce.

4 Irene Mamczarz (ed.), *Discorso della Commedia all'improvviso e scenari inediti*, Milan, 1973. As far as scenic decoration is concerned, these come closer to the earlier more serious *scenarii*. Scala includes examples of these. For the *opere regie* see Apollonio, *Storia della Commedia dell'Arte*, p. 168ff.

5 See, for example, those in the Correr collection.

6 See the introduction to Marotti's edition of Scala, *Il teatro delle Favole rappresentative*, Milan, 1976; a contrary view has been argued by Tim Fitzpatrick, 'Commedia dell'Arte and performance: the scenarios of Flaminio Scala', *Renaissance Drama Newsletter*, suppl. 3, Warwick, 1985.

7 Flaminio Scala, *Il teatro delle Favole rappresentative*, giornata 36.

8 Scala, ibid., Preface to the Reader. Yet the very regularity of the Scala *scenarii* too may indicate that they were improved for publication.

9 Niccolò Barbieri, *La Supplica*, 1634, chapter VIII and p. 253 below. For an account of the language of the *commedia dell'arte* see P. Spezzani, 'L'arte Rappresentativa di Andrea Perrucci e la lingua della Commedia dell'arte', in Lingua e struttura del teatro italiano del Rinascimento, *Quaderni del circolo filologico – linguistico padovano*, No. 2, Padua, 1970.

10 Domenico Bruni, cited here from Ms in Biblioteca Bridense, Milan, AG XIV 24, p. 23.
11 Here we follow Povoledo, 'I Comici professionisti'.
12 Taviani and Schino, *Il segreto della Commedia dell'Arte*, argue indeed that it was the appearance in the mid 1560s of poetess-actresses that was crucial to the early development of the *commedia dell'arte*.
13 They may be compared with materials in Domenico Bruni's *Dialoghi*, MS37 Burcardo from the early seventeenth century, or with the Adriani (above p. 175) Perugia A 20 materials.

CHAPTER 7 IMPROVISATION AND PERFORMANCE

1 Apollonio, 'Il duetto di Magnifico e Zanni' and *Storia della Commedia dell'Arte*, p. 73ff.
2 Molinari, *La Commedia dell'Arte*, p. 18ff.
3 For a modern edition of Perrucci and discussion of his work see A. G. Bragaglia, *Andrea Perrucci: Dell'Arte rappresentativa premeditata*, Florence, 1961. An important indication of the amateur dimension is provided by the so-called *commedia ridicolosa*, scripted plays often peformed by *dilettanti* but drawing on the materials and strategies of the improvised theatre: see L. Mariti, *La Commedia Ridicolosa*, Rome, 1978.
4 Gozzi attempted to defend improvised playing by arguing that at its best such acting was more spontaneously creative, but rather begged the main objection of his contemporaries that while it may once have been, it was so no longer. Molinari, *La Commedia dell'Arte*, has a perceptive discussion of this, p. 38ff.
5 See G. Manfredi, *L'Attore in scena*, Verona, 1746. Sìro Ferrone suggests that improvisation gradually gave way to the regular use of memorized material: *Paragone*, April, 1983.
6 Molinari, *La Commedia dell'Arte*, has a good discussion of these points, pp. 25–6 and p. 37ff.; cf. also Tessari, *La Commedia dell'Arte nel Seicento*, on players 'composing' plays. Taviani and Schino, *Il segreto della Commedia dell'Arte*, see improvisation as combining use of spontaneous and premeditated dialogue.
7 These contrasts particularly appealed to engravers and painters.
8 In his *Della poesia rappresentativa*, Ferrara, 1598, Angelo Ingegneri writes interestingly, if from an academic perspective, of costume, lighting, voice and gesture. For useful accounts of actors at this time, see G. Calendoli, *L'Attore: storia di un'arte*, Rome, 1959, p. 157ff. and Zorzi, Innamorati and Ferronę, *Il teatro del cinquecento*, pp. 59–79.
9 For these *scenarii* in English see Henry F. Salerno's translation of Scala, *Scenarios of the Commedia dell'Arte*, New York, 1967. For play on gender difference see, for example, *Il ritratto*.
10 Even serious *scenarii* include much pitched at a familiar level. For the function of masks in the improvised drama, see F. Taviani, 'Position du masque dans la commedia dell'arte', in *Le Masque: du rite au théâtre*, CNRS, Paris, 1985, pp. 119–34.
11 Apollonio, *Storia della Commedia dell'Arte*, p. 191ff.
12 For a survey of the issues regarding satire, see R. Erenstein, 'Satire and

the Commedia dell'arte', in D. Mayer and K. Richards, *Western Popular Theatre*, London, 1977. In the preface to his important edition of Ruzante's plays, L. Zorzi remarks that a weakness of the *Commedia dell'arte* was that it lacked any clear moral and social significance; that may, in due course, have helped further the demise of improvised playing in the eighteenth century.

13 For opposing views of the social composition of the Elizabethan audience see A. Harbage, *Shakespeare's Audience*, New York, 1941, and Anne Jennalie Cook, *The Privileged Playgoer*, Princeton, 1982. For the influence of the popular tradition see R. Weimann, *Shakespeare and the Popular Tradition in the Theater*, Baltimore, 1978; see too M. Hattaway, *Elizabethan Popular Theatre*, London, 1983. For a general view of popular culture at this time, see M. Bakhtin, *Rabelais and His World*, Cambridge, Mass., 1968.

CHAPTER 8 SOME LEADING PLAYERS

1 See Pandolfi, *Il Teatro del Rinascimento*, p. 139ff.

2 Barbieri, *La Supplica*. Actors too were drawn from a range of professions: Andreini was a soldier, Valerini a doctor, Cecchini a dyer.

3 The academic drama is discussed in, for example, F. Doglio, *Teatro in Europa*, I, and F. Cruciani, *Teatro nel Rinascimento*.

4 See Carlo Goldoni, *Memoirs*, trans. John Black, 2 vols, London, 1814. An important qualification here, however, is that the eighteenth century scene was significantly different as the increased commercialization of leisure produced many more troupes and different working situations. The difficulty in distinguishing between acting companies and other entertainer troupes we have already emphasized. The emergence in the mid to late sixteenth century in Italy, England and elsewhere in Europe of a new theatrical formation, organized professional acting companies, tended to displace downwards in status the remaining itinerant 'popular' entertainers. Their fate, however, like their activities, has been little examined. Some current discussion of the Italian players has emphasized their involvement in the 'high' culture and with the courts, perhaps to the neglect of less successful players and troupes.

5 Rasi, *I Comici, passim.*

6 The actor's complaint of Domenico Bruni, see p. 218, is intentionally comic, but for all that to the point. For an amusing account of eighteenth century travelling players on the move see the passage from Goldoni p. 292.

7 See G. Wickham, *Early English Stages*, London, 4 vols, 1969–80, and M. C. Bradbrook, *The Rise of the Common Player*, London, 1972. Whether the major Italian performers were able to accumulate as profitably as did, say, Alleyn and Shakespeare in England is a moot point: Scala, for example, on retirement opened a shop in Venice. That some Italian players owned money in costumes and properties is clear from Ottonelli's comment p. 219.

8 Among such paintings are figures, 40 and 41.

9 Malherbe waspishly noted the advanced age of the Italian players he saw in Paris in 1613: see p. 272.

10 H. Prunières, *L'opera italien en France avant Lulli*, Paris, 1913.

11 Ottonelli described Scapino as 'the best *zanni* of our times, inventor of fantastic instruments, and of delightful songs and airs': *Della Christiana Moderatione del Theatro*, IV, 1652, p. 26.

12 Jarro (G. Piccinni), *L'epistolari di Arlecchino*, Florence, 1895. Zan Ganassa is another possibility. Martinelli acted with nearly all the major companies of his day.

13 If the *bravure* are a guide, Andreini seemed rather to favour the verbal.

14 Ottonelli admired his talents, and linked him with Isabella and Giovan Battista Andreini as one of the outstanding players of the time: *Della Christiana Moderatione del Theatro*, IV, 1652, p. 28ff. Cesare Molinari has a most valuable study of Cecchini, 1983; it includes too an edition of his plays.

15 Mamczarz (ed.), *Discorso della Commedia all'improvviso*.

CHAPTER 9 OPPOSITION AND DEFENCE

1 An invaluable analysis of the polemic occasioned by theatre is Taviani, *La Commedia dell'Arte*, which includes a large selection of primary documents. There is a succinct account of the arts and Church reform in R. Wittkower, *Art and Architecture in Italy 1600–1750*, Harmondsworth, 1958, p. 21ff.

2 See J. Barish, *The Anti-theatrical Prejudice*, Berkeley, 1981.

3 See Zorzi, Innamorati and Ferrone, *Il teatro del cinquecento*.

4 Taviani usefully draws attention to the similarity between criticism of the erotic effects of actresses on audiences and contemporary polemic on nudity in fine art: see Barbieri, *La Supplica*, ed. F. Taviani, Milan, 1971, p. XXXVIII ff. and LIV. Aristocrat and plebeian alike were more tolerant than the bourgeois of the bawdy and scatological. Again, while courtesans could enjoin high social position, the extent to which they were socially accepted varied greatly.

5 G. D. Ottonelli, *Della Christiana Moderatione del Theatro*, 1646, cited Nicoll, *Masks, Mimes and Miracles*, p. 221. Masking, too, at Carnival time, was regarded with suspicion by many moralists who believed, with some justification, that the mask freed its wearer of many social and psychological restraints.

6 Taviani, *La Commedia dell'Arte*, includes much of the important Ottonelli material. Ottonelli took as theological authority for his 'liberal' view of theatre the writings of St. Thomas Aquinas.

7 Ottonelli refers to the way a troupe of players in 1635 deceived a leading churchman by promising restraint in their performance, but then ignored their promise when they came to perform: *Della Christiana Moderatione del Theatro*, V, 1652, p. 167.

8 Legal regulation of players and companies was real, but complicated by their itinerancy, and much was resolved at local administrative level. As the economic advantages of playing in halls rather than in the open air, to a captive rather than a passing audience, became a part of professional practice, the more performance in halls attracted the opposition of theatre's opponents. Ottonelli, for one, thought theft and immorality more easily pursued in the *stanze*.

9 See particularly chapter XLVIII of *La Supplica*. Defence of the morals, particularly the sexual morals, of players bulks large in Barbieri.
10 See particularly chapter XXIX of *La Supplica*.
11 Scala, *Il teatro delle Favole rappresentative*.
12 Taviani and Schino, *Il segreto della Commedia dell'Arte*, remark that some early actresses were courtesans or the daughters of professional prostitutes, a background which opponents of theatre were able to exploit. Taviani has a valuable further article, 'Un vivo contrasto: seminario su attori e attrici della Commedia dell'Arte', in *Teatro e storia*, I, 1986.

CHAPTER 10 DIFFUSION IN EUROPE

1 The most substantial account of the early Italian players in France is A. Baschet, *Les Comédiens Italiens à la Cour de France sous Charles IX, Henri IV et Louis XIII*, Paris, 1882.
2 See, for example, the accounts of travelling in E. S. Bates, *Touring in 1600*, Boston, 1911. Ottonelli writes of players regularly taking boats at Genova and Livorno, and of using the river-ways of Lombardy: *Della Christiana Moderation del Theatro*, IV, 1652. p. 5.
3 Shergold, 'Ganassa and the Commedia dell'Arte'.
4 The most detailed account in English of the *commedia dell'arte* in Spain is Shergold, 'Ganassa and the Commedia dell'Arte'.
5 Fynes Moryson remarks on this habit, and it was certainly practised by some English monarchs: Charles II so honoured Biancolelli and Fiorilli when they performed in London in 1673. Rasi remarks that the Duke of Guise in 1645 gave elegant clothes to departing players, a practice found too at the Elizabethan and Restoration courts.
6 See, for example, the work of dramatists like Jean-François Régnard.
7 For the later fortunes of the Italian players in France see H. C. Lancaster, *The Comédie Francaise 1680–1700*, Baltimore, 1941, and G. Attinger, *L'Esprit de la Commedia dell'Arte dans le Théâtre Francais*, Paris, 1950.
8 E. K. Chambers, *The Elizabethan Stage*, Oxford, 1923, vol. IV, pp. 261–5.
9 See Lea, *Italian Popular Comedy*, vol. II, *passim*.
10 V. Capocci, *Genio e mestiere. Shakespeare e la Commedia dell'arte*, Bari, 1950.
11 Lea, *Italian Popular Comedy*, Vol. II provides examples of these.
12 Sybil Rosenfeld, *Foreign Theatrical Companies in Great Britain in the 17th and 18th Centuries*, London, 1955.
13 Lea, 'Sir Aston Cokayne and the *Commedia dell'Arte*, *MLR*, xxiii, 1928, pp. 47–51.
14 For Inigo Jones's designs, and the texts of the relevant masques, see S. Orgel and R. Strong, *Inigo Jones and the Theatre of the Stuart Court*, New York, 1973; see also Kenneth Richards, 'The Commedia dell'Arte and the Caroline Stage', in Sergio Rossi (ed.), *Italy and the English Renaissance*, Milan, 1989.
15 Richards, ibid., and 'Inigo Jones and the Commedia dell'Arte', in *The Commedia dell'Arte from the Renaissance to Dario Fo*, ed. C. Cairns, Lampeter, 1989.

16 Ifan K. Fletcher, 'Italian Comedians in England in the 17th Century', *Theatre Notebook*, vol. 8, 1954.
17 A. L. Bader, 'The Modena Troupe in England', *MLN*, 1935.
18 See Rosenfeld, *Foreign Theatrical Companies*, for details.
19 For the influence of the Franco-Italian comedy on English Restoration drama, see Leo Hughes, *A Century of English Farce*, Princeton, 1956.
20 E. C. Selzer, 'La commedia italiana dell'arte alla corte viennese', *Rivista Italiana del dramma*, II, 1938, pp. 84–5.
21 For an account of the *commedia dell'arte* in many parts of Europe, see Kindermann, *Theatergeschichte Europas*, particularly vols 3 and 4.
22 It is perfectly possible that Pickelharing, who was the English actor Robert Reynolds (*fl.* 1610–40), had direct contact with Italian players.

CHAPTER 11 LATER FORTUNES

1 For instance Manfredi, *L'Attore in scena.* Mic additionally links the decline to the decay of Italian literature and literary taste, and to the contamination and corruption of the players' materials by foreign cultural influences. Nicoll sees the players' attraction to fashionable seventeenth-century forms like tragi-comedy as similarly contributive.
2 By Molinari, *La Commedia dell'Arte*, p. 94.
3 For the emergence of *opera buffa* see M. F. Robinson, *Naples and Neapolitan Opera*, Oxford, 1972. For the artists see the exhibition catalogue, *Les Arts du Théâtre de Watteau à Fragonard*, Galerie des Beaux Arts, Bordeaux, 1980.
4 Mamczarz (ed.), *Discorso della Commedia all'improvviso*, prints this and other *scenarii* and has a valuable commentary.
5 Two good studies of Goldoni are S. Ferrone, *Carlo Goldoni*, Florence, 1975, and F. Fido, *Guida a Goldoni*, Turin, 1977. The best overview of *settecento* comedy as a whole is Roberta Turchi, *La commedia italiana del Settecento*, Florence, 1985.
6 For Goldoni's contribution to the development of *opera buffa* see D. de Paoli, 'Goldoni librettista', *Il veltro*, 1/2, 1975.
7 There is a good English overview of Gozzi's work in the introduction to J. A. Symonds, *The Useless Memoirs of Count Carlo Gozzi*; for a recent account in English of Gozzi's best known play, *Turandot*, see D. Nicholson in *Theatre Journal*, December, 1979. The best account of Goldoni in English is J. S. Kennard, *Goldoni and the Venice of his Time*, New York, 1920.
8 The important involvement of the *commedia dell'arte* in the early development of opera is discussed by N. Pirrotta, 'Commedia dell'Arte and Opera', *Musical Quarterly*, 1955, xli, pp. 305–24.

CONCLUSION

1 P. Hartnoll (ed.), *The Oxford Companion to the Theatre*, 4th ed, and Havely, Lawrence and Richards, *Comedy*.
2 The most comprehensive and seminal examination of the ways in which the 'idea' of the *commedia dell'arte* was generated and sustained is Taviani and Schino, *Il segreto della Commedia dell'Arte*. For the

influence of a particular mask see R. Storey, *Pierrot. A Critical History of a Mask*, Princeton, 1978.

3 Some of the Russian uses of the *commedia dell'arte* are well examined in an essay by Carla Solivetti in her Italian version of Mic's *La Commedia dell'arte*, Venice, 1981. See also C. Moody, 'Meyerhold and the Commedia dell'Arte' *MLR*, 73, 1978. For the Sartoris' work see Donato Sartori and Bruno Lanata, *Arte della maschera nella Commedia dell'Arte*, Florence, 1983. For an English account of the influence of the *commedia dell'arte*, and more particularly of the 'masks', in the twentieth century, see Green and Swan, *The Triumph of Pierrot*. Taviani has a valuable and succinct account in *Enciclopedia del teatro del '900*, ed. A. Attisani, Milan 1980, p. 390ff.

4 Nicoll, *The World of Harlequin*, op. cit.

5 Although Fo tends to look more to the activities of the medieval *giullari*. For an example of the current vitality of theatre inspired by the *commedia dell'arte* see the brochure and programmes of the festival mounted in 1983 by the Théâtre Roman Rolland de Villejuif: catalogue edited by Corrado Simioni, Montgeron, 1983.

Bibliography

A Collections of *Scenarii* and Materials

About eight hundred *scenarii* (also called *soggetti* or *canovacci*) have survived, most of them in manuscript collections formed in the seventeenth and eighteenth centuries. An early important collection, and the only one published during the great period of the *Commedia dell'Arte*, was Flaminio Scala's *Il teatro delle favole rappresentative* (Venice, 1611), of which included here is *Il vecchio geloso* (*The Jealous Old Man*); many of the rest were probably gathered in random fashion, eventually finding their way into libraries. Among the most important collections are:
(i) the Locatelli collection, in the Biblioteca Casanatense in Rome, containing more than a hundred scenarios probably dating from 1618–22, and in all likelihood prepared by and for amateurs;
(ii) also in the Casanatense, the Ciro Monarca collection of forty eight pieces from the early to mid seventeenth century, of which the piece translated here, *L'ateista fulminato* (*The Atheist Damned*), is one;
(iii) the Corsini collection, now in the Biblioteca of the Accademia dei Lincei, Rome, which contains one hundred, each of which is prefaced by a water colour illustration of a stage scene, perhaps ultimately of professional provenance and dating from the first half of the 17th century;
(iv) the Passanti collection of one hundred and eighty three in the Biblioteca Nazionale of Naples;
(v) twenty four later seventeenth century *scenarii* in the Biblioteca Vaticana in Rome;
(vi) the important, although amateur and eighteenth century, collection of materials by Placido Adriani in the Biblioteca Comunale, Perugia;
(vii) the Correr collection of fifty one pieces, in the Museo Correr in Venice, which seem to have been used by Venetian professionals and are of the late seventeenth century.

In addition, some *scenarii* survive singly or in small collections, like that of the Biblioteca Estense in Modena, which includes *La schiava*, translated here.

For published *scenarii* see particularly A. Bartoli, A. G. Bragaglia, and A. Valeri, below under B, and for valuable check-lists, V. Pandolfi, and below under B, and K. M. Lea, under C. For English translations of some pieces see K. M. Lea and G. Oreglia below under C. H. Salerno, below C, has translated Scala's 1611 collection. For the late seventeenth and the eighteenth century Franco-Italian pieces see particularly materials of Domenico Biancolelli, in a French version by T. S. Gueullette, in the Biblioteque de l'Opera, Paris, and *scenarii* of Evaristo Gherardi, *Le théâtre italien*, Paris, 1694, together with the many later and supplementary editions of this, more particularly that published in six volumes in Amsterdam (1701), which is the text cited here. For Luigi Riccoboni's interestingly detailed early eighteenth century *scenarii* see I. Mamczarcz below under B. For published *bravure* see particularly F. Andreini, below under B.

B Primary Works, Printed *Scenarii* and Editions

Andreini, Francesco	*Le Bravure del Capitano Spavento divise in molti ragionamenti in forma di dialogo*, Venice, 1607.
Andreini, Giovan Battista	*La Florinda*, 1603
	L'Adamo, Milan, 1610.
	Lo schiavetto, Venice, 1612
	La Centaura, Paris 1622
	La Ferinda, Paris, 1622
	Le due commedie in commedia, 1623
	Lo Specchio, composizione sacra e poetica, Paris, 1625.
Andreini, Isabella	*Mirtilla*, 1588
	Rime, 1601
	Lettere, 1607
Aretino, Pietro	*I ragionamenti*, 1534 (1584 ed. cited here)
Barbieri, Niccolò	*La Supplica, discorso famigliare di Niccolo Barbieri detto Beltrame diretto a coloro che scrivendo o parlando trattano de' comici trascurando i meriti delle azzioni virtuose*, Venice, 1634. A modern edition is that by F. Taviani, Milan, 1971.
Bartoli, Francesco S.	*Notizie istoriche de' comici italiani che fior irono intorno all' anno MDL fino ai giorni presenti*, Padua, 2 vols, 1782.
Bartoli, Adolfo	*Scenari inediti della Commedia dell'Arte, Florence, 1880.*

Beltrame, T. 'Gli scenarii del Museo Correr', in *Giornale Storico della Letteratura Italiana*, xxxx, pp. 1–48.

Beolco, Andrea *Tutte le opere del famosissimo Ruzante*, Vicenza, 1567.
Tutte le opere, Vicenza, 1617.

Bertelli, Pietro *Diversar nationum habitus*, Padua, 1594.

Bertarelli, F. *Il Carnovale italiano mascherato*, Venice, 1643.

Borget, J. *The Divels Legend*, London, 1595.

Bragaglia, Anton G. *Andrea Perrucci: Dell'Arte rappresentativa premeditata*, Florence, 1961.

Bruni, Domenico *I Prologhi*, Turin, 1621.
Le Fatiche Comiche, Paris, 1623.

Castiglione, G. B. *Sentimenti di S. Carlo Borromeo intorno agli spettacoli*, Bergamo, 1759.

Cecchini, Pier Maria *Brevi discorsi intorno alla Commedia, Comedianti e Spettatori de P. M. Cecchini Comico Acceso et Gentilhuomo de S. M. Cesarea dove si comprende quali rappresentationi si possimo ascoltare e permettere*, Naples, 1616.
Frutti delle moderne comedie et avvisi a chi le recita, Padua, 1628.
Discorso sopra l'arte comica, circa 1612, printed in V. Pandolfi below.
Tutti i trionfi, carri, mascherate o canti carnascialeschi, 2 vols., Florence, 1559.

Cocco, E. 'Una compagnia comica della prima meta del secolo XVI', in *Giornale Storico della letteratura italiana*, 1915, LXV, p. 55 ff.

Compositions de Rhétorique de M. Don Arlequin, Lyons, 1601 (possibly by Tristano Martinelli).

Costantini, Angelo *La Vie de Scaramouche*, Paris, 1695.

Cotolendi, C *Arlequiniana*, Paris, 1694.

De'Sommi, Leone *Quattro dialoghi in materia di rappresentazioni sceniche*, ed. F. Marotti, Milan, 1968.

Essarts, N. T. Le Moyne des *Les Trois Théâtres de Paris ou abrégé historique de Etablissements de la Comédie Francoise, de la Comédie Italienne e de l'Opéra*, Paris, 1777

Le fabriche, e vedute di Venetia, Venice, 1709.

Falavolti, Laura ed. *Commedie dei comici dell'Arte*, Turin, 1982.

Ferrone, Siro — *Commedie dell'Arte*, 2 vols, Milan, 1985.

Fiorilli, Silvio — *La Ghirlanda*, Paris, 1611.

Franco, Giacomo — *Habiti d'huomini et donne Venetiane*, Venice, 1609.

Garzoni, Tommaso — *La Piazza universale di tutte le professioni del mondo, nobili e ignobili*, Venice, 1585 (cited here from the 1595 edition).

Gherardi, Evaristo — *Le Théâtre Italien de Gherardi* Paris, 1695 (cited here from the Amsterdam edition, 6 vols, 1701).

Gozzi, Carlo — *Memorie inutili*, Venice, 1797. (See also Symonds 1890–C).

Grazzini A. F. — See *Tutti i trionfi, carri, mascherate.*

Gueullette, T. S. — *Traduction du Scenario de Joseph Dominique Biancolelli, dit Arlequin. Et l'Histoire du Théâtre Italien, depuis l'année 1577 jusqu'à 1750 at les années suivantes.*

Notes et Souvenirs sur le Théâtre Italien au XVIII siècle, Paris, 1938, reprinted Geneva, 1976.

Hurtado de Mendoza, Petrus — *Scolasticae et morales disputationes*, 1631.

Ingegneri, Angelo — *Della poesia rappresentativa e del modo di rappresentare le favole sceniche*, Ferrara, 1598.

Jarro (G. Piccinni) — *L'epistolario di Arlecchino*, Florence, 1895.

Lambranzi, Gregorio — *Deliciae Theatrales*, Nürnberg, 2 vols., 1716.

L'Estoile, Pierre de — *Memoires-Journaux*, ed. Brunet, vols. 1, 2 and 7, Paris, 1855–90.

Malherbe, F. — *Oeuvres de Malherbe*, ed. L. Lalanne, 6 vols., 1862.

Martinelli, Tristano — See *Compositions de Rhétorique* above.

Monmerqué M. ed. — *Les Historiettes de Talemant de Réaux*, Paris, n.d.

Montaigne, Michel — *Journal du voyage de Michel de Montaigne en Italie en 1580–81*, 3 vols, Rome, 1774.

Neri, Ferdinando — *Scenari delle maschere in Arcadia*, Città di Castello, 1913.

Ottonelli, G. D. — *Della Christiana Moderatione del Theatro*, Florence, 1655, 5 vols (various earlier editions cited here as indicated).

Pandolfi, Vito — *La Commedia dell'Arte, Storia e testi*, 6 vols., Florence, 1957–61.

Parfaict, Les frères — *Histoire de l'Ancien Théâtre Italien*, Paris, 1753.

Pavoni, Giuseppe — *Diario Descritto de Giuseppe Pavoni*, Bologna, 1589.

Perrucci, Andrea — *Dell'Arte rappresentativa premeditiata ed all'improvviso*, Naples, 1699.

Petraccone, Enzo — *La Commedia dell'Arte*, Naples, 1927.

Porcacchi, Tommaso — *Le attioni d'Arrigo terzo Re di Francia*, Venice, 1574.

Re, Emilio — 'Scenarii Modenesi', *Giornale Storico della Letteratura Italiana*, LV, 1910, p. 2 ff.

Riccoboni, Luigi — *Histoire du Théâtre Italien depuis la décadence, de la Comédie Latine, avec un catalogue des Tragédies et Comédies imprimées depuis l'an 1500 jusqu'à l'an 1600 et une dissertation sur la tragédie moderne*, Paris, 1728.

Reflections historiques et critiques sur les differens theatres de l'Europe, Paris, 1738.

Discorso della Commedia all' improvviso e scenarii inediti, ed. Mamczarz, Irene, Milan, 1973.

Sanuto, Marino — *Diarii*, ed. various hands, Venice, 58 vols, 1879–1903.

Scala, Flaminio — *Il teatro delle Favole rappresentative overo la ricreatione comica, boscareccia e tragica, divisa in cinquanta giornate*, Venice, 1611. There is a modern edition, Ferruccio Marotti (ed.), Milan, 2 vols, 1976. (There is an English version of Scala, *Scenarios of the Commedia dell'Arte*, translated and edited by H. F. Salerno, New York, 1967).

Il finto marito, Venice, 1619.

Troiano, Massimo — *Discorsi delli trionfi, giostre, apparati e delle cose piu notabili fatte nelle sontuose Nozze dell'Illustrissimo & Excellentissimo Signor Duca Guglielmo*, Munich, 1568. (A later edition with slightly different wording is *Dialoghi di Massimo Troiano*, Venice, 1569).

Tutti i trionfi, carri, mascherate o canti carnascialeschi, 2 vols., Florence, 1559.

Valeri, A. — *Gli scenari inediti di Basilio Locatelli*, Florence, 1894.

Valerini, Adriano — *Afrodite*, Verona, 1578.

Vecchi, Oratio — *L'amfiparnasso*, Venice, 1597.

C Select Works in English

And, M. — *A History of Theatre and Popular Entertainment in Turkey*, Ankara, 1963.

Andrews, Richard — 'Scripted Theatre and the Commedia dell'Arte', in *The Theatre of the English and Italian Renaissance*, ed. R. Mulryne and M. Shewring, Macmillan, 1990.

'Arte dialogue structures in the comedies of Molière', in *The Commedia dell'Arte from the Renaissance to Dario Fo*, ed. C. Cairns, Lampeter, 1989.

Bader, A. L. — 'The Modena Troupe in England', *Modern Language Notes*, L, 1935.

Bakhtin, M. — *Rabelais and His World*, Cambridge, Mass., 1968.

Barish, J. — *The Anti-theatrical Prejudice*, Berkeley, 1981.

Bates, E. S. — *Touring in 1600*, New York, 1911.

Boughner, D. C. — *The Braggart in Renaissance Comedy*, Minneapolis, 1954.

Beaumont, C. W. — *The History of Harlequin*, London, 1926.

Beckerman, Bernard — *Shakespeare at the Globe*, New York, 1962.

Bentley, G. E. — *The Profession of Dramatist in Shakespeare's Time*, Princeton, 1976.

The Profession of Player in Shakespeare's Time, Princeton, 1984.

E. Bentley (ed.) — *The Classic Theatre*, vol I, New York, 1958.

Bieber, M. — *The History of the Greek and Roman Theater*, Princeton, 1961.

Bjorstrom, Per — *Giacomo Torelli and the Baroque Stage*, Stockholm, 1964.

Bradbrook, M. — *The Rise of the Common Player*, London, 1972.

Brenner, C. — *The Théâtre Italien: Its Repertory 1716–93*, California.

Chambers, E. K. — *The Elizabethan Stage*, Oxford, 4 vols., 1923.

Cipolla, C. M. — *Fighting the Plague in Seventeenth Century Italy*, Wisconsin, 1981.
'The decline of Italy: the case of a fully matured economy', *Economic History Review*, 5, 1952.

Cook, Anne Jennalie — *The Privileged Playgoer*, Princeton, 1982.

Corrigan, Beatrice — 'Commedia dell'Arte Portraits in the McGill Feather Book', *Renaissance Drama*, N. S. II, 1969.

Coryate, Thomas — *Coryate's Crudities*, London, 1611.

Costantini, Angelo — *The Life of Scaramouche*, trans, A. R. London, 1696.

Day, John — *The Travailes of the Three English Brothers*, London, 1607.

De Brosses — *Selections from the Letters of De Brosses*, London, 1897.

Didier, Limojon de S. — *The City and Republick of Venice*, London, 1699.

Donington, Robert — *The Rise of Opera*, London, 1981.

Duchartre, Pierre-Louis — *The Italian Comedy*, London, 1928, (From French, 1925); reprinted with Receuil Fossard illustrations, New York, 1966.

Duckworth, G. E. — *The Nature of Roman Comedy*, Princeton, 1952.

Economy and Society in Early Modern Europe, ed. P. Burke, London, 1972.

Erenstein, Robert — 'Satire and the Commedia dell'Arte', in *Western Popular Theatre*, ed D. Mayer and K. Richards, London 1977.

Europe in Crisis 1550–1660, ed. T. Aston, London, 1965.

Felver, Charles S. — 'The Commedia dell'Arte and English Drama in the Sixteenth and Early Seventeenth Centuries,' *Research Opportunities in Renaissance Drama* VI, 1966.

Fido, Franco — 'An Introduction to Ruzante', in *Renaissance Drama*, ed. A. Dessen, N. S., Illinois, 1973.

Firth, Felicity — 'Comedy in Italy', in *Comic Drama: the European Heritage*, ed. W. D. Howarth, London, 1978.

Fitzpatrick, Tim — *Commedia dell'Arte and Performance: the Scenarios of Flaminio Scala*, Renaissance

Drama Newsletter, Supplement 3, Warwick, 1985.

Fletcher, Ifan Kyrle — 'Italian Comedians in England in the 17th Century', *Theatre Notebook*, vol. 8, 1954.

Foakes, R. — *Illustrations of the English Stage 1580–1642*, London, 1985.

Goldoni, Carlo — *Memoirs*, translated by John Black, London, 2 vols, 1814.

Gordon, Mel — *Lazzi: the comic routines of the Commedia dell'Arte*, New York, 1983.

Green M. and Swan J. — *The Triumph of Pierrot: The Commedia dell'Arte and the Modern Imagination*, New York, 1986.

Gurr, Andrew — *The Shakespearean Stage*, Cambridge, 1975. *Playgoing in Shakespeare's London*, Cambridge, 1987.

Harbage, Alfred — *Shakespeare's Audience*, New York, 1941. *Annals of the Early English Stage*, London, 1964.

Hattaway, Michael — *Elizabethan Popular Theatre*, London, 1983.

Havely, Cicely Lawrenson T. and Richards K. & L. — *Comedy*, Open University Press, 1977.

Herrick, M. — *Italian Comedy in the Renaissance*, Urbana, 1950.

Italian Tragedy in the Renaissance, Urbana, 1954.

Howard, Daniel — *The Commedia dell'Arte and Jacques Callot*, Sydney, 1965.

Howarth, W. D. ed. — *Comic Drama: The European Heritage*, Methuen, 1978.

Hughes, Leo — *A Century of English Farce*, Princeton, 1956.

Kamen, Henry — *The Iron Century: Social Change 1550–1660*, London, 1971.

Katritsky, M. A. — 'Lodewyk Toeput some pictures related to the *commedia dell'arte*', *Renaissance Studies*, 1, 1, March, 1987.

'Italian comedians in Renaissance prints', *Print Quart.* Vol. 4, Sept., 1987.

'The Recueil Fossard', in *The Commedia dell'Arte from the Renaissance to Darie Fo*, ed C. Cairno, Lampeter, 1989.

Kawachi, Y. *Calendar of English Renaissance Drama*, New York, 1986.

Kennard, J. S. *A History of the Italian Theatre*, New York, 1932, 2 vols.

Masks and Marionettes, New York, 1935.

Lea, Kathleen M. *Italian Popular Commedy: A Study in the Commedia dell'Arte, 1560–1620 with Special Reference to the English Stage*, Oxford, 2 vols., 1934.

'Connections and Contrasts between the Commedia dell'Arte and the English Drama,' *Rivista di studi teatrali*, 9–10, 1954.

'Sir Aston Cockayne and the Commedia dell'Arte', *Modern Language Review*, XIII, 1928.

Lee, Vernon *Studies of the Eighteenth Century in Italy*, London, 1880.

Limon, Jerzy *Gentlemen of a Company: English Players in Central and Eastern Europe*, Cambridge, 1985.

Lough, J. *Paris Theatre Audiences in the 17th and 18th Centuries*, Oxford, 1957.

McDowell, John H. 'Some Pictorial Aspects of Early Mountebank Stages', in *Studies in Philology*, vol. 37, 1940, pp. 84–96.

'Some pictorial aspects of early *commedia dell'Arte acting', in Studies in Philology*, vol. 39, 1942, pp. 47–64.

McKerrow, R. B. See Thomas Nashe.

Moore, J. R. 'Pantaloon as Shylock', *Boston Public Lib. Q.*, Vol. I, 1949.

Moryson, Fynes *Shakespeare's Europe, Unpublished Chapters of Fynes Moryson's Itinerary*, ed. Charles Hughes, London, 2 vols., 1903.

An Itinerary, Glasgow, 4 vols., 1907.

Nagler, A. *Theatre Festivals of the Medici 1539–1637*, Yale, 1964.

Nashe, Thomas *Pierce Penilesse*, London, 1592.

The Works of Thomas Nashe, ed. R. B. McKerrow, 5 vols., Oxford, 1904–10.

Nicoll, Allardyce *Masks, Mimes and Miracles; Studies in the Popular Theatre*, London, 1931.

The Development of the Theatre, London, 5th ed. 1966.

The World of Harlequin: A Critical Study of the Commedia dell'Arte, Cambridge, 1963.

Oreglia, Giacomo — *The Commedia dell'Arte*, London, 1968.

Oxford Companion to the Theatre, ed. Phyllis Hartnoll, Oxford, 4th ed., 1983.

Permann, R. — 'The Influence of the Commedia dell'Arte on the French Theatre before 1640', *French Studies*, ix, 1955.

Philias, P. G. — 'Massinger and the Commedia dell'arte', *Modern Language Notes*, 65, 1950.

Pirrotta, N. and Povoledo, E. — *Music and Theatre from Poliziano to Monteverdi*, Cambridge, 1982 (English translation of *Li due Orfei*, Turin, 1969).

Pirrotta, N. — 'Commedia dell'arte and Opera', in *Musical Quarterly*, 1955, xli, pp. 305–24.

Redfield, R. — *Peasant Society and Culture*, Chicago, 1956.

Renaissance Drama, ed. A. Dessen, N. S., Illinois, 1975.

Riccoboni, Luigi — *An Historical and Critical Account of the Theatres in Europe*, London, 1741.

A General History of the Stage, London, 1745.

Richards, Kenneth — 'The Commedia dell'Arte and the Caroline Stage', in *Italy and the English Renaissance*, ed. S. Rossi, Milan 1989.

'The Commedia dell'Arte and Dance', in *International Encyclopaedia of Dance*, vol. I, forthcoming.

'Inigo Jones and the Commedia dell'arte', in *The Commedia dell'Arte from the Renaissance to Dario Fo*, ed. C. Cairns, Lampeter, 1989.

Richards, Kenneth and Laura — 'The Commedia dell'Arte', *Oxford Companion to the Theatre*, ed. Phyllis Hartnoll, Oxford, 1983.

Robinson, M. F. — *Naples and Neapolitan Opera*, Oxford, 1972.

Rosenfeld, Sybil — *Strolling Players and Drama in the Provinces 1660–1765*, Cambridge, 1939.

Foreign Theatrical Companies in Great Britain in the 17th and 18th Centuries, London, 1955.

The Theatre of the London Fairs in the Eighteenth Century, Cambridge, 1960.

Royce, Anya P. — 'The Venetian Commedia: Actors and Masques in the Development of the Commedia dell'Arte'.
Theatre Survey, Vol. XXVII, nos. 1 and 2, 1986.

Sand, Maurice — *The History of the Harlequinade*, London, 1915, 2 vols.

Schrickx, William — 'Commedia dell'Arte players in Antwerp in 1576,' *Theatre Research International*, 1976, No. 2.

Scott, Virginia — 'The Infancy of the English Pantomime: 1715–1723', *Educational Theatre Journal*, May 1972.
'The *Jeu* and the *Role*: Analysis of the Appeals of the Italian Comedy in France in the time of Arlequin-Dominique,' in *Western Popular Theatre*, ed. D. Mayer and K. Richards, London, 1977.
'Saved by the Magic Wand of *Circe',* *Theatre Survey*, 1986.

Shergold, N. D. — 'Ganassa and the Commedia dell'Arte in Sixteenth Century Spain,', *MLR*, I i, 1956.

Skippon, Philip — His account of his time in Paris in 1666, published as *An Account of a Journey through Part of the Low Countries, Germany, Italy and France* in *A Collection of Voyages and Travels*, London, 1732, vol. 6.

Smith, Winifred — *The Commedia dell'Arte*, New York, 1912.
Italian Actors of the Renaissance, New York, 1930.

Sterling, Charles — 'Early Paintings of the Commedia dell'Arte in France,' *Bulletin of the Metropolitan Museum*, 1943.

Strong, Roy — *Inigo Jones and the Theatre of the Stuart Court*, San Marino, 1973.
Art and Power: Renaissance Festivals 1450–1650, Woodbridge, Suffolk, 1984.

Symonds, J. A. — *The Useless Memoirs of Count Carlo Gozzi*, 2 vols., translated and with an introduction by John Addington Symonds, London, 1890.

Wadsworth, P. A. — *Molière and the Italian Theatrical Tradition*, York, S. C., 1977.
Weimann, Robert — *Shakespeare and the Popular Tradition in the Theater*, Baltimore, 1978.
Weinberg, B. — *A History of Literary Criticism in the Italian Renaissance*, 2 vols., Chicago, 1963.
Welsford, Enid — *The Fool*, London, 1935.
Western Popular Theatre, ed. D. Mayer, & K. Richards, London, 1977.
White, J. — *The Birth of Pictorial Space*, London, 1957.
Wickham, Glynne — *Early English Stages*, 4 vols., London, 1969–80.
Wiley, W. L. — *Early Public Theatre in France*, Harvard, 1960.
Worsthorne, T. — *Venetian Theatre in the 17th Century*, Oxford, 1954.

D Select Works in Italian and Other Languages

Ademollo, A. — *Il Carnevale di Roma*, Rome, 1883.
Aleati, G. and Cipolla, C. M. — 'Il trend economico nello Stato di Milano durante i secoli XVI e XVII: il caso di Pavia', *Bollettino della Società Parse di Storia Patria*, 1950.
Apollonio, Mario — *Storia della Commedia dell'Arte*, Rome, 1930.
Storia del Teatro Italiano, 2 vols, Florence, 1981.
'Il duetto di Magnifico e Zanni alle origini dell'Arte', in *Studi sul Teatro Veneto tra Umanesimo e Rinascimento,* edited Maria Teresa Muraro, Florence, 1971.
Arts du Théâtre de Watteau a Fragonard, Les, Galerie des beaux Arts, Bordeaux, 1980.
Attinger, G. — *L'Esprit de la Commedia dell'Arte dans le Théâtre Français*, Paris, 1950.
Attolini, Giovanni — *Teatro e spettacolo nel Rinascimento*, Bari, 1988.
Baroja, J. Caro — *El Carneval*, Madrid, 1965.
Baschet, Armand — *Les Comediens Italiens a la Cour de France sous Charles IX, Henri IV et Louis XIII*, Paris, 1882.
Bec, C. and Mamczarz I. — *Le Théâtre Italien et l'Europe*, Paris, 1983.

Beijer, M. 'Documents sue les farceurs francais et italiens', *Revue d'Histoire du Theatre*, IX, 1952.

Bevilaqua, F. 'G. B. Andreini e i Fedeli', *Giornale storico della letteratura italiana*, XXIII & XXIV, 1894–5.

Bragaglia, Anton G. *Pulcinella*, Rome, 1953.

Brahmer, M. 'La commedia dell'arte in Polonia', *Ricerche slavistiche*, 3, 1954.

Brouwer, F de S 'Due scenari inediti del secolo XVII', *Il Giornale storico della letteratura italiana*, XVIII, 1891, p. 277.

'L'ateista fulminato', *Rendiconti dell'Accademia dei Lincei*, 10, V, 1901, p. 400.

Calendoli, G. and Vellucci, G. eds. *Convegno internazionale di studi sul Ruzante*, Venice, 1987.

Calendoli, G. *Ruzante*, Venice, 1985.

L'Attore: storia di un'arte, Rome, 1959.

Capocci, Viola *Genio e mestiere: Shakespeare e la Commedia dell'arte*, Bari, 1950.

Civiltà di Venezia, ed. G. Perocco and A. Salvadori, 3 vols., Venice, 1976. *Il contributo dei giullari alla drammaturgia italiana delle origini*, Atti del convegno Viterbo, Rome, 1978.

Courville, X. de *Un artisan de la rénovation théâtrale avant Goldoni: Luigi Riccoboni dit Lélio (1676–1715); Un Apôtre de l'Art du Théâtre; au XVIII siècle: Luigi Riccoboni (1716–1731); Lélio premier historien de la Comédie Italien*, 3 vols, Paris, 1943–58.

Cozzi, G. 'Appunti sul teatro e teatri a Venezia agli inizi del seicento', *Bollettino dell'Istituto di Storia della Società e dello Stato Veneziano*, 1959, I, p. 187.

Croce, Benedetto *I Teatri di Napoli nei secoli XV–XVII*, Naples, 1891.

Pulcinella e il personaggio del napoletano in commedia, Rome, 1899.

Saggi sulla letteratura italiana del Seicento, Bari, 1911, and *Nuovi saggi*, 1931.

Poesia popolare e poesia d'arte, Bari, 1957.

Cruciani, Fabrizio *Teatro nel Rinascimento. Roma 1450–1550*, Rome, 1984.

D'Ancona, A. *Origini del teatro italiano*, 2 vols, Turin, 1891.

Driesen, O. *Der Ursprung des Harlekin* Berlin, 1904.

Doglio, Federico *Teatro in Europa I and II*, Milan, 1982 and 1988.

Duchartre, Pierre-Louis *La Commedia dell'Arte et ses enfants,* Paris, 1955.
Enciclopedia dello Spettacolo, Rome, 1956–61.
Esrig. D. *Commedia dell'Arte*, Nordlingen, 1985.
Erenstein, Robert *De Geschiedenis van de Commedia dell'Arte*, Amsterdam, 1985.
Evangelista, Annamaria 'Il teatro della commedia dell'arte a Firenze', *Quaderni di Teatro*, 7, 1980, p. 169 ff.
'Le compagnie dei Comici dell'Arte nel teatrino di Baldracca a Firenze: notizie dagli epistolari (1576–1653)', *Quaderni di Teatro*, 24, 1984, p. 50 ff.
Ferrone, Siro *Carlo Goldoni*, Florence, 1975.
Fido, Franco *Guida a Goldoni*, Turin, 1977.
Gambelli, Delia *Quasi un recano di concertate pezzette: le composizioni sul comico dell'Arlecchino Biancolelli, in Biblioteca Teatrale*, No 1, 1971.
'Arlecchino dalla preistoria a Biancolelli, *Biblioteca Teatrale* No 5, 1972.
Gigente, M. *Rintone e il teatro in Magna Grecia,* Naples, 1971.
Heck, Thomas F. *Commedia dell'Arte. A Guide to the Primary and Secondary Literature*, New York, 1988.
Jesi, F. *La festa*, Turin, 1977.
Kindermann, Heinz *Die Commedia dell'arte und das Deutsche Volkstheater*, Leipzig, 1938.
Theatergeschichte Europas, Salzburg, 10 vols, 1957–74.
Krumer, W. *Die Italienische Commedia dell'arte,* Darmstadt, 1976.
Leisler, E. & Prossnitz G. *Max Reinhardt und die Welt der Commedia dell'arte*, Salzburg, 1970.
Le lieu théâtrale a la Renaissance, ed. J. Jacquot, Paris, 1963.
Magagnato, Liscio *Teatri italiani del cinquecento*, Venice, 1954.
Mamone, Sara *Il teatro nella Firenze medicea*, Milan, 1981.
Manfredi, G. *L'Attore in scena*, Verona, 1746.
Mangini, Nicola *I Teatri di Venezia*, Milan, 1974.
Mariti, L. *La Commedia Ridicolosa. Comici di professione, dilettanti, editoria teatrale nel Seicento. Storia e testi*, Rome, 1978.
Alle origini del teatro moderno: La Commedia dell'Arte, Rome, 1980.

Marotti, Ferruccio — *Lo spettacolo dall'Umanesimo al Manierismo*, Milan, 1974.
Lo spazio scenico, Rome, 1974.
Masque: du rite au théâtre, Paris, 1985.
Mastropasqua F. and Molinari, C. — *Ruzante e Arlecchino*, Parma, 1970.
Mic [lashevski], C. — *La Commedia dell'Arte, ou le théâtre des comédiens italiens des XVI, XVII et XVIII siècles*, Paris, 1927.
Molinari, Cesare — *Pier Maria Cecchini, Le commedie. Un commediante e il suo mestiere*, Ferrara, 1983.
La Commedia dell'Arte, Milan, 1985.
Nicolini, Fausto — *Vita di Arlecchino*, Milan, 1958.
Nolhac, P de, and Solerti, A. — *Il viaggio in Italia di Enrico III re di Francia*, Turin, 1890.
Padoan, Giorgio — *La commedia rinascimentale veneta*, Vicenza, 1982.
Pandolfi, Vito — *Il Teatro del Rinascimento e la Commedia dell'Arte*, Rome, 1969.
Paoli, D. de — 'Goldoni librettista', *Il Veltro*, 1–2, 1975.
Papetti, Viola — *Arlecchino a Londra. La Pantomima ingelse 1706–28*, Naples, 1977.
Pieri, Marzia — *La nasicta del teatro moderno*, Turin, 1989.
Plauto e il teatro, Atti del V congresso internazionale di studi sul dramma antico, Siracuse, 1976.
Platter, Felix — *Felix et Thomas Platter à Montpellier*, Montpellier, 1892.
Povoledo, Elena — 'Le bouffon et la commedia dell'arte dans la fete Venitienne au XVI siecle', in *Les Fetes de la Renaissance*, 3, CNRS, Paris, 1975.
'L'architettura del teatro in Italia dall'età greca al Palladio', in *Bollettino del Centro di Studi Architettura Andrea Palladio*, Vicenza, 1974.
I Comici professionisti e la commedia dell arte: caratteri, tecniche, fortuna', in *Storia della'cultura Veneta*, ed. G. Arnaldi and M. P. Stocchi, Venice, 1983, 4/1
Prunieres, H. — *L'Opera Italien en France avant Lulli*, Paris, 1913.
Prota-Giurleo, Ulisse — *I teatri di Napoli nel Seicento. La commedia e le maschere*, Naples, 1962.
Rasi, Luigi — *I Comici Italiani: Biografia, bibliografia, iconografia*, Florence, 3 vols, 1897–1905.

La rinascita della tragedia nell'Italia dell'umanesimo, atti del convegno di studi Viterbo, 1980.

Reich Renier-Michiel, G. *Origini delle feste Veneziane*, Venice, 1817.

Roselli, P., Romby, G. C., and Micali, O. F. *I teatri di Firenze*, Florence, 1978.

Ruffini, F. *Teatri prima del teatro*, Rome, 1983.

Sand, Maurice. *Masques et bouffons*, Paris, 1962.

Sanesi, Ireneo *La Commedia*, 2 vols, Milan, 1911–35.

Sartori, Donato and Lanata, B. *Arte della maschera nella Commedia dell'Arte*, Florence, 1983.

Saviotti, A. 'Feste e spettacoli nel seicento', *Giornale storico della letteratura Italiana*, XLI, 1914.

Scherillo, M. *La Commedia dell'Arte in Italia*, Turin, 1890.

Selzer, E. C. 'La commedia italiana dell'arte alla corte viennese', *Rivista Italiana del dramma*, II, 1938. p. 84.

Sforza, Giovanni 'Commedianti Italiani e moralità', *Gazzetta Letteraria*, April and May 1890.

Solerti, A. and Lanza, D. 'Il teatro Ferrarese', *Il Giornale storico della letteratura italiano*, XVIII, 1891, p. 174.

Spada, Stefania *Domenico Biancolelli ou l'art d'improviser*, Naples, 1969.

Storia della cultura Veneta, ed. G. Arnaldi and M. P. Stocchi, Venice, 1983.

Taviani, Ferdinando *La Commedia dell'Arte e la società barocca: la fascinazione del teatro*, Rome, 1969.

Taviani, Ferdinando and Schino, Mirella *Il segreto della Commedia dell'Arte, La memoria delle compagnie italiane del XVI, XVII e XVIII secolo*, Florence, 1982.

Tessari, Roberto *La Commedia dell'Arte nel Seicento. 'Industria' e 'Arte giocosa' della civiltà barocca*, Florence, 1969.

Commedia dell'Arte: la Maschera e l'Ombra, Milan, 1981.

Thérault, Suzanne *Commedia dell'Arte vue à travers le Zibaldone de Perouse*, Paris, 1965.

Toschi, Pietro *Le origini del teatro italiano*, Milan, 1955.

Zorzi, Lodovico *Ruzante: Teatro, Prima edizione completa*, Turin, 1967.

Il teatro e la città, Turin, 1977.

'Intorno alla Commedia dell'arte', in *Forum Italicum*, XIV, 1980, p. 427.

Zorzi, L., Innamorati, G. and Ferrone, S. *Il teatro del cinquecento*, Florence, 1982.

Index